D1567659

Voices of the Iraq War

Recent Titles in Voices of an Era

Voices of Ancient Greece and Rome: Contemporary Accounts of Daily Life
David Matz, editor

Voices of Civil War America: Contemporary Accounts of Daily Life
Lawrence A. Kreiser, Jr. and Ray B. Browne, editors

Voices of Early Christianity: Documents from the Origins of Christianity
Kevin W. Kaatz, editor

Voices of Early Modern Japan: Contemporary Accounts of Daily Life during the Age of the Shoguns
Constantine Vaporis, editor

Voices of Revolutionary America: Contemporary Accounts of Daily Life
Carol Sue Humphrey, editor

Voices of Shakespeare's England: Contemporary Accounts of Elizabethan Daily Life
John A. Wagner, editor

Voices of Victorian England: Contemporary Accounts of Daily Life
John A. Wagner, editor

Voices of World War II: Contemporary Accounts of Daily Life
Priscilla Mary Roberts, editor

Voices of Ancient Egypt: Contemporary Accounts of Daily Life
Rosalie David, editor

Voices of the Reformation: Contemporary Accounts of Daily Life
John A. Wagner, editor

Voices of the Iraq War

Contemporary Accounts of Daily Life

Brian L. Steed, Editor

VOICES OF AN ERA

GREENWOOD™

An Imprint of ABC-CLIO, LLC
Santa Barbara, California • Denver, Colorado

Library of Congress Cataloging-in-Publication Data

Names: Steed, Brian L., editor of compilation.
Title: Voices of the Iraq war : contemporary accounts of daily life / Brian L. Steed, editor.
Description: 1st edition. | Santa Barbara, CA : Greenwood, an imprint of ABC-CLIO, LLC,
    [2016] | Series: Voices of an era | Includes bibliographical references and index.
Identifiers: LCCN 2015043229 | ISBN 9781440836749 (alk. paper) | ISBN 9781440836756 (ebook)
Subjects: LCSH: Iraq War, 2003–2011—Personal narratives, American. | Iraq War, 2003–2011—
    Sources. | Iraq War, 2003–2011—Public opinion. | Public opinion—United States.
Classification: LCC DS79.766.A1 V68 2016 | DDC 956.7044/30922—dc23
LC record available at http://lccn.loc.gov/2015043229

ISBN: 978-1-4408-3674-9
EISBN: 978-1-4408-3675-6

20   19   18   17   16   1   2   3   4   5

This book is also available on the World Wide Web as an eBook.
Visit www.abc-clio.com for details.

Greenwood
An Imprint of ABC-CLIO, LLC

ABC-CLIO, LLC
130 Cremona Drive, P.O. Box 1911
Santa Barbara, California 93116-1911

This book is printed on acid-free paper ∞

Manufactured in the United States of America

Disclaimer

All opinions and suppositions expressed in this work are entirely those of the author and in no way reflect the positions, opinions, or policies of the United States Army, the United States Department of Defense, or any official or agency of the United States government.

To the Iraqi people and the people who live in the Middle East:
I am most humbly sorry for the mess we have made.

To my wife whose assistance made this book a reality: Thank you!

CONTENTS

DOCUMENTS OF THE IRAQ WAR

Contents

PREFACE

The Iraq War is my war. On September 11, 2001, I was an instructor in the U.S. Army Armor School at Fort Knox. My students and I rushed to help establish an emergency operations center at that installation where we planned against an expected attack targeting the bullion depository made famous in the James Bond movie *Goldfinger*. That attack did not materialize, but since that day my life has been consumed by the Global War on Terrorism and the Middle East region. I trained many junior armor officers who deployed to Iraq in 2003 with the first invasion forces. Some of the voices in this book come from peers and former students who sacrificed and suffered from this long war.

I was deployed to Iraq in 2005 where I worked as a desk officer in the Political-Military office of the U.S. Embassy-Baghdad annex located in the Presidential Palace of Saddam Hussein. I swam in the pool, I endured the heat and dust storms, and I experienced firsthand the complexity of Iraq and the competing demands of those who we (U.S. military) believed served the interests of the Iraqi nation. My boss worked on issues related to Sunni Iraqis working in the Iraq Ministry of Defense and I was invited to several of the meetings to understand the competing interests and confrontations within the Government of Iraq.

From 2005 to 2008 I lived in Jordan and I served as an exchange officer with the Jordanian Army. My responsibilities included visits to the frontier borders of Jordan where I regularly viewed Iraq from Jordan. I visited the Iraqi-Jordanian border crossing—both sides of it—and I saw the corruption and challenges with respect to the new Iraq being created by the U.S. involvement. I was aware of all cross-border events including smuggling and violent exchanges. The invasion of Iraq had a dramatic impact on the Hashemite Kingdom of Jordan as Iraqi refugees flooded the country and challenged the humanitarian capacity of the small and poor nation. Wealthy and influential Iraqis also flooded into Amman, the capital of Jordan, where they caused real estate prices to skyrocket with their influx of money. Some of the money was U.S. dollars corruptly obtained from the U.S. government in the effort to rebuild Iraq.

I observed the effect of Iraq on U.S. military personnel as they visited Israel on official delegations while I served there from 2008 to 2010 as a liaison to the Israel Defense Forces. During one visit a sergeant needed my assistance to get him away from a crowded Arab market in the Old City of Jerusalem as he was suffering from posttraumatic stress flashbacks of previous Arab-speaking markets from his time in Baghdad. I helped him to get to a quiet place where he could reduce the anxiety. This was my first understanding of the cost of this war on otherwise healthy and capable young men and women.

In 2010–2011, I deployed to Iraq for a full year. I initially worked on foreign military sales cases; I was responsible for managing the details of numerous cases dealing with the M1A1 main battle tanks and associated ammunition and equipment. In this capacity I visited the Iraqi Armor School, training facilities, and range complexes. Later I changed positions to being an advisor and analyst for one of three deputy commanding generals for U.S. Forces-Iraq. This gave me a broader perspective as I attended meetings with senior government of Iraq and Iraq Ministry of Defense and Ministry of Interior officials. I also helped to prepare presentations to senior U.S. government visitors from the legislative and executive branches of government. I observed the decision-making process associated with the U.S. withdrawal from Iraq.

I left Iraq in July 2011 and I went to the United Arab Emirates where I worked in the United States Embassy-Abu Dhabi. From there I observed the perception of the U.S. actions and withdrawal from a regional perspective. I watched the declining U.S. influence in Iraq and in the region because of Iraq.

I returned to the United States after more than eight and a half years in the Middle East in 2013. I became a history instructor at the U.S. Army Command and General Staff College at Fort Leavenworth, Kansas. I taught military history and Middle East history. From this academic ivory tower I watched the fall of Mosul (2014) and the capture of Ramadi (2015). I returned to Iraq to help in the fight against the Islamic State in December 2014 for a little more than two months. I teach an elective titled "What Just Happened? History of the Global War on Terrorism" where I try to help U.S. military officers understand the complexities of what happened and why.

I know that I do not fully understand everything that happened and why. I want to understand it and therefore I wanted to write this book. I want to provide a resource that my high school- and college-age children can read and get some concept of what this war was about and why it was a failure. War is hard work. It is full of complexity and conflict—not just the kind with bullets—and it involves the most complex of machines ever created—a large human organization—that interacts with a foreign culture. Explaining this complexity and the reasons why mistakes were made is the driving focus of this book.

Finally, this book is a tribute to the hundreds of thousands of young men and women who sacrificed years of their lives away from family, friends, and personal interests to serve the peoples of America and Iraq. They wanted to make a difference and make the world better for Americans and Iraqis. Many died, many more are wounded physically and mentally, and even more still are confused at why their hard work and sacrifices seemed to have no positive result. This book is for them and their families. God bless them all.

Voices of the Iraq War is organized in seven sections that each deal with a distinct and important chronological period of the conflict. The first section, "Before the War," tells the story of why the United States invaded Iraq. The second section, "The Invasion of Iraq: Operation Iraqi Freedom," explains the tactical and operational plans and events that were relevant to the capture of Baghdad and the collapse of the Saddam Hussein regime in less than three weeks. Part 3 is "The Occupation (2003–2005)" and it opens a discussion on the nature of the Coalition Provisional Authority and the transition of power and authority to a sovereign Iraq. Fourth is "Insurgency Grows or Civil War (2005–2006)." This part deals with several challenging issues including the confusion about what was happening and the role of contractors on the battlefield. Fifth is "The Surge and Beyond (2006–2009)" and it discusses the most complex series of events in the entire war—why did the Sunni population reject al-Qaeda and turn toward the Shia-led government. Part 6, "A New Administration and Withdrawal: Operation New Dawn (2009–2011)," examines the dramatic transformation of the conflict as a result of the U.S. presidential administration change and the focus of the war turned from winning to leaving. Finally, there is Part 7 titled "Impact." This is the shortest part in the book, but the longest in reality as soldiers are and will continue to suffer the results of this war for decades to come.

In each case the intent is to explain the reasoning of the people making the decisions. Readers need to understand that such a perspective is not designed to advocate, but to inform. A peer history professor often focuses his instruction on World War I by trying to get his students to understand that the generals of that war were not stupid. They faced a set of circumstances beyond their experience and they struggled to solve the problems presented. The same is true of those who made decisions following the attacks on the United States on September 11, 2001. There were mistakes made. Significant, costly, life-shattering, and nation-shattering mistakes. What led them to invade Iraq is important to understand not from a position of judgment, but from their own perspective and thus better inform students and future leaders how to avoid similar challenges and mistakes in the future.

INTRODUCTION

The country Iraq has a lot of connotations that depend on the age of the hearer. For those who are older it may bring to mind the tremendous overwhelming military and technological success of Operation Desert Storm that drove the Iraqi army out of Kuwait and liberated that occupied country. For younger people it may bring to mind the memories of more than eight years of occupation during Operation Iraqi Freedom that ended with the withdrawal of U.S. forces in 2011. For the readers of this book, Iraq may bring to mind thoughts of the Islamic State and its successful campaign of conquest and occupation that was most dramatic in 2014 as thousands of Iraqi soldiers abandoned weapons and positions and fled in the face of their onslaught. These events are interconnected and are reflective of the interactions of key people and events that shaped the relationships of the United States and Iraq.

It is important to remember that Iraq represents an ancient geographic area called Mesopotamia—the Land between the Rivers—considered the cradle of civilization. It is here that things we call states were first created and the first empires formed and rose to power. Mesopotamia is a Greek word and, as is true for many things concerning this region, so much of what we know, say, and think about it is derived from external sources and an external perspective. This book provides the perspectives of outsiders, but outsiders who went inside—deployed as part of the great U.S. military machine and fought in a distant land for what they believed to be protection of the American people and the American way of life. From this perspective readers will come to understand the Iraq War in a meaningful and personal way.

When people hear about the Iraq War (2003–2011), there are themes that dominate the discussion. Many of these themes are conveyed with powerful emotion and invective. This is about the failure of U.S. military power. It is about the clash of worldviews and cultures. It is about a way of war that failed to adapt to a way of occupation. The popular notion of the war is that the American people were misled or that the purpose of the war was wrong from the beginning. Most of these judgments are derived from the outcomes. "If you knew then what you know now would you have invaded Iraq" was a question asked early in the 2016 Presidential Primary race of numerous candidates. This may be a useful question when one is trying to judge the decisiveness or judgment of a potential presidential candidate, but it is a bad way to appreciate history. No one knows "then what they know now." Everyone makes decisions based off the information they have at the moment of the decision. What is more complicated is that each person, be that the president of the United States or the common woman on the street, filters the information he or she has based off a lifetime's worth of worldview shaping experiences.

There is no attempt in this book to make a judgement of decisions made, rather the focus is on trying to present the decisions from the perspective of those who made them. In other words, why did the people involved believe that the decisions they made were correct at the time they made them? The people featured in the chapters that follow did not have the benefit of knowing what the results of their decisions would be. They simply had to trust that they were right. This book attempts to explain why things were done from the perspective of the time.

On September 11, 2001, the world changed for the leadership of the government of the United States. This was true from the president on down the chain. For the first time in nearly sixty years a foreign entity dared to attack the sovereign territory of the United States. Unlike in 1941 when the attack was made on a distant territory—Pearl Harbor, Hawaii (then a U.S. territory and not a state)—this attack was made against the financial and governmental seats of power—New York City and Washington, D.C., respectively. Additionally, in 2001 the state was the source of military power and most people believed that it maintained a monopoly on violence, especially violence against a state. This last point is so important for readers to remember. Yes, there were members of the U.S. government who knew about this organization called al-Qaeda, but the idea that a bunch of individuals from a nonstate group that was holed up in camps and caves in Afghanistan could organize and launch an attack against the United States of America was hard to fully comprehend and thus the search for responsible states was always central to the intended response.

NONSTATE ACTOR

This is a term with a loose definition. In this book the term is used to designate a group that has state-like military capabilities, but is not a state in the sense of being internationally recognized. Oftentimes the definition of a state includes a monopoly of violence within given boundaries, capable of entering into international agreements like treaties, independent sovereignty, or control of the territory of the state, and recognized by other states. Using this simple definition a nonstate actor is an entity that may demonstrate some of these characteristics, but in the end does not have all of them and is therefore relegated to be a "nonstate." al-Qaeda is a nonstate actor for the purposes of this book and so may be the Islamic State though this last group is sometimes referred to as a "post-state" actor because of its unique nature.

Saddam Hussein was always a possible source of trouble. He came to power as the President of Iraq in 1978 and violence seemed to be his preferred means of behavior. He launched a bloody and costly war against Iran in 1980 that lasted until 1988. This war featured the use of medium range rockets that targeted major urban areas with little hope of precision targeting and therefore led to indiscriminate killing of civilians. This war also saw the use of chemical weapons by Iraq against Iranian soldiers and Iraqi Kurdish civilians who were accused of siding with Iran during the war. During the Iran–Iraq War the Persian (Arab) Gulf was subjected to mining by Iranian ships to economically effect Iraq by degrading oil exports. This caused the U.S. government to eventually reflag Kuwaiti oil tankers as American ships and provide military escort craft for ships transiting the Gulf. As part of these escort operations the USS *Stark* was struck by two anti-ship missiles launched by an Iraqi aircraft killing 37 and wounding 21 (May 17, 1987). No military response followed. The United States accepted Iraq's apology for the incident. In many ways this was the first shot fired in a war that lasted more than a quarter of a century. And as was true of so much of the violent interactions between the two countries we still do not understand the full truth behind the attack—accident or deliberate.

On August 2, 1990, Saddam Hussein led his country to war again. This time against his neighbor to the south, Kuwait. Saddam made several accusations against Kuwait as justifications for the war; the most all-encompassing was that Kuwait, which had been one of many Ottoman governorates, had been a historical part of Iraq for centuries, and that European powers separated it out to be an independent state. The United States led an enormous coalition that put more than a half million soldiers on the ground in northern Saudi Arabia and led to a lopsided victory in Operation Desert Storm where, after weeks of aerial bombing, the massive land force retook Kuwait and destroyed much of the Iraqi Army in about 100 hours. The United States was now fully involved in large-scale warfare in Mesopotamia. Aircraft remained stationed in the Arabian Peninsula and land forces remained in Kuwait from Desert Storm until the present.

One justification for the attacks on September 11, 2001, was the presence of U.S. forces in lands deemed sacred by Muslims, namely the Kingdom of Saudi Arabia which serves as the protector of the holy cities of Mecca and Medina. Many Muslims view it as a place reserved only for believers of Islam.

Saddam Hussein did not go away after his military defeat. Instead he remained in power and he trumpeted his continued existence and his continued leadership of Iraq as proof that he defeated the United States and its international coalition. He moved forces toward his border again in what looked like another threatened invasion. The United States responded with a deployment of more forces back to Kuwait and an aggressive air campaign called Desert Fox. No fly zones were enforced in the south and north of Iraq because Saddam had used his helicopters to attack Shia and Kurds who revolted following the events of Desert Storm. The U.S. and coalition aircraft flying these missions were regularly engaged by anti-aircraft targeting radars and fired upon by surface to air missiles from the inauguration of the no-fly zones until the 2003 invasion.

What was known in 2001? Saddam was aggressive. He attacked his neighbors. He ignored international norms of inter-state behavior. He hated the United States. He even sent a team to attempt an assassination of former President George H. W. Bush during a visit to Kuwait following his departure from office. Saddam used chemical weapons against enemies and citizens, military and civilian targets. The 9/11 attackers were believed to need significant resources to conduct their attacks. Some state had to be linked to their efforts and their motivations or so many believed. The idea that Saddam Hussein was connected, in some way, to the attack on the United States on September 11, 2001, was not much of a stretch, and it seemed logical given a worldview that saw states as having a monopoly on violence. Even if Saddam did not conceive of or direct the attacks on that fateful day he might be inclined to use such people to deliver more destructive weapons—chemical or nuclear—to his hated adversary: the United States. He had chemical weapons and he used them against his enemies. He wanted nuclear weapons and had a very advanced program to develop them discovered by inspectors following the end of Desert Storm. Finally, he was a threat to the world order as he continued to defy 16 UN Security Council Resolutions.

The logic chain was there to connect the dots and identify Saddam Hussein as a threat that needed dealing with. In a world before 9/11 he was a nuisance and a tolerable evil. Following 9/11 it was no longer safe and acceptable to allow him to continue his control of a national military with industrial scale weapons production.

UN SECURITY COUNCIL RESOLUTIONS (UNSCR)

This is a UN resolution voted on and adopted by the 15 members of the Security Council. This body is charged with responsibility for the maintenance of international peace and security. The council has five permanent members (the People's Republic of China (which replaced the Republic of China in 1971), France, the Russian Federation (which replaced the defunct Soviet Union in 1991), the United Kingdom, and the United States) who have veto authority and ten rotating members. Resolutions are considered to be legally binding and thus are enforceable by UN member nations.

So the argument went.

It is easy to judge the early decisions of leaders based off the later failures of their actions, but it is important to keep in mind the context of thought and perception common in the military and government in the United States and the allies who participated in Operation Iraqi Freedom (OIF).

Finally, the Iraq War is an example of the change in the character of war. Historically armed conflict was based on a competition of violence—whoever won the competition of violence won the war. This held true regardless of whether the results came from an ancient battlefield with the clash of phalanxes or legions or a modern battlefield with the firepower of rifles, artillery, and aerial delivered ordnance. The new character of war is defined by a competition of narrative. Narrative, in this case, refers to a combination of permanent ideas and images based on customs, religion, culture, biases, mythology, prejudices, accepted truths, and other permanently shaping means of filtering ideas and perceiving information. It also includes transient narrative that consists of news, rumor, information, entertainment, conspiracy theories, and other time-sensitive means of information or data flow. This transient narrative is then filtered to determine whether it should be accepted or rejected into the permanent narrative.

In neither case is violence or narrative exclusive—this is really a question of emphasis or dominance. The "decisive operation" on the current Middle Eastern battlefield is narrative. Violence is still a critical portion of armed conflict, but it serves a subservient and supporting role only.

EVALUATING AND INTERPRETING
PRIMARY DOCUMENTS

The documents included in this book are, in many cases, not documents at all, but interviews. This fact tells much of the story about this war—it is recent. Archives are not opened and the "real story" is not yet available. In many ways this is the story of the participants—presidents, generals, soldiers, and Iraqis. The documents here are their thoughts and their reflections on the events. In the case of political leaders they are sending political messages. In the case of the documentary evidence they are representative of the shaping documents for the conflict and into the present. The repercussions of the Iraq War are being felt as this book is being written. The emotions associated with the "current" events have shaped the thoughts and reflections of many of the interviewees.

What are included in the pages that follow are the raw materials of a history still to be written. Though this book seeks to tie them together in a broader narrative each chapter and the associated document stands alone and thus must be critically viewed individually. There are several points worthy of consideration when providing critical analysis to these documents.

The study of the writing of history is called historiography. This branch of history explains how history changes over time for a given event or topic. Technically, the Iraq War is too recent to be considered history. Despite that there have already been some changes in the description of the events and the causes and consequences of the events in Iraq. Much as happened following the end of the Vietnam War there are also different perspectives of the events in Iraq. Some of those perspectives emphasize government and military failures. Other perspectives tend to glorify the sacrifice of military personnel and the focus on what was accomplished. This book was being written in 2014 and 2015. The events associated with a group called the Islamic State shaped the historiography of the Iraq War as both the causes of entry and exit from the country and the consequences were not simply debated by historians, but they were debated in the political campaigns for the congressional mid-term elections in 2014 and the presidential campaign that began in 2015. Some of the interviews were done in that environment and even if they weren't that environment shaped the discussions in the pages that follow.

First, there is no such thing as "real history." History began as a literary genre and this is true even today. Though, like the first historian Herodotus, modern historians try to explain not simply what happened, but why it happened they still struggle with their own personal biases and prejudices. As a result all history has some slant, some particular perspective. This is the point of reading a preface and an introduction for books. They tend to give the first and the fullest understanding of the perspective of the author and why the book was written. Understand the overall slant of the material and then take the slant into consideration with every page that continues.

As a reader evaluates the documents that follow, some of the considerations of those documents should be *who* wrote the document or, in the case of the oral interviews, *who* is being interviewed; *when* was the document written, *when* did the events transpire, and/or *when* did the interview take place; *where* was the document produced and/or *where* did the events transpire; *for whom* was the document produced; and *why* was this document created. Within each chapter is a brief discussion of aftermath, but this is not sufficient for critical analysis. It is also important to understand the results and consequences of the document.

Who is more than the name of the person who wrote the document or spoke in the interview. As with events, context is everything. *Who* is speaking? What is the person's background? Is there an obvious motive for producing the document or providing the interview? Does this motive shape the perception and reception of the document? If so, then in what way? Some of the interviewees may be sharing information in an altruistic sense, because they want their story shared or feel that their story may help inform the discussion. Other interview participants, particularly political personalities or senior military leaders may want to shape the perception of history and possibly the perception of their role in the events. Most soldiers know their story will not be part of the perception of history so their motives tend to be less about that then possibly having their story told at all. Soldiers do have a tendency for wanting the conflicts in which they fought to be considered worthwhile ventures. Another way is that they want to think that their friends did not die in vain. In the case of documents the question word *who* turns to one of author rather than speaker.

When can be as complex as *who* as there are numerous answers to this question depending on the specifics. *When* was the document written or signed? *When* was the document initiated? In some cases documents in this book began production under the Coalition Provisional Authority and yet it was finished and signed under the Iraqi Interim Government. These two periods, though close in time, had significantly different environments politically and in terms of security. In the case of interviews then the time becomes more important. *When* did the events take place? *When* was the interview conducted? The events shaped the thinking, but the interview time expresses the time lag between events and interview and can explain the change in perspective or a loss of vividness with respect to details. The timing of the interview can also give insight into the context of those times and may shed light on motivations. There is a case where the interview happened within a few days of the events and other cases where it was several years later.

Where can be similar to *when* in the questions. In many cases the interviews happened in the United States, far from the environment in which the events occurred. Some of the interviews happened in Iraq, at or near where the events happened. Each of the documents has a different location. In one case the speech is given in Amman, Jordan. Why might this be the case?

For Whom gets at the question of audience. The single biggest group of documents is interviews that were contracted by the U.S. government with the intent of capturing what happened during the war. The audience was the U.S. military in terms of lessons and academia to provide information about opinions and experiences. Other interviews, speeches, and documents each need to be looked at to determine the purpose of the speech or interview and who the person intended to influence with their remarks. The documents produced by the governments have audiences as well. Maybe it was to express to the Iraqi people that would be forever free of the brutality of the Saddam regime. It is this reason that readers need to consider.

The last of these simple questions is *why* was the document created or the interview provided. This was addressed in the previous question a bit as well in terms of audience. The purpose of the document can communicate a great deal about the trustworthiness of the source.

In each chapter the discussion on aftermath tries to discuss what comes after the events associated with the document. So readers have some context to begin understanding the consequence and results of the document. As previously stated there are, at the time of writing, conflicts throughout the Middle East and directly associated with Iraq. This goes to the heart of results and consequences. Some are short term and others last for years. Some of those interviewed discuss results and consequences within the document itself. Is there significance to this particular document that lasts beyond the immediacy of the moment?

Whenever one reads historical material it is important to do so critically. People have been providing literary and historical criticism of Herodotus for centuries. This is because of the importance of the book he wrote. Regardless of importance every reader should question what they read and seek to understand the material as free of author and documentary bias as possible.

CHRONOLOGY OF THE IRAQ WAR

1990   August 2   Iraq invades Kuwait.

                     August 7   United States begins Operation Desert Shield to protect Saudi Arabia.

            November 29   UN Security Council passes resolution (UNSCR) 678, setting a deadline for Iraq to withdraw from Kuwait before January 15, 1991, or face military action.

1991   January 12   U.S. Congress passes joint resolution authorizing use of military force to drive Iraq from Kuwait.

            January 17   Operation Desert Storm begins with air campaign.

            January 29   Iraqi forces attack into Saudi Arabia to the town of Khafji.

            February 1   Iraqi forces driven out of Saudi Arabia.

          February 24   Operation Desert Storm ground campaign begins.

          February 27   Coalition forces enter and liberate Kuwait City.

          February 28   Operation Desert Storm ceasefire declared.

              March 3   Iraq accepts ceasefire terms from the UN.

             March 20   United States shoots down Iraqi warplane over Kurdish territory and thus unofficially begins Operation Provide Comfort, which was a relief and protection effort, including a no-fly zone, for Iraqi Kurds. This operation ended on December 31, 1996.

               April 5   UNSCR 688 passed which required that Iraq cease the repression of the Iraqi people and allow international humanitarian organizations access.

1992   August 27   Operation Southern Watch established. This was a no-fly zone patrolled by aircraft from the United States, United Kingdom, and France. UNSCR 688 was used as the

		justification. This was initially established at the 32nd parallel and then later moved north to the 33rd parallel. The no-fly zone ended on March 19, 2003, with the beginning of Operation Iraqi Freedom.
1993	April 13	Kuwaiti officials foil a plan to bomb President George H. W. Bush during a visit to Kuwait following his departure from office.
1997	January 1	Operation Northern Watch begins. This was the northern no-fly zone and the continuation of the no-fly zone protection began with Operation Provide Comfort. This extended down to the 36th parallel. This operation ended on March 17, 2003, with the beginning of Operation Iraqi Freedom.
1998	December 16–19	Operation Desert Fox conducted. This was a four-day bombing campaign of Iraqi targets with the justification of obstruction of UN Special Commission inspectors.
2001	February 16–17	United States and United Kingdom conduct bombing raids of Iraqi targets attempting to disable Iraqi air defenses.
	September 11	Attacks by al-Qaeda on the World Trade Center and Pentagon. Saddam Hussein immediately declares that Iraq played no part in the attacks.
	October 7	Operation Enduring Freedom begins with attacks on Afghanistan.
	December 6–17	Battle of Tora Bora in Afghanistan to defeat remnants of al-Qaeda.
	December 7	The Taliban lose their last major stronghold in Afghanistan.
2002	March 1–18	Operation Anaconda attempts to destroy last remnants of al-Qaeda and the Taliban in Afghanistan.
	July 5	Saddam rejects new UN weapons inspectors.
	August 2	Saddam meets with chief weapons inspector Hans Blix.
	September 12	President Bush addresses UN and challenges the organization to confront "grave and gathering danger" of Iraq or allow the United States and likeminded nations to act.
	October 2	U.S. Congress passes joint resolution authorizing use of military force against Iraq.
	October 16	President Bush signs authorization for use of force against Iraq.
	November 8	UNSCR 1441 passed which requires Saddam Hussein to disarm or face "serious consequences."
	November 18	UN Weapons inspectors arrive in Iraq.

	December 7	Iraq submits a 12,000-page weapons declaration as required by UNSCR 1441. This document is seen as incomplete and insufficient to meet the requirement.
2003	January 3	UN Monitoring, Verification and Inspection Commission (UNMOVIC) inspectors have established a base of operations in Mosul to speed the inspection process.
	January 9	UN Chief Weapons Inspector Hans Blix and International Atomic Energy Agency head Mohammed El Baradei give a report to the UN Security Council that they are making progress, but the Iraqi government is not forthcoming.
	January 16	UN weapons inspectors find empty rocket warheads designed to carry chemical weapons.
	January 18	Global protests against the Iraq War occur in cities around the world, including Tokyo, Moscow, Paris, London, Montreal, Ottawa, Toronto, Cologne, Bonn, Göteborg, Istanbul, Cairo, Washington, D.C., and San Francisco, California.
	January 20	U.K. government announces the deployment of British forces to Kuwait.
	January 23	Australian forces begin deployment to Kuwait and the Gulf region.
	January 28	U.S. State of the Union address by President Bush.
	January 30	Eight nations (Britain, Spain, Italy, Portugal, Hungary, Poland, Denmark, and the Czech Republic) release a statement in support of U.S. efforts to invade Iraq.
	February 5	U.S. Secretary of State Colin Powell presents the U.S. case against Saddam Hussein to the UN Security Council to gain international support for military action against Iraq.
	February 12	Al-Jazeera releases an audio tape purporting to include a statement from Osama bin Laden recounting the Battle of Tora Bra and urges Muslims to overthrow the regime of Saddam Hussein.
	February 14	UNMOVIC chief weapons inspector Hans Blix reports to the UNSC that the Iraqis had been cooperating and that no weapons of mass destruction had been found though the government had to account for many banned weapons believed to be in the Iraqi arsenal. He also calls into question some of the information presented by Secretary Powell on February 5.

Tariq Aziz meets with Pope John Paul II. |

February 15	Largest international war protest with an estimated six million people in over 600 cities.
February 16	A missile larger than allowed by UN sanctions is found in Iraq.
February 24	Colin Powell states in a meeting in Beijing that "We are reaching a point where serious consequences must flow."
February 26	Hans Blix states there is no evidence that Iraq has weapons of mass destruction.
	Saddam appears in a televised interview with CBS News anchor Dan Rather and rules out exile as an option.
February 28	Iraq begins the destruction of banned missiles. The White House questions the validity of the effort.
March 1	Several countries call for Saddam Hussein to step down.
	Turkey votes against allowing U.S. forces to enter Turkey.
March 7	Hans Blix reports increased, but still qualified cooperation from Iraq.
March 12	Possible additional UNSCRs have been scuttled by various members of the council threatening vetoes.
March 16	Leaders from the United States, United Kingdom, Portugal, and Spain meet in the Azores to discuss the invasion timing.
March 17	President Bush gives a final ultimatum to Saddam Hussein for him to leave Iraq with his sons in 48 hours.
	UN Secretary General orders all UN personnel to leave Iraq.
March 18	Colin Powell announces a thirty-nation "Coalition of the Willing."
March 20	Operation Iraqi Freedom begins.
March 21	"Shock and Awe" aerial bombardment campaign begins.
March 26	Elements of 173rd Airborne Brigade parachute into Bashur Drop Zone in northern Iraq.
April 2–4	Battle of the Karbala Gap.
April 4–9	"Thunder Run" into Baghdad by 2nd Brigade, 3rd Infantry Division.
April 10	Baghdad is secured by coalition forces.
	Kurdish forces capture Kirkuk.
April 15	Coalition forces control Tikrit, Saddam's hometown.

April 21   Retired Lt. Gen. Jay Garner becomes the civilian leader of Iraq with the establishment of the Office for Reconstruction and Humanitarian Assistance (ORHA).

April 23   Coalition forces enter Fallujah.

April 28   200 protestors defy the coalition-imposed curfew in Fallujah and organize a protest. During the protest soldiers occupying a schoolhouse claim to have been fired upon, and kill 15 in returning fire. No U.S. casualties were reported.

May 1   President Bush announces an end to major combat operations.

May 12   Paul Bremer arrives in Iraq as the head of the newly formed Coalition Provisional Authority (CPA) and replaces General Jay Garner as the civil leader of Iraq.

May 15   U.S forces launch Operation Planet X, capturing hundreds of people.

May 23   L. Paul Bremer issues CPA Order Number 2 disbanding the Iraqi Army.

June 15   Operation Desert Scorpion begins. It consisted of a series of raids across Iraq intended to find resistance members and heavy weapons.

June 24   Six British soldiers killed by a mob in Southern Iraq.

July 2   President Bush says, "My answer is, bring 'em on," in responding to the growing violence in Iraq.

July 6   Joseph C. Wilson IV refutes the evidence of yellow cake uranium used to justify the invasion of Iraq in the *New York Times'* editorial page.

July 7   General John Abizaid replaces General Tommy Franks as CENTCOM commander.

July 13   The Iraqi Governing Council is established under the authority of the U.S. Coalition Provisional Authority.

July 22   Uday and Qusay Hussein are killed during a three-hour battle in Mosul, Iraq by elements of the 101st Airborne Division.

August 7   The first car bomb of Operation Iraqi Freedom explodes outside the Jordanian embassy in Baghdad killing 17.

August 19   Truck bomb explodes outside the UN headquarters killing the top UN envoy, Sergio Vieira de Mello, and 21 others and leading to the withdrawal of the UN from Iraq due to security concerns.

August 29	The Imam Ali Mosque in Najaf, Iraq, is attacked by a suicide car bomb resulting in at least 85 killed.
September 3	First post-Saddam government.
September 20	Aquila al-Hashimi, a member of the Iraq Interim Governing Council, is shot. She dies five days later.
September 23	Gallup poll shows majority of Iraqis expect better life in five years. Around two-thirds of Baghdad residents state the Iraqi dictator's removal was worth the hardships they've been forced to endure.
October 2	David Kay's Iraq Survey Group report finds little evidence of WMD in Iraq.
October 16	UNSCR passed which envisions a multinational force and preserves Washington's quasi-absolute control of Iraq.
October 27	Baghdad bombings, beginning of the Ramadan Offensive.
November 2	Heaviest single loss for the coalition troops up to that time—two U.S. Chinook helicopters are fired on by two surface-to-air missiles and one crashed near Fallujah and on its way to Baghdad airport; soldiers are killed and twenty wounded.
November 12	A suicide truck bomb blows up the Italian headquarters in Nasiriyah, killing 19 Italians (17 of them soldiers) and 14 Iraqis.
November 15	The Governing Council unveils an accelerated timetable for transferring the country to Iraqi control.
November 22	An Airbus A-300 freighter belonging to German courier firm DHL is forced to make an emergency landing with a wing fire after being struck by a shoulder-fired SA-14 missile.
November 26	Abed Hamed Mowhoush, Iraqi general, dies in U.S. custody. U.S. soldiers accused of torturing him to death.
November 27	President Bush surprises U.S. troops and accompanies them for Thanksgiving dinner.
November 30	The U.S. military reports killing 46 militants and wounding 18 in clashes in the central city of Samarra. The reports are later called into question as reporters interview residents of the city. Hospital staff only reports eight dead—most or all of them civilians, including an elderly Iranian pilgrim. No bodies of dead guerrillas are found.
December 13	Saddam Hussein is captured by soldiers from the 1st Brigade, 4th Infantry Division. He was hiding in a hole in a barn in al-Dawr, near Tikrit, Iraq. Saddam stated, "I am Saddam Hussein. I am the president of Iraq. I want to

negotiate." The U.S. soldier responded, "President Bush sends his regards."

	December 17	The U.S. 4th Infantry Division launches Operation Ivy Blizzard, lasting from dawn until mid-morning. The operation resulted in the arrest of several guerrilla fighters and possible terrorists.
2004	January 18	Suicide truck bomb detonates with 1,000 pounds of explosives outside the headquarters of the U.S.-led coalition killing about twenty people and injuring more than sixty.
	January 26	Japanese Iraq Reconstruction and Support Group: Japanese troops begin participation in most risky military expedition since World War II.
	February 1	Two suicide bombers strike Kurdish political offices in the northern city of Irbil, killing 117 and injuring 133.
	February 10	At least fifty people killed in a car bomb attack on a police recruitment center south of Baghdad.
	March 2	Multiple bombings in Baghdad and Karbala at the climax of the Shi'a festival of Ashurah kill nearly 200, the deadliest attacks up to that time.
	March 8	Provisional Iraqi government unanimously approves the country's new interim constitution.
	March 11	Madrid bombings killing 191 on commuter trains.
	March 31	Four Blackwater contractors ambushed and killed in Fallujah.
	April 4–May 1	First Battle of Fallujah (Operation Vigilant Resolve).
	April 8	Beginning of the kidnapping of foreign civilians in Iraq with the abduction of several Japanese.
		The Mahdi takes full control in Kut and partial control of Najaf, Karbala, and Kufa.
	April 16	Kut is retaken by coalition forces, but Najaf, Karabla, and Kufa remain under control of Jaysh al-Mahdi.
	April 18	Spain, led by newly elected José Luis Rodríguez Zapatero (Socialist Party), vows to withdraw its troops.
		Beginning of release of Abu Ghraib prisoner abuse images.
	April 20	Mortar rounds fired on Abu Ghraib Prison by insurgents. 22 detainees killed and 92 wounded.
	April 21	Attacks on police stations in Basra and Az Zubayr kill at least 73 people, including 17 children, along with 94 wounded.

April 26	Iraq Interim Governing Council announces a new flag for post-Saddam Iraq. The flag is later abandoned, among sentiments that it looks too much like Israel's flag.
May 17	Ezzedine Salim, head of the Iraqi Governing Council, killed in a suicide attack.
May 19	U.S. forces bomb a wedding party killing 42 people.
May 28	Iyad Allawi is chosen as the prime minister for the interim Iraqi government.
June 8	UNSCR 1546 passed which transfers sovereignty from the CPA to the Iraqi Interim Government.
June 21	Iranian seizure of Royal Navy personnel.
June 28	At 10:26 a.m., the US-led CPA formally transferred sovereignty of Iraqi territory to the Iraqi interim government, two days ahead of schedule. L. Paul Bremer departed the country two hours later.
June 30	Saddam Hussein and eleven high ex-governmental figures are put under the Iraqi Interim Government's authority.
July 1	Saddam Hussein appears at his first hearing.
July 20	President of the Philippines, confirms that hostage Angelo de la Cruz has been freed by his captors after their demands for a one-month-early withdrawal of all 51 Filipino troops from Iraq were met.
August 5–27	Battle of Najaf.
September 12	Haifa Street helicopter incident where 13 Iraqis are killed.
September 14	Baghdad car bomb near market and police station kills at least 47.
September 30	Insurgents detonate three car bombs killing 41 people (34 of them children) in the Shi'ite Amil area of southern Baghdad. The blasts, which wounded 139, occurred shortly after U.S. troops had celebrated opening a new sewage system and distributed candy to children.
October 1	Battle of Samarra.
October	Abu Musab al-Zarqawi changes his group's name to Tanzim Qaedat al Jihad fi Bilad al Rafidayn aka al Qaeda in Iraq (AQI).
Late October	United States warned that more than 300 tons of high explosives from the al-Qaqaa facility were removed.
November 7–December 23	Second Battle of Fallujah (Operation Phantom Fury).
November 8–16	Battle of Mosul.

	December 19	Suicide car bomb in Najaf, close to the Imam Ali shrine, kills 52 and wounds at least 140. On the same day, a car bomb explodes in Karbala, killing 14 and injuring at least 52.
	December 21	Attack on Forward Operating Base Marez, kills 22, including 18 U.S. personnel.
2005	January 26	31 U.S. soldiers die in a helicopter crash, deadliest day of the entire postwar period for the U.S. military.
	January 30	Iraqi legislative election. Sunnis mostly boycott.
	February 17	Full election results released.
	February 28	Al-Hillah bombing: the deadliest single blast up to that time, a car bomb kills 127 in Hillah; the identity of the bomber as a Jordanian causes a diplomatic row between Iraq and Jordan.
	March 4	Liberation of Italian journalist Giuliana Sgrena, during which secret Italian agent Nicola Calipari is killed by U.S. fire. Italian government announces a partial retreat of Italian troops from the coalition.
	March 16	First meeting of the transitional National Assembly.
	April 2	Battle of Abu Ghraib.
	April 6	Jalal Talabani (Kurd) elected president of Iraq.
	April 7	Ibrahim al-Jaafari is nominated as prime minister of Iraq.
	April 9	Tens of thousands of demonstrators loyal to Shiite cleric Muqtada Sadr march through Baghdad denouncing the U.S. occupation of Iraq.
	April 28	The parliament votes in support of the new government.
	May 8	Battle of al-Qaim.
	May 11	Suicide bombers kill at least 71 people and wound more than 160 in a crowded market and a line of security force recruits.
	May 15	Formation of the parliamentary commission to draft the new constitution.
	June 20	Suicide bomber kills 13 policemen and injured more than 100 people, in Irbil, northern Iraq.
	July 3–8	Egyptian ambassador designee to Iraq abducted while buying a newspaper. He was killed while a captive.
	July 16	Suicide bombing in Musayyib kills 100.
	August 1–4	Battle of Haditha.

August 22	Draft of constitution presented to Iraqi parliament.
August 28	Full constitution presented to parliament.
August 31	Rumors of a suicide bomber lead to a stampede on the Al-Aaimmah bridge; about 1,000 people died.
September 1–18	Battle of Tal Afar.
September 7	American hostage Roy Hallums is rescued in Iraq. He was kidnapped in November 2004 and later appeared in a video released by militants.
September 14	Bombings in Baghdad kill more than 150 and injure more than 500. Deadliest day in the insurgency so far.
September 19	British forces conduct a raid on a Basra prison to free captive SAS soldiers.
September 26	U.S. Army PFC Lynndie England is found guilty of six of seven charges by a military court in connection with the Abu Ghraib prisoner abuse scandal.
September 29	Bombings in Balad kill more than 100.
October 15	Iraqi Constitutional Referendum. Voters approve new constitution.
October 19	Beginning of Saddam Hussein's trial.
October 24	Palestine and Sheraton hotels are hit with truck bombs.
November 5–22	Operation Steel Curtain. First large deployment of Iraqi Army in support of coalition operation to remove foreign fighters.
November 15	173 prisoners are found in an Iraqi government bunker in Baghdad, having been starved, beaten, and tortured.
November 18	Suicide attacks on Shia mosques in Khanaqin, Iraq kill dozens.
November 19	Haditha killings. U.S. soldiers kill 24 unarmed Iraqi civilians.
November 24	Khadim Sarhid al-Hemaiyim, one of the most important Sunni Arab tribal leaders in Iraq, killed with his three sons and a son-in-law in Baghdad. The gunman appeared to be a member of the new Iraqi Army.
November 26–March 23	Four human rights workers of Christian Peacemaker Teams held hostage. One is killed and the rest are freed on March 23, 2006.
December 14	President George W. Bush says that the decision to invade Iraq in 2003 was the result of faulty intelligence and accepts responsibility for that decision. He maintains that his decision was still justified.

	December 15	Iraqi Legislative Election.
	December 18	Primetime Oval Office address from President Bush. He states, "Not only can we win the war in Iraq—we are winning the war in Iraq."
2006	January 5	Suicide bombers kill more than 100 people in separate attacks in Karbala and Ramadi.
	January 15	al-Qaeda in Iraq forms Mujahideen Shura Council with other groups.
	February 22	The al-Askari mosque in Samarra is bombed. No one is killed, but during retaliatory violence more than a thousand die. This is considered the start of the Iraqi Civil War.
	March 12	Abeer Qassim Hamza al-Janabi, a 14-year-old Iraqi girl raped and murdered together with her family by U.S. forces in the Mahmudiyah killings.
	April 26	Hamdania incident. Marines abduct an Iraqi civilian from a house, kill him, and place components and spent AK-47 cartridges near his body to make it appear he was planting an IED.
	May 5	Iraq was listed fourth on the 2006 Failed States Index compiled by the American Foreign Policy magazine and the Fund for Peace think-tank.
	May 20	New Iraqi government begins to function.
	June 7	Abu Musab al-Zarqawi is killed by a U.S. air strike. It was hoped that his death will ease the sectarian killings rampant in Iraq.
	June 14–October 24	Operation Together Forward. Security plan designed to reduce the sectarian violence in Baghdad since the al-Askari mosque bombing. This was deemed a failure.
	June 17–November 15	Battle of Ramadi.
	July 25–27	Operation River Falcon. Designed to remove insurgents from a region of southeast Baghdad.
	September 27–February 18	Operation Sinbad to remove corrupt police in Basra and restore law and order.
	October 15	al-Qaeda in Iraq changes its name to the Islamic State of Iraq (ISI).
	October 19–20	Battle of Amarah between members of the Jaysh al-Mahdi and the Badr Corps—competing Shia militias.
	November 7	U.S. Congressional midterm elections. Democrat party wins both chambers.

	November 23	Multiple suicide car bombs kill hundreds and wound hundreds more in Sadr City. Shiites retaliate with mortar attacks on a Sunni shrine in Baghdad and other Sunni targets.
	December 6	Iraq Study Group releases their final report.
	December 21	U.S. forces raid a building believed to contain insurgents and they instead turn out to be Iranian diplomats.
	December 25–October 1, 2007	Diyala Campaign. A coalition series of operations to secure the province.
	December 30	Execution of Saddam Hussein.
2007	January 6–9	Battle of Haifa Street rages to control a road in downtown Baghdad.
	January 10	The Iraq War troop surge of 2007 is announced.
	January 11	United States raid on Iranian Liaison Office in Arbil.
	January 15	Awad Hamed al-Bandar, former head of Iraq's Revolutionary Court; and Barzan Ibrahim, Saddam's half-brother and former intelligence chief, were both executed by hanging before dawn in Baghdad.
	January 16	Series of car bombs across Baghdad kill more than 100 people.
	January 20	The third deadliest day for U.S. troops in Iraq occurred, with at least 25 U.S. soldiers killed in a helicopter shoot down, in Anbar province, and in roadside bombings.
	January 21	Moqtada al-Sadr announces his block will return to parliament after two months of boycott.
	January 23	Five Blackwater contractors are killed in a helicopter shoot down.
	January 28–29	Battle of Najaf.
	February 3	Baghdad market bomb kills 135.
	February 6	Chinook helicopter crashes in western Iraq. This is the fifth U.S. helicopter to crash in two weeks.
	February 14–November 24	Operation Law and Order is a joint coalition-Iraqi security plan for Baghdad.
	February 15	Operation Shurta Nasir (Operation Police Victory) to remove al-Qaeda from Hit.
	February 27–September 3	Siege of U.K. bases in Basra.
	March 6	Al-Hillah bombing kills 115.
	March 10–August 19	Battle of Baqubah.

March 23	Iranian naval personnel seize 15 Royal Navy personnel conducting a search of merchant vessels in the Persian Gulf. The sailors are released on April 4.
March 27	Tal Afar bombings kill 152.
March 30	U.S. Senate approves a goal, not a requirement, of getting all combat soldiers out of Iraq by March 31, 2008.
April 6–10	Operation Black Eagle in al-Diwaniyah.
April 11	Secretary of Defense Robert Gates announces U.S. Army units will remain in Iraq for 15 months rather than twelve.
April 16	Moqtada al-Sadr's party resigns from parliament over a lack of a timeline for U.S. withdrawal.
April 18	Series of bombings across Baghdad kills nearly 200.
May 2007	Iraq oil law submitted to Iraqi Council of Representatives
May 8	144 of 275 Iraqi parliament members sign a petition requiring the Iraqi government to seek parliamentary approval before it requests an extension of the UN mandate.
June 13	Al-Askari Mosque bombing blows up two of the mosque's minarets.
June 16–August 14	Operation Phantom Thunder focused on removing al-Qaeda in Iraq and other extremist organizations.
July 12	The Apache airstrikes associated with the WikiLeaks released and edited video "Collateral Murder" occurs.
July 17	Suicide car bomb attack in Amirli kills 156.
August 14	Four coordinated suicide bombs kill an estimated 796 Yazidis in multiple locations.
August 15–January 2008	Operation Phantom Strike focused on removing al-Qaeda in Iraq and Iranian-supported extremists.
September 3	British forces finish withdrawal from Basra leaving the city in the complete control of Iraqi security forces.
September 10	General Petraeus and Ambassador Ryan Crocker submit their report to Congress on the Situation in Iraq.
September 16	Blackwater Security Consulting contractors kill 17 Iraqis during a protection mission at Nisour Square in Baghdad.
November 1	Statistics for October show a significant reduction in violence since the beginning of "the Surge."
December 16	British forces hand control of Basra over to Iraqi security forces.
December 18	UNSCR 1790 extends the UN mandate until December 31, 2008.

2008	January 8–July 28	Operation Phantom Phieonix is a continuation of Operations Phantom Thunder and Phantom Strike.
	January 11	First snowfall in Baghdad in more than 50 years.
	January 13	Iraqi government announces a law that allows former Baath Party members to have civil and military positions.
	January 22	Iraqi Parliament approves a new flag that removes the three stars symbolizing the ideals of the Baath Party.
	January 23–July 28	Ninewa Campaign, a series of offensives and counterattacks in the northern province.
	February 1	Two suicide bombs kill 99 in the Baghdad animal market.
	February 21–29	Turkey invades northern Iraq to combat Kurdish fighters from the PKK (Kurdistan Workers Party) who have launched attacks in Turkey.
	March 20	Al-Jazeera releases Osama bin Laden recording where he states that "Iraq is the perfect base to set up the jihad to liberate Palestine."
	March 23	U.S. soldiers killed in action in Global War on Terrorism exceeds 4,000.
	March 25–31	Battle of Basra begins with the Charge of the Knights led by prime minister Nuri al-Maliki to combat opposition attacks in Basra.
	March 25–May 11	Battle of Sadr City.
	April 8	General Petraeus and Ambassador Crocker testify before U.S. Senate.
	April 9	General Petraeus and Ambassador Crocker testify before U.S. House.
	May 8	Abu Ayyub al-Masri is arrested in Mosul. He is the suspected leader of al-Qaeda in Iraq.
	June 14	Iraqi forces begin an offensive against Mahdi Army in Maysan Province.
	July 29–August 11	Operation Augurs of Prosperity was intended to clear Diyala Province of opposition elements.
	September 1	United States transfers security responsibility for Anbar Province to Iraq.
	October 4	Polish forces complete mission in Iraq.
	October 26	Abu Kemal raid into Syria by U.S. special operations forces.
	October 29	United States transfers security responsibility for Wasit Province to Iraq.
	November 4	Barack Obama elected president of the United States.

November 17	U.S.-Iraq Status of Forces Agreement signed by Iraqi foreign minister and U.S. ambassador to Iraq. This agreement requires U.S. forces to be out of cities in 2009 and out of Iraq by the end of 2011.
December 4	Czech Republic forces complete mission in Iraq.
December 5	South Korean forces complete mission in Iraq.
December 9	Ukrainian forces complete mission in Iraq.
December 14	President Bush signs status of forces agreement. This was the president's fourth and final trip to Baghdad. During the press conference one of the reporters hurled two shoes at the president in protest for the chaos in Iraq.
December 17	Moldovan, Bulgarian, and Albanian forces complete mission in Iraq.
2009 January 1	United States formally transfers security responsibility for Green Zone to Iraq.
	United States opens new embassy in Baghdad.
January 20	Barack Obama sworn in as 44th president of the United States.
January 22	Estonian and Salvadoran forces complete mission in Iraq.
January 31	Iraqi Provincial Elections.
February 27	President Obama announces Christopher Hill as the new ambassador to Iraq and that U.S. combat operations will end on August 31, 2010.
April 7	Obama visits Iraq for the first time as president.
June 4	Romanian forces complete mission in Iraq.
June 30	U.S. forces withdraw from cities and towns in Iraq.
July 28	United Kingdom, Australia, and Romania complete mission in Iraq. United States is the only foreign military force in Iraq.
August 19	Numerous bombs detonate in Baghdad killing more than 100 and wounding hundreds more.
October 25	Two large car bombs kill 155 in central Baghdad and wound hundreds more.
December 8	A series of car bombs kill at least 127 people in Baghdad.
December 18	Iran invades to seize East Maysan oil field.
2010 March 7	Parliamentary Election.
April 18	A joint U.S.-Iraqi operation near Tikrit, Iraq kills Abu Ayyub al-Masri and Abu Omar al-Baghdadi. They are the

		leaders of the Islamic State of Iraq—the precursor group for the Islamic State in Iraq and al-Sham or ISIS.
	August 18	Last U.S. combat brigade departs Iraq. More than 50,000 U.S. military forces remain in Iraq conducting mostly advice and assist missions.
	August 31	Operation Iraqi Freedom formally ends.
	September 1	Operation New Dawn begins.
2011	January 8	Moqtada al-Sadr returns to Iraq and urges the rejection of violence and peaceful resistance against the country's "occupiers" in his first public address.
	January 15	Iraqi soldier kills two U.S. soldiers at a training center.
	January 17	Car bombs kill 133 across Iraq.
	April 8	Iraqi forces raid Camp Ashraf—the "refugee" camp for the People's Mujahedin of Iran—killing 34 and injuring hundreds.
	December 18	Last U.S. troops leave Iraq.
2013	April 8	The Islamic State of Iraq changes its name to the Islamic State of Iraq and al-Sham or ISIS.
	July 22	ISIS organizes a prison break-out from Taji and Abu Ghraib, Iraq.
2014	January 3	ISIS proclaims itself to be the Islamic State in Fallujah.
	June 9	Mosul, Iraq falls to ISIS.
	June 15	Operation Inherent Resolve begins with a purpose of coordinating a regional response to ISIS.
	June 29	ISIS changes its name to the Islamic State and claims to be a Caliphate.

BEFORE THE WAR

1. A Translator's Journey: Mohamed al-Shara on Leaving Iraq

INTRODUCTION

U.S. entanglement in Iraq did not begin in 2002–2003; nor is it likely to end in the foreseeable future. Direct U.S. involvement with Iraq and its neighbors began with American support of Iraq's military operations in the Iran–Iraq War (1980–1988). U.S. military operations slowly increased over the course of the war, particularly in the Persian Gulf, where Iran planted mines in an attempt to disrupt shipping. As a result, the U.S. Navy began escorting and reflagging Kuwaiti ships in order to ensure their safe passage through the gulf and protect American oil interests. In 1987 the U.S. Navy frigate, USS *Stark* was fired on by two Iraqi anti-ship missiles. U.S. officials accepted the Iraqi version that claimed it was an accident and no retaliation was conducted.

SUNNI–SHIA SPLIT

In the seventh century AD, the Muslim faith divided over a difference in succession of leadership following the death of the Prophet Mohamed. Mohamed was and is considered to be the last prophet by Muslims and all legitimate subsequent leaders of the community of believers were designated Caliph (meaning successor). Some believed that succession should be determined by a council of respected leaders who had personal association with the prophet. These men are referred to as the *Companions of the Prophet*. In such a manner, the first four Caliphs were chosen—Abu Bakr, Omar, Othman, and Ali. Others believed that Ali, who was a son-in-law of the Prophet, should be the first Caliph. Though Ali personally accepted the different choices for Caliph who preceded him the difference of opinion grew over time. Ali became the fourth Caliph following the murder of Othman. Ali was accused of not pursuing the killers of Othman by Othman's extended family. When Ali was also murdered, the division between the two opinions became a rift. It was agreed that Muawiyah, a relative of Othman, would be Caliph after Ali, but he agreed to not appoint his son as his successor. When he reneged on that promise, Hussein, Ali's son, opposed him. Hussein was killed outside the Iraqi city of Karbala in AD 680. Those who followed Ali and Hussein are called the partisans of Ali or Shiite Ali. These events gave rise to the division of those who we call Shia and Sunni (which stands for ahl al-Sunna or People of the Sunna or practices of Mohamed).

In response to the invasion of Kuwait in the summer of 1990, the United States spent nearly six months deploying about 700,000 personnel and thousands of pieces of heavy equipment to the Kingdom of Saudi Arabia as part of a powerful international coalition involving nearly a million personnel and 34 nations.

The objective of the campaign was to expel Iraq from Kuwait. The limited nature of campaign objectives was due in part to UN Security Council resolutions. The multinational nature of the coalition served as a limiting factor as well. Different nations joined the coalition with very different expectations and requirements. In particular, it was feared that the Arab members of the coalition would not go along if the United States required much beyond simply expelling Iraqi forces from Kuwait. Thus, there were severe limits.

The military campaign, known as Operation Desert Storm, took place in two parts—an aggressive air campaign that began on January 17, 1991—and a lightning fast ground campaign that began on February 24 and ended on February 28. It is sometimes referred to as the 100-Hour War. Obviously, when combining the air and the ground campaign together, it was a lot more than 100 hours. It is certain that without the extensive air campaign the ground fighting would have been longer with more coalition casualties. As it was, the coalition only suffered about a thousand casualties compared to Iraqi casualties of over one hundred thousand.

President George H. W. Bush called on the Iraqi people to overthrow Saddam Hussein as the president of Iraq. Broadcasts from Arabic language radio stations gave the impression that the coalition would support popular uprisings. This was never the intent of the coalition. Regardless of intent both the Shia in the south and the Kurds in the north began a popular uprising and enjoyed initial success against regime security forces.

The formal hostilities were brought to an end by the U.S. government in coordination with their coalition partners. Coalition and Iraqi military commanders met to discuss the cessation of hostilities and the rules for separating forces. During these discussions, the Iraqi military leaders asked to be able to fly helicopters to allow for logistics functions, as the coalition had destroyed all the major bridges over the Tigris and Euphrates Rivers. The coalition leaders agreed to what seemed to be a reasonable request.

The helicopters were instead used to suppress the uprisings and retain government authority throughout Iraq. Following the end of hostilities, a harsh sanctions regime was established that affected Iraqi life at all levels and in every way imaginable. The sanctions were regularly used as a scapegoat by Saddam Hussein for anything bad in Iraq.

The experiences from before, during, and after Operation Desert Storm would reverberate both with the U.S. government and the people of Iraq in the initial parts of Operation Iraqi Freedom.

KEEP IN MIND AS YOU READ

1. The makeup of Iraqi society is more complex than is typically described. Often one hears of Sunnis being the minority in Iraq and Shia being in the majority, but this is a religious or sectarian division. There are also ethnic divisions that matter as well. Even among the Shia, there are Persian (Iranian) and Arab Shia. Not all Shia are the same. To imply that they are would be like saying that all Christian Protestants are the same.

2. Several thousand Iraqi-Americans and other Arab-Americans served as translators for U.S. forces in Iraq. Almost all of these men and women worked as contractors for the U.S. government. Some of them have been hired as U.S. government employees.

In addition to the American citizens who worked as translators, the U.S. military and other civilian companies often hired Iraqis who had English language skills to function as translators, as very few American soldiers spoke any Arabic at all.

3. The Rafha Refugee Camp in northern Saudi Arabia referenced below, which accommodated Mohamed's family and others like it, once contained as many as 33,000 refugees and still had more than 5,000 people living there as late as 2003 when the United States went back into Iraq (more than twelve years later). In this camp, the people had no citizenship other than that of Iraq, and they waited in a form of international limbo. There were reports in 2008 that all of these people were repatriated back to Iraq.

Document 1: Excerpt from Interview with Mohamed al Shara, Cultural Advisor

Interviewer: Please share with me your experiences of coming to America and becoming a translator in Iraq.

Muhammed: It started all back during the First Gulf War, Desert Storm. There was an uprising of the people against Saddam Hussein. People felt like they were oppressed by the regime, the former regime, Saddam's regime, so people stood up. Of course, they asked for the U.S. to come in and help, but the U.S. didn't. Everything went well. All the provinces fell except, of course, the capital, which is Baghdad.

Then finally, twenty-one days—I think it lasted twenty-one days, if I remember right—I was about eleven years old back then. When Saddam was allowed to fly his helicopters, that was a big advantage to his forces. So, then he started to gain back a lot of the provinces. So what happened is my father first left. So, basically, all the men who fought against Saddam departed Iraq. We stayed behind. Uh, we stayed for about a month in Baghdad [Spring 1991]. We had to stay in Baghdad because they came into our homes. The regime knew where we lived in al Muthanna province. So we knew we had to leave, because we knew that they know that my father participated, that we participated in the uprising, so we had to leave. And the majority of the uprising started from the south, you know 'cause that's majority Shia; and they had the uprising on Saddam. So basically what happened is, we got smuggled out of the country. Uh, it was myself, my mom, and, you know, three of my sisters and two brothers.

My father already departed. We found out through a friend of my father that he made it alive. We found this out after about three weeks. We were able to pay someone to get us out of there. My father did the same thing. He went to a farm area, and from there he got smuggled to the borders. There was U.S. presence on the border of Saudi Arabia and Iraq. So we said "okay, great. That's where we want to be. We want to go there 'cause we know there's U.S. troops there. So let's go there." So finally we made it alive.

We got there. It was all crazy; it was U.S. forces mixed with Saudi forces. They put us into a camp. We stayed there for about two years. In 1993, the United Nations came in, and they had a program and they start saying, "Okay. This is—We realize this is taking too long. We cannot keep you people here forever, this is a desert. So, um, you know—you have an opportunity to leave this place at your choice. You get to pick the country that you want to go to." Some people interestingly picked Iran, because they thought that that's the best place, which is the worst place to-to choose to go to. The majority were Shia, so they said, "Okay, you know, Iran—we'll get well taken care of." Which was the opposite.

Fortunately, we had—we were the second group to leave. So, uh, communication back and forth with our relatives told us, "Hey, don't make a mistake. Make sure you come to the United States." So that's how we chose to go to the United States. Otherwise, we probably would've ended up in Europe, maybe Iran, who knows? Uh, so we said, "Okay. United States." They took us to a place called Louisville—Louisville, Kentucky. We got dropped off there in March 1993.

So I got to the United States and every time from there . . . from '93 . . . every time we talked about Iraq with my parents, I never thought that I would be coming back to Iraq before my parents do. Because they always said, "We wanna go back". Of course, I said, "No, this [meaning the United States] is my future. This is what I wanna be, this is the opportunity." I just-I had no idea that I would be back over in Iraq.

So fast-forward to 2003 when the U.S. goes into Iraq. A couple of years later, my brother-in-law goes with the military as a linguist. So I'm talking to him back and forth, and he tells me, "Hey, you know, you have an opportunity. I see a lot of people here; I don't see a lot of Iraqis. I see a lot of people from Lebanon, I see a lot of people from Egypt. We, the Iraqis, understand this. So I think you have an opportunity to come here, to make a difference. 'Cause we understand what happened here. And that's what we need right now." So I said, "Okay, great. I'll do that."

I was fortunate, because as soon as I submitted my application and it went through the process I was picked to work with Major-General Lynch, the 3rd Infantry Division commander. It was a great-great opportunity, a great experience. So I came here to Iraq.

I realized that I had an opportunity to give back to the country that took me in when we were in a really bad situation, to give back to that country, to support the military, support its military and its mission. At the same time, to try to make a better future for the country that I left in—in such bad shape.

Source: Mohamed al Shara. Interview by author. Baghdad, Iraq, February 23, 2015. Reprinted with permission.

AFTERMATH

The United States believed that it won Operation Desert Storm. It was treated as a tremendous achievement. Military units and leaders participated in victory parades—the first since World War II. President George H. W. Bush enjoyed an 89 percent approval rating in February 1991. The perception from the west was one of total victory and Iraq was quickly dismissed from major policy focus and news coverage.

The people of Iraq felt they were betrayed by the west. They were invited to topple Saddam Hussein and when they did no one came to help them. Saddam brutally repressed all those who opposed him and his regime. The international coalition of nations then imposed a brutal sanctions regime on Iraq. Though the sanctions were intended to change the behavior of the regime and its leadership, it was the people of Iraq who were punished. This further developed a sense within Iraq that the west hated the people of Iraq. When U.S. forces reentered Iraq in 2003, those feelings were soon to return as the opposition to the occupation grew.

ASK YOURSELF

1. How might you feel if you were able to escape Iraq and go to another country? What country would you chose and why? Why did some people chose Iran over the United States? Iran is the largest and most populace Shia country in the world. It is also ruled since 1979 by a Shia theocratic form of government. In this case, ethnicity and religious sectarian beliefs can be in conflict as many of the Iraqi refugees were Shia, but they were Arab Shia rather than Persian Shia. Ethnically and in terms of language they are different, but in terms of religious interpretation they are similar. Which is more powerful for you, your ethnic roots or your religious beliefs?

2. Why is there such a powerful difference of opinion about who were the victors of Operation Desert Storm? By the Spring of 1997, all of the major western leaders who opposed Saddam Hussein in Operation Desert Storm—George H. W. Bush (United States), Margaret Thatcher (United Kingdom), John Major (United Kingdom), and François Mitterrand (France)—were all out of office, defeated by the electorate yet Saddam Hussein was still president of Iraq. The power of position is significant in the Middle East.

TOPICS TO CONSIDER

1. The life of a refugee is a difficult one. Many Gulf War refugees lived in a state of statelessness for more than a dozen years. Iraqi refugees who rose up against Saddam Hussein did not know if they would ever return to their country or if they would be able to go to another country. Those who left within a couple of years were blessed with opportunities. In the aftermath of Operation Iraqi Freedom there are now thousands upon thousands of refugees from Iraq. What is the responsibility of the international community toward refugees? What effect do refuges have on regional and global stability?

2. Many people considered the United States the greatest opportunity for their family. Iraqi refugees are among those who sought out the United States as a place to live. This was despite the fact that the people of Iraq just suffered an attack upon their country directed by the United States. Why do people choose to come to the United States despite great personal hardship and sacrifice?

Further Reading

Atkinson, Rick. *Crusade: The Untold Story of the Persian Gulf War*. New York: Houghton Mifflin Company, 1993.

Scales, Robert H. *Certain Victory: The US Army in the Gulf War*. Fort Leavenworth: US Army Command and General Staff College Press, 1993.

Shadid, Anthony. *Night Draws Near: Iraq's People in the Shadow of America's War*. New York: Henry Holt and Company, 2005.

Steed, Brian L. *Bees and Spiders: Applied Cultural Awareness and the Art of Cross-Cultural Influence*. Houston: Strategic Book Publishing & Rights Agency, LLC, 2014.

Swain, Richard M. *"Lucky War": Third Army in Desert Storm*. Fort Leavenworth: US Army Command and General Staff College Press, 1994.

Woodward, Bob. *The Commanders*. New York: Simon & Schuster, 1991.

Woodward, Bob. *Bush at War*. New York: Simon & Schuster, 2002.

Woodward, Bob. *Plan of Attack*. New York: Simon & Schuster, 2004.

Zogby, James Zogby. *Arab Voices: What They Are Saying to Us, and Why It Matters*. New York: Palgrave MacMillan, 2012.

Websites

Council on Foreign Relations. "The Sunni-Shia Divide." Council on Foreign Relations. http://www.cfr.org/peace-conflict-and-human-rights/sunni-shia-divide/p33176#!/

Gallup. "Presidential Approval Ratings—Gallup Historical Statistics and Trends." Gallup. http://www.gallup.com/poll/116677/presidential-approval-ratings-gallup-historical-statistics-trends.aspx

Shuster, Mike. "Special Series: the Partisans of Ali." National Public Radio. http://www.npr.org/series/7346199/the-partisans-of-ali

The White House. "Saddam Hussein's Defiance of United Nations Resolutions." The White House of President George W. Bush official site. http://georgewbush-whitehouse.archives.gov/infocus/iraq/decade/sect2.html

Films and Television

American War Generals. Executive producers: Peter Bergen, Tresha Mabile, Jonathan Towers. National Geographic Channel, 2014.

2. Congressional Resolution Supporting Use of Force against Iraq, October 16, 2002

INTRODUCTION

Following the attacks of September 11, 2001, the United States Congress voted for an Authorization for the Use of Military Force (AUMF) for "all necessary and appropriate force against those nations, organizations, or persons he determines planned, authorized, committed, or aided the terrorist attacks that occurred on September 11, 2001, or harbored such organizations or persons, in order to prevent any future acts of international terrorism against the United States by such nations, organizations or persons" (Public Law 107–40). Operations against al-Qaeda and other organizations including the Taliban government of Afghanistan began on October 7, 2001. These operations included airpower in support of Central Intelligence Agency operatives and U.S. Army Special Operations Forces soldiers operating in concert with the Northern Alliance—an Afghan group opposed to the Taliban government. By the middle of November these forces captured most of northern Afghanistan, including the capital of Kabul. This was amazing success. It looked as if the promise of the Revolution in Military Affairs had paid off. The knowledge gained through advanced technology intelligence collection and surveillance systems created unprecedented speed.

REVOLUTION IN MILITARY AFFAIRS

This is more than a military–technical revolution which, as it states, mostly involves technology. A revolution in military affairs (RMA) is a change in society involving military matters. Many scholars think that the digital and informational technology present in the 1990s changed society. The potential of information was clear in Operation Desert Storm when U.S.-led forces identified and targeted vehicles based off moving target indicators tracked from aircraft. Precision-guided weapons flew through windows and doors to give a level of precision never before seen in war. Global positioning system allowed U.S. forces to move over featureless terrain and arrive at a destination dozens of miles away. Could knowledge combine with speed to transform war? Imagine if you had perfect knowledge of where the enemy would be at a given time. All you need to do is apply force at that one location at that given time and it may be possible to defeat the enemy in a single, surgical strike. That is the transformation and the revolution promised by the RMA of the 1990s. As the chapters in this book explain, war is never that clean. Even with great technology.

Things started going poorly a couple of weeks later. Al-Qaeda leadership was believed to be hiding in the mountainous areas called Tora Bora. In December the battles taking place in the eastern mountains of Afghanistan failed to prevent Osama bin Laden from escaping and fleeing into Pakistan. Few U.S. soldiers combined with reliance on local fighters created a weakness—U.S. priorities were not necessarily their priorities. More U.S. and coalition forces were deployed into Afghanistan in the winter and spring of 2001–2002. These forces fought Operation Anaconda in the early spring once again attempting to cut off and destroy al-Qaeda in the mountains. Though the operation had numerous problems it was still deemed necessary to demonstrate the power of U.S. aerial and helicopter delivered firepower in combination with highly trained U.S. and coalition infantry.

It was in this vein of success that senior officials looked beyond Afghanistan. Additionally, there were U.S. military deployments of special operation forces to the Philippines and Djibouti to conduct operations against al-Qaeda-linked organizations in both regions.

None of these places—Afghanistan, Philippines, Horn of Africa (mostly Somalia)—seemed capable of generating a serious threat to the United States. To do so required the resources and capabilities of a state. The state that seemed the biggest threat was Iraq. As previously stated, Saddam Hussein had demonstrated a precedent for behavior in opposition to the world order and a desire to harm the United States. Unlike the other places Iraq was an industrialized and moderately modern country against which the technological might of the coalition of countries could more effectively be used. So Iraq became the focus of planning for the next phase of the Global War on Terrorism. So went the argument employed by many in the U.S. government in 2002.

The vote on the resolution that is this chapter was moderately contentious at the time as one compares this resolution with the vote for Afghanistan.

The vote on Public Law 107–40 (Afghanistan) was as follows:

| House of Representatives: | 420 Ayes | 1 Nay | 10 Not Voting |
| Senate: | 98 Ayes | 0 Nay | 2 Present/Not Voting |

The vote on Public Law 107–243 (Iraq) was as follows:

| House of Representatives: | 297 Ayes | 133 Nays | 10 Not Voting |
| Senate: | 77 Ayes | 23 Nays | 0 Present/Not Voting |

The vote is even more remarkable when viewed through a partisan lens. Only one Republican senator (Ron Paul of Texas) opposed it and the Democrat vote was 29 in favor and 21 opposed.

KEEP IN MIND AS YOU READ

1. Following the attacks on the United States on September 11, 2001, the president of the United States advocated for a doctrine that included preemptive action as stated in the June 2002 National Security Strategy for the United States of America as follows: "The United States has long maintained the option of preemptive actions to counter a sufficient threat to our national security. The greater the threat, the greater is the risk of inaction—and the more compelling the case for taking

anticipatory action to defend ourselves, even if uncertainty remains as to the time and place of the enemy's attack. To forestall or prevent such hostile acts by our adversaries, the United States will, if necessary, act preemptively. The United States will not use force in all cases to preempt emerging threats, nor should nations use preemption as a pretext for aggression. Yet in an age where the enemies of civilization openly and actively seek the world's most destructive technologies, the United States cannot remain idle while dangers gather. We will always proceed deliberately, weighing the consequences of our actions." In this manner the Bush Administration responded to the events of 9/11 and, in some measure, viewed Iraq as a legitimate target of military action.

2. Saddam Hussein violated sixteen separate UN Security Council Resolutions. When the number sixteen is given it is important to understand that some of the resolutions were overlapping and not separate and distinct. These resolutions dated back to November 29, 1990, and began as a response to the Iraq invasion of Kuwait in August of that same year. The resolutions dealt with prisoners of war, removal and destruction of all weapons of mass destruction, and primarily access for weapons inspectors and inspectors from the International Atomic Energy Agency. In addition to these resolutions that are deemed binding on all UN member nations there are numerous other nonbinding statements from the president of the UN Security Council.

Document 2: Excerpt from Congressional Resolution Supporting the Use of Force against Iraq, October 16, 2002

Resolved by the Senate and House of Representatives of the United States of America in Congress assembled,

(a) Authorization.—The President is authorized to use the Armed Forces of the United States as he determines to be necessary and appropriate in order to—

(1) defend the national security of the United States against the continuing threat posed by Iraq; and

(2) enforce all relevant United Nations Security Council resolutions regarding Iraq.

(b) Presidential Determination.—In connection with the exercise of the authority granted in subsection (a) to use force the President shall, prior to such exercise or as soon thereafter as may be feasible, but no later than 48 hours after exercising such authority, make available to the Speaker of the House of Representatives and the President pro tempore of the Senate his determination that—

(1) reliance by the United States on further diplomatic or other peaceful means alone either (A) will not adequately protect the national security of the United States against the continuing threat posed by Iraq or (B) is not likely to lead to enforcement of all relevant United Nations Security Council resolutions regarding Iraq; and

(2) acting pursuant to this joint resolution is consistent with the United States and other countries continuing to take the necessary actions against international terrorist and terrorist organizations, including those nations, organizations, or persons who planned, authorized, committed or aided the terrorist attacks that occurred on September 11, 2001.

(c) War Powers Resolution Requirements.—

(1) Specific statutory authorization.—Consistent with section 8(a)(1) of the War Powers Resolution, the Congress declares that this section is intended to constitute specific statutory authorization within the meaning of section 5(b) of the War Powers Resolution.

Source: United States Congress Joint Resolution. Public Law 107–243, 107th Congress. Washington, DC: Government Printing Office, 2002. Available at: http://www.gpo.gov/fdsys/pkg/PLAW-107publ243/html/PLAW-107publ243.htm.

AFTERMATH

The UN Security Council voted and adopted resolution 1441 unanimously on November 8, 2002, reemphasizing the need for Iraq to provide access to inspectors under an organization referred to as the UN Monitoring, Verification and Inspection Commission (UNMOVIC) which was established in 1999. The resolution was not intended as an authorization for the use of military force. The U.S. ambassador to the United Nations, John Negroponte stated as much when he said, "The Resolution confirms what has been clear for years: that Iraq has been and remains in violation of disarmament obligations—'material breach' in lawyers' language. . . . Let us be clear: the inspections will not work unless the Iraqi regime cooperates fully with UNMOVIC and the International Atomic Energy Agency (IAEA). We hope all member states now will press Iraq to undertake that cooperation. This resolution is designed to test Iraq's intentions: will it abandon its weapons of mass destruction and its illicit missile programs or continue its delays and defiance of the entire world? Every act of Iraqi non-compliance will be a serious matter, because it would tell us that Iraq has no intention of disarming. As we have said on numerous occasions to Council members, this Resolution contains no 'hidden triggers' and no 'automaticity' with respect to the use of force."

Colin Powell, the U.S. secretary of state went before the UN Security Council on February 5, 2003, to make a further case for Iraq's "material breach" of agreements made and UN Security Council Resolutions violated.

The vote in the U.S. Congress became a major point of debate in every succeeding primary or general election for president of the United States. In 2004, by the end of the primary, the two major Democratic contenders (John Kerry and John Edwards) both voted in favor of the resolution. In 2008, then Candidate Obama used Hillary Clinton's vote in favor of the resolution as a primary point against her. Senator Obama was not in the U.S. Senate when the vote was taken and he argued that he would have voted against it. The 2012 Republican field did not really bring up the vote on this law. In 2016, the primary elections featured the infamous question "if you knew then what you know now would you have invaded Iraq?" This served as a significant vetting question for presidential candidates. The response to this question, at least in part, served as the measure of a candidate's perceived worthiness for the presidency.

ASK YOURSELF

1. The last time the U.S. government declared war was in 1942 as part of World War II when the United States declared war on Bulgaria, Hungary, and Romania. That means there was no declaration of war for the Korean War or the Vietnam War. One can make an argument for the difficulty of declaring war against a nonstate actor like al-Qaeda. Why not a formal declaration of war against Iraq? The U.S. Constitution gives the power to declare war to the legislative branch of government. Why might a president be less inclined to seek a declaration of war in present circumstances?

2. The preamble to the UN Charter states "WE THE PEOPLES OF THE UNITED NATIONS DETERMINED to save succeeding generations from the scourge of war . . . AND FOR THESE ENDS to practice tolerance and live together in peace with one another as good neighbours, and to unite our strength to maintain international peace and security, and to ensure, by the acceptance of principles and the institution of methods, that armed force shall not be used, save in the common interest . . . HAVE RESOLVED TO COMBINE OUR EFFORTS TO ACCOMPLISH THESE AIMS . . ." In consideration of this requirement what is the role of the UN with respect to conflict that a nation determines to be essential to protect its interests? More specifically, how does the UN views a concept like preemptive war?

TOPICS TO CONSIDER

1. Why is war political within the U.S. Congress? This vote is one example of a vote that seemed to be more along party lines than might be expected. Some members vote regardless of party position, but there are others that seem to shift based on the party occupying the presidency. Is this an accurate statement? If so, why might this be the case?

2. The UN Security Council is comprised of fifteen voting members. These members are broken down into two groups—permanent members with individual veto authority and temporary members who are only voting members. There are five permanent members: United States, United Kingdom, Russia, China, and France. There are ten rotating temporary members. At the time the Security Council voted on resolution 1441 the temporary members were Bulgaria, Cameroon, Colombia, Guinea, Ireland, Mexico, Mauritius, Norway, Singapore, and Syria. Notice the make-up of the member states and consider the relative representation by continent. What impact does this break-down have on the justice of this international body and the decisions made? Why is the Security Council the only body that makes and passes binding resolutions?

Further Reading

Bolger, Daniel P. *Why We Lost: A General's Inside Account of the Iraq and Afghanistan Wars.* Boston: Houghton Mifflin Harcourt, 2014.

Gordon, Michael R. and Bernard Trainor. *Cobra II: The Inside Story of the Invasion and Occupation of Iraq.* New York: Pantheon Books, 2006.

United Nations Security Council. "Resolution 1441 (2002)." United Nations, November 8, 2002.

Woodward, Bob. *Bush at War*. New York: Simon & Schuster, 2002.

Woodward, Bob. *Plan of Attack*. New York: Simon & Schuster, 2004.

Websites

Charter of the United Nations. "Preamble." United Nations. http://www.un.org/en/documents/charter/preamble.shtml

United Nations Security Council Resolution 1441. "U.S. Explanation of Vote." United Nations. http://www.un.org/webcast/usa110802.htm

United States Congress Joint Resolution. "Public Law 107–40, 107th Congress." Government Printing Office. http://www.gpo.gov/fdsys/pkg/PLAW-107publ40/pdf/PLAW-107publ40.pdf

Films and Television

Frontline: Bush's War. Director: Michael Kirk. PBS, 2008.

3. State of the Union Address, January 28, 2003

INTRODUCTION

On September 18, 2001, the United States Congress passed the Authorization for Use of Military Force in response to the attacks of September 11, 2001, and oriented against al-Qaeda and the Taliban government of Afghanistan. On October 16, 2002, the Congress again passed an Authorization for Use of Military Force, this time directed against Iraq. On November 8, 2002, the United Nations passed UN Security Council Resolution 1441 which strengthened UN inspectors and threatened additional action if support of those inspectors was not forthcoming. In less than a week after this address the U.S. Secretary of State would go before the UN Security Council to make a legal case for military action against Iraq. The case laid out by the president of the United States in this speech is the definitive U.S. position and argument for conducting a war against the state of Iraq and the regime of Saddam Hussein.

KEEP IN MIND AS YOU READ

1. Iraq used chemical weapons in war against Iran and in peace against Iraqi Kurds living in and around the village of Halabja, Iraq. These are historic facts. The idea that weapons existed was not really in question. What is being argued in this case is that the Saddam Hussein regime had an active and ongoing program to develop more chemical weapons. Additionally, the nuclear weapons inspectors who went into Iraq following the end of hostilities for Operation Desert Storm in the early 1990s found a nuclear weapons program that was much further advanced than any intelligence agency had predicted. Saddam Hussein continued to demonstrate a desire to maintain his programs and he went to great lengths to deceive and obstruct the weapons inspection teams sent to Iraq between 1991 and 2003.

2. Group think or *groupthink* is when groups of people, typically in similar professional fields, think along the same lines and interpret events and data similarly. This phenomenon has been demonstrated in numerous fields, but in 2002–2003 it was clearly evident within western intelligence agencies. Nearly every single major

intelligence agency agreed with the assessment made by the president of the United States in this State of the Union address. Though there was some disagreement on the details, as stated, the overall assessment that Saddam Hussein had an active chemical weapons program was accepted. There was less agreement on whether or not Iraq had an ongoing nuclear program, but most intelligence agencies believed that Saddam Hussein wanted to obtain nuclear weapons or materials and equipment to build nuclear weapons. Think about why this was commonly accepted as truth given that no evidence of an ongoing active chemical or nuclear weapons program was in existence following the invasion.

3. The Iraqi military did have chemical weapons. There were numerous reports of hundreds and thousands of artillery shells, rockets, and bombs containing chemical weapons collected, identified, and destroyed by coalition forces in Iraq between 2003 and 2011. These included blister and nerve agents. Many news reports and commentaries reported that no chemical weapons were found in Iraq. This is untrue. What is true is that there was no active program for the creation of new chemical weapons found. The weapons found by the coalition forces were old, many dating back to the 1980s. These were from the chemical weapons stockpiles used by Saddam against the Iranians and the Kurds.

CHEMICAL WEAPONS

Chemical weapons are munitions that use chemicals formulated to cause death or harm to human beings. They consist of a variety of types that include blister and nerve agents. Some of the earliest chemical weapons were blister agents or mustard gas. Nerve agents, or chemical weapons that attack the nervous system, were later developed. Chemical weapons are considered to be weapons of mass destruction. The largest use of such weapons was in World War I. Following that war most nations joined in a treaty to prohibit the future use of them. As stated throughout this book, these weapons were used by Saddam Hussein against Iran and against his own Kurdish people. The existence of these weapons and possible future use was one of the main justifications for going to war against Iraq.

Document 3: Excerpt from the State of the Union Address, January 28, 2003

Our nation and the world must learn the lessons of the Korean Peninsula and not allow an even greater threat to rise up in Iraq. A brutal dictator, with a history of reckless aggression, with ties to terrorism, with great potential wealth, will not be permitted to dominate a vital region and threaten the United States. (Applause.)

Twelve years ago, Saddam Hussein faced the prospect of being the last casualty in a war he had started and lost. To spare himself, he agreed to disarm of all weapons of mass destruction. For the next 12 years, he systematically violated that agreement. He pursued chemical, biological, and nuclear weapons, even while inspectors were in his country. Nothing to date has restrained him from his pursuit of these weapons—not economic sanctions, not isolation from the civilized world, not even cruise missile strikes on his military facilities.

Almost three months ago, the United Nations Security Council gave Saddam Hussein his final chance to disarm. He has shown instead utter contempt for the United Nations, and for the opinion of the world. The 108 U.N. inspectors were sent to conduct—were not sent to conduct a scavenger hunt for hidden materials across a country the size of California. The job of the inspectors is to verify that Iraq's regime is disarming. It is up to Iraq to show exactly where it is hiding its banned weapons, lay those weapons out for the world to see, and destroy them as directed. Nothing like this has happened.

The United Nations concluded in 1999 that Saddam Hussein had biological weapons sufficient to produce over 25,000 liters of anthrax—enough doses to kill several million people. He hasn't accounted for that material. He's given no evidence that he has destroyed it.

The United Nations concluded that Saddam Hussein had materials sufficient to produce more than 38,000 liters of botulinum toxin—enough to subject millions of people to death by respiratory failure. He hadn't accounted for that material. He's given no evidence that he has destroyed it.

Our intelligence officials estimate that Saddam Hussein had the materials to produce as much as 500 tons of sarin, mustard and VX nerve agent. In such quantities, these chemical agents could also kill untold thousands. He's not accounted for these materials. He has given no evidence that he has destroyed them.

U.S. intelligence indicates that Saddam Hussein had upwards of 30,000 munitions capable of delivering chemical agents. Inspectors recently turned up 16 of them—despite Iraq's recent declaration denying their existence. Saddam Hussein has not accounted for the remaining 29,984 of these prohibited munitions. He's given no evidence that he has destroyed them.

From three Iraqi defectors we know that Iraq, in the late 1990s, had several mobile biological weapons labs. These are designed to produce germ warfare agents, and can be moved from place to a place to evade inspectors. Saddam Hussein has not disclosed these facilities. He's given no evidence that he has destroyed them.

The International Atomic Energy Agency confirmed in the 1990s that Saddam Hussein had an advanced nuclear weapons development program, had a design for a nuclear weapon and was working on five different methods of enriching uranium for a bomb. The British government has learned that Saddam Hussein recently sought significant quantities of uranium from Africa. Our intelligence sources tell us that he has attempted to purchase high-strength aluminum tubes suitable for nuclear weapons production. Saddam Hussein has not credibly explained these activities. He clearly has much to hide.

The dictator of Iraq is not disarming. To the contrary; he is deceiving. From intelligence sources we know, for instance, that thousands of Iraqi security personnel are at work hiding documents and materials from the U.N. inspectors, sanitizing inspection sites and monitoring the inspectors themselves. Iraqi officials accompany the inspectors in order to intimidate witnesses.

Iraq is blocking U-2 surveillance flights requested by the United Nations. Iraqi intelligence officers are posing as the scientists inspectors are supposed to interview. Real scientists have been coached by Iraqi officials on what to say. Intelligence sources indicate that Saddam Hussein has ordered that scientists who cooperate with U.N. inspectors in disarming Iraq will be killed, along with their families.

Year after year, Saddam Hussein has gone to elaborate lengths, spent enormous sums, taken great risks to build and keep weapons of mass destruction. But why? The only possible explanation, the only possible use he could have for those weapons, is to dominate, intimidate, or attack.

With nuclear arms or a full arsenal of chemical and biological weapons, Saddam Hussein could resume his ambitions of conquest in the Middle East and create deadly havoc in that region. And this Congress and the [American] people must recognize another threat. Evidence from intelligence sources, secret communications, and statements by people now in custody reveal that Saddam Hussein aids and protects terrorists, including members of al Qaeda. Secretly, and without fingerprints, he could provide one of his hidden weapons to terrorists, or help them develop their own.

Before September the 11th, many in the world believed that Saddam Hussein could be contained. But chemical agents, lethal viruses and shadowy terrorist networks are not easily contained. Imagine those 19 hijackers with other weapons and other plans—this time armed by Saddam Hussein. It would take one vial, one canister, one crate slipped into this country to bring a day of horror like none we have ever known. We will do everything in our power to make sure that that day never comes. (Applause.)

Some have said we must not act until the threat is imminent. Since when have terrorists and tyrants announced their intentions, politely putting us on notice before they strike? If this threat is permitted to fully and suddenly emerge, all actions, all words, and all recriminations would come too late. Trusting in the sanity and restraint of Saddam Hussein is not a strategy, and it is not an option. (Applause.)

The dictator who is assembling the world's most dangerous weapons has already used them on whole villages—leaving thousands of his own citizens dead, blind, or disfigured. Iraqi refugees tell us how forced confessions are obtained—by torturing children while their parents are made to watch. International human rights groups have catalogued other methods used in the torture chambers of Iraq: electric shock, burning with hot irons, dripping acid on the skin, mutilation with electric drills, cutting out tongues, and rape. If this is not evil, then evil has no meaning. (Applause.)

And tonight I have a message for the brave and oppressed people of Iraq: Your enemy is not surrounding your country—your enemy is ruling your country. (Applause.) And the day he and his regime are removed from power will be the day of your liberation. (Applause.)

The world has waited 12 years for Iraq to disarm. America will not accept a serious and mounting threat to our country, and our friends and our allies. The United States will ask the U.N. Security Council to convene on February the 5th to consider the facts of Iraq's ongoing defiance of the world. Secretary of State Powell will present information and intelligence about Iraqi's legal—Iraq's illegal weapons programs, its attempt to hide those weapons from inspectors, and its links to terrorist groups.

We will consult. But let there be no misunderstanding: If Saddam Hussein does not fully disarm, for the safety of our people and for the peace of the world, we will lead a coalition to disarm him.

Source: George W. Bush. State of the Union Address, 2003. Available at: http://georgewbush-whitehouse.archives.gov/news/releases/2003/01/20030128-19.html. Accessed 22 December 2015.

AFTERMATH

As stated, Secretary of State Colin Powell went before the UN Security Council on February 5, 2003 and laid out a case for military action against Iraq by presenting evidence on the

Iraqi efforts to thwart weapons inspections. On February 4, 2003, Saddam Hussein gave an interview to former British Labour Cabinet Minister Tony Benn for BBC News. In this interview Saddam refuted the statements of the U.S. president and the allegations that his country had chemical weapons, obstructed UN inspectors, or wanted war. He emphasized several times the desire of the Iraqi people and his regime for peace. On March 17, 2003, President Bush appeared on television to announce to the American people that he was giving Saddam Hussein and his sons 48 hours to depart Iraq or combat operations would begin. Two days later Operation Iraqi Freedom began with an aerial bombing campaign referred to as "Shock and Awe" that targeted the Iraqi regime.

Within hours of the president's 48-hour ultimatum to Saddam Hussein to depart Iraq the U.S. intelligence community received word regarding the whereabouts of Saddam Hussein and both of his sons; they were located at a place called Dora Farms, northeast of Baghdad. Officials assured the president they could strike with reasonable certainty of killing all three. The president declined the opportunity indicating that he had given his word that Saddam had 48 hours before the attack would commence. The attack was delayed until minutes after the 48-hour deadline ended. Despite this, neither Saddam nor his sons were killed, and some reports indicated they were not even at that location. Not for the first time the U.S. government misread information and achieved nothing from a significant technological and tactical effort.

ASK YOURSELF

1. The justification for war came from a combination of events, intelligence and information. First was the reframing of thinking that the attacks on September 11, 2001, created in the minds of western leaders and most specifically the Bush Administration. Containment and patience were no longer seen as viable options with respect to the perceived possibility of a state creating weapons of mass destruction and then providing those weapons to "shadowy networks" that were not fully understood and therefore all the more frightening. Second was the connection between al-Qaeda and Iraq. It was still hard to imagine that a nonstate actor could conduct the attacks and therefore there remained a search for a state sponsor other than Afghanistan. In searching for these connections and trying to sort through the confusing information there is a tight connection between the intelligence agencies who collect, analyze, and present the information and the decision makers who use that intelligence to inform decisions. How can a national-level decision maker ensure that it receives the most accurate and independent assessments possible?

2. As the criticism followed the decision to invade Iraq much was made of the issue that there were no weapons of mass destruction. Is there a difference in this debate between the existing and hidden stockpiles and the nonexistent active program?

TOPICS TO CONSIDER

1. What is a lie? What is a mistake? Is it possible for one to cross-over into the other? Commentators on the news from the Iraq War often used the word lie with respect to President Bush and the justification for war. This includes authors of books. The data that was accumulated on the Iraq weapons programs fills thousands upon thousands of pages. There was lots of evidence, but the evidence did not lead to

a real existing program. Was Saddam Hussein lying when he told Tony Benn that he did not have weapons of mass destruction? He didn't have an active program, but he did have stockpiles. There is confusion on the records recovered from Iraq on whether or not Saddam knew that his chemical and nuclear weapons programs were stopped. He was spending money on the programs, but nothing was being developed. In 1945, prior to the death of Franklin Delano Roosevelt, if someone had asked then Vice President Harry S. Truman if the U.S. government had a nuclear weapons program he would have answered no. He would not have been lying because he was not told of the program's existence until he was sworn in as president, yet a program did exist and it was very close to being tested. This is a complicated situation and worthy of thought. How do governments communicate information that is gathered in secret or programs that are developed in secret?

2. What creates groupthink? Business and government have spent a great deal of time, thought, and money in trying to understand this phenomenon. What causes it? Is it common education, common upbringing, common experiences? More importantly, how does one overcome the model of multiple people thinking alike? In the P. W. Singer 2009 book *Wired for War: The Robotics Revolution and Conflict in the 21st Century* the author tells a story of the design for a NASA robot that is supposed to be carried by a rocket to another planetary surface. The payload is restricted to one hundred pounds. All of the scientists are trying to determine the right configuration and design for a one hundred pound robot. Another person is brought in who suggests possibly one hundred one pound robots that would set up a functioning and resilient network. This is a case where one person changed the dynamic of the discussion by reframing the problem and thereby short circuited the groupthink problem.

Further Reading

Bolger, Daniel P. *Why We Lost: A General's Inside Account of the Iraq and Afghanistan Wars.* Boston: Houghton Mifflin Harcourt, 2014.

Gordon, Michael R. and Bernard Trainor. *Cobra II: The Inside Story of the Invasion and Occupation of Iraq.* New York: Pantheon Books, 2006.

Woodward, Bob. *Bush at War.* New York: Simon & Schuster, 2002.

Woodward, Bob. *Plan of Attack.* New York: Simon & Schuster, 2004.

Websites

Benn, Tony. "Full Text of Benn Interview with Saddam." BBC News. February 4, 2003, http://news.bbc.co.uk/2/hi/uk_politics/2726831.stm (accessed June 10, 2015).

Chivers, C. J. "12 Years Later, a Mystery of Chemical Exposure in Iraq Clears." *New York Times.* May 14, 2015, http://www.nytimes.com/2015/05/15/world/middleeast/12-years-later-a-mystery-of-chemical-exposure-in-iraq-clears-slightly.html?_r=1 (accessed May 14, 2015).

Chivers, C. J. "The Secret Casualties of Iraq's Abandoned Chemical Weapons." *New York Times.* October 14, 2014, http://www.nytimes.com/interactive/2014/10/14/world/middleeast/us-casualties-of-iraq-chemical-weapons.html (accessed May 14, 2015).

Films and Television

American War Generals. Executive producers: Peter Bergen, Tresha Mabile, Jonathan Towers. National Geographic Channel, 2014.

Frontline: Bush's War. Director: Michael Kirk. PBS, 2008.

THE INVASION OF IRAQ: OPERATION IRAQI FREEDOM

4. BRIGADE COMMANDER AND THE INVASION: DAVID PERKINS

INTRODUCTION

In this chapter Colonel David Perkins discusses the training and preparation that led up to the attack and invasion into Iraq. U.S. and coalition military forces began arriving in Kuwait in the fall of 2002 and continued to assemble up to and beyond the actual beginning of the invasion. Initial plans in the U.S. Central Command called for a Desert Storm like buildup of forces that took six months or more to get forces positioned and logistics stockpiled to support the attack. Secretary of Defense Donald Rumsfeld wanted a faster process this time around and the military labeled the adjusted plan "Running Start" as the idea was to get units into position as early as possible so that they would be ready whenever the order was given. 3rd Infantry Division (3 ID) was part of this initial deployment.

The environment for coalition military forces in Kuwait was austere. Most large units had their people sleeping in tents or on their vehicles and they ate meals ready to eat (MREs) most days. For centuries the attitude of commanders has been that an idle soldier is a problem and the best way to deal with idleness is training. That is no different today. Good commanders use the time available to hone the skills of their crews and build the teamwork necessary to effectively function in austere environments.

In 2003, as in 1991, the lead units conducted breach drills to fight through obstacles along the border and then conducted long tactical movements in desert terrain before moving into the urban areas to capture key lines of communication—roads, bridges, road intersections—that would allow the larger and slower logistics formations to travel rapidly and smoothly through Iraq.

2nd brigade, 3 ID was one of the first units to make it to Baghdad. Much of the discussion in the interview focuses on the decisions associated with communicating to the Iraqi people the arrival and dominance of U.S. forces over the Iraqi military. In Iraq there was no open media. Iraqis typically received their news from government sources; therefore they knew what they were told and they believed what they knew. The U.S. military advanced the Iraqi ministry of information regularly broadcast information through press conferences and daily news reports. The main figure in this reporting was the minister of information, Muhammed Saeed al-Sahhaf. He was a former foreign minister for Iraq. He briefed the western media and regularly appeared on European and American news programs. His statements were filled with poetic exaggerations as Colonel Perkins will discuss below. In America he was given the nickname "Baghdad Bob." This follows a pattern of alliterative names given to opposing sources of propaganda (e.g., Hanoi Hannah, Seoul City Sue, or Tokyo Rose). In the United Kingdom he was referred to as "Comical Ali" as a play on words with the Iraqi general responsible for the Iraq chemical weapons program, Ali Hassan al-Majid, known as "Chemical Ali."

The decision by Colonel Perkins to go into the center of Baghdad and remain there overnight with a heavy armored force was referred to as the "Thunder Run." The importance of this event was that it provided proof that U.S. forces were present in force in Baghdad and that the Iraqi military had effectively collapsed. One of the most iconic television scenes from the war was during an interview where Muhammed Saeed al-Sahhaf was stating live on television that there were no American tanks present in Baghdad while in the background a U.S. tank was obvious coming around a building. This single image revealed all of the previous statements as clearly poetic exaggerations if not outright fabrications and lost all credibility for the Iraqi government spokesperson, if not the Iraqi government itself.

In military tactical terminology a raid is a tactical action where a force attacks an enemy objective without the intent of holding the terrain following the action. The force goes in, conducts its actions on the objective, and then withdraws back to previous positions. The "Thunder Run" was not a raid; it was intended to go in to Baghdad and hold terrain.

KEEP IN MIND AS YOU READ

1. There are competing narratives at play in this chapter. Muhammed Saeed al-Sahhaf presents an image of the Iraqi people as aggrieved and set upon by an evil and offensive west, led by the United States. The Iraqi soldiers are brave and fierce warriors who, if they fall in battle, are martyrs before God and examples to their people. In this narrative the Americans are the evil oppressors subjugating the Iraqi people and heaping suffering and humiliations upon them. In the American narrative the U.S. soldier is an honorable and noble servant of the state who is an expert in skills and abilities and who fights in behalf of human dignity and in opposition to the evils of the Saddam Hussein regime. It is easy to characterize one as false and the other as true; however, it is instructive to recognize both and see that both contain elements of fiction and reality.

2. Modern war is complex, not simply in the need for a constant flow of logistics as identified below, nor in the need for continuous and ever more increasingly technically detailed training. Warfighting is captured intellectually into warfighting functions that include intelligence, movement and maneuver, command and control (currently referred to as mission command in the U.S. Army), sustainment (logistics), protection (including issues of fortifications, force protection, military police, electronic warfare, cyber-security, etc.), fires (e.g., artillery, aerial delivered fires), and engagement. This division was deemed necessary to help commanders and staffs to think about all of the elements of the modern battlefield and to coordinate those efforts into a cohesive campaign.

3. To function effectively in this complex world leaders and soldiers need training and preparation. It is not enough to be proficient at individual tasks or even small unit tasks. Battles and wars are won by combining the effects of proficiency at multiple

levels across dozens of units to achieve a total effect of defeating the opponent. This requires weeks and months of preparation to develop the coordinated effects desired.

4. In addition to combatting idleness modern forces require lots of training because of the logistics constraints. In the comments below, Colonel Perkins mentions logistics as a part of their planning. An armored brigade, as he commanded, included something in the neighborhood of more than a hundred M1-series tanks, each one with a fuel tank carrying more than 500 gallons. These tanks burn about a gallon a minute when operating so the tanks are typically fueled once a day if idling and twice a day during combat. That is a minimum of 50,000 gallons of fuel per day requiring ten semi-truck-sized fuel tankers every day and maybe twice a day. Controlling the movement of the fuel convoys as well as the trucks carrying water, food, repair parts, ammunition, and other types of military supplies is part of the military science referred to as logistics and logistics planning. A tank without fuel becomes an expensive pillbox or fortification and military planners do everything they can to prevent that from happening.

Document 4: Excerpt from Interview with David Perkins, Brigade Commander of 2nd Brigade, 3 ID

"What did we do before we crossed the berm going into Iraq?" We had the advantage of the entire brigade combat team deploy to Kuwait in September of 2002, and lived in tents in the desert until March of 2003, so we had a lot of time on our hands, so to speak. We trained a lot. I will tell you probably one of the most important aspects of training. We trained combined arms maneuver and combined arms live fire. We had a huge training area, the Udari training area in northern Kuwait, so we fired multiple launch rocket systems (MLRS), artillery, and tanks; Bradleys.

BRADLEY

The Bradley Infantry Fighting Vehicle is more than an armored personnel carrier. It is also a mini-tank. It has a 25-mm chain gun, antitank missile launchers, and a machine gun that is mounted to point where the 25-mm gun points. It has a crew of three personnel (driver, commander, and gunner) and can carry six people in the back. It is crowded when all six people and all of their gear is back there. The vehicle is named after World War II General Omar Bradley who after the war received a fifth star and became the U.S. Army Chief of Staff. For most of the Iraq War this was the primary infantry vehicle. It is tracked and it is more than 9 feet tall.

Probably the most important thing we did is, almost every night I had what I called sort of a science project. We would get together in my tent or the brigade executive officer (XO) or the brigade operations officer (S3s) tent and we'd sit there and lay out maps and say, "I wonder what kind of things would happen to us if we had to go from here to Baghdad. How long would it take to get there? What would be the tallest poles in the tents, so to speak? How much fuel would it take? How would this happen? I wonder what the Iraqis would do." . . . We were trying to understand what the problem was. Then we would discuss, "How do you think it would unfold? What would the Special Republican Guard do? What would Saddam try to be doing?" So, what we were trying to do was gain a common visualization of how this thing would unfold, and then we would kind of discuss back and forth and then bring in the battalion commanders. What we were doing is describing to each one of us, "Okay, this is how I visualize it unfolding. Here are the problems. Fuel is going to be a problem. Class I [food and water] is going to be a problem, ammunition is going to be a problem," so we were describing back and forth and so we started to have this common visualization on how this was going to unfold. . . . We didn't have all the systems that we have now in the Army. We didn't have unmanned aerial vehicles (UAVs); we didn't have any of that. . . . Where are we going to put our Command and Control nodes because we are going to be constantly moving. . . . So, how do you conduct Command and Control of the move? We would talk through that and then go out and practice it and train it and take the entire brigade combat team and run it out across the desert and say, "How long is this? What is the pass time? What is the hourly rate of fuel consumption for a brigade combat team?" So, we would rehearse these things over and over, and train over and over and take different things; "What if we made the command post look like this? What if we made it smaller? What if we separated the tanks from the logistical assets in the brigade? How fast could you move?" And, so, there was a huge amount of discussion to understand how this would unfold and then train, train, train. . . .

We had media with us and there was media in Baghdad with "Baghdad Bob" and all that and so we had media with us, but when we were going to the airport, Baghdad Bob was over there conducting his routine press conferences that he apparently did. I obviously didn't see any of them because I did not have satellite TV in my M113. So, he was out there and being asked questions about what was going on. But, in the heart of the Regime District, there was no sign they were there. So, a reporter would ask him, "We have reports that the Americans have taken the airport. What's going on?" Baghdad Bob goes, "Look. Look out in the city. Do you see any Americans?" In the heart of downtown Baghdad, you didn't see any Americans. . . . So, the reporters . . . would look around and life was going on in downtown Baghdad and they were sort of reinforcing his narrative there. We came back and that evening in my brigade operations center, a reporter comes up to me and says, "You know, Baghdad Bob is saying that you, the brigade commander, are saying you attacked the airport. . . . [B]ut he is saying that there are no Americans in the city. That in fact this is all just a propaganda aspect on behalf of the Americans." In fact, National Public Radio (NPR) is quoted as saying that they are in the city and they didn't see any Americans, so they are buttressing his response. My response to that, at that point in time, was "Well, I was in Baghdad and I didn't see NPR, so maybe they are not in the city." I was bringing up the fact that just because you don't see it, it's not happening, but actually in this 24/7 world, that is true. I mean, perception is reality and if you don't see it and it's not on the radio, it's apparently not happening.

As we were attacking up [to] the airport that day on the 5th, we captured an Iraqi general who literally was driving to work. He was coming out of his car and I guess just went to the local Starbuck's or whatever and he pulls out on the highway and sees a US Army Armor brigade of tanks coming up the highway. So, he did the smart thing. He got out of his car and stood there with his hands up and says, "I give up." So, obviously a sort of rational-thinking person and so we take him into custody. We're talking to him and he's like, "You really surprised me when I pulled out on the highway today to see a bunch of American tanks because I'm listening to Baghdad Bob and he says the Americans are dying by the thousands at the Gate of Baghdad. Everything is good, everything is going on, and so I'm thinking, Life is good to go and I'm just going to go off to my Iraqi Army job and work through my e-mail or something." But, what that made clear to me was the Iraqi Army was getting a false sense of security. They were being falsely emboldening to stay and continue to fight the Americans that are dying by the thousands, so the information campaign has a very definite impact on people. In other words, it is emboldening their defenses. It's encouraging them to stand fast, so I could tell that it's very important that we make it abundantly clear to NPR and everybody, that the American Army is here in Baghdad.

There are not only symbolic aspects of being in the Regime Districts, but that it will have some real consequences. Therefore, if you go in and then leave, it will be turned as "We kicked them out." . . . They will spin it on all their media. The world media is there, they will see it and we will do this constantly. In other words, we would not affect regime change because they will not just put down their weapons because they're going to say, "Every time the Americans come in, they leave, so I guess we beat them." That is how we would be portrayed, so I had concerns about sort of doing a raid mentality. . . . [I]f you go in and come out, you are going to have converging forces and that's going to be a problem. Two, it's going to be spun as a strategic victory to the Iraqis. "We kicked the Americans out. Yeah, they may have been there, but see, they are gone now. Now that it is dinnertime, the Americans are gone. We are once again victorious; we have beaten them." Again, we want to bring this thing to closure as soon as possible and, quite honestly, an armored force is not the best force to take a—well, it's not the optimal force . . . to take a heavily urbanized objective. So, we sat down and were again trying to understand what we were against both from a strategic point of view, from an information campaign, from a tactical point of view, from what the intent was from General Blomford, General [William] Wallace, the US Central Command (CENTCOM) commander and everybody else. That was to obviously affect regime change and bring down the regime. So, I started planning that. I said, "You know, I think one of the best ways to do all of this is, if we can, to go in and stay because then . . . I avoid the real tactical dilemma of converging forces, number one. Number two, we avoid the strategic information loss of "We've kicked them out," and three, if we are there, we can start to control the city and force a regime change because the sooner this thing is over, the better it is for all of us. We just didn't have the numbers of forces to affect a long-term siege and build into continual raids after raids.

Source: David Perkins. Interview by Tony Carlson and Kelvin Crow, May 6, 2013. Interview Transcript. Courtesy of the Operational Leadership Experiences Digital Collection, Combat Studies Institute, Fort Leavenworth, KS. Available at: http://cgsc.contentdm .oclc.org/cdm/ref/collection/p4013coll13/id/3181 (accessed June 10, 2015).

AFTERMATH

There were two "Thunder Runs" during the effort to secure Baghdad. They occurred on April 5 and 8, 2003, the seventeenth and twentieth days since combat operations began. By April 10 the Baghdad International Airport was open for service for coalition forces within Iraq. On April 11 major coalition command posts moved to and began operations from

Baghdad. The land force commander began the repositioning for what military officials called Phase IV or stability operations on April 15 (27 days after the beginning of combat operations) and the president of the United States, as discussed in Chapter 9 of this book, declared the end of major combat operations on May 1 (43 days after the beginning of combat operations).

Based on these dates the events described by Colonel Perkins did play a critical role in breaking the formal, conventional resistance of the Iraqi military. Most U.S. and coalition military personnel believed that this was the end of the war and they would shortly be returning home.

It is in this initial conceptualization of the Iraq War that things go all wrong. Military and civilian leaders in the coalition believed this was like the world in 1945 in that when the state power is defeated the people will follow suit and submit to the conqueror. As will be discussed in later chapters and parts of the book, this was wrong. The world had changed and the people, including many in the military, did not intend to simply submit. The nature of war was changing from one of state military against state military to nonstate actors against a state military.

ASK YOURSELF

1. What is the need for training? The training described earlier costs hundreds of thousands and sometimes millions or even tens of millions of dollars. The fuel and ammunition alone are expensive. If equipment breaks it needs to be repaired. Is the professionalism and capability of a trained force worth the cost of training that force?

2. Was the military a victim of groupthink as was the intelligence community? Why did they think they could overthrow a dictatorial and authoritarian government and then simply leave within months? U.S. military forces still remain in Germany and Japan more than seventy years since the war ended and in Korea more than sixty years since that war ended.

3. How effectively do modern combat videogames reflect the complexity described earlier?

TOPICS TO CONSIDER

1. The cost and effort needed to train and prepare the U.S. military is enormous. Based off most budget figures the United States spends more on its defense budget than do the next ten nations combined. Is such a commitment to a trained and ready force exportable to other nations and cultures?

2. The difference between military success in combat and political success in war is often quite significant. In this chapter success comes from the presence of tanks that shocked individuals and leaders into surrender. The shock of invasion and the euphoria of the overthrow of the Saddam regime did not last long. By summer people were already disillusioned by the lack of electricity to cool their homes because there was no security to protect the power plant and power lines. There was no prosperity because people were out of work. Defeating a force on the battlefield is profoundly different than rebuilding societies. Look into the costs associated with the rebuilding of Iraq. These range in the trillions of dollars. Compare those costs with the costs for maintaining a trained and ready force.

Further Reading

Fontenot, Gregory, E. J. Degen, and David Tohn. *On Point: The United States Army in Operation Iraqi Freedom*. Fort Leavenworth, KS: U.S. Army Command and General Staff College Press, 2004.

Gordon, Michael R. and Bernard Trainor. *Cobra II: The Inside Story of the Invasion and Occupation of Iraq*. New York: Pantheon Books, 2006.

Lacey, James G. *Takedown: The 3rd Infantry Division's Twenty-One Day Assault on Baghdad*. Annapolis, MD: Naval Institute Press, 2007.

Woodward, Bob. *Plan of Attack*. New York: Simon & Schuster, 2004.

Zucchino, David. *Thunder Run: The Armored Strike to Capture Baghdad*. New York: Atlantic Monthly Press, 2004.

Films and Television

American War Generals. Executive producers: Peter Bergen, Tresha Mabile, Jonathan Towers. National Geographic Channel, 2014.

Frontline: Bush's War. Director: Michael Kirk. PBS, 2008.

5. Corps Staff and the Invasion: Russell Thadden and Stephen Hicks

INTRODUCTION

In this chapter there are two interviews—one from Colonel Russell Thadden and one from Colonel Stephen Hicks. Colonel Thadden was the intelligence officer or G2 for V (U.S.) Corps and Colonel Hicks was the operations officer or G3 for the same organization. This is the U.S. Army organization responsible for the ground war on the western approach to Baghdad.

These interviews provide a broader perspective of the nature of the attack north from Kuwait toward Baghdad. There is information on the impact of environment and terrain on the advance north as well as details on some of the fighting around Najaf. In this interview the relationship of the fighting is clearer. This was not an attack against a retreating opponent. There were elements in the Iraqi military and the *Fedayeen* who were committed to defeating the U.S.-led coalition. The first interview takes place before the commencement of hostilities—March 18, 2003—and the second interview happens after the V (U.S.) Corps headquarters was located in Baghdad on April 15, 2003. Thus, these comments are being made in the moment and without the benefit of reflection to change opinions and perspectives.

FEDAYEEN

This word means those who sacrifice and has been used by various Arabic-speaking groups in the Middle East for more than a thousand years. In the context of the Iraq War the group was specifically known as the *Fedayeen Saddam*. They were an unofficial paramilitary group organized in the mid-1990s to be a regime-protection force. This force operated under the control of Uday Hussein, the son of Saddam and they were used to conduct raids and ambushes of coalition forces as they advanced into the country and then some of them served as part of the nucleus for the insurgency.

KEEP IN MIND AS YOU READ

---

1. Reflect on the Iraqi perspective. Why were they defending so strongly and not just risking, but sacrificing their lives for the defense of Iraq? Didn't they know that they were going to lose this war? Some of this can be explained away as effective control of the narrative by the Saddam Hussein regime's information control. Other factors exist as well—much is related to the defending of a homeland and a civilization that is believed to be under attack by outsiders. Many thought this was their duty to defend Islam and their fellow Muslims from an attack of outsiders and unbelievers. This message was communicated early and often throughout the Muslim world. It even had an effect on some Muslims serving inside the U.S. military. Though this and other interviews come from an American perspective there are other ways of looking at this fighting—Iraq was being invaded by an enemy hostile to Iraqi civilization and culture. Iraq was the center or one of the primary centers of human civilization for several thousand years. Iraqis are proud of, and therefore eager to defend, that tradition and history.

2. Other battles, large and small were going on within the V (U.S.) Corps area of operations and outside it. The Marines were fighting to the east, the British were capturing Basra in the south. A deep attack of Apache helicopters was badly shot up in this period. The 507th maintenance company was following other units into Nasiriyah to the south and they were attacked as they made a wrong turn in the city. During this battle several members of the unit were taken captive, including Private First Class Jessica Lynch. The battle happened on March 23 and she was rescued by U.S. Special Forces on April 1, 2003. There was a lot happening all simultaneous to the events discussed in this chapter.

3. For many in the U.S. military in 2003 the image of war was that of Operation Desert Storm. In the interviews below there are references to the fighting in 1991. It is possible to see that this was the model that most leaders used in trying to understand the unknown: things will be like they were in Desert Storm.

Document 5: Excerpts from Interviews with Russell Thadden, G2 (Intelligence Officer) and Stephen Hicks, G3 (Operations Officer), V (U.S.) Corps, March 18 and April 15, 2003

Question to Colonel Thadden:	The President spoke last night to the American people. He gave Saddam Hussein and his sons 48 hours to leave Iraq. We're probably about 72 hours right now from war. Give me a thumbnail sketch of how you think the Iraqis will fight in another three days.
Colonel Thadden's Answer:	That's a good question. I think that the regular army and particularly the 11th Infantry Division, which we oppose, will not put up much of a fight. I think that a significant

number of both of their commanders and soldiers are, as a friend of mine would say, "Posturing to survive." They will wait until the last minute so that they don't get arrested or killed or that their [families] are endangered by the security services of Saddam, but that at any reasonable opportunity they will desert or surrender. I do not expect that we'll have a lot of large unit surrendering, because I do not believe the soldiers will be there for the commander to surrender them. . . . I don't expect it to be militarily effective, but there [will be] some professional officers, who out of a sense of duty and professionalism will attempt to fight and may put up some resistance. As we go further north and confront the Republican Guards, it's difficult to say how much resistance they will put forth, but I recall from last time, contrary to a lot of thoughts, that the Republican Guards did try to put up a good fight, they were under effective command and control through the end of Desert Storm. And the problem was that they didn't have the means to effectively resist. So I expect there will be some resistance—probably not as effective as in Desert Storm as far as capabilities, other than they have more restrictive terrain to call upon. And when we get to Baghdad, I expect there will be hardcore units that will, to the best of their ability, put up a serious fight. How long that will last and at what stage they will realize that Saddam is a lost cause, and give up the fight, I think it's too early to really judge. Now with that said, we have to prepare for every unit to fight hard. We can't assume away that even the 11th won't fight, and so it's a balance between being prepared to fight them hard but, if they capitulate or do surrender, to rapidly transition to humane treatment of prisoners.

Question to Colonel Hicks: Let's start with the question of how terrain and weather affected Corps operations over the course of the last three or four weeks.

Colonel Hicks' Answer: I think that the one that stands out most is the weather. If there's one point where it really affected us . . . it was the three-day sand storm where it seemed that all of the technological advantages that the corps had—from unmanned surveillance systems to attack helicopters to the ability for our [palletized loading systems] to move—really came to a grinding halt for a period of two or three days. We lost the information dominance on the enemy. We lost the ability to use the deep attack with the attack helicopters. We lost the ability to use close air support to the best extent that we could. Because of the sand storms, visibility shut down, sometimes, to the length of your arm. . . .

The terrain part of this . . . I think we picked a good way to go, to the west of the Euphrates. We did have some maneuver advantage and we did not have the issues with [lines of communication] that routes internal to the Tigris and Euphrates Rivers did have, with its complex terrain, the canals, and the road structure that didn't allow you to get off the roads, getting up through Highway 8 and Highway 1. Once we got into the urban areas, once we crossed the Euphrates, then we were into the complex terrain (e.g. areas with buildings, homes, bridges, etc.). It was very difficult, because the units could not get off of the roads, and the canals restricted the units from the maneuver. The good thing is that we were able to maneuver four hundred kilometers in fairly unrestricted terrain until we did the river crossings across the Euphrates. . . .

Question: What did the enemy do or not do that you found unusual? What is your overall assessment of the enemy?

Answer: Well, in general, what we saw was that the regular army and the Republican Guards gave up fairly quickly. The paramilitary and the death squads continued to fight. So we found we were fighting a lot of technical (improvised combat vehicles—e.g., trucks with machine-guns on the back) and death squads, many of them without a whole lot of training, but many of them very tenacious. If there was something alarming, it was the aggressiveness that they came at us with, even though we had tanks and Bradleys. It was a little disconcerting to think that a guy in a pick-up truck, with an air defense system in the back, would try to charge a tank or a Bradley. We knew that we had some fairly aggressive guys, if they were trying that technique. The same with the death squads on the ground-their "wave" attacks, although many of those were piecemeal attacks—that they ran against the 3–7 Cavalry (reconnaissance and security element for 3 ID) and the 101st Airborne Division and a number of other units that had to deal with them. That was . . . I guess it would be the tenacity and aggressiveness that they showed in putting up light-skinned vehicles against Bradleys and tanks that surprised me.

The other thing is that they really didn't adapt very well to the situation. They used basically the same tactics, techniques, and procedures all the way through the campaign, in every city, every time we engaged them. Generally, that showed their lack of understanding of our capabilities, and particularly of our night vision devices and our ability to detect and engage them at night. A lot of them just continued to use technical and infantry against us, time after time, all night in some cases, and for two or three days in other cases with infantry coming at us. It was interesting and a little unusual that they did not adapt. It was unusual that they came and met us on our terms, rather than on their terms. It was very unusual that they would all empty out of a city and come after us, when they could have stayed in the city and forced us to come in and fight in urban terrain. Time after time, and even in Baghdad, once you went through an intersection or a crossroad somewhere, they came out after us, these paramilitary forces came out after us, rather than staying in a building and forcing us to come in after them.

Question: I have heard that all of those paramilitary forces were not Iraqis—that some were foreigners. What can you tell me about that?

Answer: What we saw, and I think what all the units saw, was that the paramilitary forces that fought the hardest, and the ones that were the last ones fighting, tended to be from other countries. Whether that was because they came to Iraq specifically to kill Americans and had a "higher calling" of sorts to come after us, or whether they didn't have any place to go once the fighting was over and this was their "last stand," I don't know. . . .

There are other points that I think were extremely important. The attack up to cut Highway 8 and Highway 1 was an important part of the whole fight. The Iraqis did not expect us to come up through the Karbala Gap. All of the intel and all of the maps and all of the prisoners of war we talked to indicated that the Iraqis believed we were coming up Highways 8 and 1, and that the main attack was on those highways—and that the Karbala Gap was a supporting attack. The maps that we captured all showed that. Our deception operations to Objectives Jenkins (north of Najaf), Murray (Hindiyah, along Euphrates river southeast of Karbala), and Floyd (south of Najaf) all made the Iraqis believe, since we owned the river, that we were crossing and coming up Highway 8. That added to the deception that led them to placing the Medina Division along Highway 8. . . . When we cut Highway 8 [by seizing the Karbala Gap], we left most of the Medina south of Highway 8, Al Hillah, and Highway 1, and there were whole enemy battalions sitting in revetments, looking south, that we policed up over the next few days. There was a night of killing as they tried to get out of the pocket from Al Hillah, across to the Tigris River. That night, it was CAS (close air support) mission after CAS mission, coming in after numerous tanks, [artillery pieces], and artillery units that were trying to get out of the pocket. . . .

What has amazed me is that our soldiers have quickly adapted to the enemy. They will find ways to adapt. Where we found tanks being destroyed by RPGs fired into the grills early in the campaign, our soldiers learned how to beat that, against thousands of enemy soldiers, by the time we reached downtown Baghdad. They made changes in the way they fight in the turret, how they covered each other as they moved, the weapons the gunner and loader carried—they found ways to combat the capability of the enemy. The enemy would come up real close to the road, so our gun tubes could not depress to reach them, but our loaders would have M-4 rifles and so forth, shooting right down into the enemy. So there were five or six weapons on that tank that could be used to cover the vehicle in an urban environment. They learned that starting with the very first contact with the enemy, and moving north, they developed their skills. The soldiers adapted to the enemy. We thought we were going to need reactive armor on the tanks, and some other things. The troopers simply found ways—tactics, techniques, and procedures—that allowed them to overcome the RPG threat. Armored vehicles can survive in urban environments. That is one thing we found in Baghdad. They can survive if we use the right [tactics, techniques, and procedures] and train the right way. . . .

I think the battle of 3–7 Cavalry at Objective Jenkins and Objective Floyd at An Najaf was probably one of the fiercest fights of the whole campaign. They sat down there on the opposite side of the river and had a bridge partially blown behind them. They had to sit there in complex terrain in tanks and Bradleys and had to fight technicals. They couldn't get off the roads. For three or four nights, they fought without any kind of relief up there. They had to get vehicles refueled. There were points where we had to go down and bulldoze Iraqi bodies off of the bridge, there were so many of them. A very fierce fight by 3–7 Cavalry. One of the hardest fights. It was well over five hundred enemy dead, really over two thousand over the two nights. The 3–7 Cavalry lost two tanks and a Bradley down there. That was against an RPG that fired into the grille of the tank. We've since gotten some plates that we are going to put on the back of tanks to try to prevent that from happening. . . . [The enemy] knew where the Abrams tank weakness was, in the engine compartment. They were firing the engine compartment, getting a mobility kill, and then swarming RPGs at them. We had a soldier stay in the tank while all the rounds cooked off, so our blow-out panels worked properly. He got out with some singes on him. Everybody escaped from those two tanks and that Bradley without getting hurt. . . From that, we learned how to cover the engine compartments with tanks behind and Bradleys behind, and loaders and tank commanders carrying certain kinds of weapons. There is always a trade-off in a tank, you know. Do you want to go buttoned up or hatches open? Most of the time, we found, the drivers were buttoned up, but because of the amount of infantry and the amount of space you had to scan to keep the death squads from getting to you, and even in the cities, the TCs (tank commanders) and the loaders had to be up and be part of the overall tank survivability, engaging the enemy with their own personal weapons. We had TCs engaging enemy with their 9mm pistols in Baghdad. . . .

The first thing I'd say is that it isn't over until it's over. There's still the whole business of the relief in place to go through, getting forward, getting Baghdad under one command. In every war, you end up having some morphing of the way the enemy is going to fight. I think we have fought through a regular, conventional force; we have fought through a paramilitary force; I think that's not over yet. There may yet be other phases of this as we move into stability and support operations. Perhaps the next phase will be terrorists. It's one thing to deal with car bombs when you are in a conventional fight. When you tum to a [security and stability] operation, the ability to fight a terrorist threat of car bombs and suicide bombers in that kind of environment, where you have to have closure and get close to the people, becomes very important. We can stay away from the people in a conventional fight. We can force that to happen. When you get into stability operations, [which] requires you to get close to the population. When you do that, the threat of terrorism goes right up. We are going to fight another fight, here, which is probably a terrorist-type fight of people that want to harm Americans and will have more of an opportunity in stability operations than in a conventional fight to do that. We are going to continue fighting some of the paramilitary forces that are still feeling strong enough to continue to fight, or else don't have any other option because they can't fit back into society. That hard part is probably done, but this thing is not completely over. If we can do it quickly, it will be better. If we can normalize Iraq quickly, that would be good. We have preserved a lot of the infrastructure so that can be done quickly. Maybe in a year or two, if we put our minds to it.

Source: Stephen A. Hicks. Interview by French MacLean, April 15, 2003, and Russell H. Thaden. Interview by French MacLean, March 18, 2003. Interview Transcripts. V (U.S.) Corps Historian Office. Courtesy of the Operational Leadership Experiences Digital Collection, Combat Studies Institute, Fort Leavenworth, KS.

AFTERMATH

As stated, the final interview was completed on April 15, 2003. The last U.S. forces left Iraq in December 2011. The plan for departure from Baghdad and Iraq was to quickly hand over authority for the country to an Iraqi interim government and U.S. forces were to depart and return to the United States all within a matter of months.

The United States sent more than 319,000 forces to the Middle East to support Operation Iraqi Freedom. Only about 150,000 entered Iraq and supported the attacks to overthrow Saddam Hussein. The coalition sent an additional 22,000 into Iraq from twelve countries. The cost in terms of lives lost was 138 from the U.S. and 33 from the United Kingdom. There are only estimates for Iraqi casualties, but they range into the tens of thousands and more depending on the time frame specified.

Colonel Hicks was prescient in his prediction of what the enemy would do next as readers will see as this book progresses. Though many in the capital cities of the coalition believed that things were winding down those in country were starting to experience and witness the chaos of looting that was running rampant throughout Iraq as the people realized that the security apparatus of the Iraqi state was no longer in place.

ASK YOURSELF

1. These interviews were conducted in the middle of preparations for and conduct of combat operations. Both of the gentlemen being interviewed held critical positions in the organization and they were extremely busy. Despite this they made time for the corps historian to interview them and took the time to provide thoughtful responses. There is significant importance placed on the collection of lessons learned during and immediately after combat and training events in the U.S. military. It is part of the culture. Unlike academic history, the military applies lessons learned and history reordered to the conduct of training and operations in relatively short order. Or, at least that is the intent. Why might that be the case? Is the collection of lessons that important to military people? If so, why?

2. There is a lot of emphasis placed on the ability of technology to overcome the elements and the challenges of basic problems like darkness, cold, adverse weather. In this case, as was also true in Desert Storm, it becomes clear that technology has its limits. Sandstorms and fog can defeat thermal imaging more than any manmade efforts. If technology can still be defeated by a sandstorm, does its cost have reasonable value?

3. If these senior staff officers understood the enemy as well as they seem to have, based on their predictions that proved true, both before the fighting began about the fighting itself and after the main fighting ended about the next phase, then why did the U.S. government and more senior leaders miss the rise of the insurgency?

TOPICS TO CONSIDER

1. What is the nature of a society? Do polls and activities of portions of a population reflect the will of the people? In this war the two cultures fighting were significantly different and, as a result, often did not understand each other. They did not understand their enemy's commitment or desired goals and objectives. The nature of cultural identity is crucial in understanding motivation.

Further Reading

Atkinson, Rick. *In the Company of Soldiers: A Chronicle of Combat.* New York: Henry Holt and Company, 2004.
Fontenot, Gregory, E.J. Degen, and David Tohn. *On Point: The United States Army in Operation Iraqi Freedom.* Fort Leavenworth, KS: U.S. Army Command and General Staff College Press, 2004.

Hughes, Christopher P. *War on Two Fronts: An Infantry Commander's War in Iraq and the Pentagon*. Philadelphia: Casemate, 2007.

Lacey, James G. *Takedown: The 3rd Infantry Division's Twenty-One Day Assault on Baghdad*. Annapolis, MD: Naval Institute Press, 2007.

Zucchino, David. *Thunder Run: The Armored Strike to Capture Baghdad*. New York: Atlantic Monthly Press, 2004.

Films and Television

American War Generals. Executive producers: Peter Bergen, Tresha Mabile, Jonathan Towers. National Geographic Channel, 2014.

6. British Perspective in Basra: Johnny Austin

INTRODUCTION

As V (U.S.) Corps attacked along the west generally following the Euphrates River valley, the Marine Expeditionary Force (MEF) attacked the east. Under the overall command of the MEF was the 1st United Kingdom Armored Division who attacked with an orientation on Basra. United States Marine Corps (USMC) elements accompanied the division. The U.K. division breached the obstacles along the Iraq border and conducted the attack to seize the Basra airport and bridges across the Shatt al-Basra waterway—an artificial waterway built to the west of the city. It was a critical obstacle to be crossed prior to taking the city of Basra itself. The U.K. forces came into contact with a mixture of Iraqi conventional military and Fedayeen militia fighters. The bridges were wired for demolition, but the British force took the bridges intact and then moved on to capture the airport and later the city.

The Iraqi resistance was seen as tenacious but ill trained. One example was the use of multiple RPG teams; the people firing the RPGs regularly failed to arm the grenades thus some British armored vehicles had undetonated grenades stuck in their armor. Attacks continued for several days against the bridges. Most of the later attacks were mounted by the Fedayeen militias. During the fighting there were several friendly force–on–friendly force engagements that resulted in casualties. U.S. Marines attacked up the al-Faw Peninsula from the south and as they approached the city there was a coordinated attack to take Basra.

The city fell into coalition hands with much less conventional resistance than expected. Once the city was taken, the British forces conducted a transition from warfighting to policing.

> All in all, it was a very rapid transition from general warfighting to becoming the law of the city and conducting a police operation. It was almost imperial policing. We'd established ourselves as the police force. Crime was pretty high because Saddam had let out all the people from jail, so there were a lot of things for us to deal with. We transitioned pretty rapidly, probably too rapidly in some cases. Moving soldiers from the, "Go and kill everything" mode to, "All these people are our friends now." That probably didn't lie very well with some of our soldiers and it took a long time to change people's attitudes.

KEEP IN MIND AS YOU READ

1. Twelve nations entered Iraq in the spring of 2003 as combat forces and they fought alongside American forces in a coalition. That often means that forces from one nation take orders and follow the directions of leaders from another nation. This has been going on for more than seventy years as it was quite common in World War II. The establishment of the North Atlantic Treaty Organization (NATO) was instrumental in solidifying the nature of command relationships between organizations of different nations. Forces from the United Kingdom and the United States have interacted in this environment on many occasions. Despite the administrative relationships being smoothed over there are always national differences in perception and preference.

2. The British Army first entered Basra in 1914 as part of World War I. The campaigns in Mesopotamia were instrumental in shaping the British relationship with the Middle East. Johnny Austin is quoted above using the phrase "imperial policing." This was a term quite common in the 1920s, following World War I. The British used military means to keep the local populace in line. This was especially true in Iraq where Royal Air Force aircraft often bombed villages as a part of the "policing" to ensure their compliance with British directives. When the British entered Basra in 1914 they were supported by the Emir of Kuwait who was then a governor under Ottoman authority. For their support of British interests Kuwait was declared an independent country under British protection.

3. As stated in previous chapters there were a lot of connections back to 1991. Many Shia in Basra rose up to oppose the regime of Saddam Hussein and the regime used attack helicopters to regain authority over the area. Shia in Basra and elsewhere in the south of Iraq remembered that the United States and its coalition allies did not come to their assistance in opposing Saddam Hussein then. The feelings of distrust between Shia Iraqis and coalition forces continued into the invasion and occupation in 2003 and beyond.

Document 6: Excerpt from Interview with Johnny Austin, Mortar Officer and Platoon Commander with 1st Battalion, Royal Regiment of Fusiliers

Question: While you were in your policing role, what kinds of interaction did you have with the local Iraqis?

Answer: We worked very closely with the Iraqis. At that time, everything had been disbanded. There wasn't any police force or army. The instruments of local and national government were nonexistent to say the least. No ex-policemen in Basra were willing to show themselves because they tended to be Sunni. Being a Sunni in Basra at that time wasn't a good thing. I remember there being a lot of celebrating and we spent a lot time seizing weapons. Rather than dancing in the streets, they tended to fire [Soviet made heavy machine guns].

Unfortunately, when we seized their weapons we incurred the wrath of a lot of tribes, so we ended up being engaged in some small-scale firefights, sometimes quite large-scale firefights. It basically came down to who wielded the biggest stick and, at the time, it was us. We were able to sort of pacify these people.

The Arabs see force as something good. If you seem to be weak, they'll exploit you and if you seem to be strong, they'll toe the line. We spent a lot of time facilitating things within the city. For example, we protected money moving around the city so they could pay government employees. We tried to impose a certain element of rule of law within the city, but in a city of one million people a battle group of a thousand isn't going to have that much effect. We certainly tried to make life easier for people. We assisted in the distribution of gas bottles—that's how people cooked—and, by doing so, we averted a number of riots that could have ensued. Just before we left, we started to recruit a local militia force to provide port security. The battle group had been tasked to screen former military and police individuals to bring them back into law enforcement. There was certainly a three-week period where Basra really degenerated. After the warfighting and after the euphoria wore off, things got unpleasant and whole families were being ethnically cleansed. We spent a lot of time dealing with that. It was difficult, though, because we were stuck in a city where we didn't really speak the language and we weren't overly comfortable with the culture. We were fortunate that people volunteered to be interpreters for us, but what we failed to realize was that those people who could speak English tended to be Sunni, not Shi'a.

In some cases, that worked to our advantage. I had a very good interpreter who used to be a Super Frelon pilot. He was Sunni and quite high up in the regime, or at least a Ba'ath Party member, and he was very adept at getting people to tell the truth. I certainly enjoyed having him because he spoke both English and French and he spoke them fluently. He'd been imprisoned by Saddam because he'd refused to fly his helicopter to invade Kuwait. He didn't think one Arab nation should invade another Arab nation.

Question: Was it difficult getting the kind of interpreter support you needed when and where you needed it?

Answer: We didn't have too much of a problem initially because we paid very well for it, but we then found ourselves undermining the economy. The key people like doctors and lawyers were the ones who had the ability to speak English and we paid much larger sums than the doctors and lawyers in the communities were earning, so we caused a few problems there. Once we'd gone static, we had countless people coming to us asking for help but also offering help as well. We very quickly had the ability to locally employ people to do things for us, and one of those things was to be interpreters.

We found out very quickly that we needed to be quite robust in our attitudes towards these people. They may say they could speak English, but there were others who were just trying to get the money because they'd heard about it. We instigated a very complicated testing process and, as such, we were able to get some very good interpreters. We generally had interpreters available 24 hours a day. They would come in for eight-hour shifts and live inside our base. We'd feed them and pay them and they proved to be very effective—or maybe they just seemed to be more effective than they were because we'd had so little before. I remember moving on the roads up to the contact point with 3/4 Marines and we had to pretty much use sign language to let people know what we wanted. Now, we had interpreters who could generally understand what I was saying and who could make me understood to the people.

Question: Did the interpreters help you understand the local tribal structure?
Answer: Yes. We came across some who were experts in tribal culture. Given the nature of Iraqi society, we had to very quickly understand what tribes our interpreters came from, too, and then use them for certain purposes but not for others. The intelligence officer, a number of other captains and I sat down and conducted our own social network analysis of what was going on in Basra and who were the major opinion leaders. From there, we had to work out where we could direct interpreters. That took an awful lot of brainpower and I don't think we ever really got it right, but I also don't think we made that bad a hash of it either. It did take a lot of time to do and I wasn't particularly pleased to have to go to those meetings.

Source: Johnny Austin. Interview by Laurence Lessard, May 7, 2008. Interview Transcript. Courtesy of the Operational Leadership Experiences Digital Collection, Combat Studies Institute, Fort Leavenworth, KS. Available at: http://cgsc.contentdm.oclc.org/cdm/singleitem/collection/p4013coll13/id/1056/rec/1 (accessed June 12, 2015).

AFTERMATH

Basra was initially a quiet and relatively well-governed area or so it seemed in 2003 and 2004. The British military took a very hands-off approach and allowed locals to quickly regain control. This often led to significant corruption as bribes and intimidation were used to control the flow of material into and out of the only major port city. By 2005 the situation deteriorated with sectarian groups taking control from the organized crime to then pursue a more cohesive agenda of control of the resources and intimidation of the people. The British forces moved onto forward operating bases (FOBs) where most of their forces remained. As will be discussed in a later chapter it required significant effort to regain the lost initiative and territory conceded to the criminal and sectarian militias.

In this vignette it is possible to see how the differences in national culture and historical experience shaped the different approaches to the transition from invasion to occupation to sovereignty. This will continue to be observable as one proceeds through this book.

ASK YOURSELF

1. As stated earlier there is no one single experience in Iraq. There are different Iraqs based on the ethnic, sectarian, and tribal divisions within the country. There were also different coalition experiences based off national identities, history with Iraq and Arabs, in general, and views toward casualties with respect to the domestic political environment. The U.K. government was the most supportive of the

U.S. government in invading Iraq. They were also the most criticized as the years progressed. Iraq became a poisonous political association to the point that when the United Kingdom intended to send trainers to teach counterimprovised explosives device training to the Iraqis in 2015 the U.K. prime minister overruled it as there was a contentious election going on and any mention of U.K. deployments to Iraq were deemed as disastrous for the party making the decision even though the proposed training was innocuous and would have been supported in nearly any other location on the planet. This level of complexity is what modern conflict is about. It isn't enough to understand the country in question, but one needs to understand the variations and details in the city or neighborhood. How can soldiers learn such details?

2. Consider the challenge of working with an interpreter. How do you know they are communicating what you'd like them to communicate? How do you know who you can trust? What is the best way to vet people being considered for such a position?

TOPICS TO CONSIDER

1. The British had tremendous experience in Iraq prior to 2003, much more than the United States. Much of that experience would not be deemed applicable in a modern context as the means and ways used in the 1920s and 1930s were no longer acceptable in the 21st century. That said, there was a lot that could have been learned from other nations as part of a coalition.

2. Different nations have different pieces of equipment and different types of ammunition. Think about the complexity of supporting tens of thousands of people and thousands of pieces of equipment. This is a challenging task even if all the equipment is similar. Now consider how to do that when the pieces and parts are different. Not to mention different tastes in food.

3. In this excerpt he mentions that the police and army were disbanded and the city government was nonexistent. This was done because the coalition viewed the police and military as instruments of the tyrannical Baathist regime and felt it was important to communicate to the people that this regime was finished. Once the security apparatus is removed then how does a foreign power gain or regain control in a city? What are the instruments of governance without a government?

Further Reading

Fontenot, Gregory, E. J. Degen, and David Tohn. *On Point: The United States Army in Operation Iraqi Freedom.* Fort Leavenworth, KS: U.S. Army Command and General Staff College Press, 2004.

Gomez-Granger, Julissa, ed. *CRS Report for Congress: Medal of Honor Recipients: 1979–2008* (Updated June 4, 2008). Washington, DC: Congressional Research Service, 2008.

Gordon, Michael R. and Bernard Trainor. *Cobra II: The Inside Story of the Invasion and Occupation of Iraq.* New York: Pantheon Books, 2006.

Lacey, James G. *Takedown: The 3rd Infantry Division's Twenty-One Day Assault on Baghdad.* Annapolis, MD: Naval Institute Press, 2007.

Websites

Democratic Policy and Communications Center. "Iraq by the Numbers." December 19, 2011. www.dpc.senate.gov/docs/fs-112–1–36.pdf (accessed June 12, 2015).

Home of Heroes. "U.S. Army Awards of the Silver Star." http://www.homeofheroes.com/valor/08_WOT/ss_GWOT/citations_USA-M.html (accessed June 12, 2015).

U.S. Army Human Resources Command. "Awards and Decorations by Conflict." https://www.hrc.army.mil/TAGD/Awards%20and%20Decorations%20Statistics%20by%20Conflict (accessed June 12, 2015).

7. The Close and Chaotic Fight for Invasion: David A. Miles

INTRODUCTION

The battle in and around the Karbala Gap was significant in breaking through to Baghdad. Tenacious defense was demonstrated by supporters of the Iraqi regime and significant efforts were shown by coalition forces as they continued their attack toward the capital city.

In addition to the conventional forces of infantry and armor battalions conducting the main attacks there were operational detachment alpha (ODA) units conducting a variety of special operations forces assignments. This chapter includes an account of a special forces ODA fighting alongside conventional forces underneath an overpass. This is a small and isolated action, but it communicates in many ways the complexities and chaos of battle. It can be difficult to follow the narrative in terms of who is where and what they are each doing, but that is part of the point—trying to understand or communicate the events that transpired in close combat is difficult as each person's perspective of the battle is limited to whatever lies within their view. Decisions are made based on immediate need and perceived importance.

The subject of this chapter, Sergeant First Class David A. Miles, was an assistant operations sergeant with ODA 583 belonging to 3rd Battalion, 5th Special Forces Group (SFG) at the time of the incident described here.

KEEP IN MIND AS YOU READ

1. SFC Miles is being interviewed about his experiences in combat. Because he is talking he does not have time to carefully formulate his responses. Add to that the fact that he is speaking of intense situations that elicit strong emotions and it is easy to see why his account is, at times, sporadic and disjointed. In many ways this adds to the authenticity of his narrative despite the challenges it may present to the reader.

2. Land and places matter. As one advances north along the Euphrates River valley toward Baghdad the land is generally open with complex agricultural fields and irrigation ditches that constrain maneuver to roads. About 140–160 kilometers

south-southwest of Baghdad is the city of Karbala which is rich with religious and historical significance. To the west of the city is a large wet area called Lake Milh (also known as Lake Razazah). The lake and the Euphrates River serve to create a channel and this geographic narrow area is referred to as the Karbala Gap.

3. In a Special Forces unit a sergeant first class is one of twelve team members and is typically trained with a specialty. SFC Miles is an operations sergeant and he had his two medic-trained team members with him.

Document 7: Excerpt from Interviews with David A. Miles, Assistant Operations Sergeant, Operations Detachment Alpha (ODA) 583, Forward Operating Base 53 (3rd Battalion, 5th Special Forces Group (3–5SFG))

So the next morning we were sitting on the side of the road and tanks and Bradleys are just rolling past us. As the last tanks were rolling past, we were laughing because we figured that the first ones already had to be in Baghdad considering the number that had rolled past. After the last one rolled by, we sat there for about fifteen minutes and nothing else came by.

So he [the captain] called Giant X-ray . . . the brigade TOC [tactical operations center]. He asked if that was the column that we were supposed to be following and they said, yes, get in behind them.

So we took off running and caught up with them. At first we didn't see anyone, but the further north we got we could see people beginning to come out. We went through a mine-field that had been cleared a day or two before. We were just looking around and we were pretty apprehensive.

The closer we got to the cloverleaf, and we could hear the gunfire picking up. About 200 meters short of the cloverleaf, sporadic fire began in our area.

Our three trucks were lined up. We weren't under the underpass. I liked where we were at because we had two mortar tracks behind us and a couple of HMMWVs moved around behind us; they were about another 200 meters down the road. So here [were] my little pickup trucks sitting out in nothing. There [were] a couple of M113s and a Bradley or two underneath the overpass at the time. There were a couple more on the eastern side and the western side of the overpass.

We stayed there for a few minutes, and returned some fire. A couple of RPGs were fired and one hit the guardrail; they were being shot close—I mean, they were not being fired from far away. They were landing close, too. One hit the guardrail and another went over us. Just sporadic fire; you could see the spark every now and then.

To the south and west of us, we were receiving a lot of fire, but it was not accurate. We would occasionally receive rounds from the northeast under the overpass. Then a figure in uniform got up and took off running from underneath the bridge. We thought that he was Iraqi, but later found out that he was Syrian or whatever. In any case, he was a soldier. He was running from one position to another. Shane was up on the M240 and I called to him,

"Under [the] bridge by the palm trees," and Shane took him down. We were just kind of happy sitting there for a few minutes.

Then the captain came over and he was kind of concerned. There were two M113s there and one was a medic track and I don't know what the other one was. Some genius sends these three guys over to clear the area underneath this bridge. The captain comes running over and says, "Dave, we've got to get these guys or they're going to be in trouble." I looked over and see these three guys, and it takes them a few minutes to figure out what they're going to do with the hand grenade, and they finally pull the pin and throw it. You could tell they were all nervous and kids—they just didn't know what the hell they were doing. One had a pistol, one had an M16A2, and the third had a crew-served machine gun. I mean, what the hell is that?

We're seeing more sporadic fire from underneath there, and he says we've got to get a team and go get them. Roger that.

So I took three of the four guys on my truck to come with me.

The captain said, "I've got Steve." I said OK, you guys cover us, and Ken, Chris and I started running out to the first set of abutments. When we got there, I called back, "Set!," so the captain and Steve could run up to where we were, maybe 75–100 feet.

Somehow we determine that these three guys up in front us were all medics, because the one guy has a pistol or something; I don't know. So these guys—they were kids—they were scared shitless. SO I'm yelling, "Hold on! Hold on!" They were getting ready to go to another one, and I yelled, "Stay there!"

So the captain and Steve, so I said, "You guys set?," and he said, "Yeah, we're set."

So I went over to the north side of the abutment and I peered around and I asked Ken and Chris, "Are you guys ready?" They said yes. So I said, "Let's go."

I looked down around the corner and said, "Let's go," and then just sparks and the shit hit the fan and both those guys went down. And it was crazy because the guy who was shooting was damn near in line with the captain and Steve and my two guys and me. Why he didn't shoot the captain and Steve, I don't know.

So I spun around to get back in the middle of them and put out a burst or whatever. Ken hit the ground . . . holding his leg. And I look over and . . . Chris looked like a yard sprinkler, man, blood just shooting up out of his damned leg, you know? So I ran over and jumped on him and started working on him. I tell Ken I'm working on Chris . . . I didn't want Chris to know but by then he was . . . white and his eyes were rolling back and sometimes he wasn't listening to me anyway. So I yelled over at Ken and I told him arterial bleeding . . .

Steve was . . . yelling at me to get down or whatever. I just pretty much had to stay there.

. . . I remember they were shooting but I don't know where it was coming from. Initially when I went over and jumped on . . . Chris we were in the dirt. There wasn't anything there, you know. There's always a sandbag wrapper or something. There wasn't shit there. So I ripped his belt off, wrapped it around his leg, got on top of his leg, and cinched it down as tight as I could. Ken was still yelling at me, and that's when I told him [it was] arterial bleeding.

Steve was saying that they're shooting at us, and I told Steve that I couldn't move Chris. The captain had his back to me and was shooting at guys to the south, and so was Steve, I guess.

So I started digging through Chris' shit and I got out his, uh—he was talking to me and, God, he was white as a sheet and there was probably an area this big covered with blood. He was—ah, what was he saying? It was something funny. Anyway, his eyes were rolling back and he was going in and out. I started digging through his medical stuff and pulling out bandages and trying to rip them open with my teeth because the other hand was holding the belt.

So I got most of them out, and by then Ken had gotten over to me. He asked me, "What have we got?" . . . initially when he went down and the blood was squirting out and like I said there wasn't anything there to stop it, you know? So initially I grabbed it like that and on the back of his leg there was like a huge fricking hole, you know? So I just took my hand and jammed that in there. And I was holding the belt with that hand, and I was trying to get into all these little zippers and pouches and stuff to get his medical stuff out, and holding it with one hand.

And then Ken got finally there and I start throwing it at Ken. Ken, bless his heart, had crawled all the way over there. He had bandaged himself up, you know. And I was thinking he just got some shrapnel or something because I couldn't even see him bleeding much. Ken is a pretty tough dude; he crawled over there himself. He [was] probably hurt, I guess. So he got there and he finally gets one unwrapped. So I changed over to the left hand and I hold one and Ken wraps it. I can't remember what the hell we did with the tourniquet at that time—tucked it off, tied it off, whatever. Anyway, Ken and I got it wrapped off. Chris was looking pretty rough. I was yelling at him and talking to him.

And I guess then, after we got him bandaged, Ken took a pulse and Ken freaked out, man. It was like somebody flipped the switch and he started yelling, "Don't you leave me!" and "You're not going to die. Don't you die on me, motherfucker!" It was funny, Ken yelling at him. Then he took his blood pressure and he really thought he was in trouble now.

So now there's five of us. Two of us are down shot . . . and now the three dudes had come back. What the captain had done was he yelled and told those guys to come back . . . So now I told Steve to come over here with us, leave one of the young guys over there with the captain, so Steve and one of the kids were to take Chris back. And then I would take Ken back, and then the captain and these two young guys would come back all at once.

Everybody ready? Yeah. Covering fire! And we're just laying down rounds all over the place, covering everything, staggering magazines. So we do that for like thirty seconds. And I turn around and I check and damned if Steve isn't still sitting there right next to me!! I'm like, that's when you guys were supposed to run, you know? And what they did was they picked him up and there was a mound of dirt there and they just rolled down the other side of the mound, and they were trying to get all their crap together and by then we had stopped firing. That's why they hadn't gone anywhere.

So I said, are you ready to go again? So we starting firing again and that's when they dragged him over there. And I reached back and grabbed Ken and we jumped up . . . Ken and I both grew up back in West Virginia and we were kind of laughing and carrying on and it was like a potato sack race so like both of our inside feet were together. We were hopping along pretty good and we had almost got there, and Steve ran back out from the abutment and came forward and hooked up under Ken's other arm to help me try to get him back there because Ken's a big guy. I don't know how we did it, but somehow Steve and I launched Ken face first into the dirt. We tried to pick him back up and he says, no, I'll crawl the rest of the way. It was only like two feet . . .

Well, when we got them back on that side of the abutment, none of the three kids were medics. I don't know who the hell they were but they weren't medics. I know they weren't infantrymen; I hope they weren't. Then when we got back to the medic track, there were four guys there. What do we do? Well, for Christ's sake, you're medics!! So Ken was telling them what to do. I don't really know what happened after that as far as them going in the track or whatever.

. . . apparently another five Joes (common, generic term for soldiers) showed up from somewhere—the captain and I took off and went around the corner and told those guys, hey, this is where they're popping up at and we suspected that there was a tunnel over there. That's why we went over to get these guys (the three under the overpass) to start with because we were afraid they would get out there and get cut off.

Of course, we didn't realize it at the time but, while we were getting shot up underneath there, there were shots coming from the other areas, too. They had moved up another 88 and 113 and everybody was starting to cluster up underneath this bridge because we were getting sporadic fire from all over the dang place.

So I left the captain in the corner with those guys and walked back down the road . . . I got Gary and his trucks and Greg and his truck and I went ahead and jumped in to drive my truck. We started pulling in underneath the bridge and pulled the captain's truck in so it was facing north down the northbound lane. Gary's truck was directly behind him; the middle lane was open; and then up against the right hand side lane, I spun my truck around facing south so that Shane could be a gunner there—suppressing back underneath the overpass where we were. Steve was pretty hyped up right now and I was afraid he'd go running off somewhere. He just gets kind of high strung. So I had Mark get out of the truck off the 240 and had Steve get back up in the truck on the 240. Steve's a lot more aggressive gunner, too, so I knew that if anybody came down from the north, Steve would fire them up with the 240. Shane was on the other gun . . .

Source: David A. Miles. Interview by Dennis P. Mroczkowski, April 26, 2003. Interview Transcript. Courtesy of the Operational Leadership Experiences Digital Collection, Combat Studies Institute, Fort Leavenworth, KS.

AFTERMATH

SFC Miles was awarded the Silver Star for his actions during the incident described above. The Silver Star is considered the fourth highest award that a soldier can receive and is typically the third highest award with respect to valor or gallantry in combat. Out of over 1.5 million U.S. service members who served in Iraq during Operation Iraqi Freedom, 229 were awarded the Silver Star. SFC Miles's citation reads as follows:

The President of the United States takes pleasure in presenting the Silver Star Medal to David Miles, Master Sergeant, U.S. Army, for conspicuous gallantry and intrepidity in action while serving with Operational Detachment Alpha 583 (ODA-583) 5th Special Forces Group (Airborne) in support of Operation Iraqi Freedom in Iraq, on 7 April 2003. During the invasion of Baghdad, Master Sergeant Miles and his team were ambushed by enemy fighters at a bridge overpass in southern Baghdad. Outnumbered 20-to-1, three members of Master Sergeant Miles' group got pinned down under the intense firefight and were unable to escape. Master Sergeant Miles organized the recovery mission as the enemies continued to attack. He performed first aid on two of his team members, one of whom would have bled to death without treatment. He was able to carry both of them to safety. In all, Master Sergeant Miles killed or directed the killing of up to 20 Saddam loyalists. (Home Town: Powellton, West Virginia)

ASK YOURSELF

1. As mentioned above, the soldiers who fought together under this overpass were from several different units and branches of service. SFC Miles and his men did not know the soldiers who were sent to clear the area under the bridge yet they risked their lives to save them. What causes soldiers to behave in such altruistic ways toward people they've never met? Can you think of other circumstances in which people have been known to lay aside their personal welfare in order to help a stranger in need?

2. The life of soldiers in combat situations can be very trying. Prior to the battle under the overpass, SFC Miles and his team endured numerous hardships. They worked for days with very little sleep. Their vehicles repeatedly got stuck in the challenging terrain. One vehicle broke down entirely requiring them to wait in place exposed and alone until a replacement part could be delivered under the cover of darkness. The sandstorms were so bad that they had to use a GPS to locate vehicles fifty feet from them. In addition, they had other encounters with the enemy. At no point did they consider giving up despite their many hardships. What is it that drives soldiers to rise above adversity and press on in the face of danger and extreme difficulty? Can you think of a time in your life when you were driven to push on despite tremendous opposition? How does problem-solving your way through setbacks and trials affect a person's outlook?

TOPICS TO CONSIDER

1. A euphemism is a mild, indirect, or vague term used to refer to something that is unpleasant, unseemly, or disreputable. Soldiers often use euphemisms when referring to the things they are required to do in combat. In his account, SFC Miles uses phrases such as "took him down" and "fire them up" what he means is that he or a member of his team has killed an enemy combatant. These expressions are suggestive yet ambiguous. Everyone knows what is meant, but everyone is spared having to verbalize the harsh realities. In what ways might the use of euphemisms helps soldiers to process and ultimately accept their actions in war?

2. Another method soldiers have for dealing with the often inhumane and otherwise unethical acts committed in war is to dehumanize the enemy. This is frequently accomplished through the use of derogatory terms. How does dehumanization of the enemy help people to justify their actions with regard to that enemy? Do you think most people realize they are dehumanizing others when they invent such terms? Look for other examples in history of groups of people who were dehumanized by their enemies in some way.

Further Reading

Fontenot, Gregory, E. J. Degen, and David Tohn. *On Point: The United States Army in Operation Iraqi Freedom.* Fort Leavenworth, KS: U.S. Army Command and General Staff College Press, 2004.

Gomez-Granger, Julissa, ed. *CRS Report for Congress: Medal of Honor Recipients: 1979–2008* (updated June 4, 2008). Washington, DC: Congressional Research Service, 2008.

Gordon, Michael R. and Bernard Trainor. *Cobra II: The Inside Story of the Invasion and Occupation of Iraq*. New York: Pantheon Books, 2006.

Lacey, James G. *Takedown: The 3rd Infantry Division's Twenty-One Day Assault on Baghdad*. Annapolis, MD: Naval Institute Press, 2007.

Weinberger, Caspar W. and Wynton C. Hall (May 29, 2007). *Home of the Brave*. New York: Macmillan. pp. 201–217.

Websites

Democratic Policy and Communications Center. "Iraq by the Numbers." December 19, 2011. www.dpc.senate.gov/docs/fs-112-1-36.pdf (accessed June 12, 2015).

Home of Heroes. "U.S. Army Awards of the Silver Star." http://www.homeofheroes.com/valor/08_WOT/ss_GWOT/citations_USA-M.html (accessed June 12, 2015).

Iraq Coalition Casualty Count, icasualties.org. "Operation Iraqi Freedom." http://icasualties.org/Iraq/index.aspx (accessed June 12, 2015).

U.S. Army Human Resources Command. "Awards and Decorations by Conflict." https://www.hrc.army.mil/TAGD/Awards%20and%20Decorations%20Statistics%20by%20Conflict (accessed June 12, 2015).

Films and Television

American War Generals. Executive producers: Peter Bergen, Tresha Mabile, Jonathan Towers. National Geographic Channel, 2014.

8. Medal of Honor:
Paul R. Smith, April 4, 2003

INTRODUCTION

In this chapter the citation for a Congressional Medal of Honor recipient is presented. The Congressional Medal of Honor is the highest award possible for U.S. military personnel. The award is presented to service members, or to their families in the case of posthumous awards, by the president of the United States. The Medal of Honor (MoH) is given for service above and beyond the call of duty that essentially means heroic action conducted outside of direct orders. The process for each award includes twelve steps of review before it comes before the president of the United States.

Since its first presentation in 1863, 3,467 MoHs have been awarded to a total of 3,448 individuals (there have been nineteen double recipients).[1] Only four MoHs were awarded for Operation Iraqi Freedom. The four men so awarded are Jason L. Dunham, Ross A. McGinnis, Michael A. Monsoor, and Paul R. Smith. All of them received their awards posthumously. In the case of Jason, Ross, and Michael each sacrificed himself by covering a hand grenade in order to protect fellow service members.

Every event associated with a MoH is amazing in its details and demonstrates a tremendous disregard for personal safety in behalf of others. The focus of this chapter is Sergeant First Class Paul R. Smith, a platoon sergeant in B Company, 11th Engineer Battalion, 3rd Infantry Division.

On the day in question, April 4, 2003, the 1st Brigade Combat Team, to which Smith's unit was attached, seized the Baghdad International Airport. Blocking positions were established along the four-lane highway leading to the airport. Large masonry walls lined the highway with towers positioned approximately 100 meters apart. SFC Smith's platoon was given the task of constructing a holding area for enemy prisoners of war on the far side of the wall lining the road behind the forward most blocking position.

KEEP IN MIND AS YOU READ

1. During combat operations the U.S. Army reorganizes different types of military specialties (infantry, armor, artillery, engineers, logistics, etc.) to create a combined arms team that is more effective in engaging and defeating the enemy. Normally, an

infantry battalion is between 500 and 700 people, but once organized for combat with the other specialties it can grow to almost twice that size. A sergeant first class usually helps to lead a platoon of about thirty to fifty people.

2. Military units are given missions that focus their activities. In this case the engineers seemed to have a mundane task of building a camp to hold prisoners of war. This is crucial since large numbers of prisoners would completely complicate the operation for the attacking infantry and armor units. Surrendering and captured Iraqi soldiers needed a safe place that was easy to secure for the U.S. soldiers who needed to guard them.

Document 8: Citation for Congressional Medal of Honor Award to Sergeant First Class Paul R. Smith

For conspicuous gallantry and intrepidity at the risk of his life above and beyond the call of duty: Sergeant First Class Paul R. Smith distinguished himself by acts of gallantry and intrepidity above and beyond the call of duty in action with an armed enemy near Baghdad International Airport, Baghdad, Iraq on 4 April 2003. On that day, Sergeant First Class Smith was engaged in the construction of a prisoner of war holding area when his Task Force was violently attacked by a company-sized enemy force. Realizing the vulnerability of over 100 fellow soldiers, Sergeant First Class Smith quickly organized a hasty defense consisting of two platoons of soldiers, one Bradley Fighting Vehicle and three armored personnel carriers. As the fight developed, Sergeant First Class Smith braved hostile enemy fire to personally engage the enemy with hand grenades and anti-tank weapons, and organized the evacuation of three wounded soldiers from an armored personnel carrier struck by a rocket propelled grenade and a 60mm mortar round. Fearing the enemy would overrun their defenses, Sergeant First Class Smith moved under withering enemy fire to man a .50 caliber machine gun mounted on a damaged armored personnel carrier. In total disregard for his own life, he maintained his exposed position in order to engage the attacking enemy force. During this action, he was mortally wounded. His courageous actions helped defeat the enemy attack, and resulted in as many as 50 enemy soldiers killed, while allowing the safe withdrawal of numerous wounded soldiers. Sergeant First Class Smith's extraordinary heroism and uncommon valor are in keeping with the highest traditions of the military service and reflect great credit upon himself, the Third Infantry Division "Rock of the Marne," and the United States Army.

Source: Julissa Gomez-Granger, ed. CRS Report for Congress: Medal of Honor Recipients: 1979–2008 (updated June 4, 2008). Congressional Research Service: Washington, DC, 2008.

AFTERMATH

This was a fight led by noncommissioned officers with Sergeant First Class Smith's actions supporting other small unit attacks led by other sergeants to silence enemy fire. Following the battle Sergeant First Class Smith was found slumped at the M113 caliber .50 machine-gun position. He was dead from a bullet to the neck.

His actions were credited with protecting more than a hundred other soldiers who were in positions behind the compound that Sergeant Smith and his engineers and infantrymen protected; 3rd Infantry Division went on to capture Baghdad four days later. Exactly two years later President George W. Bush presented the shadowbox containing the MoH to Sergeant First Class Smith's eleven-year-old son, David.

ASK YOURSELF

1. Combat is confusing and fighting at the small-unit level is particularly difficult as a soldier or Marine only knows what they can personally see or hear. In the engagement discussed earlier the Bradley Fighting Vehicle (BFV) provided the greatest firepower with its 25-mm gun and possessed the greatest armor protection. During the fighting the vehicle expended all of its ammunition so the crew pulled back to rearm. The soldiers remaining to fight were unaware of the reason for the BFV's withdrawal and many felt that the crew was abandoning them. The crew of the M113 APC were wounded by a rocket propelled grenade and mortar round. They were evacuated to safety leaving the caliber .50 machine-gun unmanned and silent. This was the largest caliber weapon available to the Americans following the departure of the BFV. Could this confusion have played a role in Sergeant Smith's decision to risk his personal safety in order to protect his fellow soldiers?

2. The location of Iraqi enemies was unknown until Sergeant Smith drove an armored vehicle through one of the compound's walls to prepare the holding facility for future prisoners of war. How might this engagement have evolved differently if he had not breached that wall in an unexpected place?

TOPICS TO CONSIDER

1. What is the nature and meaning of heroism? What does it mean to go "beyond the call of duty"? In the period after the attacks on the United States on September 11 U.S. military personnel were regularly referred to as heroes. From that time until the U.S. departure from Iraq in 2011 about 2.3 million people served in Iraq or Afghanistan. Less than 1 percent of the American population served in the military at any given time during this war with about 7 percent becoming veterans of the war. Seventy-four Americans died in Iraq in April 2003. What is the difference between standard service to the country and the type of personal sacrifice and selflessness recognized in the MoH citation above?

2. During the MoH ceremony President Bush joked that Sergeant Smith had gotten into trouble for partying earlier in his career. Paul Smith was not born serious nor was he always the ideal solider. Over the course of his career and through his experiences he became more serious and strict in his service. In the other MoH cases mentioned above both Jason Dunham and Ross McGinnis were young men who lacked the benefit of years of service to shape their characters. Is heroism predictable? Is the level of heroism represented by the MoH something that is trained or innate?

Note

1. Julissa Gomez-Granger, editor, *CRS Report for Congress: Medal of Honor Recipients: 1979–2008* (updated June 4, 2008). Washington, DC: Congressional Research Service, 2008, i.

Further Reading

Weinberger, Caspar W. and Wynton C. Hall (May 29, 2007). *Home of the Brave*. New York: Macmillan, pp. 201–217.

Websites

Iraq Coalition Casualty Count, icasualties.org. "Operation Iraqi Freedom." http://icasualties .org/Iraq/index.aspx (accessed June 12, 2015).

"Navy Christens Newest Arleigh Burke-Class Ship Jason Dunham," http://www.Navy.mil/ submit/display.asp?story_id=47354 (accessed April 1, 2015).

"SECNAV Names New Zumwalt-Class Destroyer USS Michael Monsoor," http://www .defense.gov/releases/release.aspx?releaseid=12320 (accessed April 1, 2015).

9. *MISSION ACCOMPLISHED*: PRESIDENT BUSH'S REMARKS TO THE CREW OF THE USS *ABRAHAM LINCOLN*, MAY 1, 2003

INTRODUCTION

President George W. Bush was a pilot in the Air National Guard and on May 1, 2003, he became the first sitting president to make an arrested landing on an aircraft carrier. Of note, his father had been a navy carrier pilot in World War II and thus had made numerous arrested landings. President Bush arrived on an S-3 Viking as a passenger in the plane using the call sign *Navy One*. President Bush arrived on the USS *Abraham Lincoln* off the coast of San Diego to welcome the crew home after a ten-month deployment—one of the longest carrier deployments since the end of the Vietnam War. The ship bore a banner that said "Mission Accomplished." The banner was to celebrate the crew's end of mission but the White House emphasized that this was not to state that the war was over or that the fighting was complete in Iraq.

The fighting in Iraq was changing in tone and character from an invasion to an occupation with the ultimate goal of transitioning to Iraqi sovereignty and American and coalition departure. Looting was ending and the transition was beginning. In January 2003 the White House designated retired Lieutenant General Jay Garner to lead the transition team for Iraq. He had previously been responsible for securing the Kurds in northern Iraq following Desert Storm. Therefore, he seemed a logical choice. The intent was to transition to Iraqi elections in a matter of months—something like ninety days—and depart Iraq by the end of 2003. By nearly all reports there was friction between Jay Garner's efforts and the efforts of the Pentagon which included support for Iraqi exile Ahmed Chalabi. Neither Chalabi nor Garner liked the other and this created problems from the beginning of Garner's time in Iraq.

The official part of the transition within Iraq began on April 15, 2013, with a conference held in Nasariyah attended by approximately hundred Iraqi political leaders. A follow-up meeting was held on April 28 with about 250 Iraqi leaders. In this second meeting leaders of various political parties were designated and it looked as if the process was moving forward according to plans.

KEEP IN MIND AS YOU READ

1. Consider the connection between words, deeds, and images. The president stated and implied that there was much more to do in Iraq and elsewhere in the war on terrorism that he was leading. The major fighting—what appeared to be war—was over; the focus in Iraq had shifted to policing and reconstruction. As he spoke, the president stood before a banner that said "Mission Accomplished." Which had more power? The words he spoke, the events that followed with the rise of an insurgency, or the image of a banner in your mind? Do the more sober words change the opinion of the meaning of the later violent events?

2. Who was selecting leadership in Iraq? Under the regime of Saddam Hussein many intellectuals and political leaders fled Iraq to live and work elsewhere. Many of these exiles worked with the Bush administration either through the Pentagon or the department of state to assist in designing the post-invasion Iraq. In this effort Secretary of Defense Donald Rumsfeld and the department of defense took the primary position. Rumsfeld requested to lead the reconstruction effort because he had the forces and resources on the ground at the time that the reconstruction would begin. What impact might a military-led reconstruction have? In what ways does the perspective of the military vary from civilian leadership?

Document 9: Excerpt from President Bush's Remarks to the Crew of the USS Abraham Lincoln, *May 1, 2003*

Thank you all very much. Admiral Kelly, Captain Card, officers and sailors of the USS Abraham Lincoln, my fellow Americans: Major combat operations in Iraq have ended. In the battle of Iraq, the United States and our allies have prevailed. (Applause.) And now our coalition is engaged in securing and reconstructing that country.

In this battle, we have fought for the cause of liberty, and for the peace of the world. Our nation and our coalition are proud of this accomplishment—yet, it is you, the members of the United States military, who achieved it. Your courage, your willingness to face danger for your country and for each other, made this day possible. Because of you, our nation is more secure. Because of you, the tyrant has fallen, and Iraq is free. (Applause.)

Operation Iraqi Freedom was carried out with a combination of precision and speed and boldness the enemy did not expect, and the world had not seen before. From distant bases or ships at sea, we sent planes and missiles that could destroy an enemy division, or strike a single bunker. Marines and soldiers charged to Baghdad across 350 miles of hostile ground, in one of the swiftest advances of heavy arms in history. You have shown the world the skill and the might of the American Armed Forces.

This nation thanks all the members of our coalition who joined in a noble cause. We thank the Armed Forces of the United Kingdom, Australia, and Poland, who shared in the hardships of war. We thank all the citizens of Iraq who welcomed our troops and joined in the liberation of their own country. And tonight, I have a special word for Secretary

Rumsfeld, for General Franks, and for all the men and women who wear the uniform of the United States: America is grateful for a job well done. (Applause.)

The character of our military through history—the daring of Normandy, the fierce courage of Iwo Jima, the decency and idealism that turned enemies into allies—is fully present in this generation. When Iraqi civilians looked into the faces of our servicemen and women, they saw strength and kindness and goodwill. When I look at the members of the United States military, I see the best of our country, and I'm honored to be your Commander-in-Chief. (Applause.)

In the images of falling statues, we have witnessed the arrival of a new era. For a hundred of years of war, culminating in the nuclear age, military technology was designed and deployed to inflict casualties on an ever-growing scale. In defeating Nazi Germany and Imperial Japan, Allied forces destroyed entire cities, while enemy leaders who started the conflict were safe until the final days. Military power was used to end a regime by breaking a nation.

Today, we have the greater power to free a nation by breaking a dangerous and aggressive regime. With new tactics and precision weapons, we can achieve military objectives without directing violence against civilians. No device of man can remove the tragedy from war; yet it is a great moral advance when the guilty have far more to fear from war than the innocent. (Applause.)

In the images of celebrating Iraqis, we have also seen the ageless appeal of human freedom. Decades of lies and intimidation could not make the Iraqi people love their oppressors or desire their own enslavement. Men and women in every culture need liberty like they need food and water and air. Everywhere that freedom arrives, humanity rejoices; and everywhere that freedom stirs, let tyrants fear. (Applause.)

We have difficult work to do in Iraq. We're bringing order to parts of that country that remain dangerous. We're pursuing and finding leaders of the old regime, who will be held to account for their crimes. We've begun the search for hidden chemical and biological weapons and already know of hundreds of sites that will be investigated. We're helping to rebuild Iraq, where the dictator built palaces for himself, instead of hospitals and schools. And we will stand with the new leaders of Iraq as they establish a government of, by, and for the Iraqi people. (Applause.)

The transition from dictatorship to democracy will take time, but it is worth every effort. Our coalition will stay until our work is done. Then we will leave, and we will leave behind a free Iraq. (Applause.)

The battle of Iraq is one victory in a war on terror that began on September the 11, 2001—and still goes on. That terrible morning, 19 evil men—the shock troops of a hateful ideology—gave America and the civilized world a glimpse of their ambitions. They imagined, in the words of one terrorist, that September the 11th would be the "beginning of the end of America." By seeking to turn our cities into killing fields, terrorists and their allies believed that they could destroy this nation's resolve, and force our retreat from the world. They have failed. (Applause.)

In the battle of Afghanistan, we destroyed the Taliban, many terrorists, and the camps where they trained. We continue to help the Afghan people lay roads, restore hospitals, and educate all of their children. Yet we also have dangerous work to complete. As I speak, a Special Operations task force, led by the 82nd Airborne, is on the trail of the terrorists and those who seek to undermine the free government of Afghanistan. America and our coalition will finish what we have begun. (Applause.)

From Pakistan to the Philippines to the Horn of Africa, we are hunting down al Qaeda killers. Nineteen months ago, I pledged that the terrorists would not escape the patient justice of the United States. And as of tonight, nearly one-half of al Qaeda's senior operatives have been captured or killed. (Applause.)

The liberation of Iraq is a crucial advance in the campaign against terror. We've removed an ally of al Qaeda, and cut off a source of terrorist funding. And this much is certain: No terrorist network will gain weapons of mass destruction from the Iraqi regime, because the regime is no more. (Applause.)

In these 19 months that changed the world, our actions have been focused and deliberate and proportionate to the offense. We have not forgotten the victims of September the 11th—the last phone calls, the cold murder of children, the searches in the rubble. With those attacks, the terrorists and their supporters declared war on the United States. And war is what they got. (Applause.)

Our war against terror is proceeding according to principles that I have made clear to all: Any person involved in committing or planning terrorist attacks against the American people becomes an enemy of this country, and a target of American justice. (Applause.)

Any person, organization, or government that supports, protects, or harbors terrorists is complicit in the murder of the innocent, and equally guilty of terrorist crimes.

Any outlaw regime that has ties to terrorist groups and seeks or possesses weapons of mass destruction is a grave danger to the civilized world—and will be confronted. (Applause.)

And anyone in the world, including the Arab world, who works and sacrifices for freedom has a loyal friend in the United States of America. (Applause.)

Our commitment to liberty is America's tradition—declared at our founding; affirmed in Franklin Roosevelt's Four Freedoms; asserted in the Truman Doctrine and in Ronald Reagan's challenge to an evil empire. We are committed to freedom in Afghanistan, in Iraq, and in a peaceful Palestine. The advance of freedom is the surest strategy to undermine the appeal of terror in the world. Where freedom takes hold, hatred gives way to hope. When freedom takes hold, men and women turn to the peaceful pursuit of a better life. American values and American interests lead in the same direction: We stand for human liberty. (Applause.)

U.S. DOCTRINE OF FREEDOM

The three presidential addresses mentioned in this speech allude to three founding doctrines with respect to U.S. foreign policy regarding human rights and liberties.

- In the 1941 State of the Union speech, January 6, 1941, President Franklin Roosevelt enumerated four freedoms that people "everywhere in the world" should enjoy. Those freedoms are: freedom of speech, freedom of worship, freedom from want, and freedom from fear.
- On March 12, 1947, President Harry Truman addressed Congress concerning a request for aid for Greece and Turkey. In this address the president laid out a philosophy of U.S. interests with respect to supporting free peoples against oppression.
- President Ronald Reagan first used the phrase *evil empire* to refer to the Soviet Union on March 8, 1983. In this speech and others rhetorically and philosophically linked to it the president expressed a vision where confrontation of the Soviets was akin to an extension of the age-old fight of good versus evil.

The United States upholds these principles of security and freedom in many ways—with all the tools of diplomacy, law enforcement, intelligence, and finance. We're working with a broad coalition of nations that understand the threat and our shared responsibility to meet it. The use of force has been—and remains—our last resort. Yet all can know, friend and foe alike, that our nation has a mission: We will answer threats to our security, and we will defend the peace. (Applause.)

Our mission continues. Al Qaeda is wounded, not destroyed. The scattered cells of the terrorist network still operate in many nations, and we know from daily intelligence that they continue to plot against free people. The proliferation of deadly weapons remains a serious danger. The enemies of freedom are not idle, and neither are we. Our government has taken unprecedented measures to defend the homeland. And we will continue to hunt down the enemy before he can strike. (Applause.)

The war on terror is not over; yet it is not endless. We do not know the day of final victory, but we have seen the turning of the tide. No act of the terrorists will change our purpose, or weaken our resolve, or alter their fate. Their cause is lost. Free nations will press on to victory. (Applause.)

Other nations in history have fought in foreign lands and remained to occupy and exploit. Americans, following a battle, want nothing more than to return home. And that is your direction tonight. (Applause.) After service in the Afghan—and Iraqi theaters of war—after 100,000 miles, on the longest carrier deployment in recent history, you are homeward bound. (Applause.) Some of you will see new family members for the first time—150 babies were born while their fathers were on the Lincoln. Your families are proud of you, and your nation will welcome you. (Applause.)

We are mindful, as well, that some good men and women are not making the journey home. One of those who fell, Corporal Jason Mileo, spoke to his parents five days before his death. Jason's father said, "He called us from the center of Baghdad, not to brag, but to tell us he loved us. Our son was a soldier."

Every name, every life is a loss to our military, to our nation, and to the loved ones who grieve. There's no homecoming for these families. Yet we pray, in God's time, their reunion will come.

Those we lost were last seen on duty. Their final act on this Earth was to fight a great evil and bring liberty to others. All of you—all in this generation of our military—have taken up the highest calling of history. You're defending your country, and protecting the innocent from harm. And wherever you go, you carry a message of hope—a message that is ancient and ever new. In the words of the prophet Isaiah, "To the captives, 'come out,'—and to those in darkness, 'be free.'"

Thank you for serving our country and our cause. May God bless you all, and may God continue to bless America. (Applause.)

Source: The White House. "President Bush Announces Major Combat Operations in Iraq Have Ended." Available at: http://georgewbush-whitehouse.archives.gov/news/releases/2003/05/20030501-15.html (accessed June 11, 2015).

AFTERMATH

The images associated with this speech became some of the most iconic for the entirety of the Bush administration. The words of the speech are nearly forgotten which is interesting as they lay out elements of what might be called the Bush Doctrine as clearly as any speech President Bush gave. In this speech the president reaffirmed his belief in the connections between Iraq, al-Qaeda, and weapons of mass destructions. Efforts would prove with the release of the Iraq Survey Group study that no active programs existed. As early as October 3, 2003, with the release of the interim report it seemed that despite evidence of activities relating to weapons of mass destruction, no actual active weapons programs were then identified. The study group head, David Kay, resigned January 23, 2004, stating that he did not believe weapons programs existed. The links between Iraq and al-Qaeda were tenuous at best from the beginning. Abu Musab al-Zarqawi was in northern Iraq at the time of the invasion, but he was there because he had fled from Afghanistan following the U.S. invasion of that country in 2001–2002. Zarqawi grew a violent organization that made claims of allegiance to al-Qaeda, but this took place mostly after the U.S.-led invasion.

As things got worse with respect to U.S. casualties in Iraq and the 2004 election approached the images of this speech, the banner, and the president walking across the flight deck of the USS *Abraham Lincoln* in a flight suit were broadcast and rebroadcast as a form of satire or sarcasm to communicate that the president did not understand Iraq and what was happening there.

ASK YOURSELF

1. Was Iraq an ally of al-Qaeda? From where did this idea come? As stated above the links were mostly based off the location of Zarqawi in Iraq in 2002 and not material support from the Iraqi regime to al-Qaeda members or al-Qaeda operations. Why then did this seem like a logical connection? Remember the way senior leaders in Washington, D.C., imagined threats to the United States. They thought mostly in terms of states rather than nonstate actors.

2. This is not the first time that President Bush indicated that this war was different from previous wars. He had previously said that there would not be armistice signings nor would there be surrenders or ticker-tape parades. If all of this is true, what does victory against a nonstate opponent look like?

3. Based on the words in this speech and the words in the State of the Union address in Chapter 3, did the president adequately prepare the American people for the kind of war this turned out to be?

TOPICS TO CONSIDER

1. Over the course of the twentieth century the nature of victory in war evolved. In World War II, President Roosevelt indicated that the United States was seeking unconditional surrender from Nazi Germany. This statement was blamed during and after the war for hardening the resolve of the German people who believed, as a result, that they had no alternative but to fight for their lives. In the Korean War the final objectives of the war were uncertain as they repeatedly changed from restoring the status quo to uniting the Korean Peninsula to defeating the Communist Chinese to finally restoring something like the 38th Parallel. The Vietnam War presented an even more complex set of victory criteria; ultimately the final output was peace with honor. What does that actually mean? How does one define victory

in war? Has the nature of conflict changed as warfare has evolved from the near total commitment to war demonstrated in World War II to something significantly more limited in every conflict since?

2. In 1935 a German filmmaker named Leni Riefenstahl made one of the most critically acclaimed propaganda films ever—*Triumph of the Will* about the 1934 Nazi Party Congress. In the early 1940s, Frank Capra made a series of propaganda films for the U.S. government to show to military members and then later to the public at large communicating the reasons for opposing Nazi Germany and Imperial Japan and outlining why Americans should support the war effort. Both Capra and Riefenstahl (more so Riefenstahl) used images masterfully to communicate the motivations for service and sacrifice as well as the costs of less significant efforts. Images are powerful. It is certain that President Bush and his communications team felt that the image of the president landing on an aircraft carrier as a fellow combat pilot would generate some of the positive war images they desired. How do images shape the character of a war in the hearts and minds of citizens, the combatant nations, or the opposing ideologies?

Further Reading

Bolger, Daniel P. *Why We Lost: A General's Inside Account of the Iraq and Afghanistan Wars.* Boston: Houghton Mifflin Harcourt, 2014.

Gordon, Michael R. and Bernard Trainor. *Cobra II: The Inside Story of the Invasion and Occupation of Iraq.* New York: Pantheon Books, 2006.

Shadid, Anthony. *Night Draws Near: Iraq's People in the Shadow of America's War.* New York: Henry Holt and Company, 2005.

Woodward, Bob. *Plan of Attack.* New York: Simon & Schuster, 2004.

Zogby, James Zogby. *Arab Voices: What They Are Saying to Us, and Why It Matters.* New York: Palgrave Macmillan, 2012.

Films and Television

Frontline: Bush's War. Director: Michael Kirk. PBS, 2008.

THE OCCUPATION
(2003–2005)

10. Disbanding the Army: Coalition Provisional Authority Number 2, May 23, 2003

INTRODUCTION

Jay Garner was designated to be the director of the Office for Reconstruction and Humanitarian Assistance (OHRA) for Iraq in January 2003. This organization was intended to serve as a caretaker administration until a democratically elected Iraqi government could take over. This organization lasted less than a month; retired Lieutenant General Garner arrived in Baghdad on April 21, 2003, and he was replaced on May 11, 2003, by L. Paul Bremer. There are differing accounts regarding the reasons for this abrupt transition. Garner had experience with Iraq and Iraqis as the former manager of Operation Provide Comfort in northern Iraq. L. Paul Bremer had no prior experience in Iraq or the Middle East. He served as a U.S. ambassador to the Netherlands at the culmination of a full career in Foreign Service. After retiring he worked in a variety of government-consulting organizations and positions. One of the arguments offered is that Garner was not moving quickly enough to remove Ba'ath Party members from positions of authority.

When Bremer arrived in country he was the U.S. Presidential Envoy and Administrator in Iraq and the Chief Executive for the coalition provisional authority (CPA). In this position he worked directly for the U.S. Department of Defense. The CPA deputy administrator was Jeremy Greenstock, an experienced British career diplomat who was sent to Iraq as the U.K.'s Special Representative. Unlike Bremer, he had previously worked in Dubai and Saudi Arabia so he had Middle Eastern experience.

The CPA was headquartered in Saddam Hussein's palaces in and around Baghdad.

If the criticism of Garner was that he did not move fast enough for de-Ba'athification, then the CPA under Bremer did the opposite. CPA Order 1 was the order to remove all members of the Ba'ath Party from the public sector and ban them from future public sector employment. That order was issued on May 16, 2003, just five days after Bremer's arrival in Iraq.

KEEP IN MIND AS YOU READ

1. Most public sector employees in Iraq were members of the Ba'ath Party. Under Saddam Hussein membership in the party was a near requirement for public jobs and a definite requirement for advancement to management positions within

government positions. It is important to keep in mind the fact that these were the people who understood how to manage the utilities, to provide the water and electricity, to remove the trash, and all other aspects necessary to healthy urban life. They, or a significant majority of such people, were now gone. How might removing this expertise affect urban life?

2. In Iraq the military and government service was used as a form of welfare. Military and government work was not about efficiency, it was about giving people a job to do, a paycheck to earn, and a sense of honor and respect in society. Most of the senior positions in the Ba'ath party, the government, and the military were held by Sunnis. Even discounting CPA Order 1 and CPA Order 2 below the idea of western efficiency in manufacturing would still have put thousands of people out of work. Many people in Iraq who had jobs simply came to work and received a paycheck. They did not have a necessary part in the manufacturing of a product. By western capitalist standards these are unnecessary jobs, but by the standards of welfare employment in Iraq it kept people off the streets, fed, and in their homes—not protesting against the government.

3. The coalition and especially the CPA presented a challenge to the Iraqi young man. First and foremost, they humiliated the Iraqi military. While some who opposed Saddam Hussein saw the military as an extension of his regime, many in Iraq viewed the military as an honorable profession and valued their service in the Iraqi army of the past. When the coalition ended all military service and sent the army home millions of families were affected. Worse still, pensions were cancelled, and those people of colonel rank and higher were cut off and dishonored. The army contained the people who were trained to use weapons and explosives and knew how to obey orders. They all were now unemployed and angry.

Document 10: Excerpt from Coalition Provisional Order Number 2, May 23, 2003

Coalition Provisional Authority Order Number 2: Dissolution of Entities

Pursuant to my authority as Administrator of the Coalition Provisional Authority (CPA), relevant U.N. Security Council resolutions, including Resolution 1483 (2003), and the laws and usages of war, Reconfirming all of the provisions of General Franks' Freedom Message to the Iraqi People of April 16, 2003, Recognizing that the prior Iraqi regime used certain government entities to oppress the Iraqi people and as instruments of torture, repression and corruption, Reaffirming the Instructions to the Citizens of Iraq regarding Ministry of Youth and Sport of May 8, 2003, I hereby promulgate the following:

Section 1

Dissolved Entities

The entities (the "Dissolved Entities") listed in the attached Annex are hereby dissolved. Additional entities may be added to this list in the future.

Section 2

Assets and Financial Obligations

1) All assets, including records and data, in whatever from maintained and wherever located, of the Dissolved Entities shall be held by the Administrator of the CPA ("the Administrator") on behalf of and for the benefit of the Iraqi people and shall be used to assist the Iraqi people and to support the recovery of Iraq.

2) All financial obligations of the Dissolved Entities are suspended. The Administrator of the CPA will establish procedures whereby persons claiming to be the beneficiaries of such obligations may apply for payment.

3) Persons in possession of assets of the Dissolved Entities shall preserve those assets, promptly inform local Coalition authorities, and immediately turn them over, as directed by those authorities. Continued possession, transfer, sale, use, conversion, or concealment of such assets following the date of this Order is prohibited and may be punished.

Section 3

Employees and Service Members

1) Any military or other rank, title, or status granted to a former employee or functionary of a Dissolved Entity by the former Regime is hereby cancelled.

2) All conscripts are released from their service obligations. Conscriptions is suspended indefinitely, subject to decisions by future Iraq governments concerning whether a free Iraq should have conscription.

3) Any person employed by a Dissolved Entity in any form or capacity, is dismissed effective as of April 16, 2003. Any person employed by a Dissolved Entity, in any from or capacity remains accountable for acts committed during such employment.

4) A termination payment in an amount to be determined by the Administrator will be paid to employees so dismissed, except those who are Senior Party Members as defined in the Administrator's May 16, 2003 Order of the Coalition Provisional Authority De-Ba'athification of Iraqi Society ("Senior Party Members") (See Section 3.6).

5) Pensions being paid by, or on account of service to, a Dissolved Entity before April 16, 2003 will continue to be paid, including to war widows and disabled veterans, provided that no pension payments will be made to any person who is a Senior Party Member (see Section 3.6) and that the power is reserved to the Administrator and to future Iraqi governments to revoke or reduce pensions as a penalty for past or future illegal conduct or to modify pension arrangements to eliminate improper privileges granted by the Ba'athist regime or for similar reasons.

6) Notwithstanding any provision of this Order, or any other Order, law, or regulation, and consistent with the Administrator's May 16, 2003 Order of the Coalition Provisional Authority De-Ba'athification of Iraqi Society, no payment, including a termination or pension payment, will be made to any person who is or was a Senior Party Member. Any person holding the rank under the former regime of Colonel or above, or its equivalent, will be deemed a Senior Party Member, provided that such persons may seek, under procedures to be prescribed, to establish to the satisfaction of the Administrator, that they were not a Senior Party Member.

Source: Coalition Provisional Authority. "Order Number 2: Dissolution of Entities." May 23, 2003. Available at: http://www.iraqcoalition.org/regulations/20030823_CPAORD_2_Dissolution_of_Entities_with_Annex_A.pdf (accessed June 12, 2015).

AFTERMATH

This order along with CPA Order 1 have been given the distinction of doing more than anything else to generate the opposition to the occupation and to fuel the sectarian violence to come. If there was going to be a spark for revolution and opposition then this order provided the fuel that lit the spark turning it into an inferno.

On July 13, 2003, the Iraqi governing council was formed and it continued its service until June 1, 2004, when the Iraqi interim government took over. That government was in turn replaced by the Iraqi transitional government in May 2005. It was in 2006 that the first permanent Iraqi government finally took office and the rotation of authorities ended. One of the primary responsibilities of this governing council was the drafting of a temporary constitution or transitional administrative law. This law delineated that the council would cease to function on June 30, 2004, when Iraq would become fully sovereign.

ASK YOURSELF

1. There were two different ways of handling de-Ba'athification. One was supported by Jay Garner and was much slower and less inclusive of all senior party officials and the other was executed by Paul Bremer and was more rapid and sweeping. In the discussion and blame that followed during the war and after many people pointed to CPA Order 2 and CPA Order 1 as the causes of much of the violence. In making decisions about very difficult issues like who rules and who is removed from power, who is responsible for the sins of the past, and who is forgiven? Is it possible that there is neither right nor wrong? If so, then what is the basis for judgment? Can a person judge based off pragmatic reasoning rather than moral reasoning, meaning what is best and expedient rather than what is good or evil?

2. The phrase "second and third order effects" is often thrown around as if human beings think about such things on a regular basis. What is a second-order effect? The first order effect of removing Ba'ath Party officials from their positions was to communicate to Iraqis that the era of Saddam Hussein was over. Is that what it communicated? The second-order effect was that people were out of work—professional people who were important to the daily functioning of the government and the country. How does an occupying authority make things happen without those people around to run the programs? Unemployed and humiliated soldiers provided a ready and trained force to violently oppose the occupation. Was that a second- or third-order effect? Societies are complex and making decisions that reshape entire societies has effects that cannot be foreseen. This is what some refer to as the law of unintended consequences.

TOPICS TO CONSIDER

1. Is it possible to work with your enemy? There is an entire field of conflict resolution studies that deals with reconciliation and the processes by which reconciliation can occur. One of the most important elements is to break the cycle of vengeance. At some point the opponent needs to be forgiven for whatever they have done and allowed to rejoin society.

2. Germany faced serious de-Nazification issues following World War II. It was a political issue in Germany and in the occupying and victorious powers. The Nazi Party ruled Germany for about twelve years. The Ba'ath Party ruled Iraq for about 35 years. That means that it impacted three or four generations of Iraqis whereas the Nazi Party only directly influenced two generations of Germans in terms of workers. This is a powerful issue when dealing with peace concerns. In resolving the conflict how much do you have to redesign the society? Look at the reconciliation and peace processes of previous wars to see how effectively integration of societies occurred. In some cases this was an extremely violent process as opponents were killed.

Further Reading

Bolger, Daniel P. *Why We Lost: A General's Inside Account of the Iraq and Afghanistan Wars.* Boston: Houghton Mifflin Harcourt, 2014.

Bremer, L. Paul. *My Year in Iraq: The Struggle to Build a Future of Hope.* New York: Threshold Editions, 2006.

Gordon, Michael R. and Bernard Trainor. *Cobra II: The Inside Story of the Invasion and Occupation of Iraq.* New York: Pantheon Books, 2006.

Woodward, Bob. *Plan of Attack.* New York: Simon & Schuster, 2004.

Wright, Donald P. and Timothy R. Reese. *On Point II: Transition to the New Campaign: The United States Army in Operation Iraqi Freedom May 2003–January 2005.* Fort Leavenworth, KS: U.S. Army Command and General Staff College Press, 2008.

Websites

Coalition Provisional Authority. "Coalition Provisional Authority Order Number 1: De-Ba'athification of Iraqi Society." May 16, 2003. http://nsarchive.gwu.edu/NSAEBB/NSAEBB418/docs/9a%20-%20Coalition%20Provisional%20Authority%20Order%20No%201%20-%205–16–03.pdf (accessed June 12, 2015).

Palast, Greg. "Jay Garner." *BBC Newsnight.* http://news.bbc.co.uk/2/hi/programmes/newsnight/3552737.stm (accessed June 12, 2015).

Films and Television

American War Generals. Executive producers: Peter Bergen, Tresha Mabile, Jonathan Towers. National Geographic Channel, 2014.

Frontline: Bush's War. Director: Michael Kirk. PBS, 2008.

11. Iraqi Advisor to U.S. Military Personnel: Nasier Abadi

INTRODUCTION

At the time of the interview Lieutenant General Nasier Abadi was the deputy chief of staff of the Iraqi Joint Forces, the second ranking officer in the Iraqi military. When coalition forces arrived in Iraq he was retired. He was subsequently recalled to active duty where he provided advice to coalition forces and served in senior positions as indicated. He was initially recalled

> . . . to active military service in 2003 as the senior Iraqi advisor to the Coalition Military Assistance Training Team (CMATT) during the formation and development of the new Iraqi Joint Forces. He is a decorated Iraqi Air Force veteran with over 4,200 flying hours operating more than 50 different types of aircraft. As the deputy chief of Staff of the Iraqi Joint Forces, Lieutenant General Abadi oversaw the operation of the headquarters joint staff in order to ensure that current and future military operations are well planned and supported. He also provides advice to the chief of staff of the joint forces and the civilian government of Iraq in developing and implementing the national security and military strategies.

The comments below fit within the context of the previous chapter in that this is an Iraqi reaction to the disbanding the Iraqi military. The role of security forces in Arab culture is important. They are seen as honorable—the warrior is an iconic image in Arab history and society and it is therefore valued across sects and ethnicities. It was Coalition Provisional Authority (CPA) Order 2 that disbanded the Iraqi Army and security forces and wiped out the pensions for Iraqi soldiers and their families. That order was issued on May 23, 2003.

KEEP IN MIND AS YOU READ

1. No two cultures see the world the same way. This chapter is an Iraqi perspective of a decision by the CPA. It is important to note that many American officials in Iraq and in Washington did agree with CPA Order 2 though there were prominent

voices in opposition. Very few Iraqis felt this was a good idea as communicated below. Most of the reasons given below are practical. It is important to also think about the social impact of removing family leaders from the respected positions of army officers or soldiers.

2. The different perspectives matter. This is not simply about opinion, but about how people receive and process information—how they filter what they see and hear and therefore how they determine meanings from events. The Iraqi's believed that the United States and other coalition countries wanted Iraq to be weak and damaged. Removing the army from service accomplished that end. The CPA leadership thought it was removing a symbol of Saddam Hussein's power and dictatorial rule. Both perspectives had value and were correct, but neither perspective addressed the value or accuracy of the counterpart position.

Document 11: Excerpt from Interview with Nasier Abadi, August 2005

Question: Did you agree with the decision to disband the military forces?

Answer: There are numerous instances in history in which a victorious force thought it had its enemy defeated and ignored the problems of controlling cities and populations. Certainly, that was the case in a number of ancient examples in this very region. The coalition did not take into account the foreseeable consequences of having inadequate forces to secure cities and populations. Moreover, the coalition had no provisions in case its optimistic projections of a peaceful aftermath of major combat operations failed. There was no contingency plan for something going wrong such as an outbreak of public disorder, looting, and crime and revenge killings. Neither was the coalition prepared for the virtual disappearance of the police and in effect all public order forces. The coalition had no plan for the total lack of public order forces in the wake of the success of the coalition forces and the disappearance of the Iraqi Army. The vacuum that resulted was enormous.

The coalition also had no plan in place that I could see to control the flow of funds from Iraq to the outside, from legal and illegal operations. Therefore, much of the flow of funds could be made available to terrorists, former Baath Party officials, insurgents, and ordinary criminals. These funds, as we now know, fueled the violence that is still dominating Iraqi life.

I don't think the coalition was right in dissolving the Army. Because, from my perspective the negatives really outweighed the positives and what we see now is proof that the coalition wasn't forward thinking in making the decision. The vacuum and insecurity that caused all this to take place could have been reduced if we had the Army. By reducing the Army, by removing the age groups that were not required in the Armed Forces, we would have had about what we are thinking of developing, 150,000 to 200,0010 soldiers which are required to fight the insurgency.

Had there been no insurgency, we could have reduced the numbers even further. Had we controlled security and started the infrastructure and development of the water, electricity and oil, we would have had new companies to invest in Iraq. Things would have been much, much different. We could have advanced by leaps and bounds and not gone back as the case is now where we are fighting for survival and to safeguard the pipeline and the electricity. There is only one hour of electricity in Baghdad for every six hours. With the heat of the summer in July and August, with temperatures over fifty degrees Celsius, people don't have cold air or cold water, since even the water was hit by the terrorists.

Source: Nasier Abadi. Interview by David J. Conboy, August 2005. "An Interview with Lieutenant General Nasier Abadi, Deputy Chief of Staff, Iraqi Joint Forces." US Army War College, Carlisle Barracks, Pennsylvania. Interview Transcript. Courtesy of the Operational Leadership Experiences Digital Collection, Combat Studies Institute, Fort Leavenworth, KS.

AFTERMATH

As stated in the previous chapter and quite well in the statement above—no security force empowered the conduct of opposition groups. At the time of writing this book the violence in Iraq was primarily sectarian in nature and this gives the impression that this was typically true. The first prominent violence in Iraq was mostly criminal. Kidnappings for ransom were common in the early years of the occupation. The civil war/sectarian strife grew over time. It may be possible to imagine a less violent Iraq if there had been a greater security presence from the beginning.

ASK YOURSELF

1. Why did the coalition forces miss the difference in narratives? When L. Paul Bremer signed the first two orders that denied public sector employment to former senior Ba'ath Party officials and disbanded the Iraqi Army what prevented him from seeing beyond the coalition perspective of ridding Iraq of Saddam's influence to the Iraqi perspective of dishonoring those who served and opening the way for criminal activity?

TOPICS TO CONSIDER

1. Cultural and narrative filters shape how we see and perceive all information. If this is true then is it possible for a person from one culture to actually see the world through a different cultural filter?

Further Reading

Al-Ali, Zaid. *The Struggle for Iraq's Future: How Corruption, Incompetence and Sectarianism Have Undermined Democracy.* New Haven, CT: Yale University Press, 2014.

Bremer, L. Paul. *My Year in Iraq: The Struggle to Build a Future of Hope.* New York: Threshold Editions, 2006.

Gordon, Michael R. and Bernard Trainor. *Cobra II: The Inside Story of the Invasion and Occupation of Iraq.* New York: Pantheon Books, 2006.

Woodward, Bob. *Plan of Attack*. New York: Simon & Schuster, 2004.

Wright, Donald P. and Timothy R. Reese. *On Point II: Transition to the New Campaign: The United States Army in Operation Iraqi Freedom May 2003–January 2005*. Fort Leavenworth, KS: U.S. Army Command and General Staff College Press, 2008.

Websites

Coalition Provisional Authority. "Coalition Provisional Authority Order Number 1: De-Ba'athification of Iraqi Society." May 16, 2003. http://nsarchive.gwu.edu/NSAEBB/NSAEBB418/docs/9a%20-%20Coalition%20Provisional%20Authority%20Order%20No%201%20-%205-16-03.pdf (accessed June 12, 2015).

Coalition Provisional Authority. "Order Number 2: Dissolution of Entities." May 23, 2003. http://www.iraqcoalition.org/regulations/20030823_CPAORD_2_Dissolution_of_Entities_with_Annex_A.pdf (accessed June 12, 2015).

Films and Television

American War Generals. Executive producers: Peter Bergen, Tresha Mabile, Jonathan Towers. National Geographic Channel, 2014.

Frontline: Bush's War. Director: Michael Kirk. PBS, 2008.

12. A Journalist's Perspective on Combat: Ann Barnard

INTRODUCTION

Ann Barnard served as co-Iraq bureau chief for the *Boston Globe* in 2003–2004. She was in and out of Iraq several times during the course of the war starting from April to May 2003 and then full time from December 2003 through the summer of 2004. She returned to Iraq again in late 2004 and early 2005. Much of her time in Iraq was spent in Fallujah before, during, and after Operation Al Fajr: the November 2004 combined-joint assault to retake the city of Fallujah from insurgent control.

During the November 2004 campaign Barnard was embedded with Alpha Company, 2-63 Armor, part of the Army's Task Force 2-2 Infantry, commanded by Captain Paul Fowler. She rode around with soldiers and Bradley crewmembers as they actively engaged insurgents in high-intensity urban fighting. Her goal was to live as soldiers lived in order to better understand and represent the war from their perspective.

KEEP IN MIND AS YOU READ

1. In the previous chapter the rules of engagement (ROE) were introduced. These give rather broad guidelines for how, in what circumstances, and against whom it was appropriate to engage the enemy. Review that chapter prior to reading the excerpts below.

2. Some say that the reason why soldiers fight is for the "buddy in their foxhole." This is a social activity and the associations with peers form some of the tightest bonds similar to being on a championship sports team that sacrificed a great deal to earn the championship. Only in this case the team members are risking their lives.

Document 12: Excerpt from Interview with Anne Barnard, *Boston Globe* Reporter—Rules of Engagement

On Rules of Engagement and Their Interpretation Down the Line

During an ongoing skirmish at the hospital, our squad ended up in a scrap heap of rusted cars. They were really excited to be out of the Bradley and walking around these spare parts workshops. Then a sniper started shooting and Lieutenant Gregory said, "Everybody back in the Bradley!" and the soldiers were like, "Well, there's nothing for us to do. We get one shot and we get back in the Bradley." They were really young guys and didn't want to get back in the Bradley. Then I sat in on the meeting with Captain Fowler and his platoon commanders. They took out maps and spread them out in an auto repair shop. There was a whole row of auto repair shops on the southern side of Route Fran. They were covered with graffiti, some of it supporting different insurgent groups or just criticizing the Americans or other political slogans. Captain Fowler was spread out in one of those areas talking about the next set of objectives. I remember the first set of objectives were all named Coyote or Wolf or something like that. The second set, in the southern half of the city, they were all named after different beers. I don't know if the Fallujans would appreciate that so much, but the troops did. So there was Objective Miller, Objective Lite and Objective Bud. The idea was that in this southern industrial section of the city they thought there were car bomb factories, lots of other arms storage and maybe places where people were going to be hiding out—maybe tunnels. There were all these storage areas or shop fronts that had corrugated metal gates that were pulled down to close them. Captain Fowler said he didn't want the guys going into those places. He wanted them to shoot out the gate first, and the same thing about houses. No boots on the ground until you put some rounds through the door. Earlier, in briefings before the battle, here's what Fowler and First Sergeant Richard told their platoon leaders: "The first time you get shot at from a building, it's rubble," Fowler said. "No questions asked." Richard said insurgents might be wearing the same uniforms as the troops. An Iraqi in a uniform but no flak vest was likely hostile. "Be safe," he said. "Don't beat yourself up if you shoot one." Suspected enemy buildings were to be "cleared by fire" before troops entered. "No boots on the ground unless you're looking for body parts," Fowler said. Nonetheless, he said, "The object is to give Fallujah back to the Fallujans. Not to give them back a pile of rubble."

Question: Were those rules of engagement coming down from Lieutenant Colonel Newell (commander Task Force 2-2 Infantry)?

Answer: I believe so but I don't know for sure. I know I repeatedly heard everybody from Major General Richard Natonski (USMC commander of 1st Marine Division and ground force commander for Operation al-Fajr) on down saying we have to be careful about causing any more damage than we need to. We can't give them back a destroyed city. But the closer down you got to the frontline enlisted men, the guy who's responsible for his men . . . In other words, the message was always basically the same: "We have to take over the city and we've got to do it fast and efficiently, but we also have to do it with as little destruction as possible because we have to have something left to hand back to the Fallujans. At the same time, we need to protect our troops and your first duty is to not let your buddy get killed unnecessarily." Okay, that was always the message, but the emphasis switched as you went further down the chain of command to, "Don't feel bad if you kill some guy, because you've got to take precautions to protect your fellow soldiers." I felt that Fowler, especially afterwards, was introspective. He would say things like, "Wow, we're tank guys and look what we had to do to the city—and what's going to happen next?" So it's not that he was ignoring what had been said higher up; the problem is, how do you . . .?

Question: There's just an inherent disconnect between those two stated goals, so to speak.
Answer: Absolutely.

Observations of Soldiers' Introduction to Combat

So anyway, they laid out their plans and we went back into the Bradleys, and this was the toughest combat that my specific platoon saw. I can tell you later exactly what day this was. Either November 10 or November 11. We're going south and there were a lot of narrow alleys where the Bradley couldn't get through and they had to ram into a wall and knock it down. At different times they would take fire and try to pursue who was shooting at them. But in the most dramatic case, the Bradley was going through a very narrow space between buildings and they saw some guys outside taking shots at them. There was always a fear that guys would come up and actually stick an explosive to the vehicle. That didn't happen in this case but the Iraqi guys they had seen had gone into a building. This was an area of auto body shops.

At one point they were ramming the Bradley into a wall to get through a narrow passage. They saw a man fire an RPG at the Bradley from just a few yards away. The driver, Specialist Doyle Grubaugh, was shouting, "He's in the wall to our left!" Another squad threw a grenade. Then Harkleroad's squad, from our Bradley, dismounted. I was still in the Bradley when I saw Sergeant Harkleroad lead the squad into this concrete building and I immediately heard a volley of shots. Before I could even do anything I saw the other guys dragging Harkleroad back out by his shoulders, and he was completely limp. I didn't know how badly he was hurt. They dragged him up onto the ramp of the Bradley and then I could see that he just had a leg wound. Their demeanor had completely changed. They had been so bored and so antsy, and all of a sudden they were fired up. After he was medically evacuated out, these guys were red, sweaty and breathing hard and they explained that they had gone into the building and immediately a guy had popped up from one of those wells that you use if you're fixing a car. There's a well in the floor that you can get into. A guy popped up and shot Harkleroad just like that, and they immediately fired on the guy and killed him. There were three other guys in there with him, and they thought later those guys might have been already killed by the grenade, but they shot them all. So it was really an intense moment to see these four guys, who were probably all under 22, discussing in sort of breathless terms how they had gotten shot at and killed at least one of these guys. I think it was the first time they had killed anybody up close like that, if at all. It might have been the first time they had killed anybody that they knew of for sure, but certainly it was the first time they saw a guy that close. Specialist Todd Taylor was yelling to Harkleroad, "You're not going down like this! We killed those f—ers! They're dead! We knocked 'em out!" The other guys were PFC

Jeremy DeGraw, Specialist Michael Roberge and Andrew Hodge. They asked each other stuff like, "Have you ever seen close combat before? Can you believe that guy survived the grenade?" And they repeated details, half to themselves: "I emptied a magazine into him." Then it kind of went on like that for hours. By the end of the night, the four squad guys left in my Bradley killed another four guys in a trench at close range. It was a very intense day and night of moving around the southern part of the city.

Source: Barnard, Anne. Interview by John McCool, September 14, 2007. Interview Transcript. Courtesy of the Operational Leadership Experiences Digital Collection, Combat Studies Institute, Fort Leavenworth, KS. Available at: http://cgsc.contentdm.oclc.org/cdm/singleitem/collection/p4013coll13/id/749/rec/1 (accessed June 15, 2015).

AFTERMATH

The events described above were part of Operation Al-Fajr which is the Second Battle of Fallujah. The battle is a topic for more discussion in Chapters 16 and 17. Anne Barnard went on to be a reporter for the *New York Times* where she was, at the time of writing, the Beirut bureau chief.

ASK YOURSELF

1. Did the soldiers follow the ROE? Did the leaders give guidance that would lead to adherence or to disregard of the rules? Were they right to take the position they did? It may be easy to criticize the realities of fighting when one is not personally at risk of injury or death through hesitation.
2. Is it possible to return a functioning city after full-blown combat? How can that be done better? The cost of war in material damage is significant. This is especially true if soldiers are trying to protect their lives in the process. It's much easier to risk the armored vehicle by driving through a wall than to risk your own life by going through a door.
3. What were the Iraqis thinking about all of this? They were the ones being attacked. How would you view the coalition if this was happening in your city or to members of your family?

TOPICS TO CONSIDER

1. Following My Lai and other infamous atrocities in history there is typically a discussion of who was at fault—those who executed the orders or those who gave the orders. In this simple vignette there is room to consider the longer term challenges of the orders given. No one was prosecuted for what was done in Fallujah. Does that make it right?
2. In 1994 and again in 1996 the Russian military went into the city of Grozny. In 1994, it was a disaster for the Russians. In 1996, they flattened the city and inflicted mass suffering on tens of thousands of people. In the first battle they clearly lost. In the second battle, what was the result?

MY LAI MASSACRE

On March 16, 1968, soldiers from C Company, 1st Battalion, 20th Infantry Regiments of the 23rd (Americal) Division committed the biggest atrocity of the Vietnam War when they assaulted, raped, and murdered hundreds of villagers from two hamlets named My Lai and My Khe from the Son My village.

The events associated with the massacre and the subsequent attempt to cover up those events made this a media sensation at a time when the Vietnam War was beginning to lose popular support in America. Eventually, 26 soldiers were charged with crimes, but only Lieutenant William Calley Jr., a platoon leader during the actions that day, was convicted of a crime.

Further Reading

Danner, Mark. *Torture and Truth: America, Abu Ghraib, and the War on Terror*. New York: New York Review of Books, 2004.

Kyle, Chris and Scott McEwen. *American Sniper: The Autobiography of the Most Lethal Sniper in U.S. Military History*. New York: HarperCollins, 2013.

Shadid, Anthony. *Night Draws Near: Iraq's People in the Shadow of America's War*. New York: Henry Holt and Company, 2005.

West, Bing. *No True Glory: A Frontline Account of the Battle for Fallujah*. New York: Bantam Books, 2005.

Wright, Donald P. and Timothy R. Reese. *On Point II: Transition to the New Campaign: The United States Army in Operation Iraqi Freedom May 2003–January 2005*. Fort Leavenworth, KS: U.S. Army Command and General Staff College Press, 2008.

Website

Barnard, Anne. "Inside Fallujah's War: Empathy, destruction mark a week with US troops." *The Boston Globe*, November 28, 2004. http://www.boston.com/news/world/articles/2004/11/28/inside_fallujahs_war/?page=full (accessed August 12, 2015).

Films and Television

American Sniper. Director: Clint Eastwood. Warner Bros., 2014.

American War Generals. Executive producers: Peter Bergen, Tresha Mabile, Jonathan Towers. National Geographic Channel, 2014.

Frontline: Bush's War. Director: Michael Kirk. PBS, 2008.

Generation Kill. Director: Susanna White, Simon Cellan Jones. Blown Deadline Productions, 2008.

13. Abu Ghraib, a Guard's Perspective: Samuel J. Provance

INTRODUCTION

The images revealed in late 2003 of Iraqi detainees in various stages of undress and electrical wires attached to their appendages became sensational and opened a broad discussion on prisons and prisoner treatment by U.S. forces throughout the Middle East. The single most significant location brought to light was Abu Ghraib prison in Iraq. Abu Ghraib became nearly synonymous with the perceived excesses of the Bush administration in prosecuting what they characterized as the global war on terrorism. For many people in America and around the globe, Abu Ghraib and the images associated with it epitomized the U.S. occupation of Iraq.

The passage below was provided by Samuel J. Provance a soldier from the 302nd Military Intelligence Battalion. He was a system administrator at the prison and not a direct participant in the events. He was not the first soldier to bring forward concerns about the actions happening within the walls of the prison, but he was asked to testify before a U.S. Congressional subcommittee because of the retaliation that he received from his command as a discussion on whistleblower protection.

Abu Ghraib was one of the most infamous prisons under the Saddam Hussein regime. It was where unspeakable acts of torture were conducted by that regime. These included attaching live electric wires to body parts, including genitals; removing of toenails; poisoning; amputations, including burning off limbs. These physically destructive methods of torture were well documented and publicized to the world beyond Iraq and rumored and reported amongst citizens within Iraq. The initial liberation of the Abu Ghraib prison by coalition forces was heralded as a blow to inhumane treatment and a sign of better things to come. Shortly after being liberated, the prison was reused by the coalition as they were capturing more people than they had places to detain them.

KEEP IN MIND AS YOU READ

1. Earlier in this book the concept of a competition of narrative was discussed. The images and actions associated with Abu Ghraib and the reactions to those images

get at the heart of the competition of narrative. Readers should consider their reactions to the account described later and think about how that expresses their own perceived notions of the role of Americans and Iraqis in the war. Is this account expected or disturbing to preconceived ideas of U.S. behavior?

2. When an army occupies a country it is inevitable that some individuals will rise up in opposition to that occupation and in the process break the law. The challenge in such circumstances is to have a complete system of governance in place which goes beyond mere apprehension and incarceration. The system must include judges and a manner of progressing people through the full process of judicial hearing and review to incarceration and release. If that process is not fully developed, as was the case in Iraq in the early period of the occupation, then what is the role and purpose of detention? Interrogation has a very relevant purpose in an occupation in that it provides information on those opposing the government. In this process it is important to consider whether or not everyone who needs interrogation also needs detention.

3. With the collapse of the Iraqi government and the disbanding of the Iraqi army and police force there was a period of chaos and looting followed by sustained turmoil that increased into violent opposition and eventually blossomed into a full-blown insurgency. In fighting the chaos and the insurgency coalition forces rounded up hundreds and thousands of young and middle-aged men who needed to be placed somewhere while their value for intelligence purposes or the extent of their crimes was determined. This was the reality. Abu Ghraib was a logical, existing structure so it was utilized.

4. What training is necessary to conduct interrogations and evaluate detainees? What are the numbers that need to be trained and did that training exist when the soldiers deployed into theater?

Document 13: Excerpt from Prepared Statement by Samuel Provance, Abu Ghraib Prison Guard

(Note: The following statement was part of an online version of the report. Based on legal concerns, names of personnel are not provided. Original statement: This statement has been redacted at the request of the Department of Defense to eliminate the names of personnel whose identities have not yet been publicly disclosed.)

My name is Samuel Provance and I come from Greenville, SC. I enlisted in the United States Army in 1998 and sought a specialization in intelligence in 2002. I was drawn to the Army by the professional training and good life it promised, but also because it provided me an opportunity to serve my country.

The Army has stood for duty, honor and country. In wearing my country's service uniform and risking my life for my country's protection, it never occurred to me that I might be required to be a part of things that conflict with these values of duty, honor and country. But my experience in Iraq and later in Germany left me troubled by what has happened to the Army. I saw the traditional values of military service as I understood them compromised or undermined. I am still proud to be a soldier and to wear the uniform of the United States Army. But I am concerned about what the Army is becoming.

While serving with my unit in Iraq, I became aware of changes in the procedures in which I and my fellow soldiers were trained. These changes involved using procedures which we previously did not use, and had been trained not to use, and in involving military police (MP) personnel in "preparation" of detainees who were to be interrogated. Some detainees were treated in an incorrect and immoral fashion as a result of these changes. After what had happened at Abu Ghraib became a matter of public knowledge, and there was a demand for action, young soldiers were scapegoated while superiors misrepresented what had happened and tried to misdirect attention away from what was really going on. I considered all of this conduct to be dishonorable and inconsistent with the traditions of the Army. I was ashamed and embarrassed to be associated with it.

When I made clear to my superiors that I was troubled about what had happened, I was told that the honor of my unit and the Army depended on either withholding the truth or outright lies. I cannot accept this. Honor cannot be achieved by lies and scapegoating. Honor depends on the truth. It demands that we live consistently with the values we hold out to the world. My belief in holding to the truth led directly to conflict with my superiors, and ultimately to my demotion.

I welcome the opportunity to speak to you today and to answer your questions. . . .

Duty Position from Abu Ghraib to Present

In September 2003, I was sent to the Abu Ghraib prison to replace SGT Andreas Zivic, who had been wounded in a mortar attack. I replaced him as the NCO in charge (NCOIC) of System Administration at the prison. We first had to recover the site that had been mortared. They had been working out of an unprotected and fully exposed tent, which was very unsafe as the site had been receiving mortar fire almost every day. A request had been made to move the operation into the hardened building right next to it prior to the fatal attack. The request was denied by COL Pappas—there was a great deal of sensitivity about what was going on in that hardsite and access to it was severely limited. As a result of conducting the operations in an unsheltered position, two soldiers were killed and numerous wounded, some disabled for life and chaptered from the Army. I later came to understand that this was one of the direct costs to my unit of the abuses that occurred at Abu Ghraib. I also served as the local Security Officer until relieved by CWO ????? in January 2004.

At first there were only a couple companies of military intelligence (MI) soldiers (from the 325th Reserve and 519th Airborne) and a handful of computers, but then a group came from Guantanamo Bay (GTMO), Cuba to "make the place better run" (as we were told). There was a conflict between the GTMO soldiers and those who were already at Abu Ghraib, having to do with the way interrogations were being conducted and reported (I do not remember the specifics of the conflict, but in general our people wanted to use the techniques we were trained to use at Ft. Huachuca, and the GTMO people had very different ideas). After this period, the number of civilian contractors who reported in increased significantly. These contractors were principally from CACI and Titan Corporations, and were functioning as interrogators, translators and linguists. The interrogators were principally Americans, but the others were frequently Arab-speaking Middle Easterners, but not Iraqis. In the course of my duties, I would see some of these civilians regularly, others maybe only once or twice. Soldiers from other MI units then came, as well as even more civilians.

I worked the night shift (from 8 p.m. until 8 a.m. the following morning). My nightly routine consisted of making accounts for new users, troubleshooting computer problems, backing up the secret shared drive, maintaining the secret and top secret network connectivity, and manning the top-secret part of the Joint Interrogation and Debriefing Center (JIDC). SPC ????? worked with me and handled the day shift.

Mistreatment of Prisoners at Abu Ghraib

I had many discussions with different interrogators and analysts. Being "the computer guy," my job required me to interact with most of the MI team, and I often had the time to speak with them personally. Over time I began to get a pretty clear picture of what was being done to the detainees at Abu Ghraib. What I learned surprised and disturbed me.

The first alarming incident I heard about was that some of the interrogators had gotten drunk, and then under the guise of interrogation, molested an underaged Iraqi girl detainee. It could have been worse, but MP on duty stopped them. Friends of some of the interrogators involved were concerned that COL Pappas would deal severely with the incident. They asked me to recite a falsehood about COL Pappas, in the hope that he would be disqualified from serving as convening authority. I refused to do this.

I befriended SPC ?????, an analyst who was being retrained to be an interrogator (many others were being retrained in this same way). ????? told me detainees were routinely stripped naked in the cells and sometimes during interrogations (she said one man so shamed had actually made a loin cloth out of an MRE (Meal Ready to Eat) bag, so they no longer allowed him to have the MRE bag with his food). She said they also starved them or allowed them to only have certain items of food at a time. She said they played loud music—"Barney I Love You" being the interrogators' favorite. I was shocked by this and told her I couldn't understand how she could cope with the nudity. Wasn't it embarrassing or at least uncomfortable? ????? said that this was one of the new practices and they got used to it. Moreover, she got a thrill out of being a woman interrogating them, knowing how much it angered and offended them to have a woman in a position of authority and control over men. She said they used dogs to terrify and torment the prisoners. She also said they deprived them of sleep for long periods of time. This was all part of a carefully planned regimen that had been introduced after the arrival of the teams from GTMO.

????? once invited me to accompany her to the hardsite, where I observed the MP's were constantly yelling at the detainees. One detainee was being made to repeat his number over and over again.

I also befriended SPC ?????, who was with the first MP units that set up Abu Ghraib after the war. ????? told me that she had witnessed abuses of Iraqi people and even seen some of them murdered. She said she documented these things in diaries that she sent home to her family in case someone killed her before she made it home to do something about it. She particularly mentioned fearing her chain of command. Her view, that anyone disclosing these incidents of abuse would face swift and severe retaliation, was widespread among soldiers at Abu Ghraib.

SPC ?????, an analyst I had known from training at Ft. Huachuca, told me that he had seen some detainees handcuffed together in contorted positions as punishment for raping a boy. He also said the interrogators were using the detainee's faith in Islam as a tool to break them and get them to talk. He said he was bothered by these practices—felt they were wrong—but wasn't in a position to do anything about it.

While eating at the dining facility at Camp Victory, SPC ?????, an MI guard, told an entire table full of laughing soldiers about how the MP's had shown him and other soldiers how to knock someone out and to strike a detainee without leaving marks. They had practiced these techniques on unsuspecting detainees, after watching, he had participated himself.

In discussions I had with some of my colleagues, brutal treatment of the detainees was justified by the fact that they were "the enemy" and that they "belonged here." But to my surprise, I learned that a large number of the detainees had no business being there at all. SSG ?????, who worked in the outprocessing office, told me that most of the detainees had just been picked up in sweeps for no particular reason, and that some of them weren't even being tracked or registered. She also said they were all being kept there "indefinitely." Sometime later, I learned that a few detainees had been released and they were telling stories on the outside about having been abused while interrogated. The accounts at the time involved cigarettes being put in their ears and being told that American soldiers would be sent to rape their families. I was surprised about these claims and asked SSG ????? what she thought. She said not only were these claims probably true, she had a good idea just which soldiers would have been involved.

SGT ?????, whom I knew from my company, told me his soldiers (MI guards) were being subjected to and made to do things he did not like. He said when he and others from 302nd got to the prison, they were told they could "do whatever they wanted to the detainees," particularly while making them do exercises (a practice known as "smoking"). He described an incident in which SPC ????? grabbed the ankle of one detainee, causing him to hit his head on the floor. They all laughed.

SPC ?????, also from my company, gave me essentially the same account as SGT ?????.

I was told that SPC ????? and ????? were relieved from interrogation duty by LTC Jordan: ????? for being too brutal and ????? for escorting a detainee naked in front of the general population.

A unit of MI guards was formed because the MP's no longer wanted to do the things they were being asked to do by interrogators. The MI guards were well known for being extremely rowdy at night, drinking bottles of Robitussin DM with tablets of Vivarin, and then partying in a dark room full of blinking lights and loud music. They were even doing this with one of the civilian interrogators ("DJ"), whom they worked for directly during interrogations. One night they came back with rings on their fingers and I asked where they got them, and they said they got them from detainees.

?????, a civilian interrogator, requested that I give him access to highly classified information. He said it was vital, and despite the fact that he had no clearance through the Brigade S-2, tried to convince me he had a clearance and demanded I give him this information. I declined his requests and reported the matter to the Brigade S-2. I nevertheless had the impression that civilian contractors were being given access to highly classified information notwithstanding the lack of proper clearance. Moreover, these civilian contractors involved in interrogation frequently behaved as if they were the superiors of the uniformed military interrogators, giving them directions and instructions. Their presence and activities clearly seemed to undermine or confuse the chain of command at Abu Ghraib and to undermine discipline and morale.

I spoke with a number of other interrogators and analysts, and most corroborated in some way the accounts of abuse and mistreatment I have described here. Most everything I note here was either widely known or openly discussed. The community there was very small, so even the mechanics and cooks knew a lot of what was going on. Because of these facts, I was amazed that so few soldiers provided accounts of what happened during the official investigations undertaken by [Major General] Taguba and then [Major General] Fay.

In October 2003, one day I noticed that a delegation from the Red Cross was at Abu Ghraib performing some sort of mission. Word got around that the Red Cross had been very critical of what they saw at the prison. I hoped that this would lead to some changes. However, shortly after their visit, LTC Jordan spoke to our unit telling us of the Red Cross visit. He said they had made many complaints about the conditions in which the detainees were held. Jordan said by contrast their conditions were far better off than they were under Saddam Hussein. The message seemed to be that nothing was going to change, that everything was going on just the way the command authority wanted.

In December 2003, SPC Wilson and I were in COL Pappas' office fixing his printer. COL Pappas and his staff captain were discussing staging a mock fast rope attack (in which assault troops would repel down ropes from helicopters) in the middle of the hardsites as a "Christmas present for the detainees." They laughed together about it, saying it would scare the bejeezus out of the detainees. I thought they were joking at the time, but it further convinced me that they had an attitude of indifference or even hostility towards detainees and that they wanted to use fear and intimidation as the main tools against them. Later, I read MG Taguba's interview with COL Pappas, and learned that he in fact staged this exercise, and defended it to MG Taguba as necessary to prevent a possible prison uprising.

Source: Samuel J. Provance. Prepared Statement as part of National Whistleblowers in the Post-September 11th Era: Lost in a Labyrinth and Facing Subtle Retaliation. Given before U.S. House of Representatives Subcommittee on National Security, Emerging Threats, and International Relations of the Committee on Government Reform, February 14, 2006. Washington, DC. Available at: http://fas.org/irp/congress/2006_hr/whistle.pdf (accessed June 13, 2015).

AFTERMATH

Earlier in this book the concept of a competition of narrative was discussed. The images and actions associated with Abu Ghraib and the reactions to those images get at the heart of the competition of narrative. The American public was revolted by the images because they ran in direct contradiction to the narrative of the U.S. military—defending freedoms, human rights and liberties, and promoting western values. The Iraqi public and people throughout the Middle East viewed the photos as proof of the narrative they accepted—Americans are brutal invading oppressors, all of the good things are a façade covering an uglier reality, all the rumors of abuse are true.

This was the ugliest revelation in the Iraq War. It created problems at every level of the conflict and in every location. It was a problem for soldiers walking on the streets of Iraqi towns and cities. It was a problem for leaders at every level in the military as this revealed a great deal of the behavior of soldiers and leaders under stress in dealing with a foreign culture. This caused a change in the command structure in Iraq. Originally the military command was a three-star level commander—LTG Ricardo Sanchez. Shortly following the release of the reports of Abu Ghraib and some of the early findings of U.S. military investigations it was decided to replace a three-star commander with a four-star commander. This also played significantly at the U.S. and coalition capitals. In the United States there were Congressional hearings and investigations that revealed that this problem was bigger than the events in a single prison or with a group of bad soldiers from a single unit.

It was from this catalyzing event that the revelations about a system of prisons existed throughout Afghanistan and Iraq and in other countries in the Middle East and elsewhere in the world. In these prisons, some run by the military and others run by the Central Intelligence Agency the guards and interrogators used enhanced interrogation techniques that some referred to as torture. These revelations were as damaging to U.S. respect and influence as were the images of Abu Ghraib. Many people assumed what was shown represented something like the tip of an iceberg. This brought into question what else might be happening that wasn't being shared.

ASK YOURSELF

1. Why do atrocities occur? Is everyone capable of committing heinous and shameful acts? The soldiers who committed these acts discussed in the testimony above were not identified as abnormal in their prior behavior, nor were they seen as deviant in earlier periods of their lives. Why would apparently normal and average people commit acts that they would not normally do? Was it peer pressure? These are profound questions that get at human nature. Those who perpetrated these acts and those who committed worse atrocities in other wars do not typically stand out before or after the events as aberrant personalities thus revealing something about every one of us.

2. Samuel Provance was a Specialist in the U.S. Army, a rank of little authority and recognized as needing to follow orders rather than to give them. The fact that he was disturbed by what he saw and heard to the point of willingly sharing those concerns with investigators was a critical part of this story. Not just one, but many junior-ranking soldiers spoke out against what they knew was happening. This is a different kind of discipline from the standard view—obeying orders. Provance and others like him obeyed their consciences and did what they knew was right. It is this level of personal discipline and courage that is critical in warfare as much as the other kind—obedience to orders. However, in war discipline is preeminent and thus following orders becomes critical to life. Can those soldiers who performed these acts be protected by saying that they were following orders?

3. What is torture? The United States ratified the UN definition of torture on October 21, 1994. It reads as follows:

   For the purpose of this Convention, the term "torture" means any act by which severe pain or suffering, whether physical or mental, is intentionally inflicted on a person for such purposes as obtaining from him, or a third person, information or a confession, punishing him for an act he or a third person has committed or is suspected of having committed, or intimidating or coercing him or a third person, or for any reason based on discrimination of any kind, when such pain or suffering is inflicted by or at the instigation of or with the consent or acquiescence of a public official or other person acting in an official capacity. It does not include pain or suffering arising only from, inherent in, or incidental to, lawful sanctions.

   This definition is broad and includes a considerable amount of things radically different than the standard definitions and images of torture and torture chambers such as those operated by Saddam Hussein. Thus, there is a vigorous debate about whether or not sleep deprivation crosses the line from acceptable interrogation technique to torture?

TOPICS TO CONSIDER

1. The events of Abu Ghraib were graphically depicted on media outlets of every fashion. The *Economist* magazine included a man standing with a hood on with wires connected to his fingertips on its cover. This iconic image is one of the

most recognized symbols of the U.S. occupation of Iraq. The military tried to sell the events as reprehensible events limited to bad actors in a unit suffering from poor leadership. Others portrayed it as indicative of bad policies and a culture of lawlessness that extended from the highest levels of the U.S. government on down to the lowly soldier operating in the prison. Others argued that the attention given to these abuses was out of proportion to the abuse. Most of what happened in Abu Ghraib was humiliation. No electric shock was used—just threatened. No fingernails were pulled. Was the coverage requisite for the crimes? Was the harm from the media broadcast justifiable based on the crimes committed?

2. Think about concentration camp and death camp guards in World War II, the officials who rounded up Japanese Americans to be transported to relocation camps, the police in Alabama who turned firehoses on Civil Rights protestors, and many others who committed various forms of atrocity over the decades and generations. Are they that different from you, the reader? If so, then what made them different? Was it the acts they committed? Was it the mere thought of acting out against another human being? Was it considering another person to be less of a human being than themselves? Where do atrocities begin?

Further Reading

Al-Ali, Zaid. *The Struggle for Iraq's Future: How Corruption, Incompetence and Sectarianism Have Undermined Democracy.* New Haven, CT: Yale University Press, 2014.

Danner, Mark. *Torture and Truth: America, Abu Ghraib, and the War on Terror.* New York: New York Review of Books, 2004.

Hersh, Seymour. *Chain of Command: The Road from 9/11 to Abu Ghraib.* New York: Harper-Collins Publishers Inc., 2004.

Shadid, Anthony. *Night Draws Near: Iraq's People in the Shadow of America's War.* New York: Henry Holt and Company, 2005.

Wright, Donald P. and Timothy R. Reese. *On Point II: Transition to the New Campaign: The United States Army in Operation Iraqi Freedom May 2003–January 2005.* Fort Leavenworth, KS: U.S. Army Command and General Staff College Press, 2008.

Website

United Nations. "Convention against Torture and Other Cruel, Inhuman or Degrading Treatment or Punishment." United Nations Human Rights, Office of the High Commissioner for Human Rights. Adopted by General Assembly resolution 39/46 of 10 December 1984. http://www.ohchr.org/EN/ProfessionalInterest/Pages/CAT.aspx (accessed June 13, 2015).

Films and Television

American War Generals. Executive producers: Peter Bergen, Tresha Mabile, Jonathan Towers. National Geographic Channel, 2014.

Frontline: Bush's War. Director: Michael Kirk. PBS, 2008.

Frontline: The Torture Question. Director: Michael Kirk, 2005.

Generation Kill. Director: Susanna White, Simon Cellan Jones. Blown Deadline Productions, 2008.

Zero Dark Thirty. Director: Kathryn Bigelow. Columbia Pictures, 2012.

14. The Battle of Fallujah from a USMC Information Operations Perspective: Andy Dietz

INTRODUCTION

There were two Battles of Fallujah. The first battle began on April 4, 2004. The second began on October 31, 2004. They both happened in the same locations and for many of the same reasons, but they were conducted in different ways and with significantly different outcomes. Fallujah had a reputation of being something like the wild west of Iraq, even during the reign of Saddam Hussein. During the Iraq War it was part of the Sunni Triangle—an area of violence and difficulty for United States and coalition forces that extended from Baqubah in the east to Ramadi in the west to Bayji in the north. Fallujah sits in the middle of the east-west axis. Throughout the entire eight years of the U.S. occupation Fallujah was a consistent problem for both coalition and Iraqi leadership. Following the disbanding of the Iraqi Army there were approximately 70,000 unemployed young men in the city. The city is heavily influenced by tribal structures and the religion tends to be more conservative.

The attack launched in April was smaller and less prepared than the one later in the year. In March 2004 the first Marine Expeditionary Force (MEF) replaced the 82nd Airborne Division of the U.S. Army. The Marines took a different approach to their duties—they sought to win the hearts and minds of the local populace. The biggest catalyst event was the March 31, 2004, ambush of Blackwater Security Contractors. Four were killed and their charred bodies were hung from a prominent overpass entering the city. At about this time Shiite militias under Muqtada al-Sadr rose up and began protests around the country. The coalition faced its hardest challenge to date. On April 4 the coalition launched Operation Vigilant Resolve to capture or kill those responsible for the murders and to restore control of the city to coalition forces and the Iraqi Governing Council. The Marine leadership wanted to take a softer approach, but the CPA and leaders in Washington, D.C., felt strong action needed to be taken. Four Marine battalion assaulted positions in the city following aerial and artillery precision strikes and for five days the fighting went on. Several key members of the Iraq Governing Council threatened to desert the coalition if the attacks did not stop. The CPA suspended offensive operations. In early May the Marines withdrew from the city and handed security over to an ad hoc organization raised from local former military personnel called the *Fallujah Brigade.*

Things did not get better over the summer. The *Fallujah Brigade* was ineffective in restoring order and by October the coalition, now under the direction of Iraqi transition leaders ordered another attack on the city. This time leaflets were dropped and people were warned to leave the city. On October 31 the artillery and aerial bombardment began.

Major Andy Dietz is a United States Marine Corps (USMC) field artillery officer who worked as the information operations officer for Marine Regimental Combat Team 1 in the Second Battle of Fallujah.

KEEP IN MIND AS YOU READ

1. What is the responsibility of the local populace versus the governing authority for security? The Iraqi people in Fallujah felt that opposition to the Shia-led puppet government in Baghdad was worth any cost to their city. This was their duty to resist.
2. What does precision mean in times of war? There are few truly precise weapons. As will be clear in the aftermath of the fighting, this battle will displace large numbers of people. Where do they go?

Document 14: Excerpt from Interview with Andy Dietz, Second Battle of Fallujah

Question: How did you handle getting the civilians out? It's my understanding that, over a length of time, you guys attempted to do that.

Follow-up Question: Was that part of the [Information Operation] piece?

Answer: Yes, that was part of the [Information Operation] piece. The other half of it was getting the city prepared for combat operations. There has been, of course, a lot of argument about us letting everybody leave and we let some of the big fish leave. But our way of looking at it was: we did not want to go into a built-up city that size with potentially 250,000 non-combatants, so we wanted to get the people out. The problem was that if we tell people to leave, then by international law we're responsible for taking care of them. We also knew that most of those people could leave and they'd be just fine with family support structures from Baghdad all the way to Saqlawiyah, and even further to Habbaniyah. We always had a campaign to try to drive a wedge between the civilians and the insurgents. We saw a lot of them as being fence-sitters, and with their culture the ascendant power is the one they're going to lean towards. So that was something we were working on even before we started getting people out of the city. Since we couldn't go into the city proper, we utilized a lot of leaflet drops over the city. We did things such as tell them how much money had been allocated for Fallujah for reconstruction and why that money wasn't coming—and we'd do it sequentially. First week, "We would have already been spending X-million number of dollars to repair your city with these projects and now we can't." The next drop would up the ante on what projects weren't getting done, the money, so we kept doing that. Other methods we used were radio messages, some of which were generic to the Al Anbar Province, but a lot of them were targeted to the people in Fallujah. We would do loudspeaker broadcasts from the periphery of the city, especially on Fridays doing counter-mosque messages. And then the last thing, we would pass out handbills in places we knew people were transiting into the city. We couldn't go into the city itself, but we knew if we gave these handbills in certain spots they were going to wind up in the city, and that's what we wanted to happen as well. So that was trying to get the fence-sitters and basically make it as difficult as possible for the insurgents to operate in the city. Toward the latter phase before Al Fajr, we focused on getting people out of the city, and we did that with a variety of methods. First we changed the tone of the radio broadcasts. We started spreading our messages, both through the radio and through leaflet drops, that said things like, "In the event of combat operations, please do the following things: stay inside your home; don't get involved; if you have to come outside, don't come out with a weapon." Basically messages that were gearing people towards the fact that something was going to happen. We started changing the tone of those, kind of ratcheted them up a little bit as we got closer; and we also started sending messages to the insurgents. They're the target audience now: "Defeat is inevitable. There's no way you're going to win." So we're getting a trickle of people coming in and out, and they would know when we were going to come because they'd have to see the troop buildup. . . . We basically culminated our IO efforts by firing illumination missions over the city, usually around two to three o'clock in the morning. Lighting it up, which had unintended consequences which were actually of great benefit to us. We did that for several nights in a row, and then we culminated with illumination rounds and Marine F-18 sonic passes over the city. After that, everyone knew the game was on; people left in droves and they quite literally emptied the city. We encountered very few civilians in the city. Most of them were males that stayed behind to watch their houses. We would transport them out of the city, usually up to Saqlawiyah where we had a civil-military operations center (CMOC) set up that would take people, give them some food, and get them on their way to their families. . . .

Question: Are there ways IO could have been better employed or is that too difficult to quantify?

Answer: . . . [W]e knew what we wanted to tell them; but I don't think we necessarily knew what they wanted to hear. I think we got better at that as we went along because we started finding out what it was they wanted hear. But we just didn't have that up front, and I think we may have wasted some resources that had little effect.

Question: What did they want hear?

Answer: They wanted to hear specific things like when the essential services were going to be up, how were they going to get their house rebuilt, what the Iraqi government is going to do to help. Some of those things we had answers to and some of them we didn't, and we would make assumptions. Part of the city is actually lower than the river so when a lot of the pump stations were out—which many of them were out when we went in—a lot of water collects in the streets. They were flooded. So we'd get the pump stations fixed at great cost and effort and risk to peoples' lives and pump the water out, and we assumed people realized that that means progress. Well, it doesn't necessarily mean progress because they don't really understand how the whole pump system works, and we don't bother telling them about it. "Why should I tell them this has been fixed? They can see it themselves." Well, maybe not necessarily—and guys that live in unaffected areas certainly don't know that. We made it easier for them to report possible insurgents trying to infiltrate back into the city and report unexploded ordnance and weapons caches. They didn't know what to do if they found them, even though we handed out these things telling them what to do. Well, we started putting English on the back of these things that said, "If an Iraqi gives this to you, they have information about the following." Because a lot of times, they'd hand these thing to a Marine or a soldier and, "Great, what does this mean?" Well, now they can flip it over and show you. Once these things started to work, more and more people started giving us actionable tips. There was another thing that worked really well that we didn't even think about for a while. Even though we have one of the hospitals running a couple clinics and one or two ambulances, people don't really know that's available, so we put out a handbill that said, "If you need emergency medical attention, find the nearest Iraqi security force or multinational force to get help." We put on the back side in English that if someone hands you this, they need emergency medical help. Lo and behold, a couple days after we started handing those out, we actually had a father who ran out and stopped a Marine convoy going through the center of the city in the middle of the night, well past curfew. They stopped and he hands them the thing. His daughter had gotten burned with cooking oil on both hands really bad. They take her and the father, bring them back to our FOB, she gets immediate medical attention, and it paid huge dividends because that person is now going to go back in the city and say, "Hey, this a great thing." We were slow on the uptake on a lot of that stuff because we just didn't know what they wanted to hear. We had put up water tanks that were erected all over the city, and we assumed they would realize they could go and get their water there. We didn't know we had to tell them. Of course, on the flip side, we didn't think we would have to tell them, "Hey, stop taking the pipes and spigots from these things because the water doesn't work then." I don't know how we could've gotten information like that, but we could've been more effective had we known that. . . .

Question: . . . [D]id you guys have reporters with you?

Answer: Yes. . . . We determined our threshold was usually five media teams per battalion and we were more than maxed out when we went into the city. Everybody had multiple reporters. Shortly after *Fox News* did a big two-hour report on the thing in Fallujah—Greg Palkot was one of the embeds—we had embeds everywhere and we did everything we could to facilitate them getting the story out. I don't want to say they helped us, but they helped report the steps we were taking to mitigate certain types of collateral damage. They would report on how we would approach a mosque we were taking fire from. They knew we wouldn't blow it up. They would help us explain to the world: "Hey, look, we're returning fire in kind, trying to limit the collateral damage. We've gone through every possible step we can and we have no choice left now but to do X." We can't task them and we can't tell them what to report, but if they sit there and see everything we're doing and they report it, then that's a good thing and that happened. We had more press than we probably could have handled, but we did; and with the exception of one case, they were completely cooperative and played by the rules. In that one case they didn't, they were asked to leave and were replaced by a different reporter team. . . . Unfortunately, after the fighting was over and Fallujah became one of the safest places in all of Iraq and there were really great things going on, none of them wanted to come because there was no story then. . . .

On Election Day in Fallujah, where half of all the votes from Al Anbar were cast—the entire province, half of them, 8,000 of them, were cast in Fallujah, which we figured was 30 to 40 percent of the eligible voting population for the city. On that day, there were two reporters in the city, and one was a local radio reporter from Chattanooga. Nobody wanted to come and cover the story. They didn't want to cover the hundreds and thousands of people that were in line. They didn't want to report on the fact that we ran out of voting material and had to run some of the Independent Electoral Commission of Iraq (IECI) workers back to our FOB to get more. They didn't want to report any [of] that . . . but, yes, we did have them and they helped show the truth of what was going on, to dispel any kinds of rumors. Before we went into the city, there would still be news stories that would come out of the city, and usually they would hit Al-Jazeera because they'd placed stringers in the city. They didn't necessarily have to be credentialed; they could be anybody who writes a story. Even though we know they're not telling the truth, it was very difficult for us to counter that in the Arab world because we don't have anybody on the ground. So once we got reporters in the city, that was huge because now these are agencies that have a better reputation, perhaps less biased, less of an agenda than someone reporting for Al-Jazeera. We actually took one embed team from Al-Arabiya. We put them in the city with one of our civil affairs (CA) teams, ran them around for a while. We had been telling them, "Hey, you guys can come," and one of them finally said, "Yeah, we'll do it." The Marines weren't exactly thrilled when they found out who it was going to be at first, but they worked great. . . .

Question: Are there any other things you'd like to touch on or other things you think deserve special attention about Fallujah or anything else?

Answer: I will say one thing: Fallujah was a unique city. It's traditionally been along smuggling routes. It recently had a big criminal element and also a big former Ba'athist element down there, which also made it kind of a unique city. Something we really had to focus on was that most of the rest of Iraq didn't really care what happened in Fallujah. An Iraqi I knew and worked with from time to time—who was not from Fallujah; he was from Baghdad—he said, "Iraqi population: 25 million. Big bomb"—meaning Fallujah—"Iraqi population: 24 million. Nobody really cares." That was kind of the perspective most people outside the city really had, which I think helped us to realize that, while we want to avoid collateral damage as much as possible, we may have a slight window here where we can go a little heavier. Also, when we started talking to people afterwards—and we leveled, Lord knows, probably half the city and damaged the other half—and people are walking up and don't have a house anymore, we're thinking they're going to be really upset with us. Actually, they said, "You know, I don't have a house, but I also don't have to worry about my kids anymore." We were shocked that people in this city are talking like that. Election Day turned into a mob in that city. We couldn't stop our vehicle because if we stopped, we probably wouldn't be able to start them again because people would be coming all around us. Shock. We had no idea that the people in the city were that anti-insurgent and were probably wanting us to come in. We had no idea, and that would've been a really nice thing to know. The uniqueness of the city gave us more of a free hand in being heavy handed when we needed to be.

Source: Andy Dietz. Interview by John McCool and Matt Matthews, February 21, 2006. Interview Transcript. Courtesy of the Operational Leadership Experiences Digital Collection, Combat Studies Institute, Fort Leavenworth, KS. Available at: http://cgsc.contentdm.oclc.org/cdm/singleitem/collection/p4013coll13/id/188/rec/1 (accessed June 15, 2015).

AFTERMATH

Between 75 and 90 percent of the population of the city fled before the battle took place. That is something like 150,000–200,000 people. A total of 38 U.S. personnel were killed as well as six Iraqi soldiers serving alongside coalition forces. It is estimated that between 1,200 and 2,000 Iraqi opposition fighters or insurgents were killed in the fighting with another 1,000–1,500 captured. Over 60 percent of the buildings in the city were damaged and 20 percent destroyed including sixty of the more than 200 mosques. The destruction of the city enraged the Sunni population and led to an increase of insurgent activity. It was in the period that al-Qaeda in Iraq began to grow (it was designated by this name in October 2004).

Once the fighting was done the coalition went to work to rebuild Fallujah. Elements of this are addressed in Chapter 18. Additionally a new civil government and a new security force were created. Residents did not begin returning until mid-December. They were warned that they could be displaced for 75–90 days at the conflict's beginning. Some reports indicated that Operation al-Fajr destroyed the insurgent's grip on the city and only sporadic insurgent attacks continued throughout the rest of the U.S. occupation in Iraq. Though this may be technically accurate, it is important to note that when the Islamic State in Iraq and al-Sham entered Fallujah in January 2014 it was greeted with popular acclaim. The reason for this welcome goes back to the social structure of Fallujah and the opposition to the U.S.-led occupation and the Shia-led government in Baghdad.

ASK YOURSELF

1. Was it possible for the soldiers heading into Fallujah to meet the intent of their commanders? Could they preserve the city and still defeat the opposition fighters they were going against? What risks are entailed in preserving the city? Are those risks you might be willing to make?

2. The United States has not fought a war on its soil since 1865. Imagine how you might feel if soldiers were destroying your city to get at a minority of trouble makers. How would that change if you viewed the "trouble makers" as defending your honor and your liberty?

3. Would you stay or would you go if leaflets were dropped in your neighborhood warning of an impending attack?

TOPICS TO CONSIDER

1. In 2014 and 2015 the United States witnessed riots and mass demonstrations in Ferguson, Missouri, and Baltimore, Maryland, that began as a result of people feeling humiliated by police forces. Similar events happened in 1992 in Los Angeles when a verdict was communicated about police brutality that the community did not agree with. In some ways these events get at similar emotions to those experienced by the people in Fallujah. How does the perception of government disinterest or hostility affect the relationship between citizen and government?

2. Where do people go when they are driven from or flee from their homes? Often the world focuses on refuges at the moment of crisis, but as was earlier stated some of them might be in camps for years or even decades. How does this shape societies and families?

3. The media tends to focus on events deemed newsworthy. This means that systems that work properly do not get the same coverage as bombs and riots and bodies hanging from overpasses. What should the role of media be with respect to telling a complete story? Do they have this obligation? Has the media been consistent in their portrayal of conflict over generations?

Further Reading

Kyle, Chris, and Scott McEwen. *American Sniper: The Autobiography of the Most Lethal Sniper in U.S. Military History.* New York: HarperCollins, 2013.

McCool, John, and Kendall D. Gott. *Eyewitness to War, V. 1: US Army in Operation AL FAJR: An Oral History.* Government Printing Office, 2006. http://1.usa.gov/19vFnjH (accessed June 15, 2015).

McCool, John, and Kendall D. Gott. *Eyewitness to War, V. 2: US Army in Operation AL FAJR: An Oral History.* Government Printing Office, 2006. http://1.usa.gov/1h8UDHi (accessed June 15, 2015).

Shadid, Anthony. *Night Draws Near: Iraq's People in the Shadow of America's War.* New York: Henry Holt and Company, 2005.

West, Bing. *No True Glory: A Frontline Account of the Battle for Fallujah.* New York: Bantam Books, 2005.

Woodward, Bob. *State of Denial: Bush at War, Part III.* New York: Simon & Schuster, 2006.

Films and Television

American Sniper. Director: Clint Eastwood. Warner Bros., 2014.
American War Generals. Executive producers: Peter Bergen, Tresha Mabile, Jonathan Towers. National Geographic Channel, 2014.
Frontline: Bush's War. Director: Michael Kirk. PBS, 2008.

15. A Journalist's Perspective on Combat (2): Ann Barnard

INTRODUCTION

Ann Barnard served as co-Iraq bureau chief for the *Boston Globe* in 2003–2004. She was in and out of Iraq several times during the course of the war starting from April to May 2003 and then full time from December 2003 through the summer of 2004. She returned to Iraq again in late 2004 and early 2005. Much of her time in Iraq was spent in Fallujah before, during, and after Operation Al Fajr: the November 2004 combined-joint assault to retake the city of Fallujah from insurgent control.

Following the retaking of Fallujah, Barnard was able to view firsthand the aftermath of the battle, its impact on the city's residents, and the difficult challenge of reconstruction. She interacted closely both with the city's residents and with the Marine Corps civil affairs unit tasked with restoring such things as water, electricity, banking, and local government.

Of Fallujah Barnard said, "Fallujah has always been sort of a Wild West city, even in the minds of other Iraqis. The tribes are very strong. Many of them did not like submitting to Saddam. They didn't welcome control by outsiders of any kind. There was a tradition of highway robbery going back hundreds of years. Drivers who used to take us when we used to drive from Jordan into Baghdad would always say that you have to drive quickly through Fallujah or drive through very early in the morning so you don't get stuck up on the roads. On the other hand, there were some elite members of Saddam's military who lived there. There were some tribes that Saddam was able to co-opt. The Dulaymi tribe was very strong there. The Dulaymis sometimes resisted Saddam and sometimes supported him, but they were a very strong, traditionally powerful tribe that he had to bargain with. Fallujah has a reputation of fierceness, independence and stubbornness, I would say."

In this chapter the discussion is on the events following the conclusion of the Second Battle of Fallujah. This is a look at reconstruction efforts and what was going wrong.

KEEP IN MIND AS YOU READ

1. These are the recollections and experiences of a newspaper reporter. She is not obligated to present a particular perspective or interpretation of the events she witnessed. Does that make her more objective or accurate?

2. The operation of a city of hundreds of thousands of people is complex with numerous skills and abilities needed to make it happen. The training provided to military personnel from the United States or other countries does not include the operation of major utilities.

Document 15: Excerpt from Interview with Anne Barnard, Boston Globe Reporter—Reconstruction of Fallujah

[The 4th Civil Affairs Group out of Anacostia Naval Station in Washington, DC.] roll into the city and they're looking for any local representatives of the Iraqi ministries—and of course there's already a disconnect between the bureaucracy in Fallujah and the bureaucracy in Baghdad because the bureaucracy in Baghdad is increasingly Shi'ite controlled and Fallujah is almost all Sunni. People in Fallujah are suspicious of them and they're suspicious of people in Fallujah. They have this sort of life and death suspicion between them, so that was adding to the problem probably already, even though that was before the sectarian conflict really exploded.

It would be funny if it wasn't so sad, but the scene I remember is going around with these Marines with two Iraqi guys someone had found who were employees of the city water department. They were trying to get these guys to take them to the pumping stations and show them how to turn the pumps back on. But as they went around, it transpired that these guys might have worked for the water department but they were like security guards. They weren't engineers or technicians. They knew where the pumps were but how they worked was anyone's guess. They weren't able to immediately get them going, and then they finally brought in some American engineers. I don't know if these were Seabees but they were American military and they worked with them on some of these pumps. At one point, a more senior Marine actively staged a photo to make it look like these Iraqi guys were the ones who were fixing the pump. Of course the narrative is supposed to be, "Americans go in and they're just facilitating and now the Iraqis are taking over, doing everything for themselves." But really it was just these American military guys who fixed it.

I later witnessed this Marine officer, who was also a major but was senior to Weems because he was the commanding officer of the unit, reporting to Colonel Mike Shupp in a battalion briefing that the Iraqis had actually fixed the pumps. You know, it's a small thing, but that's the way things don't get communicated correctly up the chain about what's really going on. That kind of thing just repeated again and again in Iraq. These Marines were trying their best but they were supposed to restart the water system, the electrical system, the local government and everything else, even the banking system, and they didn't have information about who the people were or how the infrastructure physically worked. It was really difficult. Again, they put them in these tough positions so some of them, in November 2004, were kind of on their own trying to figure out how to do this.

Weems' commanding officer was talking about, "Maybe we should create mandatory work brigades." I think there were orders from higher up that there were going to be special IDs and retina scans to allow in only official Fallujah residents, and this civil affairs guy thought maybe these people should be required to join work brigades—essentially forced labor. Some higher up guys were talking about this out loud but Weems and the guys below him were thinking that wasn't really going to work. I wrote a story about it because they were talking about all these really draconian measures they were going to take. That thing about the work brigades, of course, ended up getting scrapped, but they did have very tight control of the city, which continued for months. There were checkpoints at every entrance to the city, there were no cars allowed in the city, so you had a paradox. In order to make it safe for the Americans to operate in there and arguably safe for normal people as well, you had to have so much control over the town that it felt like it was really under occupation, that it was like a police state. Give any flexibility or any opening . . . they were sure insurgents were going to come back in.

It's another one of those things where there's a disconnect between your two goals. You want normal life to start again in Fallujah but people couldn't really come home and live there, because if they had business in Baghdad and they have to come and go, it's just going to take hours each way. They would be fully searched, you couldn't take your car in and out, and it just wasn't normal life. Again, remember what I said about Fallujah being this extremely proud city. You had residents who I met—and this is already on my second visit—who had to come in and out of these checkpoints and they just said, "Please, we've been living like this for a couple years now with one group and then another taking over our city. Now the Americans are taking over and we're so humiliated that we have to go in and out this way." It was a paradox. What's the solution? I don't know.

Source: Anne Barnard. Interview by John McCool, September 14, 2007. Interview Transcript. Courtesy of the Operational Leadership Experiences Digital Collection, Combat Studies Institute, Fort Leavenworth, KS. Available at: http://cgsc.contentdm.oclc.org/cdm/singleitem/collection/p4013coll13/id/749/rec/1 (accessed June 15, 2015).

AFTERMATH

In this chapter there is a window of the challenges associated with the U.S. military rebuilding a society. The U.S. military has a "can do" culture where results are paramount and people do what it takes to accomplish the mission. Depending on the product read it is easy to see very different interpretations of the battles in Fallujah. It is unclear that the battle for Fallujah was as much a success as Andy Dietz states in his interview in Chapter 15 or if it was ultimately a failure. It is certain that insurgent opposition to the coalition decreased following the battles. Soldiers and Marines did not go back into Fallujah in a combat role throughout the rest of the civil war. It was more about minor attacks, improvised explosive devices (IEDs), and insurgent facilitation than a source for major violent opposition to the Iraqi government or the coalition.

ASK YOURSELF

1. Were the U.S. military personnel capable of both operating the essential services of the city and facilitating the Iraqi's success in operating and maintaining the operation of the city? This is a tall order and a demanding task. Advising and facilitating someone else in a complex task typically is a full-time job. Operating a major city is also a full-time job.

2. When the officer mentioned above stated that the Iraqis put the plant into operation that was factually inaccurate—maybe even a lie. The USMC values integrity as a core virtue. Why would an officer lie about something like that? What was he gaining or trying to communicate such that he was willing to make an inaccurate statement?

TOPICS TO CONSIDER

1. T. E. Lawrence (the famous *Lawrence of* Arabia) gave 27 articles for working with Arabs. He worked with the Arab Revolt in World War I for which he became internationally famous. Number 15 of his 27 articles says: "Do not try to do too much with your own hands. Better the Arabs do it tolerably than that you do it perfectly. It is their war, and you are to help them, not to win it for them. Actually, also, under the very odd conditions of Arabia, your practical work will not be as good as, perhaps, you think it is." This truism is repeated in almost every U.S. military (and most coalition militaries include it as well) publication that deals with advising foreign forces. Is he correct?

Further Reading

Gordon, Michael R. and Bernard Trainor. *Cobra II: The Inside Story of the Invasion and Occupation of Iraq*. New York: Pantheon Books, 2006.

Kyle, Chris, and Scott McEwen. *American Sniper: The Autobiography of the Most Lethal Sniper in U.S. Military History*. New York: HarperCollins, 2013.

West, Bing. *No True Glory: A Frontline Account of the Battle for Fallujah*. New York: Bantam Books, 2005.

Woodward, Bob. *State of Denial: Bush at War, Part III*. New York: Simon & Schuster, 2006.

Wright, Donald P. and Timothy R. Reese. *On Point II: Transition to the New Campaign: The United States Army in Operation Iraqi Freedom May 2003–January 2005*. Fort Leavenworth, KS: U.S. Army Command and General Staff College Press, 2008.

Websites

Barnard, Anne. "Returning Fallujans will face clampdown." *The Boston Globe*, December 5, 2004. http://www.boston.com/news/world/articles/2004/12/05/returning_fallujans_will_face_clampdown?pg=full (accessed August 12, 2015).

Ramsey, Robert D. III. *Advice for Advisors: Suggestions and Observations from Lawrence to the Present. Global War on Terrorism Occasional Paper 19*. Fort Leavenworth, KS: Combat Studies Institute Press, 2006. http://1.usa.gov/16fYgn9 (accessed June 16, 2015).

Films and Television

American Sniper. Director: Clint Eastwood. Warner Bros., 2014.

American War Generals. Executive producers: Peter Bergen, Tresha Mabile, Jonathan Towers. National Geographic Channel, 2014.

Frontline: Bush's War. Director: Michael Kirk. PBS, 2008.

Lawrence of Arabia. Director: David Lean. Columbia Pictures, 1962.

16. Counterinsurgency from the Ground: John Nagl

INTRODUCTION

The subject of this chapter, John Nagl, is both an author and a practitioner of counter-insurgency. He is a graduate of the U.S. Military Academy at West Point and a Rhodes scholar at Oxford University where he earned a doctorate. His dissertation was published as *Learning to Eat Soup with a Knife: Counterinsurgency Lessons from Malaya and Vietnam*. This book became a major intellectual force in the U.S. military as things started going poorly in Iraq.

This interview is about his time in Iraq as an operations officer in a battalion/task force. From September 2003 to September 2004 Nagl, then a major, served as the operations officer for Task Force 1–34 Armor that was part of the 1st Brigade Combat Team for the 1st Infantry Division. Nagl's unit was assigned to Al Anbar province for the entirety of their time in Iraq where they faced continual challenges with insurgents.

Nagl would return from Iraq and become one of the authors of the U.S. Army and USMC field manual on counterinsurgency which has an excerpt later in this book.

KEEP IN MIND AS YOU READ

1. This is a controversial topic and not all military professionals nor all national security experts agree with all of the ideas espoused by John Nagl. Regardless, he is probably the most widely read author who was also a practitioner and thus regardless of controversy his material deserves or demands consideration.
2. In limited warfare the challenge is to use violence to decrease violence.
3. War is serious and the requests placed upon locals constitute a life and death issue.

Document 16: Excerpt from Interview with John Nagl, Operations Officer for Task Force 1–34 Armor, 2003–2004

Question: Could you discuss the nuts and bolts of TF 1–34 Armor's efforts to recruit, organize and train Iraqi security forces?

Answer: The recruiting and basic training of what was then called the Iraqi Civil Defense Corps (ICDC) was centralized under brigade control in Ramadi. About six months into our deployment, in the spring of 2004, we received operational control of an ICDC battalion. We refurbished barracks for the ICDC, provided them with additional weapons and training, and mentored their leadership. We chose not to embed advisors with our ICDC 24/7 because of the very tenuous relationship between the Sunni ICDC forces and the local population, particularly after the Sunni uprising after the first battle of Fallujah in April 2004. Indeed, it was extremely dangerous for both our ICDC and our Iraqi police comrades to be seen working with us at all. Two police chiefs were assassinated in Khalidiyah between May 2003 and our arrival in September, and Brigadier Ishmael, the third chief, survived at least two attacks during our year with him. We knew he was supporting the insurgency to some extent but assessed that he had to do so to stay alive. We were assigned responsibility for a second ICDC battalion in May or June 2004 and I worked closely with its commander, Lieutenant Colonel Sulieman. He was beaten to death in Fallujah in August 2004 for his relationship with us. Lieutenant Colonel Hussein, the S3 of our ICDC battalion, was later killed as well. We left behind a police force and an Iraqi Army battalion that showed some promise but were far from ready to conduct independent operations when we departed in September 2004.

Question: In the Peter Maass article, you discussed "calibration of force and discrimination in the use of firepower" (p. 24). Could you elaborate on your remarks and thoughts?

Answer: The key to success in a counterinsurgency environment is not to create more insurgents than you capture or kill. A stray tank round that kills a family could create dozens of insurgents for a generation. Thus, it is essential to use force as carefully and with as much discrimination as is possible. This is especially important at situations like checkpoints when soldiers must be given the non-lethal tools to protect themselves from possible car bombers without relying upon deadly force. Always consider the long-term effects of operations in a counterinsurgency environment. Killing an insurgent today may be satisfying, but if in doing so you convince all the members of his clan to fight you to the death, you've actually taken three steps backwards.

Question: Maass discusses your book and academic credentials and quotes you as saying, "[T]he 'expert' thing just kills me. . . . I thought I understood something about counterinsurgency until I started doing it" (p. 24). Where were the largest gaps between what you did in Iraq and your comparison of British and American counterinsurgency approaches and results?

Answer: The environment in Khalidiyah was far more difficult than I had imagined it could be—more dangerous, I think, than most places in Vietnam were for most of that conflict. It was therefore far more difficult to conduct any operation involving contact with the local population than I had ever considered. Protecting members of the population who wanted to help us but who faced assassination at night if they were seen talking to us during the day was an immensely difficult challenge. It was also harder working through interpreters than I had imagined it would be, and interpreters were in much shorter supply than I had thought they would be as well. Clausewitz talks about friction with the words, "In war, everything is very simple, but the simplest things are very difficult." In an insurgency, a smart, committed, ruthless enemy dedicates himself to adding friction to everything we do and with greater effect than I could have imagined before doing it myself.

Source: John A. Nagl. Interview by Christopher K. Ives, January 9, 2007. Interview Transcript. Courtesy of the Operational Leadership Experiences Digital Collection, Combat Studies Institute, Fort Leavenworth, KS. Available at: http://cgsc.contentdm.oclc.org/cdm/singleitem/collection/p4013coll13/id/331/rec/7 (accessed July 17, 2015).

AFTERMATH

As stated, John Nagl went on to coauthor *FM 3–24: Counterinsurgency* for the U.S. Army and USMC. His ideas and lessons shaped the perspective in Iraq for the last four years of the war and also helped to shape the thinking with respect to Afghanistan as well. Gian Gentile went on to write a counterpoint to this notion of the U.S. military as counterinsurgents and others have come out as part of a robust argument about the war. Some have characterized the pro-counterinsurgency argument as the *Good War* argument, meaning that in Iraq there was a good war possible and if the United States had only fought the war smarter or better then a positive result would have happened. This debate grew more intense with the publication of Lieutenant General (retired) Bolger's book in which he states that the United States lost the war in Iraq. The debate still goes on at the time of writing this book. It is uncertain how things will end though the Islamic State seems to have influenced many to accept the need for counterinsurgency.

ASK YOURSELF

1. If a major role of the U.S. military is to destroy things and kill people then why would an officer in that military advocate for less destruction and killing? Is his argument valid? Often some of the biggest advocates against violence are soldiers. Why might that be the case?

2. If association with the U.S. military threatens the lives of people with whom that organization needs to work then what are the ethical obligations of the U.S. military toward those people?

TOPICS TO CONSIDER

1. Innovation is critical to organizational development. The U.S. military prides itself on its ability to learn and adapt. Does learning equal innovation? Is adjustment to enemy action or reaction the same as innovating and developing new ideas? If not, then how is it possible to innovate in times of conflict? U.S. forces are and were not the only ones innovating. Typically, in war, both sides innovate and the innovation of one side tends to drive the need for innovation on the other side. Opponents of the U.S.-led coalition adapted and evolved throughout the Iraq War driving the need for U.S. innovation and change

Further Reading

Gentile, Gian. *Wrong Turn: America's Deadly Embrace of Counterinsurgency*. New York: The New Press, 2013.

Kilcullen, David. *Counterinsurgency*. Oxford: Oxford University Press, 2010.

Kilcullen, David. *The Accidental Guerilla: Fighting Small Wars in the Midst of a Big One*. Oxford: Oxford University Press, 2011.

Nagl, John A. *Learning to Eat Soup with a Knife: Counterinsurgency Lessons from Malaya and Vietnam*. Westport, CT: Praeger Publishers, 2002.

Nagl, John A. *Knife Fights: A Memoir of Modern War in Theory and Practice*. New York: Penguin Press, 2014.

Website

Maass, Peter. "Professor Nagl's War." *The New York Times*, January 11, 2004. http://www.nytimes.com/2004/01/11/magazine/professor-nagl-s-war.html (accessed July 17, 2015).

Films and Television

American War Generals. Executive producers: Peter Bergen, Tresha Mabile, Jonathan Towers. National Geographic Channel, 2014.

Eagle Eye. Director: D. J. Caruso. Dreamworks SKG, 2008.

Frontline: Bush's War. Director: Michael Kirk. PBS, 2008.

17. Perspective from the Commander of Multi-National Forces-Iraq: George Casey

INTRODUCTION

George Casey was the longest-serving commander in Iraq from July 2004 to February 2007. He took the U.S. and coalition command and made it into a massive semipermanent military structure. He came in on the tail of the Abu Ghraib prison scandal and the transition of authority to the Iraqi Interim Government through the growth of the insurgency into a near civil war. His brief memoir from which these excerpts are taken shows a leader who is struggling to understand the situation and to implement the best organization and plan he possibly can. These are his words and therefore show him in a favorable light.

These comments come from his efforts to understand the situation and craft the plan to lead the transition to Iraqi sovereignty and U.S. and coalition departure.

KEEP IN MIND AS YOU READ

1. General Casey was sent to Iraq to extricate the United States from the country and the increasing violence within eighteen months. He was expected to have all U.S. forces out of Iraq by early 2006. His early thinking and assessments are shaded by this expectation.

2. General Casey had not served in the Middle East prior to this assignment other than in Operation Desert Storm. He had never worked as an advisor to a foreign military nor had he worked in an environment where the other agencies of the U.S. government were important players in his operations. His career had always been focused on the U.S. military. His position immediately preceding his command in Iraq was as the deputy chief of staff for the U.S. Army.

Document 17: Excerpts from Strategic Reflections by George Casey, Commander, Multi-National Forces-Iraq, July 2004–February 2007

Going in, I believed that the U.S. objective was to facilitate the establishment of a representative Iraqi government that respected the human rights of all Iraqis and had sufficient security forces to maintain domestic order and deny Iraq as a safe haven for terrorists. I knew that I needed to quickly make an on-the-ground assessment, develop a strategy and a campaign plan to achieve our objective, and then work with Ambassador Negroponte to build our team and organize the mission for success—all while working to build a strong partnership with the newly sovereign Iraqi government. We would have plenty to do. While I knew the mission in Iraq would not be easy, I was just starting to understand its complexity. . . .

Following the change of command, I met with my immediate boss, General Abizaid, to receive his oral and written guidance for the mission. . . . He told me to focus on setting the conditions for the January elections while building loyal Iraqi security forces and institutions and respecting Iraqi sovereignty. He told me to let him know the adequacy of the rules of engagement and support from his headquarters, and informed me that I was authorized to communicate directly with the Chairman and Secretary of Defense on "matters relating to the operational and tactical direction of the force." He asked only to be kept informed in these instances. This would substantially increase our agility to prosecute tactical actions, and I resolved not to abuse this trust. . . .

At that time, MNF-I [Multi-National Forces-Iraq] consisted of around 162,000 coalition forces from 33 countries that had been organized into five Multi-National Division (MND) areas of operation and one Multi-National Brigade (MNB) area of operation in northwest Iraq. MND–South East was commanded by a UK two-star general, and MND–Center South was commanded by a Polish two-star general. These two divisions contained the preponderance of non-U.S. coalition forces. MND-Baghdad, MND-North Central, and MNF-West, the USMC sector, were commanded by U.S. two-star generals, and MNB-North West was commanded by a U.S. one-star general. While the U.S. units contained some multinational forces, they were predominantly U.S. organizations. These units reported directly to the Multi-National Corps-Iraq commander, a U.S. three-star general who was responsible for orchestrating the operational aspects of our mission. . . .

The Red Team was led by a senior Foreign Service officer with an Army two-star general as his deputy. Their task was to take an independent look at both the nature of the threat and the nature of the war, and to give us recommendations on how we should proceed. The team consisted of handpicked senior members of the Embassy and Central Intelligence Agency (CIA), the British embassy and Special Intelligence Service, and MNF-I. The Ambassador and I gave them 30 days to do their work, with the intent of bringing it together with the ongoing MNF-I campaign planning effort. We planned to issue the joint mission statement and campaign plan by early August. I felt very strongly that it was my responsibility to ensure that every member of the coalition clearly understood what it was that we were trying to accomplish in Iraq so each one could contribute to our success. These two documents would go far in helping me do that.

In late July, after several productive sessions with them, the Red Team reported back to the Ambassador and me. They concluded that we were fighting an insurgency and that it was "stronger than it was nine months ago and could deny the [Iraqi Interim Government] legitimacy over the next nine months." In their view, the insurgency was primarily led by well-funded Sunni Arab "rejectionists" who had lost power with the overthrow of Saddam Hussein and rejected the new order. The rejectionists centered around former regime elements, members of the former Ba'ath Party, and former Iraqi security and intelligence forces who had the wherewithal to challenge the formation of a democratic government in Iraq. The Red Team felt that there was "not a monolithic Ba'ath Party" controlling the insurgency, but a "loose system of leadership with no single leader," and that many of the key leaders and facilitators were based outside of Iraq, primarily in Syria. The insurgents shared a range of motivations from "the explicitly religious to Arab nationalists to Saddam loyalists." They felt that foreign Islamic extremists (al Qaeda) were a "small if lethal problem in Iraq" (numbering fewer than 1,000) and that "Iran is hoping to win influence over Iraq's political and electoral process without having to provoke a Shia-based insurgency (for which it is preparing, nonetheless)." Despite their different objectives, all insurgents shared a common goal—the failure of the coalition mission. We accepted this view of the threat. . . .

The campaign plan, issued August 5, 2004, laid out direction for the next 18 months. The plan put the Iraq mission in the context of our efforts up to that time (the Liberation and Occupation Phases of Operation Iraqi Freedom), and focused primarily on the next 18 months (the Partnership Phase), which entailed the completion of the UNSCR timeline and the formation of a constitutionally elected Iraqi government by 2006. The plan looked beyond January 2006, but only broadly, to the Iraqi Self-reliance Phase, where Iraqis would assume security responsibility. As we were still early in the mission, we purposely did not assign a timeline for this phase. . . .

Working directly from the Red Team assessment, the Ambassador and I crafted a joint mission statement for our respective organizations and signed it on August 18. In this first critical document, we formally defined our objective: "To help the Iraqi people build a new Iraq, at peace with its neighbors, with a constitutional, representative government that respects human rights and possesses security forces sufficient to maintain domestic order, and deny Iraq as a safe haven for terrorists." We stated that the IIG shared this objective, but was "in the early stages of consolidating the aspects of national power," so we aimed "to bolster the IIG's legitimacy in perception and fact," acknowledging this would be a major challenge. We also conveyed our common view of the threat, noting that the gravest immediate threat to IIG legitimacy was an insurgency principally led by well-funded Sunni Arab rejectionists drawn from former regime elements. To deal with that threat, we laid out a series of tasks in three interrelated categories: political, security, and economic, and asserted that these tasks would be the "focal point of integrated efforts mounted by everyone operating in Iraq under our authority [emphasis added]." . . .

Armed with these insights, I returned to Washington in mid-December for consultations on the situation in Iraq and to provide my thoughts on the way ahead after the January elections. I met with the President, Secretary Rumsfeld, and the Joint Chiefs and shared the findings of our Campaign Progress Review, COIN [Counter Insurgency], and Red Team studies, and reported on our preparations for the upcoming elections. I also began to discuss the concept of placing coalition advisor teams alongside Iraqi military, police, and border forces to hasten the development of our "capable indigenous partner." I told the national security team that we would be ready to conduct the January elections, but that there would be violence as insurgents and terrorists attempted to disrupt the elections. I also warned them to expect a loss of momentum during the government formation process after the elections, and—to emphasize our thinking on how long this might take—I stated that even if the UNSCR [United Nations Security Council Resolution] 1546 process was completed on schedule, the Iraqis would still face an insurgency, long-term development challenges, and meddling neighbors. I also pointed out that a year from then, the ISF would still not be capable of independent COIN operations. My message was that the mission in Iraq was going to extend beyond the 18 months of the UN timeline, but we would be ready for the first democratic elections in over five decades.

Source: George Casey. *Strategic Reflections: Operation Iraqi Freedom July 2004–February 2007.* Washington, DC: National Defense University Press, 2012.

AFTERMATH

Obviously the eighteen-month expected withdrawal of U.S. forces was inaccurate. General Casey continued to command for two and a half years. He disagreed with the increase of U.S. forces and believed that more U.S. soldiers simply created more targets for the insurgents and the civil war participants. He wanted to reduce the U.S. footprint in country and believed that this would reduce the violence. He was replaced by General Petraeus after the 2006 midterm elections and the decision to change the strategy in Iraq.

General Casey departed Iraq to become the 36th chief of staff for the U.S. Army.

The Iraq War continued and the U.S. involvement did not end for nearly five years after his departure.

ASK YOURSELF

1. *Strategic Reflections* gives insights into a person who, by his description, seemed to understand the challenging dynamics of Iraq and what was happening in the country. If this was true then why did the violence increase throughout his time in command?

2. Under Saddam "elections" were held regularly. How did the election discussed in this chapter differ from those held by the old regime? Americans tend to think a democratically elected government is right for every nation and culture, but is that necessarily true? Given the nature of Arab culture, what form of government might best meet the needs of the Iraqi people? Would it have been admitting defeat for the United States to encourage a form of government for Iraq that was different from our own?

TOPICS TO CONSIDER

1. President Bush laid out the U.S. policy with respect to Iraq in several speeches where he stated that "We will not leave until victory has been achieved." He also stated that in the war against terrorism there would not be a surrender of the enemy on the deck of the USS *Missouri* as there was with the Japanese at the end of World War II. These two notions seem to be at odds. On the one hand there is bellicose rhetoric not unlike in previous wars where victory was definable and visible; at the same time there is an acknowledgement that we were fighting a different kind of war. How do wars end in the modern world?

Further Reading

Al-Ali, Zaid. *The Struggle for Iraq's Future: How Corruption, Incompetence and Sectarianism Have Undermined Democracy*. New Haven, CT: Yale University Press, 2014.

Bolger, Daniel P. *Why We Lost: A General's Inside Account of the Iraq and Afghanistan Wars*. Boston: Houghton Mifflin Harcourt, 2014.

Gordon, Michael R. and Bernard Trainor. *Cobra II: The Inside Story of the Invasion and Occupation of Iraq*. New York: Pantheon Books, 2006.

Woodward, Bob. *State of Denial: Bush at War, Part III*. New York: Simon & Schuster, 2006.

Wright, Donald P. and Timothy R. Reese. *On Point II: Transition to the New Campaign: The United States Army in Operation Iraqi Freedom May 2003–January 2005*. Fort Leavenworth, KS: U.S. Army Command and General Staff College Press, 2008.

Website

National Security Presidential Directive 36, "United States Government Operations in Iraq," May 11, 2004. http://fas.org/irp/offdocs/nspd/nspd051104.pdf (accessed July 15, 2015).

Films and Television

American War Generals. Executive producers: Peter Bergen, Tresha Mabile, Jonathan Towers. National Geographic Channel, 2014.

Frontline: Bush's War. Director: Michael Kirk. PBS, 2008.

18. Iraqi Constitution: Preamble and Basic Rights, October 15, 2005

INTRODUCTION

The creation of an Iraqi constitution by Iraqis was deemed to be one of the most important aspects of establishing sovereignty in Iraq. The process took longer than expected. It began with the establishment of the Iraqi Governing Council on or about July 13, 2003, and concluded with the publication of the final document on October 15, 2005. As will be noted there is a lot of compromise captured in the document.

This chapter includes parts of the rights that make clear some of the trauma experienced in the past and the desire to legally preempt a recurrence of that trauma in the future.

KEEP IN MIND AS YOU READ

1. This U.S. Constitutional Convention lasted less than four months (May 25–September 17, 1787) and in that process established the longest-standing current constitution in the world. It is important to reflect on the make-up and dynamics of the convention itself. The members of that convention, though with different political perspectives, were generally homogeneous in terms of ethnicity and worldview. Slavery was the single biggest separating idea though there were others. This homogeneity led, at least in part, to a relatively quick and less specific document. A lot of the enumerated rights were not as spelled out as they are in the Iraqi constitution because there was less common ground and common perspective in Iraq.

2. The history of Mesopotamia is long and deep. As you read this preamble you can see the connection to Hammurabi and the Babylonian, Assyrian, and Persian Empires as well as the rise and dominance of Islam and Islamic Caliphates ruled from Baghdad and elsewhere in Iraq. Reflect also on the tortured nature of that history and the abuses against minorities and majorities as well as the excesses of despotic rulers. Many of the rights and protections are intended to prevent the treatment endured under Saddam Hussein and other similar rulers.

3. U.S. citizens and leaders view the Constitution as the touchstone document. It is the source from which all other laws flow. This is not a common perspective of

constitutions around the world. The U.S. Constitution has only been amended 27 times and never fundamentally changed. Other nations have changed constitutions numerous times when they no longer seemed relevant to the times or there was a significant transition in leadership.

Document 18: Excerpt from the Iraqi Constitution and Basic Rights, October 15, 2005

(Note: The following is heavily edited to express some key points of interest.)

THE PREAMBLE

In the name of God, the most merciful, the most compassionate. We have honored the sons of Adam. We are the people of the land between two rivers, the homeland of the apostles and prophets, abode of the virtuous imams, pioneers of civilization, crafters of writing and cradle of numeration. Upon our land the first law made by man was passed, the most ancient just pact for homelands policy was inscribed, and upon our soil, companions of the Prophet and saints prayed, philosophers and scientists theorized and writers and poets excelled. Acknowledging God's right over us, and in fulfillment of the call of our homeland and citizens, and in response to the call of our religious and national leaderships and the determination of our great (religious) authorities and of our leaders and reformers, and in the midst of an international support from our friends and those who love us, marched for the first time in our history toward the ballot boxes by the millions, men and women, young and old, on the 30th of January, 2005, invoking the pains of sectarian oppression sufferings inflicted by the autocratic clique and inspired by the tragedies of Iraq's martyrs, Shiite and Sunni, Arabs and Kurds and Turkmen and from all the other components of the people and recollecting the darkness of the ravage of the holy cities and the South in the Sha'abaniyya uprising and burnt by the flames of grief of the mass graves, the marshes, Dujail and others and articulating the sufferings of racial oppression in the massacres of Halabja, Barzan, Anfal and the Fayli Kurds and inspired by the ordeals of the Turkmen in Bashir and as is the case in the remaining areas of Iraq where the people of the west suffered from the assassinations of their leaders, symbols and elderly and from the displacement of their skilled individuals and from the drying out of their cultural and intellectual wells, so we sought hand-in-hand and shoulder-to-shoulder to create our new Iraq, the Iraq of the future free from sectarianism, racism, locality complex, discrimination and exclusion.

Accusations of being infidels, and terrorism did not stop us from marching forward to build a nation of law. Sectarianism and racism have not stopped us from marching together to strengthen our national unity, and to follow the path of peaceful transfer of power and adopt the course of the just distribution of resources and providing equal opportunity for all.

We the people of Iraq who have just risen from our stumble, and who are looking with confidence to the future through a republican, federal, democratic, pluralistic system, have resolved with the determination of our men, women, the elderly and youth, to respect the rules of law, to establish justice and equality to cast aside the politics of aggression, and to tend to the concerns of women and their rights, and to the elderly and their concerns, and to children and their affairs and to spread a culture of diversity and defusing terrorism. We the people of Iraq of all components and shades have taken upon ourselves to decide freely and with our choice to unite our future and to take lessons from yesterday for tomorrow, to draft, through the values and ideals of the heavenly messages and the findings of science and man's civilization, this lasting constitution. The adherence to this constitution preserves for Iraq its free union, its people, its land and its sovereignty.

Section One: Fundamental Principles

Article 1:

The Republic of Iraq is a single federal, independent and fully sovereign state in which the system of government is republican, representative, parliamentary, and democratic, and this Constitution is a guarantor of the unity of Iraq.

Article 2:

First: Islam is the official religion of the State and is a foundation source of legislation:

- A. No law may be enacted that contradicts the established provisions of Islam
- B. No law may be enacted that contradicts the principles of democracy.
- C. No law may be enacted that contradicts the rights and basic freedoms stipulated in this Constitution.

Second: This Constitution guarantees the Islamic identity of the majority of the Iraqi people and guarantees the full religious rights to freedom of religious belief and practice of all individuals such as Christians, Yazidis, and Mandean Sabeans.

Article 3:

Iraq is a country of multiple nationalities, religions, and sects. It is a founding and active member in the Arab League and is committed to its charter, and it is part of the Islamic world. . . .

Article 9:

First:

- A. The Iraqi armed forces and security services will be composed of the components of the Iraqi people with due consideration given to their balance and representation without discrimination or exclusion. They shall be subject to the control of the civilian authority, shall defend Iraq, shall not be used as an instrument to oppress the Iraqi people, shall not interfere in the political affairs, and shall have no role in the transfer of authority.
- B. The formation of military militias outside the framework of the armed forces is prohibited.
- C. The Iraqi armed forces and their personnel, including military personnel working in the Ministry of Defense or any subordinate departments or organizations, may not stand for election to political office, campaign for candidates, or participate in other activities prohibited by Ministry of Defense regulations. This ban includes the

activities of the personnel mentioned above acting in their personal or professional capacities, but shall not infringe upon the right of these personnel to cast their vote in the elections.

D. The Iraqi National Intelligence Service shall collect information, assess threats to national security, and advise the Iraqi government. This Service shall be under civilian control, shall be subject to legislative oversight, and shall operate in accordance with the law and pursuant to the recognized principles of human rights.

E. The Iraqi Government shall respect and implement Iraq's international obligations regarding the non-proliferation, non-development, nonproduction, and non-use of nuclear, chemical, and biological weapons, and shall prohibit associated equipment, materiel, technologies, and delivery systems for use in the development, manufacture, production, and use of such weapons.

Second: Military service shall be regulated by law.

Article 10:

The holy shrines and religious sites in Iraq are religious and civilizational entities. The State is committed to assuring and maintaining their sanctity, and to guaranteeing the free practice of rituals in them. . . .

Section Two: Rights and Liberties
Chapter One: [Rights]
First: Civil and Political Rights

Article 14:

Iraqis are equal before the law without discrimination based on gender, race, ethnicity, nationality, origin, color, religion, sect, belief or opinion, or economic or social status.

Article 15:

Every individual has the right to enjoy life, security and liberty. Deprivation or restriction of these rights is prohibited except in accordance with the law and based on a decision issued by a competent judicial authority.

Article 16:

Equal opportunities shall be guaranteed to all Iraqis, and the state shall ensure that the necessary measures to achieve this are taken.

Article 17:

First: Every individual shall have the right to personal privacy so long as it does not contradict the rights of others and public morals.

Second: The sanctity of the homes shall be protected. Homes may not be entered, searched, or violated, except by a judicial decision in accordance with the law.

Article 18:

First: Iraqi citizenship is a right for every Iraqi and is the basis of his nationality.

Second: Anyone who is born to an Iraqi father or to an Iraqi mother shall be considered an Iraqi. This shall be regulated by law.

Third:

A. An Iraqi citizen by birth may not have his citizenship withdrawn for any reason. Any person who had his citizenship withdrawn shall have the right to demand its reinstatement. This shall be regulated by a law.

B. Iraqi citizenship shall be withdrawn from naturalized citizens in cases regulated by law.

Fourth: An Iraqi may have multiple citizenships. Everyone who assumes a senior, security or sovereign position must abandon any other acquired citizenship. This shall be regulated by law.

Fifth: Iraqi citizenship shall not be granted for the purposes of the policy of population settlement that disrupts the demographic composition of Iraq.

Sixth: Citizenship provisions shall be regulated by law. The competent courts shall consider the suits arising from those provisions. . . .

Second: Economic, Social and Cultural Liberties

Article 22:

First: Work is a right for all Iraqis in a way that guarantees a dignified life for them.

Second: The law shall regulate the relationship between employees and employers on economic bases and while observing the rules of social justice.

Third: The State shall guarantee the right to form and join unions and professional associations, and this shall be regulated by law.

Article 23:

First: Private property is protected. The owner shall have the right to benefit, exploit and dispose of private property within the limits of the law.

Second: Expropriation is not permissible except for the purposes of public benefit in return for just compensation, and this shall be regulated by law.

Third:

A. Every Iraqi shall have the right to own property anywhere in Iraq. No others may possess immovable assets, except as exempted by law.

B. Ownership of property for the purposes of demographic change is prohibited. . . .

Article 29:

First:

A. The family is the foundation of society; the State shall preserve it and its religious, moral, and national values.

B. The State shall guarantee the protection of motherhood, childhood and old age, shall care for children and youth, and shall provide them with the appropriate conditions to develop their talents and abilities.

Second: Children have the right to upbringing, care and education from their parents. Parents have the right to respect and care from their children, especially in times of need, disability, and old age.

Third: Economic exploitation of children in all of its forms shall be prohibited, and the State shall take the necessary measures for their protection.

Fourth: All forms of violence and abuse in the family, school, and society shall be prohibited.

Article 30:

First: The State shall guarantee to the individual and the family—especially children and women—social and health security, the basic requirements for living a free and decent life, and shall secure for them suitable income and appropriate housing.

Second: The State shall guarantee social and health security to Iraqis in cases of old age, sickness, employment disability, homelessness, orphanhood, or unemployment, shall work to protect them from ignorance, fear and poverty, and shall provide them housing and special programs of care and rehabilitation, and this shall be regulated by law.

Article 31:

First: Every citizen has the right to health care. The State shall maintain public health and provide the means of prevention and treatment by building different types of hospitals and health institutions.

Second: Individuals and entities have the right to build hospitals, clinics, or private health care centers under the supervision of the State, and this shall be regulated by law.

Article 32:

The State shall care for the handicapped and those with special needs, and shall ensure their rehabilitation in order to reintegrate them into society, and this shall be regulated by law. . . .

Chapter Two: [Liberties]

Article 37:

First:

A. The liberty and dignity of man shall be protected.

B. No person may be kept in custody or investigated except according to a judicial decision.

C. All forms of psychological and physical torture and inhumane treatment are prohibited. Any confession made under force, threat, or torture shall not be relied on, and the victim shall have the right to seek compensation for material and moral damages incurred in accordance with the law.

Second: The State shall guarantee protection of the individual from intellectual, political and religious coercion.

Third: Forced labor, slavery, slave trade, trafficking in women or children, and sex trade shall be prohibited.

Article 38:

The State shall guarantee in a way that does not violate public order and morality:

A. Freedom of expression using all means.
B. Freedom of press, printing, advertisement, media and publication.
C. Freedom of assembly and peaceful demonstration, and this shall be regulated by law.

Article 39:

First: The freedom to form and join associations and political parties shall be guaranteed, and this shall be regulated by law.

Second: It is not permissible to force any person to join any party, society, or political entity, or force him to continue his membership in it.

Article 40:

The freedom of communication and correspondence, postal, telegraphic, electronic, and telephonic, shall be guaranteed and may not be monitored, wiretapped, or disclosed except for legal and security necessity and by a judicial decision.

Article 41:

Iraqis are free in their commitment to their personal status according to their religions, sects, beliefs, or choices, and this shall be regulated by law.

Article 42:

Each individual shall have the freedom of thought, conscience, and belief.

Article 43:

First: The followers of all religions and sects are free in the:
   A. Practice of religious rites, including the Husseini rituals.
   B. Management of religious endowments (waqf), their affairs, and their religious institutions, and this shall be regulated by law.

Second: The State shall guarantee freedom of worship and the protection of places of worship.

Article 44:

First: Each Iraqi has freedom of movement, travel, and residence inside and outside Iraq.

Second: No Iraqi may be exiled, displaced, or deprived from returning to the homeland.

Article 45:

First: The State shall seek to strengthen the role of civil society institutions, and to support, develop and preserve their independence in a way that is consistent with peaceful means to achieve their legitimate goals, and this shall be regulated by law.

Second: The State shall seek the advancement of the Iraqi clans and tribes, shall attend to their affairs in a manner that is consistent with religion and the law, and shall uphold their noble human values in a way that contributes to the development of society. The State shall prohibit the tribal traditions that are in contradiction with human rights.

Article 46:

Restricting or limiting the practice of any of the rights or liberties stipulated in this Constitution is prohibited, except by a law or on the basis of a law, and insofar as that limitation or restriction does not violate the essence of the right or freedom.

Source: Government of Iraq. Final Draft of Iraqi Constitution: Baghdad, Iraq, October 15, 2005. Available at: www.iraqinationality.gov.iq/attach/iraqi_constitution.pdf (accessed June 16, 2015).

AFTERMATH

The events following the 2005 adoption of the constitution challenge the notion that the document was transformative for Iraq. Sectarian and ethnic tensions have increased over the time and based on events before 2011 and after 2011 it seems that it was the coalition presence rather than the constitution as an inspirational document that kept the lid on the tension and conflict. Despite this negative assessment, the document provides tremendous insight into the political dynamics of Iraq and allows readers to understand the tensions existing within the country and the society prior to and following the adoption of this document.

ASK YOURSELF

1. Why enumerate specific rights? Why does the U.S. Constitution use vague terms with respect to rights versus the specific terms in the Iraq constitution?
2. What does the preamble say of how the Iraqi people see themselves? What is their shared sense of identity?

TOPICS TO CONSIDER

1. Trace the history of Mesopotamia and Iraq with respect to the empires that controlled the area. How does this affect the perspective of the people?
2. Compare the Preamble of the U.S. Constitution to that of the Iraqi Constitution. In what ways are they similar? In what ways do they differ? What might account for these differences?

3. Compare the rights and liberties outlined in the Iraqi constitution to the U.S. Bill of Rights. How do they differ? In what ways are they similar? What might account for the differences?

4. Another thing to consider would be an exploration of parliamentary government. How does it differ from our system of government?

Further Reading

Al-Ali, Zaid. *The Struggle for Iraq's Future: How Corruption, Incompetence and Sectarianism Have Undermined Democracy*. New Haven, CT: Yale University Press, 2014.

Bremer, L. Paul. *My Year in Iraq: The Struggle to Build a Future of Hope*. New York: Threshold Editions, 2006.

Shadid, Anthony. *Night Draws Near: Iraq's People in the Shadow of America's War*. New York: Henry Holt and Company, 2005.

Woodward, Bob. *State of Denial: Bush at War, Part III*. New York: Simon & Schuster, 2006.

Wright, Donald P. and Timothy R. Reese. *On Point II: Transition to the New Campaign: The United States Army in Operation Iraqi Freedom May 2003–January 2005*. Fort Leavenworth, KS: U.S. Army Command and General Staff College Press, 2008.

Films and Television

Frontline: Bush's War. Director: Michael Kirk. PBS, 2008.

INSURGENCY GROWS
OR CIVIL WAR
(2005–2006)

19. Noncommissioned Officer and the Close Fight: Hans Hull

INTRODUCTION

Improvised explosive device or IED is an innocuous term used first by the British in trying to describe nonmilitary constructed weapons used by the Provisional Irish Republican Army. Weapons like these have been used for decades by nonstate actors who struggled to get military-grade weaponry. In the failure to do so they used the materials readily available. In Iraq IED became a common acronym, and more than 60 percent of coalition casualties came from these weapons. They were constructed from a variety of sources. Unlike other conflicts there was not a shortage of military-grade explosives material. The use of the word improvised in Iraq is based on the use of military weapons in nontraditional ways. Following the initial invasion there was a period of heavy looting. Many of the groups who later opposed the U.S.-led coalition found weapons and stored them away for future use or they went to hidden weapon caches that the Iraqi Army made prior to the invasion. Common IEDs included artillery rounds and other military weapons that were then tied into some detonator for effect against coalition convoys.

Over time the devices and the detonators became more complex. Some detonators were pressure plates. Later, washing machine or dryer timers were used. Some were command detonated by electrical wire and others by cell phones, car key fobs, or garage door opener remotes. The attacks also became more complex as those planting the devices observed coalition reactions and then planned to include and target the reactions. For example, one IED was detonated and then another would wait until the crowd gathered or the ambulance or maintenance personnel arrived and then be detonated to ensure maximum casualties.

The most deadly innovation was the explosively formed penetrators (EFPs). This was a complex, yet still IED device. A copper plate was used with a shape charge of explosives. The explosive would create a projectile of the copper plate and this projectile had the capacity to pierce armored vehicles. Shia militias were the predominant users of these devices as they were typically brought in from Iran or the experts were Iranian or Lebanese Hezbollah fighters who trained Iraqis to create and use the devices.

Oftentimes IEDs were used beside or under a road to target coalition convoys of vehicles. This use gave rise to the name "roadside bomb."

In this chapter the interview is with First Sergeant (Ret) Hans Hull who was the first sergeant for Charlie Company, 1st Battalion, 12th Infantry, 4th Infantry Division during the unit's deployment in support of Operation Iraqi Freedom (OIF) from December 2005 to

November 2006. A first sergeant is the senior enlisted noncommissioned officer for a company. He essentially has responsibility for the care, training, and welfare of 100–200 people. During the deployment, 1SGT Hull's company was detached from their battalion and attached to a light Infantry battalion from 101st Airborne Division and that was 2nd Battalion, 506th Infantry. The company was responsible for running an outpost that required traversing IED-infested roads back and forth between the outpost and camp to include Route Redwings. The company operated from forward-operating base (FOB) Falcon south of Baghdad Green Zone.

KEEP IN MIND AS YOU READ

1. United States and coalition forces operated from FOBs and moved from these locations to areas of operation in this period of the war and, for the most part, throughout the war. The story discussed below is dealing with the challenges that happened along the routes of movement from FOB to area of operation.
2. For a coalition soldier nowhere was safe. There was always the possibility of engagement from objects in or near the road or from attackers adjacent to the road. Every movement was deliberate and required thought and risk mitigation.
3. Every unit left behind some level of rear detachment and family members met in organizations called family readiness groups. This was the official way for unit leaders to communicate with family members back home about the status of the unit and issues that affected the entire unit. Individual issues were handled through email, Skype, or in the case of official notifications of death or injury through casualty-notification officers designated from the parent organization. In the case of a death, these notification officers were dispatched to notify the family in person of the soldier's passing. Additionally, unit leaders typically sent letters to the families of fallen soldiers expressing their condolences and their gratitude.
4. Soldiers often use the euphemism "kinetic" to designate lethal fire. Because moving objects have kinetic energy munitions such as bullets, artillery rounds, and bombs are kinetic weapons. Kinetic activity or kinetic operations involve the use of such weaponry or the risk of injury or death from enemy action involving them. In this sense an IED is a kinetic engagement.
5. Military personnel use code names for various features. Most roads in Iraq had code-name designations. These were rarely, if ever, the Iraqi name for the road. Usually they were memorable and linked to American culture, for example, sports teams, beverages, animals.

Document 19: Excerpt from Interview with Hans Hull, First Sergeant for C Company, 1st Battalion, 12th Infantry

Question: How kinetic was the activity at this time?
Answer: It was kinetic to a degree. We would have little fights from time to time, but they were very short and sharp . . . We had a lot more experience with indirect

fires, mortars, rockets, IEDs. Though once in a while, we did get into a small arms fight.

Question: Was there a lot of IEDs at this time?

Answer: There were a lot of IEDs . . . personally, our company would run into two or three IEDs every week. Though . . . in our . . . two or three battalion sector, somebody was getting hit on a daily basis . . .

Question: Were the IEDs big enough that they would damage the tanks or have you run into any explosively formed penetrators (EFPs) at this point?

Answer: We wouldn't run into EFPs until later in the year. Christmas day was the first day we went on patrols and from Christmas until about . . . mid-February of 2006, when we had the outpost, we ran into quite a few IEDs. Typically, 155 mm shells, artillery shells, a number of 125 mm buried tank projectiles. These were buried under the road. Route Redwings, a couple years before, had been an unpaved country road and one of the previous divisions had contracted to have the road paved. Unfortunately, and . . . I don't really know the details—somehow the insurgents were able to lay a large number of IEDs in the road before it was paved. . . . So, basically we were . . . running them out of their ammunition by driving up and down the road. They weren't able to put more, but they had quite a few to go off of. Now as far as damage goes, they would typically damage the running gear of the tanks, . . . but tanks would suffer a lot of damage from running gear. Bradley's would suffer damage from running gear. We did have half an attached mortar platoon with us and I really feared for them, because all they had was their [armored] HMMWVs. So, I was hoping they wouldn't get [hit] too hard. A route clearance package came down our road in January. One of our sister tank companies and they lost a tank, literally, to a buried aircraft bomb. So, yes, there were some highly destructive IEDs down there.

Question: Wow. How was your Soldiers morale?

Answer: . . . At the time, morale was pretty good. They were irritated. They really did not like being hit by IEDs. They wanted to get into a straight up fight so they could shoot at somebody if they needed to . . .

Question: Looking over your deployment experience is there any specific memories that stand out?

Answer: Oh, wow. Yeah. There are a few. Probably the starkest is people we lost. One of our Infantry squad leaders was killed in a fight and I had to go identify him. That stands out. I don't want to focus on all the bad things, but the tank that was blown up, Delta 2–3, SSG Chase and PFC Wagler were killed. I remember, even though SSG Chase was in a different company, I remember talking to him. He was a good guy. That was very stark, because when that tank was lost, I was part of the folks that went out there to pick up the pieces. Yeah, that's pretty tough. Another would be our loss of SSG Christopher Schornak, a squad leader in our attached mechanized Infantry platoon. On 26 February 2006, the platoon was involved in a nighttime cordon and search in sector, looking for a local insurgent leader. SSG Schornak's squad surprised two enemy mortar teams that were trying to escape the area, and the squad, supported by the platoon, killed several insurgents and scattered the rest. Unfortunately, while he was directing the squad against the insurgents, SSG Schornak was hit by enemy rifle fire and killed. SSG Schornak's actions allowed the squad to react against the enemy more quickly and prevent more friendly casualties. The second would be the death of 1LT James Lyons, the platoon leader for Second Platoon. On 27 September 2006, while commanding a combined section (two M1A2 tanks and an M1114 HMMWV) near an old sewage treatment plant, he responded to a request for help from a nearby Iraqi National Police patrol. The friendly patrol had come under attack from enemy dismounted fighters, so 1LT Lyons brought his section forward to hit the enemy with heavier weapons. During the fighting which was at very close quarters among palm groves and farm buildings, 1LT Lyons, who was manning his machine gun at the hatch of his tank, was hit and killed by enemy fire. The rest of the Soldiers in the section kept the enemy pinned down in a nearby palm grove until a combination of the rest of C Co and supporting attack helicopters could arrive and join the fight. 1LT Lyon's actions took the pressure off of the friendly Iraqi forces and allowed C Co to defeat the enemy. Both of these leaders were well liked in the company and we all took it pretty hard. But as we had to, we said our goodbyes and continued the mission. Finally, a very, very, I guess, momentous moment was in October of that year, when the Mahdi Militia was able to drop mortar rounds into our ammunition supply point. They set it on fire. The fire department was unable to put it out and we got a ringside seat to watch an ammunition supply point burn for, I don't know, 12/13 hours and blow up. It was very, very—I don't want to minimize it. I don't want to say entertaining, though, different groups of people might see it differently. Yes, it stood out. It was very, very—you'll remember something like that.

Question: I'm assuming you weren't too close to that.

Answer: We were 300 meters away. We couldn't go anyway. So, we sat next to a burning ammunition dump for about 12/13 hours. It'll get your attention to be sure.

Question: Is there anything else you'd like to add that we haven't covered?

Answer: . . . As a leader, making sure that Soldiers are doing the right thing, whether it's checking on a weapon, whether it's making sure somebodies awake on their guard post, whether they're doing maintenance on their vehicle, whether they're making sure their Soldiers hydrated or maybe just calling home. Leaders checking on each other and checking on Soldiers, I think is really very important. That's something I'd have to add. That also includes the right arm checking on the leader. Like, I'd check on the [company commander] to make sure he was squared. He wasn't running down. He didn't have something that he couldn't handle, because, of course, the first sergeant and the CO have to be—have a tight working relationship. Because, if those leaders, someone isn't looking out for them, they can get run down too.

Source: Hans Hull. Interview by Lisa Beckenbaugh, June 26, 2014. Interview Transcript. Courtesy of the Operational Leadership Experiences Digital Collection, Combat

Studies Institute, Fort Leavenworth, KS. Available at: http://cgsc.contentdm.oclc.org/cdm/singleitem/collection/p4013coll13/id/3192/rec/1 (accessed June 16, 2015).

AFTERMATH

Most U.S. units arrived in Iraq, did their work in their assigned area for however long they were deployed, and then they went home. Depending on the time of the war this became something of a routine for soldiers: prepare to deploy to theater, deploy and do your mission, return from theater and recover equipment, rest with family, and then get ready to do it all over again. The casualties mentioned in this piece get at some of the personal aspects of the loss felt by fellow soldiers for the 4,803 U.S soldiers who died during their service in Iraq. Those numbers include both hostile and nonhostile deaths which is a distinction without a difference as the death of a fellow-soldier is a personal loss for each of those who serve with them regardless of the reason for the loss.

ASK YOURSELF

1. How might the need to traverse the same route every day when soldiers have died on that road affect a person over time? Even if a soldier doesn't personally experience direct fire engagement can this daily stress result in the same posttraumatic stress experienced from specific episodes of trauma?
2. Hans Hull mentions that soldiers wanted to face their opponents. How might an unseen opponent effect how soldiers perceive risk, threat, and the local populace? What effect might it have on the stress level of soldiers?

TOPICS TO CONSIDER

1. On November 19, 2005, 24 Iraqis, including women, children, and elderly, were killed by U.S. Marines. This event is referred to as the Haditha killings or massacre. Initial reports indicated that 15 of the people were killed by a roadside blast and eight were killed by the marines when they returned fire following the roadside bomb detonation. Some have suggested that the Marines lost control when one of their fellow Marines was killed in the blast. An investigation, prompted by media reports, concluded that Marines killed unarmed civilians in the engagement. Part of the power insurgents wield against state militaries is their ability to disperse and hide among the populace. Is such a reaction justified in an environment where the enemy is often hidden within the crowd?
2. Consider how often media coverage of an event determines the seriousness of the event. In other words, those events singled out by the media as significant often receive more legal and political attention than other similarly heinous or unfortunate events. Atrocities happen every day around the world, but many of them go unknown to the general public.
3. On March 12, 2006, five soldiers from the 502nd Infantry Regiment operating close to the town of Mahmudiyah killed the parents and family of a 14-year-old Iraqi girl and then raped and murdered the girl. The girl lived in a home about

200 meters from a six-person checkpoint. According to reports five of the soldiers left the checkpoint with the intent to rape the girl who they had watched over the preceding days and weeks. Two of the soldiers were convicted of the crimes and three others plead guilty. As with the event above, consider the long-term impact of serving in an environment where the enemy is unseen and the culture is foreign. This separation of us and them can create an environment where those perceived as "them" are no longer viewed as equal in terms of consideration, rights, or propriety.

Further Reading

Al-Ali, Zaid. *The Struggle for Iraq's Future: How Corruption, Incompetence and Sectarianism Have Undermined Democracy.* New Haven, CT: Yale University Press, 2014.

Bolger, Daniel P. *Why We Lost: A General's Inside Account of the Iraq and Afghanistan Wars.* Boston: Houghton Mifflin Harcourt, 2014.

Frederick, Jim. *Black Hearts: One Platoon's Descent into Madness in Iraq's Triangle of Death.* New York: Broadway Paperbacks, 2010.

Woodward, Bob. *State of Denial: Bush at War, Part III.* New York: Simon & Schuster, 2006.

Websites

Green, Steven D. Court Statement of Steven D. Green as part of the court martial for the rape and murder of Abeer Qasem Hamza. http://i.cdn.turner.com/cnn/2009/images/05/28/statement.pdf (accessed June 16, 2015).

The War Profiteers—War Crimes, Kidnappings & Torture. "The Massacre of Haditha—The Revenge Killing of 24 Iraqi Civilians." The War Profiteers—War Crimes, Kidnappings & Torture, Killing of Iraqi Civilians Index. http://www.expose-the-war-profiteers.org/DOD/iraq_II/haditha.htm (accessed June 16, 2015).

Tilghman, Andrew. "I came over here because I wanted to kill people." *Washington Post*, June 30, 2006. http://i.cdn.turner.com/cnn/2009/images/05/28/statement.pdf (accessed June 16, 2006).

Films and Television

American Sniper. Director: Clint Eastwood. Warner Bros., 2014.

American War Generals. Executive producers: Peter Bergen, Tresha Mabile, Jonathan Towers. National Geographic Channel, 2014.

Frontline: Bush's War. Director: Michael Kirk. PBS, 2008.

Generation Kill. Director: Susanna White, Simon Cellan Jones. Blown Deadline Productions, 2008.

20. British Perspective in Basra (2): Johnny Austin

INTRODUCTION

This chapter updates events in Basra from those described in Chapter 6. The subject of this chapter remained with his same unit from the earlier chapter—1st Battalion, Royal Regiment of Fusiliers—serving as the battalion operations officer. In this deployment the battalion was the reserve for the 1st U.K. Armored Division. This meant that they provided the response force as well as the muscle for capture missions. The battalion did not have the same area of operations throughout the deployment, nor did they have the same interpreters.

Basra changed from the 2003 deployment. There was more violence and Shia militias had taken over control of the city with respect to governance issues. This played out in the intimidation and murder of interpreters and the change in how participation or support of the coalition was perceived by the local populace. The British did not deploy the same logistics support as U.S. forces and therefore lived in a more austere environment.

British officers have experience with terrorism from their deployments to Northern Ireland. This led to a particular view toward the phenomenon that shaped how the units addressed the problem and how British forces interacted with the populace. Readers will note a particular tone with respect to dealing with Iraqis and Iraqi culture.

KEEP IN MIND AS YOU READ

1. Not all Iraqis are the same. The people in Basra are not simply different than the people in Baghdad because of sectarian or tribal differences. There is also a dramatic difference in culture and history. Many of the tribes around Basra are linked with marsh Arabs. These are people who lived in the marshes along the Shat al-Arab—the confluence of the Tigris and Euphrates Rivers—and developed a lifestyle manifestly different from the desert Bedouin lifestyle significant elsewhere in Iraq. These people were harshly treated by Saddam Hussein who drained much of the marshes to better be able to control them.

2. In 2003 the Iraqi population in Basra was generally welcoming to the British, and the British force in and around the city was less aggressive and force oriented than U.S. forces elsewhere in Iraq. This led to a hands-off approach, in comparison

with U.S. leaders, which seemed to be working. By 2005 that approach was no longer effective as militias infiltrated the government and the society and began to regularly attack coalition bases. The softer approach now turned into a hard approach with a lot of emphasis on capturing and interrogating hostiles.

Document 20: Excerpt from Interview with Johnny Austin, Battalion Operations Officer with 1st Battalion, Royal Regiment of Fusiliers

Question: In terms of the partnership and mentoring that you found yourself doing, was there a visible improvement over the period of time that you worked with the Iraqi Border Police?

Answer: . . . The problem is that the Iraqi Security Forces are like an elastic band. You can stretch them so far through training but as soon as you let them go, they'll revert back to their normal shape and size. Culturally, they're very different than us and it was hard to impress upon them the importance of certain things. They were very impressed by new pieces of equipment but they weren't necessarily impressed by new pieces of instruction or new information. Their general call was, "If you buy us this, we'll be able to do it better." Having seen them go through their version of the military decision-making process (MDMP), it appears to be a very autocratic style of leadership. I watched a general plan the entire operation and not tell anyone about it until its execution. Funny enough, it worked. Maybe that is a lesson. It's very easy to impose our way of doing things on these people, but culturally it probably doesn't sit well with them. They don't want to be inclusive because knowledge is power. It was interesting for me to see how the general did his planning and how he briefed it. If that happened in the British Army or the American Army, I'm sure the operation would not have been as successful, because no one knew what the hell was going on. Yet because of operational security reasons and because of the culture, it seemed to work, which was a real surprise for me. That sort of changed my opinion of making them do everything in a Western way. Maybe they just need to do it in as efficient a way as they can.

Question: How was interpreter support this time around?

Answer: It was problematic. Clearly, intimidation was a huge problem. In the timeframe of two years, we'd gone from guys wandering around with force protection issues whatsoever, walking to work every day, to interpreters not being willing to show their faces and having to live inside the camp for their period of duty. We then had to provide methods to reinsert them back into their normal lives. There was a huge spate of executions in Basra of expected and real interpreters and they were persecuted pretty badly. As a result, the number of interpreters dropped off. The system was difficult for us and it was run at the division and brigade level. On our first deployment to Iraq, we were able to recruit our own interpreters and take care of them ourselves, which makes a big difference.

They become almost part of your equipment and you treat them better. When you're just calling on resources, the relationship between the guy who needed interpretation and the guy who is facilitating wasn't as good as it could have been. It was literally like we signed an interpreter out of a store and took him to do his job. We were lucky, though, in that we were allowed to hold onto ours for a longer period due to our notice-to-move times. We had a camp within a camp where the interpreters lived and when we needed them, we dragged them out, much to their chagrin. Operational security was a huge thing to them. They felt like they needed to be told things, so they could then focus on what they needed to do, but we couldn't do that because of the sensitivity of the operations we were conducting. Invariably, we'd drag one of them kicking and screaming out of his bed at a stupid time in the morning and stick him in the back of the vehicle. They aren't the most compliant after that.

Question: If you could make a recommendation to the British Army based on this deployment, what would you tell them to do?

Answer: I wouldn't have pursued the strategy that we've been following since our initial invasion into Iraq. We've gotten ourselves into a position now where we've distanced ourselves from the Iraqi population. I know that the plan was to transition to provincial Iraqi control and that counterinsurgency forces can be seen as more of a problem than a solution, but we allowed ourselves to be too politically correct, to allow the people in southern Iraq to have more determination than they really needed. As a result, we have these horrible infighting struggles. I'm a great believer that Iraqis, when they step out of line, they need a smack. You don't have to go over the top, but if you can prove that you're stronger than them, they'll keep the lid on things—and that's something we lost after our first deployment. We allowed the conditions to change within the city to a degree where the insurgents felt able to operate with impunity. I don't think it was until we came back in 2005–2006 that major arrests started to happen. Clearly that was the result of intelligence being built up over time, but if we hadn't allowed that situation to be created, there wouldn't have been that situation in the first place. From the time I left Basra in June 2003 until I got back in October 2005, I was shocked at how things had deteriorated. It was disappointing to me because I'd been welcomed with open arms and I could do anything I wanted in the city in 2003. That wasn't the case in 2005. In my opinion, that was clearly because we were rushing things too quickly.

Source: Johnny Austin. Interview by Laurence Lessard, May 7, 2008. Interview Transcript. Courtesy of the Operational Leadership Experiences Digital Collection, Combat Studies Institute, Fort Leavenworth, KS. Available at: http://cgsc.contentdm.oclc.org/cdm/singleitem/collection/p4013coll13/id/1057/rec/2 (accessed June 17, 2015).

AFTERMATH

Basra continued to be a challenge throughput Operation Iraqi Freedom. In 2008 the militias took over the city and the Iraqi Army, led by the prime minister deployed a large force to fight against this usurpation by nongovernment organizations. The 2008 operation was called the Charge of the Knights and will figure in Chapter 34.

ASK YOURSELF

1. Why do British forces handle problems differently? What is it about their current situation and history that informs and empowers them to make different decisions and that leads toward this different worldview?

2. How important is the relationship between interpreters and the soldiers they support? Austin gives some great points about the difference between a person who works with you all the time and one who is viewed as a temporary assistant or resource.

TOPICS TO CONSIDER

1. In discussions of occupations the word choice and analogies often used are similar to comments on parenting and the role of different forms of discipline in raising a child. On its surface this is condescending toward the population being occupied as they are the children in the analogy and the occupiers are the parents. In the excerpt mentioned earlier there is a comment about when the Iraqis step out of line "they need a smack." How might this mindset affect the relationship between occupier and occupied? Consider other occupations (e.g., U.S. forces in Germany and Japan following the end of World War II, Soviet forces in Eastern Europe during the Cold War, French forces in North Africa, or British forces in the Middle East) over the course of history. Is this analogy used in those discussions as well?

Further Reading

Stewart, Rory. *The Prince of the Marshes.* New York: Recorded Books, LLC, 2007.

Synnott, Hilary. *Bad Days in Basra: My Turbulent Time as Britain's Man in Southern Iraq.* New York: Palmgrave Macmillan, 2008.

Website

Democratic Policy and Communications Center. "Iraq by the Numbers." December 19, 2011. www.dpc.senate.gov/docs/fs-112-1-36.pdf (accessed June 12, 2015).

21. Iraqi Advisor to U.S. Military Personnel (2): Nasier Abadi

INTRODUCTION

This is the second iteration of comments from Lieutenant General Nasier Abadi. The first appears in Chapter 11. As a reminder, General Abadi was the deputy chief of staff of the Iraqi Joint Forces, the second ranking officer in the Iraqi Military. When coalition forces arrived in Iraq he was retired. He was subsequently recalled to active duty where he provided advice to coalition forces and served in senior positions. In this chapter he elucidates differences in culture between the U.S. personnel with whom he worked and Iraqis.

KEEP IN MIND AS YOU READ

1. Much of this book is telling the Iraq War from a coalition perspective. Here is refection on different ways of seeing the same problems. There is not simply a single perspective or a single solution. This is about developing a complete perspective of the entirety of the problems involved, seeing the complexity of a complex situation.
2. It is through differences that the multidimensional problem can be perceived. Knowing and understanding the different perspectives matters. Iraqis do not come from an immigrant society where everyone's immediate or distant relatives left their extended families to risk a new environment and experience new things. They are surrounded by their immediate family, extended family, and tribes. They are firmly rooted in tradition. Those connections are much more significant to them than accomplishing tasks.

Document 21: Excerpt from Interview with
Nasier Abadi, August 2005

Question: How are Iraqi and coalition cultures different and how has that impacted security efforts?

Answer: I think that the way each considers time is the big difference. The coalition follows the advice of Francis Bacon, "To choose time is to save time". The coalition is very time and schedule dependent, while Iraqis follow John Milton, "Conversing I forgot all time." Meaning that Iraqis are more relaxed about time and keeping to a schedule and they can talk on and on and on. That was an aftermath of what we had in the old regime. If you did not want to make a decision, you make a committee and let it linger for months at a time.

The other thing is that the coalition does things professionally while in Iraq we are more aware of relationships and that is the starting point for everything. A person will go back to where he comes from and who he knows and his status. Family ties and tribal affiliations are very important to Iraqis, sometimes more important than merit and qualifications. When you meet someone he will say, for example, I am Hamid, son of so, son of so, and son of so, from a certain tribe. You are supposed to have the same description, since that is who you are and not your qualifications. Now, we have something more that has come up with democracy. We have political parties and each political party is pushing their candidate to be the representative. Even in the military we have political candidates.

Question: What can the coalition learn from the Iraqis?

Answer: The coalition must focus on relationships and developing partnerships. When in Rome, do as the Romans do. When they are here they have to consider this aspect, and listen to Iraqi input and learn from their knowledge of their own country and how things are done. Iraqis operate at a much slower pace and they take more time in order to gain an understanding. The coalition can also learn better from the Iraqis in the intelligence sector. The coalition has the technology, but the Iraqis can gather and assess human intelligence better. So, I think we should have the lead in this area.

Question: What can Iraqis learn from the coalition?

Answer: Iraqis can learn to focus on merit and qualification in assignment and promotions, and not political and tribal affiliations. We can work to eliminate corruption which we inherited from before and is still creeping into the Armed Forces. The use of technology is also important, as is the development of systems, doctrine and procedures so success is not just dependent on personality. There has to be robust processes so the Iraqis can deliver and succeed.

Question: How can we better bridge the cultural gap and take the best of both cultures to ensure success?

Answer: We need time for the learning process to take place. Teamwork—when we are together, we both learn from one another and I think teamwork is foremost in this. Building trust and confidence in each other when we work together, and teamwork improves the trust and confidence. Then listening and seeking to understand each other. Iraqis love to talk and Americans have a way of listening because that's the way they are. When someone is speaking they listen. But the Iraqis keep on talking and they never stop. Because the coalition is time conscious, the meeting is over and the coalition has had . . . very little time to talk since the Iraqis use all the time and nothing has been accomplished. From that, you come to having patience on both sides to tolerate each other and a big heart and the will to bridge the gap. I think these are very important to help us succeed.

Source: Nasier Abadi. Interview by David J. Conboy, August 2005. "An Interview with Lieutenant General Nasier Abadi, Deputy Chief of Staff, Iraqi Joint Forces." U.S. Army War College, Carlisle Barracks, Pennsylvania. Interview Transcript. Courtesy of the Operational Leadership Experiences Digital Collection, Combat Studies Institute, Fort Leavenworth, KS.

AFTERMATH

Throughout the U.S. and coalition occupation of Iraq there was tension in the cross-cultural relationships. Training for deploying personnel tended to be very specific and technical in terms of phrases in the local language and cultural do's and don'ts or they tended to be academic in terms of explaining the various tribal affiliations and regions where those tribes had influence. Few deployed soldiers learned Arabic or Kurdish and many never left their coalition-only forward operating bases. Those who worked directly with Iraqis continually struggled with the differences described earlier.

To this day U.S. forces continue to fail when it comes to creating solutions that work for both the coalition and the Iraqis. The reasons for this vary, but some might include that U.S. military tends to force Iraqis to act on our timeline and do not take into account what truly matters within the Iraqi culture. This is a way of forcing U.S. perspective on Iraqis. Instead of solving the problems that exist the foreign force often adds to them by failing to see the cultural consequences of decisions and actions.

ASK YOURSELF

1. The differences between the coalition forces perspective and that of the Iraqis weren't semantic differences or differences of opinions, but rather radically different perspectives for viewing the same problem combined with radically different approaches to solving them. Why did coalition-force soldiers and leaders miss the significance of these cultural differences?

TOPICS TO CONSIDER

1. Culture is something beyond surface-level behaviors of clothing, food preferences, or language. It is inherent in shaping how people perceive and identify the world.

It is what makes a person who they are. This isn't about whether a person favors the Dallas Cowboys or the Seattle Seahawks. Nor is it about whether a person prefers American Football over Soccer. This is a core intellectual issue of perception and identity. Is it even possible for a person from one culture to truly understand and empathize with a person from another culture? It's easy to see what is wrong with other people's perspective. It's very difficult to recognize the flaws in your own. General Abadi seems to get it. He is able to identify the flaws and strengths within his own culture as well as that of the coalition. He is broad minded, but he is rare. Readers should brainstorm a plan for helping each side to work more effectively with the other—the teamwork that General Abadi refers to.

2. What is the connection between nepotism and corruption? Why is merit an important factor in selecting leaders?

Further Reading

Al-Ali, Zaid. *The Struggle for Iraq's Future: How Corruption, Incompetence and Sectarianism Have Undermined Democracy*. New Haven, CT: Yale University Press, 2014.

Bolger, Daniel P. *Why We Lost: A General's Inside Account of the Iraq and Afghanistan Wars*. Boston: Houghton Mifflin Harcourt, 2014.

Steed, Brian L. *Bees and Spiders: Applied Cultural Awareness and the Art of Cross-Cultural Influence*. Houston: Strategic Book Publishing & Rights Agency, LLC, 2014.

Woodward, Bob. *State of Denial: Bush at War, Part III*. New York: Simon & Schuster, 2006.

Films and Television

American War Generals. Executive producers: Peter Bergen, Tresha Mabile, Jonathan Towers. National Geographic Channel, 2014.

Frontline: Bush's War. Director: Michael Kirk. PBS, 2008.

22. Training the Iraqi Security Forces: David Petraeus

INTRODUCTION

Multi-National Security Transition Command-Iraq or MNSTC-I (pronounced "min-sticky") was the subordinate element of Multi-National Forces-Iraq (MNF-I) given the responsibility for developing, organizing, training, equipping, and sustaining the Iraqi Security Forces that included forces from the Ministry of Defense (MoD; including standard military services—army, navy, air force), Ministry of Interior (MoI; including the police: national, federal, and border), and counter terrorism services (CTS).

The command was established in 2004 with then Lieutenant General Petraeus as the commander. Other commanders followed as indicated below. The impetus for the command was the realization that Iraq needed to have a much more robust and capable security service than they would be able to build on their own. Additionally, the increase in violence in Iraq during this period meant that Iraq did not have the time or the luxury of security to create the institutions and organizations that it needed without significant outside assistance. MNSTC-I provided that assistance by coordinating all the efforts of the coalition countries into a consolidated whole.

The subject of this chapter is David Petraeus who was at the time of the interview was the commander of the Combined Arms Center at Fort Leavenworth, Kansas. He was then responsible for the training and education of nearly all U.S. forces. Previously he was the commander of the 101st Airborne Division during the invasion of Iraq and he finished his involvement in Iraq for that tour in the city of Mosul. He returned to Iraq as the MNSTC-I commander and began or expanded many of the training and development programs used to create and improve the Iraqi Security Forces. At the Combined Arms Center he was instrumental in publishing the counterinsurgency doctrine for the U.S. Army. He returned to Iraq as the MNF-I commander in 2007.

COMMANDERS OF MNSTC-I

David Petraeus	2004–2005	Martin E. Dempsey	2005–2007
James M. Dubik	2007–2008	Frank Helmick	2008–2009
Michael D. Barbero	2009–2010		

KEEP IN MIND AS YOU READ

1. The strategy for U.S. and coalition departure from Iraq was essentially for Iraqi forces to stand up as U.S. and coalition forces departed the country. That was the concept. This was not practical because the increase in violence tended to parallel the increase in trained Iraqi forces thus creating a continual need for additional forces along the way.

2. The U.S. and coalition countries trained hundreds of thousands of Iraqi military and police forces. At times, the insurgents and those in opposition to the coalition focused attacks on recruiting stations and buses of trainees to discourage people from joining the forces. This created an enormous task of logistics and training management. In many cases individuals or units completed training only to go immediately into some operation where they were under hostile fire within days or even hours.

3. The United States had organization that focused on training the U.S. National Guard and Reserve forces. Most of the units so designated existed within the National Guard and Reserve organization itself with some officers from the active duty component. The units mentioned in this interview who were responsible for training the Iraqis came from the reserve component. During this period the active component was standing up advise and assist teams who worked directly with Iraqi headquarters to assist in coordinating what the United States often called enablers—fire support, surveillance, signal communication, etc.—as well as provide advice on unit training. This interview is focused on the deployment of the 98th Division, which is a training unit from the U.S. Army Reserve.

Document 22: Excerpt from Interview with David Petraeus, MNSTC-I Commander, 2004–2005

Question: What was the purpose of [the trip in April/May 2004] and what was the upshot of the briefing you later gave General Abizaid on the state of the Iraqi Army?

Answer: This trip was in the wake of the poor performance in early April of the Iraqi Security Forces (ISF) as a whole—the forces of the Ministry of Interior (MOI) as well as the Ministry of Defense (MOD)—when violence broke out all over the country, incited by Moqtada al-Sadr's militia in a number of southern cities and eastern Baghdad, and also by Sunni-Arab insurgents, whose actions included the hanging of contractors in the city of Fallujah in early April. We spent about three weeks over there with a team of about a dozen commissioned and noncommissioned officers from the 101st Airborne Division who had all recently returned from Iraq in mid to late February. We were there to assess the different components of the ISF at that time, and what we found was very uneven quality among the forces. On the army side, you had no national forces at that point in time—and the one or two battalions they did have refused to go into combat in Fallujah when they were ordered in. Granted, it was a little more complex than that, but the bottom line was they didn't get into the fight. There was a cobbled-together unit called the Commando Battalion, which was a mix of different militias from the political parties that did actually do some fighting in Fallujah, and some of their members were even wounded. But by and large it did not stay on the line very long.

There were also Iraqi Civil Defense Corps (ICDC) units that were stood up by the six different coalition divisions. At that time, there was not a directed program of much detail from Combined Joint Task Force 7 (CJTF-7), or at least there hadn't been sufficient time to have real standardization across all these units. Some of these units had been treated more like real military units, for example by the British division, the 101st and later by Task Force Olympia in the north. They got their forces proper bases, paid them on time, scraped together all the equipment they could for them and partnered them with coalition forces. They would use the companies for three weeks and would then allow them their one week of leave, which enabled them to have a good battle rhythm. This worked pretty well, and the forces in those areas did relatively well in the outbreak of violence in early April. In other areas, though, where they weren't able to build the infrastructure that was required to have true bases and had a different approach, they were much less effective. The soldiers would have to walk to work in the morning and walk home at night, and sometimes the security situation in those areas was such that they found it difficult to get to work, much less to actually fight.

The Coalition Military Assistance Training Team (CMATT) was responsible for the national effort and divisions were responsible for the ICDC effort, which, by the way, we had a conference on while we were there around 1 May and all came to agreement on 10 principles for the ICDC. The Combat Studies Institute has these, incidentally. Anyway, these principles actually provided a pretty good way ahead for the ICDC, which eventually became the Iraqi National Guard and was later integrated into the Iraqi Army. The police side was being overseen by an element of the Coalition Provisional Authority (CPA). (CPA also oversaw CMATT.) That element was a mix of some soldiers—some of whom actually had experience with policing, but most did not—and some civilians who had experience in law enforcement or in actual policing. That was even more uneven and in need of additional resources, emphasis and so forth. Across the board there was a lack of the infrastructure necessary. The soldiers were not equipped adequately, they didn't have enough vehicles and there were all kinds of logistical challenges. There were also no institutions over them. A true MOD didn't exist at all and the MOI was nascent, to put it mildly. So we did that assessment, offered those observations to General Abizaid, and then I went back to Fort Campbell to resume being commander of the 101st. I got a call a couple weeks later and was told to change command out early in May and get back over to Iraq as soon as I could. So I went back to Iraq and took command of what would come to be MNSTC-I in early June.

[The Foreign Army-Training Assistance Command (FA-TRAC)] was essentially a proposal whereby one of the institutional training divisions (DIVITs) of the US Army Reserve could take on the same mission that MNSTC-I was about to embark on. . . . The 98th provided a substantial number of the officers who populated the staffs and headquarters of MNSTC-I, CMATT and the Civilian Police Assistance Training Team (CPATT). They also provided advisor teams for a substantial number of Iraqi combat, training and base support units. Over time, they additionally provided some advisors for logistical transportation units, various branch schools, the basic training program, and NCO academy courses as well. As the Iraqi units grew, the advisors—and the Iraqis—took on more and more responsibility. The 98th also provided advisors all the way up to the joint headquarters of the Iraqi MOD, which is about as high as we went at that time. . . .

The advisor team would marry up with the Iraqi battalion, originally with its officers. They'd go through training and prep with them to prepare for the conduct of basic training, after which the soldiers joined the leaders, and the advisors watched and helped as the Iraqis went through basic training for a couple months. Then they did some small unit collective training and followed that by actually stepping outside the wire. . . .

We would need them to fill a variety of staff billets, fill a number of advisor teams for combat units, base support units and others, then finally the training elements. They could also provide other elements that were sort of swing teams that we could send to help train staffs in different areas, in base support units, as well as echelons above battalion. It wasn't just battalion advisor teams; it was advisors for the headquarters of brigades, divisions and the rest. . . .

This was a "one off" organization, and again I didn't get to bring the 101st headquarters over with all its assets to serve as its nucleus. We got things more one piece at a time. The 98th did plug in a lot of stuff when they arrived, so a lot of their division staff did come. They brought their lawyers, for example, and people for a variety of staff sections; but it was certainly not like getting one of the big Active Component division staffs to come in with all their enabler battalions and combat service support units. . . .

They were fortunate to have the opportunity, in most cases, to grow with their Iraqi units. That was very positive for them. As I mentioned, that meant they usually had several months at a minimum to actually grow with their Iraqi units and go through all the basic, advanced and then small unit collective training that the Iraqi units went through before they actually went into combat. . . .

As units became operational, particularly once they settled into an area of operations, their tactical control was transferred to their respective Multi-National Corps-Iraq (MNC-I) unit in whose area they were operating. The feeling was that there needed to be an element in the headquarters of MNC-I that had an administrative responsibility with these transition teams that were out there with the Iraqi units, even though they had a partnership with the unit in whose area they were working, and even though the Iraqi unit they were advising was under the tactical control of the coalition unit. What would happen is, as replacement units would come in, they actually wouldn't even in-process at MNSTC-I. Rather, they would go directly onto the books of replacement advisor teams. They would go directly onto the books of MNC-I or the IAG and then go right out to replace them. That made sense. We still had good visibility of that and still provided the training at the Phoenix Academy, which was a seven- to 10-day final training prep conducted at Taji for all advisor teams. We started it in early 2005 to help make sure people really had a grasp of the situation in Iraq and in the areas they would be working. It was an opportunity to also give them the latest tactics, techniques and procedures (TTPs) that had just emerged or any other issues that were topical at that particular time. I volunteered General Sherlock and his cell, which was basically a 98th Division cell. . . .

Source: David H. Petraeus. Interview by Steven Clay, December 11, 2006. Interview Transcript. Courtesy of the Operational Leadership Experiences Digital Collection, Combat

Studies Institute, Fort Leavenworth, KS. Available at: http://cgsc.contentdm.oclc.org/cdm/singleitem/collection/p4013coll13/id/328/rec/2 (accessed June 18, 2015).

AFTERMATH

Throughout the U.S. occupation of Iraq the U.S. forces trained more than 900,000 Iraqi security force personnel. By the end of U.S. occupation the Iraqi forces were conducting the vast majority of operations throughout the country. In many measures it is possible to see the U.S. occupation as a success. The challenge is that the security forces trained were among those who broke and ran in 2014 when the IS came into Iraq in force.

ASK YOURSELF

1. Is military prowess translatable? Just because the U.S. military does what they do in a good way is it possible to translate those abilities to another force or another culture? As one thinks about the events described earlier consider the idea of having United States reserve soldiers who did not have combat experience train Iraqi forces who did have combat experience. This comes across as an interesting twist on the idea that U.S. ideas are more powerful than some other nationality's experience.
2. Was this plan a cure or a bandage? Did training the Iraqi security forces solve the problems plaguing the country or was this simply a way to cover over those problems and use security as an excuse for short-term action when long-term solutions were needed? What is the other way that the coalition could have used to evaluate Iraqi capability?

TOPICS TO CONSIDER

1. U.S. military forces focus on doctrine, education, and training that is expeditionary in nature whereas most other militaries around the world have their defense forces focused on domestic security. The mindset of fighting abroad versus fighting or oppressing at home is deep and significant. Consider the number of militaries that exist to deploy and conduct operations external to their country and those that exist to provide security and stability within their country or only to defend their national borders. What differences might exist in the type of training and tactics required for these different purposes?

Further Reading

Bolger, Daniel P. *Why We Lost: A General's Inside Account of the Iraq and Afghanistan Wars.* Boston: Houghton Mifflin Harcourt, 2014.

Broadwell, Paula. *All In: The Education of General David Petraeus.* New York: Penguin Press, 2012.

Robinson, Linda. *Tell Me How This Ends: General David Petraeus and the Search for a Way Out of Iraq.* New York: PublicAffairs, 2008.

Website

Cordesman, Anthony H., Sam Khazai, and Daniel Dewit. *Shaping Iraq's Security Forces: US-Iranian Competition Series.* Center for Strategic & International Studies. December 16, 2013. csis.org/files/publication/131213_Iraq_Security_Forces.pdf (accessed December 25, 2015).

Films and Television

American War Generals. Executive producers: Peter Bergen, Tresha Mabile, Jonathan Towers. National Geographic Channel, 2014.
Frontline: Bush's War. Director: Michael Kirk. PBS, 2008.

23. Perspectives on the Insurgency: Dan Darling

INTRODUCTION

Dan Darling worked as a civilian analyst for the USMC intelligence activity. He wrote a complete history of the insurgency in al-Anbar Province prior to deploying to Iraq to continue his analysis in theater from 2007 to 2008. He is one of the most well-informed individuals on the dynamics of the insurgency in Iraq.

To understand Anbar Province, the insurgency in Iraq, and, for that matter, Iraqi culture one needs to understand tribal dynamics and the social structure of the Iraqi tribes. The tribes provide much of the thread for the fabric of culture in Iraq. During the control of the Ba'ath Party and especially under Saddam Hussein there was a lot of effort made to degrade the power and influence of the tribes. Once Saddam was removed from power the tribes became much more significant very quickly. Tribes provide much of the social safety net in Iraq. If a person has a problem they seek out their tribal leaders for help; that includes financial, familial, and security assistance. Most people living outside of Baghdad, and especially in al-Anbar Province, worked in family businesses—tribal.

This chapter includes a discussion about the rise of the insurgency and the influence of several key events. Fallujah and the fighting in and around it in 2004 were instrumental to the development of the insurgency. The fighting in April 2004 is where most of the insurgent leaders made their names—where they earned their credibility. Those who survived the fighting in November 2004 continued to direct the actions of the opposition to the coalition and the Shia-led government.

KEEP IN MIND AS YOU READ

1. The toppling of Saddam Hussein unleashed decades of frustration between the Sunni and Shia in Iraq. Some of the historical tensions go back centuries, but Saddam and the Ba'ath Party were dominated by Sunnis. This gave a sense of oppression and humiliation to the Shia and an inflated sense of importance to

the Sunni. Most Americans, when taught about Iraq, hear that Sunnis make up about 20 percent of the population and Shia make up about 60 percent. Sunnis in Iraq believe they are the majority and have been taught that their whole life. They think they are the dominant group and that efforts to say otherwise are part of a conspiracy to humiliate them and to subjugate them to Shia (and typically Persian) authority. What you're taught your whole life does make a difference in how and what you think, even if what you're taught is clearly false.

2. Several significant events in Islamic history happened in Iraq and several of them involved the Sunni–Shia conflict. The al-Askari Shrine is not necessarily a site of the conflict between the sects of Islam, but it is a mausoleum for two venerated Shia Imams. For the most part all Iraqis respect the shrine, but Shia tend to consider it one of the most important shrines in all of Iraq behind only the shrines in Najaf and Karbala. Thus, it is a powerful symbol of the Shia sect. Its bombing by the group led by Abu Musaub al-Zarqawi went a long way toward creating the sectarian civil war between Sunni and Shia in Iraq.

Document 23: Excerpt from Interview with Dan Darling, USMC Intelligence Analyst

Question: April of 2004 and both the significance of it and how pivotal it was in the history of the insurgency . . .

Answer: . . . [P]eople are always looking for sort of a directing intellect, and it was sort of a strategy by committee for lack of a better term. You had a large number of groups who were not natural allies, but who understood that they could do more together than they could separately. So, they were able to bring the heat on the United States across Iraq. I mean, you saw, again, Shi'a Sadrists convoy's, like supply convoys, being sent to Fallujah loaded with fresh weapons, medical supplies . . . basically to keep the guys in Fallujah and helping them to break the siege under the guise of humanitarian aid. Similarly, you saw . . . both Sunni nationalists and jihadists formations go and attack our rear positions. In order to stir up [trouble] down in what would later be called the "Triangle of Death". . . .

[E]veryone involved in that experience became rock stars within the insurgency, because they were seen [opposing coalition forces] . . .

This is the other thing about having a national organization, you have infrastructure. Particularly, the guys in Syria, who had advantage of the sanctuary. They could live—they could think the deep thoughts [because of] it. Al-Zarqawi's group . . . had a Syria-based sanctuary, too, with the foreign fighter networks and some other aspects. They, themselves . . . had a group at the Shura council level that did engage in the sort of deep planning, "How are we going to do this?" That's what gave them the advantage over the local guys, who just had not evolved into that higher level of organization and [were] still thinking day-to-day or month-to-month . . . "We got obsessed with numbers." . . . [I]t's the false comparison to conventional forces. . . .

NICK BERG BEHEADING

On May 11, 2004, a video was released showing five men dressed in black, faces shrouded, and speaking in Arabic and one man sitting on the ground in an orange jumpsuit. The man in the jumpsuit was Nicholas Berg. He was a freelance radio tower repairman who was in Iraq looking for contracts. He had returned from a trip to Mosul in early April and he was last seen on April 10, 2004.

The five men surrounding Nick Berg included Abu Musab al-Zarqawi, who would be the one to decapitate Mr. Berg on the videotape.

The orange jumpsuit was used because that was the same color and type of clothing that prisoners in Guantanamo Bay wore and some who were held at Abu Ghraib. The justification given for the violent act was the recently released photos of prisoner abuse at Abu Ghraib (see Chapter 14 of this book).

Nick Berg's body was found on a Baghdad overpass on May 8, 2004, by a U.S. military patrol.

For the longest time, the Shi'a were told in the south by Sunni insurgent representatives that al-Zarqawi was a boogie man. He was something the US had dreamed up . . . to legitimize our presence. This was even after the Nick Berg video and everything. . . . [T]he cat being out of the bag was when [Osama] bin Laden came out and declared [Abu Musaub al-Zarqawi] his representative in Iraq in October of 2004. . . . "This is my man in Iraq." This made it clear. The other issue is that like out of the Shi'a sort of develop, at least on tribal lines, reached out to their Sunni brethren. . . .

The utter sectarian mindset of al-Zarqawi and frankly his inability to prioritize between the Americans and the Shi'a was probably one of the things that undid him. . . .

Question: So, the Omar Brigade, when does it become public in 2005, again?

Answer: Summer of 2005 is when it became public, but by that point, it already has hundreds of members and stuff like that. This is when he sort of creates it and Omar Hadid, . . . Al-Zarqawi number two in Fallujah, who is critical to his ability to get so closely tied into that town. Omar Hadid was a former member of the Iraqi military, who was involved in a whole host of Salafist activities in Fallujah in the 1990s, including the bombing of a cinema there. After which time, in order to escape arrest, he fled to Afghanistan, where he linked up with al-Zarqawi. After 2001, he went home at the very beginning of Operation Enduring Freedom (OEF) and he resettled himself in the Salafist circles in Fallujah, gaining instant credibility, because he had fought. So, he was critical to al-Zarqawi's ability to have a support network already in place in Fallujah. That's why Fallujah's important the way that other areas just are not. He's got a local guy there who's giving him a window and who has a local following. . . .

[L]ike [in] April 2004, because now you have a pecking order, they get into a hold for most of the next year and even beyond. I would actually say through the entire duration of the insurgency. Some of [the people who fought in Fallujah] were still calling the shots. [It is] like everybody . . . becomes a big shot . . . and now there's sort of an understood pecking order within the insurgency. That's sort of one of the big achievements of the April 2004 [Battle of Fallujah]. . . .

It's like mob stuff. Like all the [c]apos are understood and everyone understands who's a made man. Where before you had sort of competing factions struggling for influence. Now it's understood that like, "This is the way it is." Okay. Now what you see as a result of that, like I said, is you also see sort of a recognition among what I call the . . . neo-Ba'athists, which were people who had formerly been regional power brokers under Saddam Hussein who took advantage of Saddam's divestment of authority prior to the invasion to carve out their own little fiefdoms. This was sort of [a sorting] and you see a lot of those guys go away, who are killed off as a result of the explosion. The ones who survived, you know, again, will continue to be big shots. Their elite status—this is sort of again legitimization moment for them. You also have another aspect, which is later reversed, which is that the neo-Ba'athists, at this point in 2004 well into 2006, have sort of usurped the traditional prerogatives of the tribal leadership. They are now the ones doling out patronage. They are now the ones who are seen as the guys that can get things done. They're providing security. They're seen to like officiate disputes and other types of dynamics. You have the sort of rise, again temporarily, of this new class of people, which had not previously been the case in a lot of locations. Most of these guys having former military or intelligence backgrounds in the sort of bread and butter of Saddam's [military]. . . .

[O]ver the course of like 2005 and particularly the coalition unfortunately sort of shot itself in the foot on this regard, because we went after a number—and we did a very good job in some of these locations of going after nationalist or neo-Ba'athist leadership. . . . 2005 was basically the year that [the] entire Karbead family is taken down. So are [other senior opposition leaders]. . . . So, what this does is it weakens the hand of the nationalist insurgents outside of al-Douri and their ability to resist. Also, at this point, al-Zarqawi, because he's built up this western sort of facilitation network, is able to get easy resupply. People forget this is, that . . . the Syrian regime implemented no financial controls on gulf donations and so for al-Zarqawi's external funding, he was able [to] . . . transfer stuff directly from the gulf to Syria and then have a runner bring it over to Iraq. Then . . . he took over the Mosul mafia. Even though he didn't hold the city, what he gained was a controlling interest in the Mosul mafia. . . .

The . . . official estimates of insurgent manpower were garbage. [Coalition reported] . . . 2k, killed or captured and Fallujah had even more than that. Fallujah we estimate on the order of like 5–7k, killed or captured. If you look at the original numbers that were briefed all the way up to the President of the United States (POTUS) at the time, it was like, "Total manpower of the insurgency is like 3k or 5k." Well, unless they are all in these locations, which is completely inconsistent with the violence. I think that there was a deep reluctance [to admit to the real size of the insurgency when it was] briefed [that] the total manpower of the insurgency as like 100k plus. . . .

[B]y late 2005 in particular . . . you finally start seeing—and this is what we call proto-awakening. . . . The year before—you start seeing tribal leaders very gradually start to attempt to re-assert their influence under the leadership of a guy out west named Sheikh Nasser Kareem al-Fahdawi. Okay, now nobody knows this guy's name, even though he was involved in a lot of the political engagement efforts to try and bring in the nationalists insurgents into the fold in late 2005 and early 2006. The reason nobody knows him is because January 2006 [he was on] a list that was sent to AQI leadership for approval of people to target. They name Sheikh Nasser. . . . "Here's all the nationalist leaders he's meeting with. He's trying to bring them into the fold. Bring them into the government. We have to kill him." It's, in fact, the decision to kill basically, which is why nobody ever knows who he is frankly. . . .

[They didn't] just . . . kill him. They shot him, drug his body behind a car until it was decapitated and then they mounted the head with a plaque underneath it that said, "Mertad" or apostate in central al-Ramadi, right outside on 17th Street. So, just as a public demonstration of power—also that they could do this without anyone stopping. . . .

He's al-Fahdawi out of al-Ramadi. But, he . . . had national credentials. A lot of the Fahdawi's were very well represented in Saddam's armed forces, particularly the regular army and Republican Guard level. As a result, he had sort of prestige and clout from that. He was trying to basically create a coalition that could negotiate with the coalition in good faith. He understood it—okay, "We've got the insurgency. We need a political strategy." You know what I mean. "To gain us power, which means negotiations at some point." . . . [S]o AQI gunned him down. This was—even before . . . they [began] . . . to purge tribal leadership, which is the seed of their eventual destruction. I mean, they killed off a total, I think it's like 45 sheiks in Al Anbar alone. God knows what they did in the rest of the country, that's just because we tallied it up. . . .

[A]ll this is done in 2005 and early 2006. Because what happens—this is part of the reason why it's AQI's concern over this sort of tentative outreach efforts, is one of the decisions that drives the idea of destroying the al-Askari Mosque so that there's no way back. If you want to do something that will so permanently polarize Iraqi society to the point where there's no negotiation. . . . [This] is . . . basically . . . part of the reason. There's no coincidence that immediately during that period they also create their little mujahedeen shura to try and create an Iraqi face. . . .

In an effort to legitimize—now that they achieved their result. Iraqi society is now permanently polarized, now they need to become more representative of Iraq. They can't be seen as a foreign organization, because you have spiked up the polarization so much to a point, you've got to worry about a backlash from that xenophobia too. . . .

There's a great quote from al-Zarqawi on this point, which is like, "Now there can be no more compromise, because there is no compromise after the Golden Mosque. So, we have just sabotaged—we have thrown this . . . ". . . .

[Zarqawi] put Sunni elite in a situation where basically, "What? Are we supposed to negotiate with the people who are killing our brothers en mass in Baghdad? Who stack them up like cord wood? Are you going to negotiate with the genociders of our people?" You see the point.

This goes . . . to the higher order strategy that we miss, because we are only concentrating on our particular AORs [Areas of Responsibility]. So, we're not seeing the whole picture. That's an area where I, frankly, think that the intelligence community let the MNF-I and US national leadership down. We had no knowledge that this was going on, because a lot of these people were just assuming that sectarian violence is like rain. It just happens. . . .

They're smarter than people think. I mean, now to be fair, by the way, the Baathists were fricking terrified by what happened—the al-Askari Mosque stuff. In large part because they understood what had been unleashed. They're still Iraqis at the end of the day. This is the kind of thing that they saw—civil war is always a Baathists [worst nightmare], because the Baathists at the end of the day are Iraqi nationalists. They want a strong Iraq. Unified Iraq. This could lead to Balkanization. They were horrified by what happened. But, they had no choice. Again, you have closed off all avenues at this point. . . .

[I]f you look at the immediate . . . Shi'a reaction to [the al-Askari shrine bombing] . . . You had like 3,000 dead Sunni's within 24 hours. Then 6,000 dead by the end of the week. It just drove home [Zarqawi's point of no return] as well as the internally displaced persons (IDPs). People from al-Ramadi who were going to Salah ad-Din and other majority Sunni areas with . . . horror stories of what had happened to them. This did a lot . . . in [the] ordinary Sunni's minds—and this is where AQI was able to accelerate to achieve—in Al Anbar. Now up in north area [other Sunni leaders] maintained their fiefdoms, but AQI was able to basically establish themselves as the head of the pack. If there was going to be a sectarian fight, we want the biggest, baddest gang on our side. That was sort of AQIs genius. . . . [T]hey had established themselves as people who were utterly ruthless and were willing to do things other groups were not. Now AQI at this point then creates the Mujahedeen Shura Council to put an Iraqi face on it. . . . [T]hey were ordered to do this by Al-Qaeda senior leadership. . . . [Y]ou're going to notice a recurring pattern of behavior here—they start believing their own press. What they set out to do is they begin to implement what I can only describe as an Islamic Khmer Rouge-esque pattern of behavior. Where they . . . target the leadership of any tribe that refuses to swear loyalty on a systematic basis. I mean, tribal leaders have been killed before but it was a one on/one off kind of thing. It wasn't a deliberate policy. Here it was submit or die. Literally, they did stuff like burn sheiks alive who refused. Held them down and a guy would just chain them on two sides and a guy would come with a flamethrower and just charbroil them alive right outside his house. They would kill his kids and dump them in an ice chest and just roll them around. That was the kind of stuff that was done. . . .

Source: Dan Darling. Interview by Frank Sopcheck, May 18, 2014. Interview Transcript. Courtesy of the Operational Leadership Experiences Digital Collection, Combat Studies Institute, Fort Leavenworth, KS. Available at: http://cgsc.contentdm.oclc.org/cdm/singleitem/collection/p4013coll13/id/3249/rec/1 (accessed July 21, 2015).

AFTERMATH

Abu Musab al-Zarqawi was killed by a U.S. drone strike in 2006. The sectarian civil war that was inspired by the attack on the al-Askari Shrine was unleashed and people were dying by the hundreds on a weekly basis. This was the environment that caused the change in U.S. civilian and military leadership and what possibly cost the Republicans the 2006 midterm elections. The environment was intensely negative and it looked like Iraq would be lost to the extreme violence and reprisals to violence. As Zarqawi wanted the Shia were now full participants in fighting the Sunnis and fighting the coalition. The coalition was forced to fight on multiple fronts simultaneously and struggled to fully understand what was happening and who was the enemy.

ASK YOURSELF

1. Are religious symbols important? The al-Askari Shrine was a mausoleum for two dead people who were respected in a religion. It is difficult sometimes to imagine how the destruction of a structure could cause civil war, but it is important to understand the significance placed on religious symbols within the faith of the people.
2. Why follow a Jordanian in Iraq? Zarqawi was not Iraqi, but he became the single most significant leader in the fighting for about a year. What was it about Zarqawi that made people follow him?

TOPICS TO CONSIDER

1. During the 19th century in America the U.S. Army fought a series of tribal groups on the Great Plains. The warrior-leaders from the Indian tribes were not commanders. They did not direct the actions of a fixed number of warriors. Warriors rode with Crazy Horse or Two Moons or any other leader because that person was effective in battle and he had *good medicine* in the fight. A warrior wanted to be with such a person because they brought honor and glory. This understanding is useful when considering how tribes "organize" for fighting. It is not nearly as bureaucratic as Western militaries. How does what happened in Iraq compare with the American military's experience during the Indian Wars?

Further Reading

Al-Ali, Zaid. *The Struggle for Iraq's Future: How Corruption, Incompetence and Sectarianism Have Undermined Democracy*. New Haven, CT: Yale University Press, 2014.

West, Bing. *No True Glory: A Frontline Account of the Battle for Fallujah*. New York: Bantam Books, 2005.

Films and Television

American War Generals. Executive producers: Peter Bergen, Tresha Mabile, Jonathan Towers. National Geographic Channel, 2014.

Frontline: Bush's War. Director: Michael Kirk. PBS, 2008.

24. Contractors in War—
Blackwater: Erik Prince

INTRODUCTION

One of the most significant transformations in armed conflict that was evident in the Iraq War was the increase in private security and intelligence contractors. The U.S. government made conscious choices to move a lot of the logistics and soldier support issues out of the uniformed military and instead hire contractors to provide these crucial functions. This was an ongoing process from the beginning of the all-volunteer force in the mid-1970s until the present. What changes after Operation Desert Storm and then increases following the attacks on September 11, 2001, is the privatization of security and intelligence.

Representative Henry Waxman of California stated in the same hearing from which the below text is taken:

> Over the past 25 years, a sophisticated campaign has been waged to privatize Government services. The theory is that corporations can deliver Government services better and at a lower cost than the Government. Over the last 6 years, this theory has been put into practice.
>
> The result is that privatization has exploded. For every taxpayer dollar spent on Federal programs, over 40 cents now goes to private contractors. Our Government now outsources even the oversight of the outsourcing.
>
> At home, core Government functions like tax collection and emergency response have been contracted out. Abroad, companies like Halliburton and Blackwater have made millions performing tasks that used to be done by our Nation's military forces. . . .
>
> . . . Privatizing is working exceptionally well for Blackwater. The question for this hearing is whether outsourcing to Blackwater is a good deal for the American taxpayer, whether it is a good deal for the military and whether it is serving our national interest in Iraq.
>
> The first part of that question is cost. We know that sergeants in the military generally cost the Government between $50,000 to $70,000 per year. We also know that a comparable position at Blackwater costs the Federal Government over $400,000, six times as much . . .
>
> Blackwater charges the Government so much that it can lure highly trained soldiers out of our forces to work for them. [Defense Secretary Gates] is now taking the

unprecedented step of considering whether to ask our troops to sign a non-compete agreement to prevent the U.S. military from becoming a taxpayer-funded training program for private contractors.

The point of the hearing, conducted by the Committee on Oversight and Reform, was to question the role of Blackwater USA and its personnel in the killing of 17 Iraqi civilians at a traffic circle in Baghdad on September 16, 2007.

KEEP IN MIND AS YOU READ

1. Representative John F. Tierney from Massachusetts made the following comments about the role of contractors:

   The all-voluntary professional force after the Vietnam War employed the so-called Abrams Doctrine. The idea was that we wouldn't go to war without the sufficient backing of the Nation.

   Outsourcing has circumvented this doctrine. It allows the administration to almost double the force size without any political price being paid. We have too few regular troops and if we admitted that and tried to put in more, the administration would have to admit it was wrong in the way it prosecuted this war originally. It would have to recognize the impact on drawing forces out of Afghanistan.

   If we call up even more National Guards or Reservists, then it would cause even more of a protest among the people in this country that are already not sold on the Iraq venture. If we relied more on our allies, they would have to share the power, share the decision making and share the contract work. So private contractors have allowed, essentially, this administration to add additional forces without paying any political capital.

   . . . Figures by one account are some nine individuals a week losing their lives in the service of private contracting that are not counted in the figures of casualties reported to the American people.

2. In fighting groups like al-Qaeda and other non-state actors one of the ways that nations have responded is through the use of their own non-state actors—contractors.

Document 24: Statement of Erik D. Prince, Chairman and CEO, Blackwater for the House Committee on Oversight and Government Reform, October 2, 2007

Chairman Waxman, Congressman Davis, Members of the Committee, my name is Erik Prince and I am the Chairman and CEO of the Prince Group and Blackwater USA. Blackwater is a team of dedicated security professionals who provide training to America's military and law enforcement communities and risk their lives to protect Americans in harm's way overseas. Under the direction and oversight of the United States Government, Blackwater provides an opportunity for military and law enforcement veterans with a record of honorable service to continue their support to the United States. Words alone cannot express the respect I have for these men and women who volunteer to defend U.S. personnel, facilities, and diplomatic missions. I am proud to be here today to represent them. . . .

Blackwater personnel supporting our Country's overseas missions are all military and law enforcement veterans, many of whom have recent military deployments. No individual protected by Blackwater has ever been killed or seriously injured. There is no better evidence of the skill and dedication of these men. At the same time, thirty brave men have made the ultimate sacrifice while working for Blackwater and its affiliates. Numerous others have been wounded and permanently maimed. The entire Blackwater family mourns the loss of these brave lives. Our thoughts are with them and their families.

The areas of Iraq in which we operate are particularly dangerous and challenging. Blackwater personnel are subject to regular attacks by terrorists and other nefarious forces within Iraq. We are the targets of the same ruthless enemies that have killed more than 3,800 American military personnel and thousands of innocent Iraqis. Any incident where Americans are attacked serves as a reminder of the hostile environment in which our professionals work to keep American officials and dignitaries safe, including visiting Members of Congress. In doing so, more American service members are available to fight the enemy.

Last month, U.S. Ambassador to Iraq Ryan Crocker testified before the Senate Committee on Armed Services and addressed the vital role of Blackwater in Iraq:

> The reality is, for example, on the security function, much of our security—most of our security is provided by contractors. It is overseen by diplomatic security officers—Foreign Service officers, but there is simply no way at all that the State Department's Bureau of Diplomatic Security could ever have enough full-time personnel to staff the security function in Iraq. There is no alternative except through contracts.

Ambassador Crocker further noted "the capability and courage of the individuals who provide security under contract," calling the job they do "worthy of respect of all Americans." We are honored to be so well regarded by the head of the mission we protect.

Blackwater shares the Committee's interest in ensuring the accountability and oversight of contractor personnel supporting U.S. operations. The company and its personnel are already accountable under and subject to numerous statutes, treaties, and regulations of the United States. We also support the clarification of the Military Extraterritorial Jurisdiction Act and other measures contained in legislation authored by Rep. David Price (D-NC). I am attaching to my statement a list of existing laws, regulations, and treaties that apply to contractors and their personnel. As an additional measure of accountability, Blackwater mandates that its security professionals required to have a security clearance must take the same oath to support and defend the Constitution as is required by law for personnel of our United States Government customers.

While existing laws and regulations provide a level of contractor accountability and oversight, Blackwater believes that more can and should be done to increase accountability, oversight and transparency. Blackwater looks forward to working with Congress and the Executive Branch to ensure that any necessary improvements to these laws and policies are implemented.

The Worldwide Personal Protection Services contract, which has been provided to this Committee, was competitively awarded and details almost every aspect of operations and contractor performance, including hiring and vetting guidelines, background checks, screening, training standards, rules of force, and conduct standards. All personnel working on Department of State contracts must receive a security clearance from the U.S. Government of at least a "secret" level. In Iraq, Blackwater reports to the Embassy's Regional Security Officer, or RSO. All Blackwater movements and operations are directed by the RSO. In conjunction with internal company procedures and controls, the RSO ensures that Blackwater complies with all relevant contractual terms and conditions as well as any applicable laws and regulations. It is Blackwater's goal not just to meet the standards of the contract, but rather to continuously exceed any such standards and to continuously improve its performance.

We have approximately 1,000 professionals serving today in Iraq as part of our nation's total force. Blackwater does not engage in offensive or military missions, but performs only defensive security functions.

At this point, I would like to explain the incident of September 16, 2007 in Baghdad involving Blackwater. To put this incident into perspective and as the Department of State recently stated, in 2007 Blackwater has conducted 1,873 security details for diplomatic visits to the Red Zone-areas outside the Green Zone in Iraq since January, 2007, and there have been only 56 incidents in which weapons were discharged, or less than three percent of movements. In 2006, Blackwater conducted over 6,500 diplomatic movements in the Red Zone. Weapons were discharged in less than one percent of those missions.

My understanding of the September 16 incident is that the Department of State is conducting a full investigation, but those results are not yet available. We should await the results of that investigation for a complete understanding of that event. This is my current understanding of the facts, which has to be considered incomplete at this time.

On Sunday, September 16, 2007, at approximately noon, a Blackwater team protecting an American government official had reached its destination when a very large vehicle-born improvised explosive device, otherwise known as a car bomb, detonated in close proximity to their location. This team secured its principal and requested support for its evacuation. In support of the first group, a second Blackwater team of vehicles proceeded to an intersection approximately one mile away from the explosion site to secure a route of egress for the Blackwater convoy that was protecting the government official. As the vehicle team arrived at the intersection, they came under small-arms fire and notified the first team to proceed along a different route. The vehicle team still in the intersection continued to receive fire and some team members returned fire at threatening targets. Among the threats identified were men with AK-47s firing on the convoy, as well as approaching vehicles that appeared to be suicide car bombers. The Blackwater personnel attempted to exit the area but one of their vehicles was disabled by enemy fire. They were ultimately able to tow the armored truck out of the intersection and return to the International Zone. Some of those firing on this Blackwater team appeared to be wearing Iraqi National Police uniforms, or portions of such uniforms. As the withdrawal occurred, the Blackwater vehicles remained under fire from such personnel.

The only team to discharge weapons was the vehicle team that was fired upon in the intersection. Of the approximately twenty members of that team, only five members discharged their weapons in response to the threat. Blackwater air assets did assist in directing the teams to safety, but contrary to some reports, no one in the helicopters discharged any weapons.

To the extent there was loss of innocent life, let me be clear that I consider that tragic. Every life, whether American or Iraqi, is precious. I stress to the Committee and to the American public, however, that based on everything we currently know, the Blackwater team acted appropriately while operating in a very complex war zone on September 16.

Despite the valiant missions our people conduct each day with great success, in this September 16 instance, Blackwater and its people have been the subject of negative and baseless allegations reported as truth. There has been a rush to judgment based on inaccurate information, and many public reports have wrongly pronounced Blackwater's guilt for the death of varying numbers of civilians. Congress should not accept these allegations as truth until it has the facts. It is one thing to debate the accountability issues related to a private security company providing services to the U.S. Government, but it is quite another to attack the very brave men and women who voluntarily risk their lives on the front-lines each day serving in a very difficult situation at the request of their country and in defense of human life.

I hope you will understand that during my testimony today I cannot discuss matters that might reveal sensitive operational security and technical information that could be utilized by our country's enemies in Iraq and Afghanistan. Such disclosure should be avoided in order to safeguard lives of Blackwater and Department of State personnel. I will answer your questions with these restrictions in mind, and raise concerns as necessary.

I am prepared to answer your questions.

Source: Erik D. Prince. Prepared Statement as part of Blackwater USA Hearing. Given before U.S. House of Representatives Committee on Government Reform, October 2, 2007. Washington D.C. Available at: https://house.resource.org/110/org.c-span.201290–1.1.pdf (accessed June 17, 2015).

AFTERMATH

Blackwater USA began functioning in Iraq shortly after the invasion in 2003. Their first contract was for personal security. In 2006 they were awarded a contract for personal security for the U.S. Embassy in Baghdad. In 2007 the government of Iraq revoked the license for Blackwater to function in Iraq and they were required to depart the country. Employees of the company continued to operate in Iraq for several years. In 2009 the company changed its name to Xe Services LLC and in 2010 Erik Prince started another company in the United Arab Emirates called Reflex Responses. Xe Services was bought out and renamed Academi.

Blackwater USA and its later-named companies have had several charges and lawsuits filed against them and their employees. For the specific incidents in this Chapter 5 men were tried. One plead guilty and cooperated in the investigations, three were convicted of manslaughter, and one was convicted for murder. The appeals process was ongoing as of writing.

ASK YOURSELF

1. Is there a role for security contractors in conflict zones?
2. What are the risks associated with having contractors in a conflict zone?
3. What benefits come from contractors on the battlefield?

TOPICS TO CONSIDER

1. Contractors are sometimes referred to as mercenaries. There is a long history of mercenary service in conflict areas. As the character of war continues to devolve away from the state monopoly of violence then it should be expected there will be more and more contractors or mercenaries on battlefields and in the urban conflict areas.

Further Reading

Al-Ali, Zaid. *The Struggle for Iraq's Future: How Corruption, Incompetence and Sectarianism Have Undermined Democracy.* New Haven, CT: Yale University Press, 2014.

Bolger, Daniel P. *Why We Lost: A General's Inside Account of the Iraq and Afghanistan Wars.* Boston: Houghton Mifflin Harcourt, 2014.

Prince, Erik. *Civilian Warriors: The Inside Story of Blackwater and the Unsung Heroes of the War on Terror.* New York: Penguin Group LLC, 2013.

Scahill, Jeremy. *Blackwater: The Rise of the World's Most Powerful Mercenary Army.* New York: Nation Books, 2007.

Woodward, Bob. *The War Within: A Secret White House History.* New York: Simon & Schuster, 2008.

Website

Blackwater USA Hearing. Given before U.S. House of Representatives Committee on Government Reform, October 2, 2007. Washington, DC. https://house.resource.org/110/org.c-span.201290–1.1.pdf (accessed June 17, 2015).

Films and Television

American War Generals. Executive producers: Peter Bergen, Tresha Mabile, Jonathan Towers. National Geographic Channel, 2014.

Frontline: Bush's War. Director: Michael Kirk. PBS, 2008.

Frontline: Private Warriors. Producer: Martin Smith. PBS, 2005.

25. POLITICAL EFFORTS: GEORGE W. BUSH AND NURI AL-MALIKI

INTRODUCTION

On November 30, 2006, U.S. president George W. Bush and Iraqi prime minister Nuri al-Malaki met to discuss the upsurge in sectarian violence in Iraq. The meeting took place in Amman, Jordan. Two meetings were scheduled, one for the evening of the 29th and one on the morning of the 30th. The evening meeting, which would have included Jordan's King Abdullah II, was cancelled abruptly by Prime Minister al-Malaki. No clear reason was given as to the prime minister's withdrawal from the three-way meeting, but much speculation surrounded the apparent snub. Many in the United States felt it was meant as a boycott in response to a classified memo written by National Security Adviser Stephen Hadley which was leaked to the press. The memo in question contained some scathing criticisms of al-Malaki. Others believed that al-Malaki wanted to avoid the possibility that King Abdullah might bring the Palestinian-Israeli conflict into the discussion. Whatever the case, the two leaders met one on one the following morning as planned and issued the joint statement included in this chapter.

KEEP IN MIND AS YOU READ

1. Throughout 2005 there was only one month with fewer than 1,000 people killed. In 2006, the numbers became worse with regular deaths in excess of 2,000 and even 3,000 per month. These numbers are civilian deaths. The first month, December 2007, it was under 1,000 and then the numbers did not regularly remain under 1,000 until May 2008. The news was filled with scenes of death, destruction, and explosions. For comparison the average per month deaths in 2011 was about 350. In 2004, 2005, 2006, and 2007 the annual coalition deaths were about 900 per year with the highest being 961 in 2007.

2. The 2006 U.S. midterm elections included a great deal of discussion about the Iraq War. Much of the debate centered around the notion that the war was entirely voluntary—not a necessity. The election held on November 7, 2006, was a gain for the Democrats in the U.S. Senate (+6), U.S. House of Representatives (+31),

and state governors (+6). Many viewed this shift in party support as evidence the American public no longer supported the war in Iraq.

3. On November 8, 2006, President Bush announced the resignation of Donald Rumsfeld as secretary of defense and nominated Robert Gates to take his place.

Document 25: Joint Statement by President George W. Bush and Prime Minister Nuri al-Maliki, November 30, 2006

We were pleased to continue our consultations on building security and stability in Iraq. We are grateful to His Majesty King Abdullah II of Jordan for hosting these meetings here in Amman.

Our discussions reviewed developments in Iraq, focusing on the security situation and our common concern about sectarian violence targeting innocent Iraqis. In this regard, the Prime Minister affirms the commitment of his government to advance efforts toward national reconciliation and the need for all Iraqis and political forces in Iraq to work against armed elements responsible for violence and intimidation. The Prime Minister also affirms his determination with help from the United States and the international community to improve the efficiency of government operations, particularly in confronting corruption and strengthening the rule of law.

We discussed the plague of terrorism in Iraq which is being fomented and fueled by Al Qaeda. The people of Iraq, like the people of the United States and the entire civilized world, must stand together to face this common threat. The Prime Minister affirmed that Iraq is a partner in the fight against Al Qaeda. We agreed that defeating Al Qaeda and the terrorists is vital to ensuring the success of Iraq's democracy. We discussed the means by which the United States will enhance Iraq's capabilities to further isolate extremists and bring all who choose violence and terror to full justice under Iraqi law.

We agreed in particular to take all necessary measures to track down and bring to justice those responsible for the cowardly attacks last week in Sadr City. The Prime Minister has also pledged to bring to justice those responsible for crimes committed in the wake of this attack.

We discussed accelerating the transfer of security responsibilities to the Government of Iraq; our hopes for strengthening the future relationship between our two nations; and joint efforts to achieve greater cooperation from governments in the region and to counter those elements that are fueling the conflict.

We received an interim report from the high-level Joint Committee on Accelerating the Transferring of Security Responsibility, and encouraged the Committee to continue its good work. We agreed that reform of the Iraqi security ministries and agencies and addressing the issue of militias should be accelerated. The ultimate solution to stabilizing Iraq and reducing violence is true national reconciliation and capable and loyal Iraqi forces dedicated to protecting all the Iraqi people.

We are committed to continuing to build the partnership between our two countries as we work together to strengthen a stable, democratic, and unified Iraq.

Source: Joint Statement by President George W. Bush and Prime Minister Nuri al-Maliki of Iraq, November 30, 2006. Government Printing Office. Available at: http://www.gpo.gov/fdsys/pkg/WCPD-2006–12–04/html/WCPD-2006–12–04-Pg2112.htm (accessed July 1, 2015).

AFTERMATH

The coalition was not popular in Iraq. Most Iraqis blamed the coalition invasion and behavior for creating the chaotic situation in Iraq. Depending on region many wanted the coalition to leave immediately or to stabilize the country and then leave.

On December 6 the Iraq Study Group led by James Baker and Lee Hamilton presented their recommendations to President Bush. The report called for a reduction of U.S. forces among 79 recommendations. The following day a group of military and academic experts met with President Bush and some of the recommendations in the meeting included sending more forces. Robert Gates became secretary of defense on December 18, 2006. On January 5, 2007, several significant personnel changes were announced for the military including the replacement of General George Casey by General David Petraeus as commander of Multi-National Forces-Iraq.

On January 10, 2007, President Bush announced a new policy for Iraq. Five additional combat brigades were to deploy in support of the new commander with an emphasis on counterinsurgency.

The feelings of the Iraqi people toward President Bush were most brazenly displayed during a news conference held in Baghdad on December 14, 2008. During the meeting Muntadhar al-Zaidi, an Iraqi broadcast journalist, threw his shoes at President Bush after shouting "This is a farewell kiss from the Iraqi people, you dog." He had previously been kidnapped and ransomed. His actions, in many ways, represented the frustrations of the Iraqi people.

ASK YOURSELF

1. Most U.S. personnel believed that they were serving the Iraqi people yet throughout the conduct of the war the Iraqi people blamed the United States for their suffering which they believed to be the result of U.S. actions which created the environment of chaos. Is it possible to overthrow a country's leader without creating a vacuum of power? Is it right for one nation to decide who should or should not rule another?

2. Why were Iraqi people angry at America for overthrowing Saddam Hussein if he was so bad? Before the war Saddam Hussein was portrayed as the worst leader possible. If this portrayal was correct then why did the Iraqi people wish he were still in charge in late 2006?

TOPICS TO CONSIDER

1. What is the balance between security and freedom? Is it more important to keep a brutal leader if that person maintains security and stability in the country or is personal liberty more important than collective stability?

Further Reading

Al-Ali, Zaid. *The Struggle for Iraq's Future: How Corruption, Incompetence and Sectarianism Have Undermined Democracy.* New Haven, CT: Yale University Press, 2014.

Bush, George W. *Decision Points.* New York: Random House, Inc., 2010.

Gates, Robert M. *Duty: Memoirs of a Secretary at War.* New York: Alfred A. Knopf, Inc., 2014.

Rumsfeld, Donald. *Known and Unknown: A Memoir.* New York: Penguin Group, 2011.

Websites

Cordesman, Anthony H. *Iraqi Perceptions of the War: Public Opinion by City and Region.* Washington, DC: Center for Strategic and International Studies, 2007. http://www.comw.org/warreport/fulltext/0705cordesman.pdf (accessed July 1, 2015).

Iraq Body Count. Documented civilian deaths from violence. https://www.iraqbodycount.org/database/ (accessed July 1, 2015).

icasualties.org. Operation Iraqi Freedom: Iraq Coalition Casualties: Fatalities by Year. http://icasualties.org/Iraq/ByYear.aspx (accessed July 1, 2015).

Films and Television

American Sniper. Director: Clint Eastwood. Warner Bros., 2014.

American War Generals. Executive producers: Peter Bergen, Tresha Mabile, Jonathan Towers. National Geographic Channel, 2014.

Frontline: Bush's War. Director: Michael Kirk. PBS, 2008.

THE SURGE AND BEYOND
(2006–2009)

26. FIELD MANUAL 3–24: COUNTERINSURGENCY, 2006

INTRODUCTION

During World War II and the Cold War it was common to hear about German or Soviet officers who said that the U.S. military does not follow its own doctrine. Many of these "quotes" are suspect and probably not true. Despite this there has been a perception that the United States is non-doctrinal. Since the creation of the all-volunteer force in 1973 and the U.S. Army Training and Doctrine Command (TRADOC) in 1974 there has been an invigoration of the importance of doctrine. By the time of the fighting in Iraq doctrine was a critical component of training and education in the U.S. military.

Doctrine refers to the foundational concepts and principles for military action. It is not designed to communicate what to do in a specific circumstance, but rather the general guidelines and principles that shape thinking and promote good decision making in preparation for and execution of military operations. As such, doctrine serves an important role in providing the context for thought and it does matter.

Within TRADOC there is the Combined Arms Center at Fort Leavenworth, Kansas. This command is responsible for overseeing the actions and activities of numerous schools within the U.S. Army. It also serves and served as the place for thinking about how to fight the, then current, war in Iraq. It was here that General Petraeus was assigned to command and he took the responsibility for completing the doctrine for counterinsurgency or COIN.

KEEP IN MIND AS YOU READ

1. Military innovation is most often linked to things—equipment, technology, etc.—rather than ideas. Throughout warfare it can be argued that ideas have had more effect on the battlefield than equipment or technology. It is interesting to note which precedes which. Did the idea lead to the new gear or did the new gear lead to a new way of thinking about the task? By the time the new COIN doctrine was published leaders throughout Iraq were already doing most, if not all, of the things recommended in the manual.

2. Within most militaries there are two components. The operational element is responsible for the actual fighting. The institutional element resources the fighting by providing the training, procurement, and ideas necessary to support the military in a fight. Doctrine typically comes from the institutional military even though, as stated earlier, it may be strongly influenced by the actions of the operational military.

Document 26: Excerpt from U.S. Army Field Manual 3–24 (Counterinsurgency), 2006

1–159. COIN is an extremely complex form of warfare. At its core, COIN is a struggle for the population's support. The protection, welfare, and support of the people are vital to success. Gaining and maintaining that support is a formidable challenge. Achieving these aims requires synchronizing the efforts of many nonmilitary and HN [Host Nation] agencies in a comprehensive approach.

160. Designing operations that achieve the desired end state requires counterinsurgents to understand the culture and the problems they face. Both insurgents and counterinsurgents are fighting for the support of the populace. However, insurgents are constrained by neither the law of war nor the bounds of human decency as Western nations understand them. In fact, some insurgents are willing to commit suicide and kill innocent civilians in carrying out their operations—and deem this a legitimate option. They also will do anything to preserve their greatest advantage, the ability to hide among the people. These amoral and often barbaric enemies survive by their wits, constantly adapting to the situation. Defeating them requires counterinsurgents to develop the ability to learn and adapt rapidly and continuously. This manual emphasizes this "Learn and Adapt" imperative as it discusses ways to gain and maintain the support of the people.

1–161. Popular support allows counterinsurgents to develop the intelligence necessary to identify and defeat insurgents. Designing and executing a comprehensive campaign to secure the populace and then gain its support requires carefully coordinating actions along several [logical line of operations] over time to produce success. One of these [logical line of operations] is developing HN security forces that can assume primary responsibility for combating the insurgency. COIN operations also place distinct burdens on leaders and logisticians. All of these aspects of COIN are described and analyzed in the chapters that follow.

Table 1–1 Successful and unsuccessful counterinsurgency operational practices

Successful Practices	Unsuccessful Practices
• Emphasize intelligence.	• Overemphasize killing and capturing the enemy rather than securing and engaging the populace.
• Focus on the population, its needs, and its security.	
• Establish and expand secure areas.	• Conduct large-scale operations as the norm.
• Isolate insurgents from the populace (population control).	• Concentrate military forces in large bases for protection.
• Conduct effective, pervasive, and continuous information operations.	• Focus special forces primarily on raiding.

Successful Practices	Unsuccessful Practices
• Provide amnesty and rehabilitation for those willing to support the new government. • Place host-nation police in the lead with military support as soon as the security situation permits. • Expand and diversify the host-nation police force. • Train military forces to conduct counterinsurgency operations. • Embed quality advisors and special forces with host-nation forces. • Deny sanctuary to insurgents. • Encourage strong political and military cooperation and information sharing. • Secure host-nation borders. • Protect key infrastructure.	• Place low priority on assigning quality advisors to host-nation forces. • Build and train host-nation security forces in the U.S. military image. • Ignore peacetime government processes, including legal procedures. • Allow open borders, airspace, and coastlines.

Source: U.S. Department of the Army. *Counterinsurgency.* Field Manual 3–24. Washington, D.C.: U.S. Department of the Army, December 15, 2006. Available at: http://usacac.army.mil/cac2/Repository/Materials/COIN-FM3–24.pdf (accessed July 6, 2015).

AFTERMATH

FM 3–24 was a watershed in that it brought back a deep discussion in the U.S. military on the notion of COIN and how this kind of fight could be effectively waged. The manual was not without critics. Some called into question the historical anecdotes used to support the arguments. The particular emphasis on the British COIN campaign in Malaysia was called into question because of its inaccuracies or, at least, the incompleteness of the story.

Despite the criticism the manual became part of a U.S. military narrative which asserted that a new doctrine and extra forces were what caused the Surge to be successful.

ASK YOURSELF

1. What is the most important form of innovation in war—ideas, technology, training? How does the innovation become manifest in the conflict? Soldiers and commanders were applying the elements of the manual before the manual was published. Did the training provide the ideas or did they come from the conflict itself?
2. Did the ideas really matter or was it really perception management? In the case of FM 3–24 were those ideas useful in changing the nature of the fighting? There were numerous incidents of people giving tremendous credit to the manual for the ideas provided and the success achieved in the Surge and beyond. Was it true or is it the perception that matters?

TOPICS TO CONSIDER

1. Remember other chapters that discuss the midterm elections in the United States in 2006 and the tremendous changes in the Pentagon and throughout the department of defense with respect to fighting the war in Iraq. This manual came in the middle of all of those changing situations. Politics are the driving impetus of conflict as Carl von Clausewitz stated. This doctrine came forward in the middle of tremendous political debate on the war.

Further Reading

Bolger, Daniel P. *Why We Lost: A General's Inside Account of the Iraq and Afghanistan Wars.* Boston: Houghton Mifflin Harcourt, 2014.

Kilcullen, David. *Counterinsurgency.* Oxford: Oxford University Press, 2010.

Kilcullen, David. *The Accidental Guerilla: Fighting Small Wars in the Midst of a Big One.* Oxford: Oxford University Press, 2011.

Mansoor, Peter. *Surge: My Journey with General David Petraeus and the Remaking of the Iraq War.* New Haven, CT: Yale University Press, 2013.

Woodward, Bob. *The War Within: A Secret White House History.* New York: Simon & Schuster, 2008.

Films and Television

American War Generals. Executive producers: Peter Bergen, Tresha Mabile, Jonathan Towers. National Geographic Channel, 2014.

Frontline: Bush's War. Director: Michael Kirk. PBS, 2008.

27. Telafar, the Example for Counterinsurgency: Paul Yingling

INTRODUCTION

If there is a single pre-*Surge* battle that is held up of what right looks like then it is the fighting by the 3rd Armored Cavalry Regiment in and around the northern Iraqi city of Telafar. The regiment did a unique and effective job in preparing soldiers for the deployment as they regularly sent soldiers for Arabic language training, they called in academic experts to speak with soldiers, and they conducted an aggressive professional development program. It is possible that this greater-than-average preparation was a contributing factor to the success of the regiment in conducting the fight against insurgents in Telafar.

Telafar was a smuggling route for decades and probably centuries. As such it also became an entry point for foreign fighters and a logical location for al-Qaeda in Iraq and other groups opposed to the U.S.-led coalition to gather and focus their efforts. The story of retaking this city was one that was used to argue in favor of getting U.S. forces off big forward operating bases and out with the population. The regimental commander was Colonel H. R. McMaster who had notoriety from his combat actions in Operation Desert Storm and his academic ability in writing a book criticizing the senior military leaders during the Vietnam War.

The interview subject in this chapter was Lieutenant Colonel Paul Yingling. This deployment was his second to Iraq. During his first tour his unit, 2nd Battalion, 18th Field Artillery Regiment, was assigned to reduce captured enemy ammunition and train the Iraqi Civil Defense Corps. During his second tour from March 2005 to March 2006 Yingling was assigned to the 3rd Armored Cavalry Regiment. He served in the somewhat ambiguous position of effects coordinator. His duties included information operations, public affairs, psychological operations, civil affairs, and Iraqi security forces development. The regiment spent its first two months in south Baghdad before moving to the western Ninevah Province where they assisted in reclaiming Telafar from insurgents, reestablishing government services, and rebuilding Iraqi civil and military forces. Yingling was and is a prolific author writing numerous pieces criticizing the conduct of the war.

KEEP IN MIND AS YOU READ

1. War, counterinsurgency, armed conflict, whatever it is called is a complex business. Soldiers and officers deploy from the United States or other coalition countries and come to a place where the people dress and speak differently. Most soldiers quickly become overwhelmed by the differences. In an attempt to simplify things, they often separate the Iraqis from the Americans in their minds. This makes communication of complex ideas even more complicated, if not impossible. Adding to these factors is the fact that nearly all communication goes through a translator who does not fully understand the intent and ideas of either speaker but is simply translating words and not the underlying ideas. This is hard stuff. Challenges and failures are not typically the result of incompetence, but rather because of the degree of difficulty involved.

Document 27: Excerpt from Interview with Paul Yingling, 3rd ACR, 2005–2006

Question: Can you detail for us the overall regimental mission and how you fit into that?

Answer: Broadly speaking, the regimental mission was to conduct combined counterinsurgency operations to enable development of Iraqi institutions in order to implement UN Security Council Resolution 1546. That was the macro mission. In terms of the regimental concept of operations, there were three components [clear-hold-build] . . .

The first thing we did was conduct Operation Veterans Forward, which was an area reconnaissance operation to get a better sense of our AO. Not just the enemy intelligence but also the civil factors, political development, economic capabilities and rule of law. What we found was that the enemy had been using western Nineveh Province as the . . . training base for the insurgency in Mosul and Baghdad. It was a sanctuary that was well suited for a couple reasons. Firstly, US and coalition forces were relatively sparse in that area. Secondly, the human capital was there. Mosul and Tall Afar are the home of a large number of retirees from the Iraqi Army . . . There were a lot of noncommissioned officers (NCOs) and warrant officers retired there and these were guys who were our equivalent of master gunners. These were guys who hold a lot of technical experience and bomb-making capabilities. They were a little older, were very capable trainers, and they were training insurgents for employment in Mosul and also elsewhere in Iraq. They had partnered with Al Qaeda in Iraq, who had a very good IO capability, access to external funding, an ideological base and religious appeal to mobilize the population. It was a very small but effective Al Qaeda leadership partnered with a very large and more capable technical and ideological base. These two forces combined to conduct these training activities and also to wage a very brutal campaign of intimidation and coercion against the population to keep them disengaged from supporting the Iraqi government . . .

We initially tried to reconstruct the Tall Afar police force and the other police forces in the [area] but we weren't able to do that because of the enemy's campaign of intimidation and coercion. What Veterans Forward did was place Iraqi Army forces on the Syrian border and in proximity to Tall Afar, and from there we developed our estimate of the [area]. What we found was that until we broke the enemy's campaign of intimidation, we couldn't proceed on the other lines of operation. We couldn't recruit security forces, couldn't encourage economic development, couldn't get contractors to come into the [area] and we couldn't encourage political participation or sectarian reconciliation.

So in August 2005, we began planning Operation Restoring Rights. This was a combined area security operation, the purpose of which was to establish security in Tall Afar and the outlying areas so we could proceed along the other lines of operation. It consisted of the 3rd Iraqi Army Division of about 8,000 troops, as well as 3rd ACR, selected Special Forces (SF), Iraqi police and also a brigade from the 2nd Iraqi Army Division. All told it was about 11,000 troops: 8,000 Iraqi and about 3,000 coalition forces in what was essentially about a three-by-three square kilometer area . . .

We isolated the town by conducting security operations in the outlying areas, established an obstacle around the town and established entry control points. We evacuated the most well defended part of the town—the enemy's ideological stronghold of Sarai—by using [information operations] and [psychological operation] broadcasts to encourage the population to leave, and almost all of them did with the exception of the hardcore Takfirist groups defending the town. We conducted a security operation in early September, which cleared the town of the insurgents; and after that we established the Iraqi police presence throughout the city: that was the "hold" part of the operation.

We were able to bring in contractors and the coalition provided about $11 million in reconstruction funds, the Iraqi government provided $37 million and we began to build the essential services, which would further isolate the insurgency from the population. As we were leaving in February/March 2006, we had a police force in Tall Afar that was broadly representative of the population. It was a Sunni/Shi'a mix: 60 percent Shi'a and about 30 to 40 percent Sunni. They were professionally educated and had gone to a police academy in Jordan. We had essential services functioning at the basic level in terms of food distribution and water, and governance functioned at the city level. A city council was in place and functioning . . . I certainly won't say we solved or defeated the insurgency throughout the province. I will say, though, that with the help of very effective Iraqi leaders—Najim Abdullah Abid al-Jibouri, the mayor of Tall Afar, and Major General Khorsheed Saleem al-Dosekey, commander of the 3rd Iraqi Army Division—we were able to establish the security conditions that allowed progress in security force development and essential services.

Question: . . . Can you discuss how effective you think the operation was in the short term and also in the long term? There have been reports lately of car bombs going off and 20-plus people being killed.

Answer: I think the model that Colonel McMaster used to visualize Restoring Rights—the clear-hold-build model—is effective. The way he visualized the operation was to examine previous operations in the area and taking lessons learned from them, specifically Black Typhoon that took place in November 2004.

As we examined these previous operations, what we found was that the enemy started a campaign of intimidation in the summer of 2004. They destroyed the police force and expelled civil authorities from the town of Biaj on the Syrian border. They next transitioned to Tall Afar in September 2004 and then Mosul in November. In each case the model was very similar. The insurgents would mass on small isolated police stations, kill or intimidate the police into quitting their posts, destroy the police stations and the other symbols of government authority, and then proceed with establishing an intimidation campaign throughout the city. When the coalition launched Black Typhoon in September 2004 to defeat the insurgents, the insurgents scattered along kinship lines to outlying communities. At the same time, they appealed to their allies both in Iraq—specifically in the Iraqi Islamic Party—and outside Iraq with the government of Turkey to convey the [information operation] theme that this was an unjust assault against the Turkmen population of Tall Afar.

Having seen that model in the past, Colonel McMaster visualized the operation as first we had to prevent the enemy from displacing along kinship lines. To prevent this, we brought most of the squadron we had on the Syrian border and used them to conduct security operations and build up the police forces in outlying areas—Avghani to the northwest of Tall Afar and other smaller communities around Tall Afar. We first established security there before we converged forces on Tall Afar. Based on the advice we got from our Iraqi allies, we established these deliberate obstacles around the town to include a berm and entry control points. This way, when we did decide to evacuate the population to prevent collateral damage, we could screen the population as they left. Although we didn't really understand it at the time, we did it anyway and it turned out to be a very good thing to do. That berm had a very powerful psychological effect on the population.

Question: The berm was an Iraqi idea?

Answer: It was. We got that advice from Mayor Najim and Major General Khorsheed as well as from some Iraqi legislators whom we were in touch with. Although we didn't quite understand it and it wasn't something doctrinally that we anticipated doing, it was very good advice. One of the lessons I learned from this was to step outside of my Western skin and see the problem through the Iraqis' eyes and take their advice when conducting operations because they have a perspective that we just can't fully appreciate.

Question: Was there any other advice they gave for the planning or execution of this operation?

Answer: There was a lot. Every part of the operation, to include the naming of the operation, was conducted in partnership with the Iraqis, with Major General Khorsheed and Mayor Najim. I will have to say that, in some sense, we got very lucky because we had two very capable partners in those two leaders. Not every unit in Iraq has been that lucky, so we felt very fortunate to have these very courageous and capable leaders to partner with. They advised us to place Iraqi Army and police partnered together at the entry control points, because the police had a very good sense of who was in the city but they did not have a good reputation among the population. The police could identify insurgents but the police often frightened the population. Partnering them with the Iraqi Army and coalition forces, then, kept the population from being intimidated by the police, but at the same time gave us a unique on-the-ground capability.

As the population was displacing through entry control points outside of the city to displaced civilian facilities we had established or to their families outside the city, the police could identify the insurgents. We had insurgents try to dress as women to escape. We had insurgents try to grab the hands of small children and claim to be their parents and the police would catch them. So, relying on this local expertise was key, because we just don't have the cultural sensitivity to see who doesn't belong and who does. Only the police had that and so we were able to leverage that and that was based on the advice of our Iraqi allies. That ability to deny the enemy the ability to hide in plain sight among the population was probably the most important thing we did.

Colonel McMaster encouraged us at the regimental staff level, as we were working on security operations, to look ahead to the essential services line. Even as we were beginning the security part and doing the security operations, we were working with the Iraqi government to provide us with reconstruction funding. We thought it was important that all the reconstruction effort was an Iraqi effort. Even when we were spending coalition money, the IO theme was that the Iraqi government was restoring essential services to the city of Tall Afar. That building of essential services and security forces was clearly important, so I think the clear-hold-build model is a very good one. I think, though, that Tall Afar was unique in some ways because it was such a small area. It was only a three-by-three kilometer city that we were able to mass our large amount of forces in. I don't know enough about the rest of Iraq to say that it would necessarily be replicable in Baghdad or Mosul or the cities in Anbar Province. But on the scale we operated on and with the forces we had available, I thought it was very effective.

Having said that, you asked about the longer term. I don't think you can say success or failure in an insurgency can be measured by single events. There are going to be attacks in Tall Afar and, in fact, I'm really surprised there haven't been more. It's been spoken about by President Bush as a success story and, after he gave that speech, I was really worried that the insurgents were going to react by attacking the institutions in Tall Afar. If the institutions hold and grow then I think we can say that Tall Afar was successful, even if there are isolated events. But if the police force or the army in Tall Afar doesn't hold or if the essential services progress doesn't continue and the population stops believing the government has their best interests at heart, then we won't have long term success. The security just buys time for those other more decisive elements to take hold. So if security forces don't continue to develop as a professional and capable force and essential services don't continue, then Tall Afar could slip back to where it was—and that would be heartbreaking, but it is possible.

Source: Paul Yingling. Interview by John McCool, September 22, 2006. Interview Transcript. Courtesy of the Operational Leadership Experiences Digital Collection, Combat Studies Institute, Fort Leavenworth, KS. Available at: http://cgsc.contentdm.oclc.org/cdm/singleitem/collection/p4013coll13/id/273/rec/1 (accessed July 18, 2015).

AFTERMATH

Telafar became a major point of fighting following the withdrawal of U.S. forces in 2011. Being somewhat isolated and close to the Syrian border it was a natural focal point for insurgents at the time of MNF-I and this continued with the rise of the Islamic State. Telafar fell under Islamic State control in the spring of 2014 and remains in that status at the time of writing. Numerous U.S. officers who served in and around the city had connections with tribal and factional leaders in the city; however, those contacts were ineffective based on the brutal nature of Islamic State occupation.

ASK YOURSELF

1. Clear-hold-build seems simple and effective. Why couldn't this have been done successfully everywhere? Yingling gives some reasons for this in his comments above.
2. What made some Iraqi officers excellent partners and others less so? In other chapters in this book there are varying degrees of success in working with Iraqi counterparts. Why might this have been so? It would seem that the motivations for Iraqis to cooperate or not cooperate should be the same throughout the country, but was that true?

TOPICS TO CONSIDER

1. Understanding an environment is considered to be among the first things that military planners do when they begin their planning process. If this is the case then why was Telafar so difficult initially and then so seemingly simple for 3rd ACR? Complexity is key here. There are numerous levels of understanding. One can understand the rules of American Football, but that doesn't mean that the same person really *understands* the game in all of its complexity, strategy, player decisions, and so on. Consider all of the complex issues that one needs to study before that person can say they understand a single city in all of its politics and social dynamics.

Further Reading

Al-Ali, Zaid. *The Struggle for Iraq's Future: How Corruption, Incompetence and Sectarianism Have Undermined Democracy*. New Haven, CT: Yale University Press, 2014.

Bolger, Daniel P. *Why We Lost: A General's Inside Account of the Iraq and Afghanistan Wars*. Boston: Houghton Mifflin Harcourt, 2014.

Mansoor, Peter. *Surge: My Journey with General David Petraeus and the Remaking of the Iraq War*. New Haven, CT: Yale University Press, 2013.

Montalvan, Luis Carlos. *Until Tuesday: A Wounded Warrior and the Golden Retriever Who Saved Him*. New York: Hachette Books, 2011.

Woodward, Bob. *The War Within: A Secret White House History*. New York: Simon & Schuster, 2008.

Films and Television

American War Generals. Executive producers: Peter Bergen, Tresha Mabile, Jonathan Towers. National Geographic Channel, 2014.

Frontline: Bush's War. Director: Michael Kirk. PBS, 2008.

28. Counter-IED: Brian Huskey

INTRODUCTION

Throughout the Iraq War the weapon that was primarily responsible for the deaths and wounds of most U.S. and coalition personnel was the improvised explosive device or IED. The U.S. military invested enormous amounts of money, time, and personnel to develop organizations, determine lessons learned, and provide a response to the weapons. This resulted in organizations being created in theater and also at the national military level. In theater it was called Task Force Troy. They were responsible for providing counter-IED efforts that included explosive ordnance disposal (EOD) as well as dealing with various countermeasures that included jamming.

Additionally, there was an organization called the Asymmetric Warfare Group that did not look exclusively at IEDs, but at all techniques used by the opponent. What made them unique was the speed with which they turned observations into solutions.

At the joint military level the organization combining all of the assets and efforts was known as the Joint Improvised Explosive Device Defeat Organization or JIEDDO. Their job was to provide oversight and control on all of the various efforts being created by each of the military services to deal with IEDs. JIEDDI was created in 2006 and continued beyond the war's end.

Most militaries use an alpha-numeric code to identify various staff positions and their responsibilities.

Letters

    S = staff
    G = general staff or staff officer for an organization directly commanded by a general
    J = joint staff for an organization that has army, air force, and navy personnel included

Numbers

1 = personnel officer (human resources)	2 = intelligence	3 = operations
4 = logistics	5 = plans	6 = signal or communications
7 = training	8 = budget	9 = civil-military operations

Captain Huskey, the subject of this chapter, began his military service as an enlisted Marine before entering the U.S. Army. Captain Huskey deployed to Iraq in 2006 as a military intelligence officer but was ultimately assigned to Task Force Troy after demonstrating a knowledge of IEDs which his superiors found valuable. While this interview discusses personnel management more than counter-IED it reinforces the importance of ingenuity and adaptability within the military.

KEEP IN MIND AS YOU READ

1. Personnel deployed to Iraq typically as part of a preexisting unit that came together into theater from their home station wherever that might be in the United States or somewhere else in the world. Another way that soldiers reached theater was through the worldwide individual augmentation system or WIAS. In this manner individual skills were requested and people were pulled from their units to meet the specific requirements. The policy of deploying units came about as a result of lessons from the Vietnam War where the majority of those who served deployed individually. This method failed to develop the unit cohesion that was valuable in time of war.

Document 28: Excerpt from Interview with Brian Huskey, Military Intelligence, 2006–2007

When I originally showed up [in Iraq] there was an officer and she was not that good and the battalion commander basically said, "Whoever comes in next. I don't care if it's a warrant officer or whoever but you're fired and they're going to be the next personnel officer (S1). I just happened to be the next person who showed up. I think she had the job for five months and then made me the S1. I [hadn't] trained for the S1 and they told us that we were not going to switch out at all so I was not happy about deploying to theater to be the S1 because it wasn't what I had trained to do. When you spend 10 years jumping out of planes and all this other stuff and suddenly you're the S1 for an MI battalion, it wasn't fun.

LTC Chavez came in as our battalion commander and said, "I don't want this guy because I need him doing something," but everyone's jobs had already been laid out for them. He put another captain he got from the 25th ID to be the S1 and they looked at my background and said, "Oh you went to school in Britain and you've majored in British Military History and you know all of this British stuff and you drive a British car. We need someone to be the liaison officer (LNO) to Great Britain in Basra. You're the perfect guy for that." I said, "Okay." They told me, "Start learning all of these units in Basra and what their missions are." That's what I did. I could tell you everything there is to know about Basra or who the movers and shakers were; I knew all the generals and their backgrounds and everything. We show up and everyone goes to do their job. I had packed my bags and waited two days for a plane and they tell me, "Okay you're going to fly down to Basra." The plane starts to spin up and take off and then it lands. It takes off and then the engine starts winding down and no one knows what's going on. They come up and the deck opens and the British corporal came in and says [in a British accent], "Is there a

CPT Huskey on this plane?" I say, "Yes." And he says, "Sir you have to get your bags and get the bleep off." I say, "What's going on?" Then he replies, "I don't know sir but you gotta go; you gotta go right now!" So I grab my bags and didn't know what was going on. I got back on the high mobility multipurpose wheeled vehicle (HMMWV) and got back to our base.

The division intelligence officer (G2) LTC Kyper—apparently the job I was filling was supposed to be a worldwide individual augmentation system (WIAS) tasker. That's where they just look and pull one guy, "You're going to do a job." They always had so many extra officers, why make someone leave his family or something? They said, "We'll just fill it out of this." I trained to do that job [go to Basra as the liaison to the British] the whole time and I got pulled back and COL Kyper said, "Why are we sending Huskey to go do this job? According to my modified table of organization and equipment (MTOE)," or whatever he had, "This is a WIAS tasker." They said, "Well, yeah it is but we have extra people and that's the job that he had trained to do; the job he said he was going to do." He said, "Well no. We'll keep him here and he will do something." There was nothing for me to do. All of the slots had already been filled. We were literally packed so then they had to pull somebody else and had to fill it. So now some poor guy who was spending time with his wife and kids had to go fill this WIAS tasker. I trained for that job and literally there was nothing for me to do. They said, "We're going to make you the night assistant battle captain." We had a battle major and a battle captain and I was the assistant battle captain. It was horrible because I was used to being this man of action and I had nothing to do and the job I trained for was nothing.

How I got the job was—there was a Marine major there who had been in Vietnam. His peer was a three-star general. He had been in the Reserves and they called him up. His name was MAJ Rayfield. He still wears his Marine Corps uniform but he wore his old pistol belt and he had a 45 millimeter instead of a nine millimeter; it was really odd. MAJ Rayfield and I were talking one day and I told him, "MAJ Rayfield, I have nothing to do here, sir. This is ridiculous." He said, "What you need to do is just find something and be good at it. That's how MI works. Someday someone is going to ask a question about Peruvian crossbows and you'll be like, "Sir. I know all about Peruvian crossbows." You'll answer the question and they'll say, "I want this man on my Peruvian team. And that's how it works."

I started looking at it and was like, "What's killing all of the Soldiers over here? It's improvised explosive devices (IEDs)." I started looking at IEDs and the main thing that killed IEDs was explosively formed penetrators (EFPs) and so I studied everything there was to know about EFPs. Sure enough about two weeks later the colonel had to go to a meeting and he wanted me to take notes because his note taker had a dental appointment. He snagged me and said, "You're going to have to take notes at this meeting." I was in the meeting with General Chiarelli, who was the Multi-National Corps-Iraq (MNC-I) commander at the time, and he asked a question about EFPs. He said, "I don't understand these EFPs." There was this full-bird colonel in the room who answered the question and he answered it wrong; it was completely wrong. Everyone in the room was a general or a full-bird colonel except for me who was taking notes in the back. I stood up and said, "Actually, that's wrong." Of course everyone looked at me and said, "What?" They looked at me and the colonel I was with said, "What are you doing?" The colonel who answered incorrectly said, "What do you mean there young captain?" So I explained how they worked and said, "Sir, they're coming from this route and they're coming from this." A lot of it was classified for this forum but I told them all about the stuff that I had learned and he said, "That's outstanding! What are you doing here?" I said, "Sir, I'm the night assistant battle captain." He said, "We need you on Task Force Troy," which was the theater IED task force. He asked my colonel, "Do you mind if I pull this guy, your assistant? Do you need him as the night assistant battle captain?" My colonel said, "No. No we don't need him at all." So I was detached and I got put in Task Force Troy; that's how I got the job.

Source: Brian Huskey. Interview by Angie Slattery, December 16, 2010. Interview Transcript. Courtesy of the Operational Leadership Experiences Digital Collection, Combat Studies Institute, Fort Leavenworth, KS. Available at: http://cgsc.contentdm.oclc.org/cdm/singleitem/collection/p4013coll13/id/2164/rec/1 (accessed July 14, 2015).

AFTERMATH

The battle with IEDs and explosively formed penetrators (EFPs) lasted throughout the Iraq War to the time of this book's writing. They are cheap and they are simple and they can do a great deal of damage while creating little risk for the person using the system. Task Force Troy and other organizations provided systems to the battlefield that used technology to predetonate the charges or rendered inoperable the triggering mechanisms. Despite the solutions IEDs killed U.S. and coalition personnel throughout the war. The peak of IED use and casualties was in 2007 with dramatic decreases until the end of the war.

ASK YOURSELF

1. What does this experience teach about the value of subject matter expertise? Major Rayfield gave advice about becoming the expert at something and Captain Huskey applied himself to that effort. How would his experience in Iraq have been different if he had not listened to the advice?

TOPICS TO CONSIDER

1. Competition is the nature of conflict. Combatants will only change their behavior when they are forced to by the actions and reactions of their adversary. There was an evolution of IEDs throughout the war, but the basic idea of a remote-triggered explosive is still extremely popular on battlefields today. This will certainly remain true until a solution to the problem is developed.

Further Reading

Bolger, Daniel P. *Why We Lost: A General's Inside Account of the Iraq and Afghanistan Wars.* Boston: Houghton Mifflin Harcourt, 2014.
Kilcullen, David. *Counterinsurgency.* Oxford: Oxford University Press, 2010.
Kilcullen, David. *The Accidental Guerilla: Fighting Small Wars in the Midst of a Big One.* Oxford: Oxford University Press, 2011.
Mansoor, Peter. *Surge: My Journey with General David Petraeus and the Remaking of the Iraq War.* New Haven, CT: Yale University Press, 2013.
Woodward, Bob. *The War Within: A Secret White House History.* New York: Simon & Schuster, 2008.

Websites

Cordesman, Anthony H., Marissa Allison, Vivek Kocharlakota, Jason Lemieux, and Charles Loi. "Afghan and Iraqi Metrics and the IED Threat." Center for Strategic and International Studies, November 10, 2010. http://csis.org/files/publication/101110_ied_metrics_combined.pdf (accessed July 14, 2015). Supporting website is http://csis.org/publication/afghan-and-iraqi-metrics-and-ied-threat-afghanistan (accessed July 14, 2015).

Films and Television

The Hurt Locker. Director: Kathryn Bigelow. Voltage Pictures, 2009.

29. Congressional Testimony: David Petraeus, September 10, 2007

INTRODUCTION

On September 10, 2007 General David Petraeus and Ambassador Ryan Crocker went to Capitol Hill to brief a joint session of the U.S. Congress House Armed Services and Senate Foreign Relations committees on the situation in Iraq. More than a commander giving accountability to Congress, this hearing was part of a high stakes theater which was unfolding. The testimony of these two men was part of a larger political debate happening in Washington, D.C., about the nature of the Iraq War and the potential for further action in the country.

SUNNI AWAKENING—*SAHWA*

Organic or emergent are good words to describe what happened in the *Sahwa* or *awakening* in Anbar Province. This means that this movement grew naturally rather than being created by a person or event. The exact beginning of the *awakening* is nearly impossible to state, but in 2005 and 2006 several tribal leaders in Anbar became frustrated with the death, destruction, and chaos and they decided to oppose the foreign fighters. At first these were not senior tribal leaders, but typically sons or nephews. They gathered small groups of men and they cooperated with U.S. forces operating in their areas. By the time *The Surge* began in 2007 the *awakening* had been going on for more than a year. Sunni tribes were becoming more and more likely to oppose al-Qaeda and other similar groups and to fight against them. Because the local tribes knew who was an Iraqi tribal member and who was a foreigner it was much easier for them to identify the enemy. The intelligence provided by the *awakening* was more important than the combat actions conducted by them. In many ways, this was what changed the combat dynamic in Iraq more so than the extra deployment of U.S. soldiers. That said, extra U.S. forces did make engagement with and exploitation of *awakening* information much more effective.

In addition to the testimony a written report was released that included the assessment of both the general and the ambassador. The excerpts in this chapter are from that report.

The Surge has already become shrouded in myth by the time this book was written. It is regularly misunderstood what it was and what it did. The intent was to send 30,000 additional U.S. ground forces into Iraq to stabilize the security situation and by so doing to create an environment wherein the political problems could be solved. This meant that five additional brigade combat teams came into Iraq, many of the currently deployed brigades were extended to stay 15 months rather than twelve months as they were original sent to do. General Petraeus often spoke of a surge of ideas which was espoused primarily in the new U.S. Army and USMC field manual titled *Counterinsurgency* (refer to Chapter 27). General Petraeus taking command of Multi-National Forces-Iraq was also part of this surge. His plan was to get soldiers off the large forward-operating bases and have them be and live among the people to provide security to the populace. The idea being that if the populace believed that the United States would work and fight for them then they would be more supportive of coalition ideas. The additional U.S. forces coincided with a growing Sunni *awakening* that was leading tribal leaders to oppose al-Qaeda and other extreme groups and work with coalition forces.

The Surge was more than U.S. forces. It included the Iraqi events that most observers and commentators did not understand. When political debates rage about whether or not *The Surge* was successful it is important to understand what all was included in the years 2006–2009. It was much more than additional soldiers.

KEEP IN MIND AS YOU READ

1. MoveOn.org published a full-page ad in the *New York Times* accusing General Petraeus of "cooking the books" and labeled him as "General Betray Us," an obvious play on his name. This was the most blatant criticism of both the testimony and the conduct of the war. MoveOn.org is a progressive or liberal public policy advocacy group and political action committee.
2. Members of the Senate Foreign Relations committee in 2007 included presidential candidate and future vice president Joseph Biden, who also served as the committee chair, then candidate and future president Barack Obama, and future secretary of defense Chuck Hagel.

Document 29: Excerpt from Report to Congress on the Situation in Iraq, General David H. Petraeus, Commander, Multi-National Force, Iraq, September 10–11, 2007

Current Situation and Trends

The most significant development in the past six months likely has been the increasing emergence of tribes and local citizens rejecting Al Qaeda and other extremists. This has, of course, been most visible in Anbar Province. A year ago the province was assessed as "lost" politically. Today, it is a model of what happens when local leaders and citizens decide to oppose Al Qaeda and reject its Taliban-like ideology. While Anbar is unique and the model it provides cannot be replicated everywhere in Iraq, it does demonstrate the dramatic change in security that is possible with the support and participation of local citizens. . . . other tribes have been inspired by the actions of those in Anbar and have volunteered to fight extremists as well. We have, in coordination with the Iraqi government's National Reconciliation Committee, been engaging these tribes and groups of local citizens who want to oppose extremists and to contribute to local security. Some 20,000 such individuals are already being hired for the Iraqi Police, thousands of others are being assimilated into the Iraqi Army, and thousands more are vying for a spot in Iraq's Security Forces.

Iraqi Security Forces

Iraqi Security Forces have continued to grow, to develop their capabilities, and to shoulder more of the burden of providing security for their country. . .there are now nearly 140 Iraqi Army, National Police, and Special Operations Forces Battalions in the fight, with about 95 of those capable of taking the lead in operations, albeit with some coalition support. Beyond that, all of Iraq's battalions have been heavily involved in combat operations that often result in the loss of leaders, soldiers, and equipment. These losses are among the shortcomings identified by operational readiness assessments, but we should not take from these assessments the impression that Iraqi forces are not in the fight and contributing. Indeed, despite their shortages, many Iraqi units across Iraq now operate with minimal coalition assistance.

As counterinsurgency operations require substantial numbers of boots on the ground, we are helping the Iraqis expand the size of their security forces. Currently, there are some 445,000 individuals on the payrolls of Iraq's Interior and Defense Ministries. Based on recent decisions by Prime Minister Maliki, the number of Iraq's security forces will grow further by the end of this year, possibly by as much as 40,000. Given the security challenges Iraq faces, we support this decision, and we will work with the two security ministries as they continue their efforts to expand their basic training capacity, leader development programs, logistical structures and elements, and various other institutional capabilities to support the substantial growth in Iraqi forces.

Significantly, in 2007, Iraq will, as in 2006, spend more on its security forces than it will receive in security assistance from the United States. In fact, Iraq is becoming one of the United States' larger foreign military sales customers, committing some $1.6 billion to FMS already, with the possibility of up to $1.8 billion more being committed before the end of this year. . .

To summarize, the security situation in Iraq is improving, and Iraqi elements are slowly taking on more of the responsibility for protecting their citizens. Innumerable challenges lie ahead; however, Coalition and Iraqi Security Forces have made progress toward achieving sustainable security. As a result, the United States will be in a position to reduce its forces in Iraq in the months ahead.

Recommendations

One may argue that the best way to speed the process in Iraq is to change the MNF-I mission from one that emphasizes population security, counter-terrorism, and transition, to one that is strictly focused on transition and counter-terrorism. Making that change now would, in our view, be premature. We have learned before that there is a real danger in handing over tasks to the Iraqi Security Forces before their capacity and local conditions warrant. In fact, the drafters of the recently released National Intelligence Estimate on Iraq recognized this danger when they wrote, and I quote, "We assess that changing the mission of Coalition forces from a primarily counterinsurgency and stabilization role to a primary combat support role for Iraqi forces and counterterrorist operations to prevent AQI from establishing a safe haven would erode security gains achieved thus far."

In describing the recommendations I have made, I should note again that, like Ambassador Crocker, I believe Iraq's problems will require a long-term effort. There are no easy answers or quick solutions. And though we both believe this effort can succeed, it will take time. Our assessments underscore, in fact, the importance of recognizing that a premature drawdown of our forces would likely have devastating consequences.

That assessment is supported by the findings of a 16 August Defense Intelligence Agency report on the implications of a rapid withdrawal of US forces from Iraq. Summarizing it in an unclassified fashion, it concludes that a rapid withdrawal would result in the further release of the strong centrifugal forces in Iraq and produce a number of dangerous results, including a high risk of disintegration of the Iraqi Security Forces; rapid deterioration of local security initiatives; Al Qaeda-Iraq regaining lost ground and freedom of maneuver; a marked increase in violence and further ethno-sectarian displacement and refugee flows; alliances of convenience by Iraqi groups with internal and external forces to gain advantages over their rivals; and exacerbation of already challenging regional dynamics, especially with respect to Iran.

Lieutenant General Odierno and I share this assessment and believe that the best way to secure our national interests and avoid an unfavorable outcome in Iraq is to continue to focus our operations on securing the Iraqi people while targeting terrorist groups and militia extremists and, as quickly as conditions are met, transitioning security tasks to Iraqi elements.

Source: David H. Petraeus. *Report to Congress on the Situation in Iraq.* Headquarters, Multi-National Forces-Iraq, Baghdad, Iraq, September 10–11, 2007. Available at: https://www.gpo.gov/fdsys/pkg/CHRG-110shrg44322/html/CHRG-110shrg44322.htm (accessed December 25, 2015).

AFTERMATH

The political nature of the war by 2007 meant that this testimony would be viewed in a partisan way. Many of the members of congress accused General Petraeus and Ambassador Crocker of presenting the Bush Administration's perspective rather than an open assessment from their perspectives. This was part of the criticism in the MoveOn.org advertisement in the *New York Times* as well as other sources.

At the time of the testimony the BBC reported on a poll of the Iraqi people that stated that 70 percent (93% among Sunnis and 50% among Shia) of the Iraqi people believed that the Surge made security worse in Iraq. Simple statistics on the number of attacks provided data which indicated that by September 2007 the violence was decreasing, but it would require many more months before the violence returned to 2004 levels.

The debate of success in Iraq is linked to the notion of success or lack of success of the Surge. As noted this became a critical point in the partisan political fighting in Congress once the Democrats took control in the 2006 elections and also in the 2008 presidential campaign. The questions about success or failure in Iraq became more poignant and significant in 2014 and 2015 as the IS gained control of areas of Iraq and U.S. military forces returned to Iraq to coordinate training and air strikes.

SONS OF IRAQ

The Sunni *awakening* that grew in Anbar Province became more and more formal over time. By 2007 the U.S. military began paying Sunni "militias" to provide security and intelligence. Over time these groups of fighters gained the name the *Sons of Iraq*. The idea of U.S. leaders was to integrate these tribal fighters into something of a formal militia under the authority of the Iraqi government. During 2008 the United States exerted pressure on the Nuri al-Maliki-led government to bring these fighters into some official status. By the end of the year tens of thousands of fighters received pay from the Iraqi government. Critics of the program said that this was paying bribe money to people who had American and Iraqi blood on their hands. Those who supported the program expressed the benefits in terms of reduced violence, increased intelligence reporting on foreign fighters and al-Qaeda (and other extremist groups) operatives and operations. Payment of the Sons of Iraq was always problematic. The Iraqi prime minister did not want to pay them and it required consistent U.S. attention and pressure to make this happen. Once that pressure ended then the program rapidly ended as well.

ASK YOURSELF

1. Did the Surge work? The answer to this question is contained in the definition of success. What does success look like? What are the metrics that demonstrate whether or not success is happening on the ground? Is this measured by the number of attacks or by a general sense of the people—do they feel more secure? The answers to these questions determine whether or not someone believes the Surge worked.

2. If in fact the Surge was a success, what caused it to be successful? Was it the deployment of five U.S. combat brigades? Was it the use of a new counterinsurgency doctrine as published in FM 3–24? Was it a new, dynamic leader in Iraq? Was it the Sunni awakening? Was it the acquiescence of the Shia-led government to pay Sunni fighters in the Sons of Iraq program? Was it all of these things in some combination we do not understand?

TOPICS TO CONSIDER

1. How long does something need to be effective in order for it to be considered a success? The Surge seemed to work in that violence decreased in Iraq for a number of years. The effectiveness of the Surge was called into question in 2014 when the Islamic State swept into Iraq seizing territory. Is the failure of the Iraqi Army and government in 2014 evidence that the Surge failed? What was the actual purpose of the Surge? Was that purpose fulfilled?

2. The nature of emergent ideas and phenomenon is difficult to understand. Why do people accept new ideas? What causes people to want to change? In many ways this is the most important question to come from this war. Is it possible to make people change faster or does this need to happen at an organic pace?

Further Reading

Al-Ali, Zaid. *The Struggle for Iraq's Future: How Corruption, Incompetence and Sectarianism Have Undermined Democracy.* New Haven, CT: Yale University Press, 2014.

Kilcullen, David. *Counterinsurgency*. Oxford: Oxford University Press, 2010.

Kilcullen, David. *The Accidental Guerilla: Fighting Small Wars in the Midst of a Big One*. Oxford: Oxford University Press, 2011.

Mansoor, Peter. *Surge: My Journey with General David Petraeus and the Remaking of the Iraq War*. New Haven, CT: Yale University Press, 2013.

Woodward, Bob. *The War Within: A Secret White House History*. New York: Simon & Schuster, 2008.

Websites

BBC News. "US surge has failed—Iraqi Poll." http://news.bbc.co.uk/2/hi/middle_east/6983841.stm (accessed July 7, 2015). Specific poll data at http://news.bbc.co.uk/1/shared/bsp/hi/pdfs/10_09_07_iraqpollaug2007_full.pdf (accessed July 7, 2015).

Films and Television

American War Generals. Executive producers: Peter Bergen, Tresha Mabile, Jonathan Towers. National Geographic Channel, 2014.

30. Military Transition Team Advising the Iraqi Security Forces: Mark Hull

INTRODUCTION

The U.S. military used military transition teams (MiTTs) as the primary vehicle for training the Iraqi Army from 2006 until 2011. A MiTT could consist of 10–16 personnel from active duty, National Guard, or reserves. Many of the teams included personnel from the army, navy, Marine Corps, and air force. The ranks typically ranged from lieutenant colonel to sergeant. The teams could range in size from three up to 45, but the most common size was a force in the teens. Each team also had between two and six translators assigned. The idea was for this dozen or so people to help train and provide assistance to an Iraqi brigade which is a force commanded by a colonel usually made up of about three battalions and somewhere around 2,000 to 4,000. There were numerous types of transition teams working with different types of Iraqi Security Forces. The MiTTs were primarily with the Iraqi Army.

The relationship between the MiTT and the Iraqi force was critical to creating an environment of cooperation and development. The point of the MiTT was to build the capacity of Iraqi Army units so they could lead the fight against the insurgents and the U.S. military could depart Iraq. The experience related below is not indicative of the majority of MiTT experiences. In many cases the relationships between Iraqi leaders and U.S. personnel were excellent and the MiTT accomplished great things in terms of developing their Iraqi counterparts. There are numerous stories of MiTT leaders and Iraqi commanders forging lasting bonds of friendship. What is offered below presents an understanding of the challenges in cross-cultural relationships.

Dr. Mark Hull, a military intelligence officer with the U.S. Army Reserves, deployed to Iraq in 2006–2007 as part of a MiTT assigned to mentor and train two different units of the Iraqi Army. The first unit, 9–3 [9th Division, 3rd Brigade] IA (Iraqi Army) was located in Taji, Iraq. The second, a Kurdish brigade from northern Iraq, was assigned to join with coalition forces in supporting the Surge. Dr. Hull's unit was responsible for bringing the Kurdish unit to Baghdad and working with them during the Surge. In the final months of his deployment, Hull's team worked with an Iraqi police unit. Dr. Hull was also a civilian lawyer with experience as a prosecutor.

KEEP IN MIND AS YOU READ

1. The requirement to advise someone from a foreign culture while having limited language experience places a great deal of stress on the ability of the leaders. This can be problematic in the best of circumstances.
2. The violence in Iraq in 2006 until 2008 was high and was not solely directed against those in uniform who were fighting in official capacities. Families were attacked. Children were kidnapped. This environment caused many, if not all, Iraqis to question their service and dedication.

Document 30: Excerpts from Interview with Mark Hull, Military Transition Team Member, 2006–2007

PRT Construction vs. Iranian Reconstruction

Question: How did the Iraqis respond to you?
Answer: [Concerning the 1–2 IA [1st Division, 2nd Brigade], specifically] They were outwardly polite and seemingly cooperative. Once you got a closer look at the way that they did business and the way they operated, you realized what essentially was a criminal enterprise. Everybody from the division commander to the brigade commanders to the battalion commanders were on the take. There were established procedures—I think my law or prosecution background either helped me or hurt me, depending on how you want to look at it. I was able to piece together how they were stealing money and moving money and it was vast.

Question: It was an established kind of practice?
Answer: Yes. Everything from taking kickbacks from contractors to selling equipment, pretty much any kind of equipment. There was a distribution chain that started at the very top and depending on what level of officer you were, you got a percentage every month.

Question: It wasn't like it was ad hoc or something that was brand new to the Army?
Answer: It was the mafia.

Question: Within the military?
Answer: Sure. In fact, the structure was eerily almost exactly like the mafia, in terms of the organizational relationships and how things got moved. It was not a happy parallel.

*****

Question: Okay. What was their [Kurdish unit] experience level?
Answer: They had fought, I think, in tribal or regional conflicts going back to the Saddam area, some of them, although many of them not. They had the same issues

in terms of maybe half the brigade was imaginary and similar sorts of corruption issues. That got worse once we got to Baghdad.

Question: Was there a benefit to having all these imaginary soldiers? Now you have run across this in two different units.

Answer: Well, it's free money if you're the commanding officer or the senior members of the brigade, because you're still receiving payroll, except some of the people don't actually exist so the money goes directly into the kickback scheme.

Question: Okay. So, they keep the names on the role in order to get that extra money and then they distribute that among the people making sure that there's the names on the roles.

Answer: It goes to the syndicate and again, it's very clear [to the people involved] how much money or what percentage each person gets. If you're an officer who doesn't take money, you're not there very long.

Question: You get drummed out or moved?

Answer: You are not—you don't stay and certainly don't stay in the brigade. I had suspicions that perhaps worse things were going on, but I couldn't prove that.

Question: Not good to be an honest Iraqi military officer?

Answer: It would be very dangerous to you and your family if you reported corruption inside the unit.

*****

Answer: The thing that happened at the end of the deployment was, I thought, was sort of telling. I received a report from [U.S. Army 1st Cavalry] Division that they'd intercepted a phone call between one of our staff colonels and the Jaish al Mahdi militia—the guys we were fighting. The [Iraqi] colonel had offered to sell my team to the Mahdi militia in exchange for—or I mean, they would allow us to get killed to, in exchange for the Mahdi militia not attacking the Kurds.

Question: So, the Kurdish colonel . . .

Answer: Sold my team.

Question: Was he making this deal?

Answer: Yes.

And we were still obligated to give them [the Iraqi brigade] money every month and make sure that they had new equipment. All this for people that were going to have us killed. It wasn't a good working relationship.

Question: I can imagine. With regard to equipment you said that you were giving them new equipment every month, is that because they were selling off their current . . .

Answer: Yes.

Question: Who were they selling it to?

Answer: Black market. They would send truck loads back to Kurdistan from Baghdad that had ammunition, clothing, weapons, air conditioners, anything with copper, light fixtures, light bulbs, pencils, I mean, anything that they could conceivably take, you could open a tent and sell on the black market up in Erbil. They took all of it back home.

Question: Then we turned around and gave them more?

Answer: Yes.

*****

Question: Okay. So then, they transfer you to the national police. Did you have a different experience with the national police?

Answer: It was worse.

They were serious thugs. I mean, they were killing people and kidnapping people. They were serious, serious mobsters.

Question: Okay. So beyond criminal enterprise they had other activities?

Answer: They were manning checkpoints—and they [the unit personnel] were all Shi'a—they were manning checkpoints with Shi'a militia guys and we had pretty substantial reports, I think high reliability reports, that they were pulling people out of cars that were Sunnis and making them disappear.

Question: So, they were carrying out their own ethnic . . .

Answer: Cleansing. That was the idea, which was—I think, the reason that people have said the surge worked in our area wasn't because it really necessarily worked, but it was because the Shi'a militia were able to get rid of the people that they needed to make disappear. . . .

If you ethnically cleanse a group, there is no need for violence anymore, because you won.

Question: So, their main goal in the surge . . . was just to get rid of all the Sunnis?

Answer: Force them out, I mean either you could scare them and intimidate them, which they tried to do or you could kill them or kill their families. Either way you end up with the territory and they don't, so violence drops quite a bit.

*****

Question: Have you faced any difficult challenges post deployment?

Answer: I struggled for a long time to try to resolve, I think, the basic conflict of it. I used to pride myself on trying to do the right thing or the legal thing. I never completely, I think until maybe here recently, resolved the fact that I was helping people that I knew were doing bad. That just kept going around in my head—like a never-ending circle. That's gotten very much better here in the last six, seven, eight months. I mean, noticeable better. I'm doing more law classes now and I think that's helped me out to try to find my mental and emotional center.

Source: Mark Hull. Interview by Lisa Beckenbaugh, April 22, 2013. Interview Transcript. Courtesy of the Operational Leadership Experiences Digital Collection, Combat Studies Institute, Fort Leavenworth, KS. Available at: http://cgsc.contentdm.oclc.org/cdm/singleitem/collection/p4013coll13/id/3099/rec/1 (accessed July 9, 2015).

AFTERMATH

In terms of its action in Iraq, the United States was consistently criticized for the corruption on the part of the Iraqi military leadership and poor management of resources on the part of the U.S. personnel. The U.S. Congress created a special inspector general for Iraq reconstruction in 2004 to provide oversight of the U.S. support to Iraq. Nearly every report to Congress included tremendous incidents of mismanagement or improper use of U.S. funds and failure on the part of the Iraq government to manage resources.

ASK YOURSELF

1. The Special Inspector General for Iraq Reconstruction (SIGIR) stated that he believed $8 billion was wasted outright in Iraq. Why was there so little outcry from the American people for this amount of waste?
2. While this number is shocking, to a certain extent there is waste, fraud, and abuse in every bureaucratic organization. What, if anything, can taxpayers and voters do to prevent such a blatant misuse of funds within the government?
3. Why would the U.S. leadership continue to partner with units which seemed to be working in direct opposition to stated U.S. goals and objectives?

TOPICS TO CONSIDER

1. Mark Hull stated, "I think we [the Army] did overall this job very poorly and I think it was because we were trying to do something that we knew wasn't going to be achievable. I'm still angry about people that we lost for no good purpose. I don't know if that's a lesson learned or anything. I wish it were one I hadn't had to learn." What affect does it have on the outcome of a mission if those executing the policy do not believe in the policy?

Further Reading

Al-Ali, Zaid. *The Struggle for Iraq's Future: How Corruption, Incompetence and Sectarianism Have Undermined Democracy*. New Haven, CT: Yale University Press, 2014.
Bolger, Daniel P. *Why We Lost: A General's Inside Account of the Iraq and Afghanistan Wars*. Boston: Houghton Mifflin Harcourt, 2014.

Websites

Ackerman, Spencer. "Over $8B of the Money You Spent Rebuilding Iraq was Wasted Outright." Wired. http://www.wired.com/2013/03/iraq-waste/ (accessed July 9, 2015).
Special Inspector General for Iraq Reconstruction. Archived Site. http://cybercemetery.unt.edu/archive/sigir/20130930184730/http://www.sigir.mil/ (accessed July 9, 2015).

Films and Television

American War Generals. Executive producers: Peter Bergen, Tresha Mabile, Jonathan Towers. National Geographic Channel, 2014.

Iraq for Sale: The War Profiteers. Director: Robert Greenwald. Brave New Films, 2006.

Frontline: Losing Iraq. Director: Michael Kirk. PBS, 2014.

31. British Perspective in Basra (3): Stephen Campbell

INTRODUCTION

The British mainly controlled the area around Basra and what was known as Multi-National Division South or MND-S throughout most of the war. As previously stated, the British had a history in Basra that dated back to their original occupation in 1914. For much of the war Basra appeared to be the model city and the British conducted themselves as the model occupiers. Numerous articles appeared touting British success in keeping peace. The peacefulness was a façade; as seen in previous chapters, insurgents were infiltrating the society and slowly making life for the British operating in and around Basra more and more painful. In 2008 this exploded with Sadrist militias taking control of the city. This forced a powerful response from Prime Minister Nuri al-Maliki and the Iraqi Army in what was known as the charge of the knights. This was nearly simultaneous with fighting happening in Sadr City.

Major Stephen Campbell, an intelligence officer in the U.K. Army, deployed to Iraq three times in support of Operation Iraqi Freedom. His deployments took place in 2004, 2005–2006, and 2008. During his deployments he served in Basra with the 1st U.K.

CHARGE OF THE KNIGHTS

Basra was a troubled city from early on in the coalition occupation. Several Shiite militias dominated the security and governance of the city running things like a mafia-style organization rather than a representative and responsive government. Basra became a major transit point for opium and other drug smuggling. It was also a hub of Iranian influence. The Iranians brought in explosively formed penetrators (EFPs) that were used by the insurgency to attack and penetrate coalition armored vehicles. British forces handed over security of Basra to Iraqi "officials" in 2007 though those officials tended to be in the employ or under the influence of one or more of the militia. The situation grew so dire by late March 2008 that the prime minister ordered additional Iraqi Army and police units from the center and west of Iraq to move to Basra and he took charge there himself. This rapid movement of forces was designated the charge of the knights by the Iraqi military and it was their first all-Iraq operation since 2003. U.S. and coalition forces would play a very small role in the actual fighting though they provided surveillance and targeting assistance.

Armoured Division and the 3rd U.K. Mechanized Division. His first deployment from February to August, 2004, began just two months after his commissioning from the Royal Military Academy in Sandhurst, England.

By deploying multiple times to the same area Major Campbell was able to experience various stages of the war in Iraq and to witness the shifts in focus that took place within the local populace, the British Army, and the coalition.

KEEP IN MIND AS YOU READ

1. Information is a critical currency in military operations. The challenge is that different armies and different cultures communicate information in different ways and with different precision. Throughout the Iraq War one of the greatest benefits of the Military Transition Teams (MiTTs) was their ability, when working with an Iraqi unit, to provide information on what was happening in a U.S. or NATO format that was understood and accepted at the headquarters level that controlled the supporting firepower; thus fires could be delivered in support of Iraqi units.

2. Cell phones provided command communications throughout the Iraq War for the senior Iraqi leaders. Senior commanders and political leaders called subordinates and discussed tactical actions and directed operations over the phone.

3. In what became known as *the Charge of the Knights* Prime Minister Maliki did not spend a lot of time in planning. Once he decided to go to Basra, he went and then he coordinated on the fly, as it were.

Document 31: Excerpts from Interview with Stephen Campbell, British Military Intelligence Officer, 2008

So, I went out to Iraq [with] three days' notice, beginning March of 2008 as an acting major . . . I was arriving at the time when the headquarters, the sole remaining British base in Iraq, was being rocketed four or five times a day, night and day. The campaign narrative for us was, "We are the last headquarters to see this through to an exit." . . .

. . . It was kind of the perfect storm of unexpected events that kind of resulted in me arriving in Basra in the beginning of March. I arrived there and I was horrified at what I saw . . .

For us to be so, kind of, woefully impotent in 2008 really, you know, just kind of aggravated me that our operational approach had been so shallow, hollow, I don't know, bankrupt. It hadn't achieved any of the goals that we had set for ourselves and yet we seemed to be kind of lying to ourselves about that. We talked about stuff a lot and tried to work out a way ahead. To be fair to [the British force commander], when I arrived he was already concerned that the deal we'd done in Basra had basically hung the Iraqi Security Forces out on their own, left the population to the mercy of the Mujahideen basically and that things were getting worse. . . .

[The J2] just had that [intelligence] collection done. He'd done the analysis. Had the report written and I arrived as the deputy commander, the British one-star, was sending the report back to him through his aide de camp (ADC), who was a junior captain, saying, "This report is alarmist. I want you to delete all these passages." I basically got to the level of, I was about to give him my rank slide in my weapon and say, "I'm refusing to soldier in this environment. He is manipulating intelligence for political ends. This is unacceptable. I refuse to take part in this. I'm quitting. I insist you either arrest me or stop what you're doing." I even asked the legal representative quietly what position I would be in if I did that, because I took it that seriously. I thought, "Well, if [we] can't collect intelligence. If we can't then write and brief that intelligence to the commander and to a wider audience that things are going wrong, because the commander's telling us 'We're not allowed to say they're going wrong.' I refuse to take part in the army. That's not why I joined. That's not what we're here to do." . . .

The thing that people never really got was that the Iraqis were real people and they had their own view of the world. They had their own view of their own country. If you were a Shi'a politician, whose powerbase was in southern Iraq, you probably knew what was going on in southern Iraq. You can only brief them so many times in Baghdad not to worry about Basra and have his relatives on the phone telling him that doctors and lawyers and women were being murdered in Basra by the Jaish al Mahdi before he gets a little bit sick of that and wants to do something about it. It will be interest[ing] if this ever comes out formally in history, but I got told multiple stories about how this happened from people who were involved. The one I think is given most credibility is that Nuri al-Maliki had some family connections and these are very loose Iraqi family connections, within the Iraqi Security Forces, particularly Iraqi Special Forces, but also living in Basra. He found out about a friend of the family or a member of the family who was a doctor who was killed and he had a nephew or a distant cousin in the Iraqi Special Forces. He basically pulled all this different information from different sources together and thought, "What I'm being told about Basra isn't right." The way the political calculus for him changed whereby he though, "Okay, I need to do something about the Sadrists even though they were kind of complicit in me becoming prime minister within the Shi'a block. I need to do something about this. This can't stand. I've got to do something about it. I can do something about it. Let's do something about it." . . .

We didn't have any embedded people on the ground with [the Iraqi] units that were fighting. They would tell us, "There's militiamen on this block shooting at us, level it." We'd say, "Well, we can't level a block." We'd put a [aerial reconnaissance] platform over it, look down there and not really see anything, just some people moving around. Then we'd go, "Well, we can't see troops in contact. We don't have anyone that can confirm that there's not going to be a punitive collateral damage issue, so we can't fire." You can very quickly see how we're in the right from our perspective and they're in the right from their perspective, because they're fighting. Very quickly we're not really adding any value, are we? Then also, because we don't have anyone embedded on the ground with them, we can't have any situational awareness or understanding. We don't know where the Iraqi Security Force units are, because Nuri al-Maliki essentially just pulled a division from here, a division from there, and just chucked them into Basra. They've got no maps, there's no plan, there's no operations process for having them go, there's no sensible, "Okay, you'll base here and then we'll have FOBs here, project power here." They just got chucked into this meat grinder that was . . . central and southern Basra.

The way Basra is, you've got three big housing estates that kind of ring it. You've got old Basra in the center on the Shatt al-Arab River, which is the old historic Basra, which was the Venice of the Middle East. The Iran-Iraq War ruined that; the sewage is a mess. The place is shattered. The Iran-Iraq War caus[ed] internal refugees, displaced people, and then the Marsh Arabs have been moved off the land, creating even more. So, you have this city of slums sort of surrounding the old town. In front of the city of slums, Sadrists, they're all from Maysan to a large extent. They're a great recruiting ground for Shi'a extremists. Because they surround the city, they dominate all the routes in. Once you get your way in, you're kind of surrounded, because just the geography of the thing. So, the Iraqi Security Forces in the first 48-hours were in a really bad position, really bad position. . . .

Our infantry unit that was doing the training for the Iraqi Security Forces on the Friday, it was doing it detached. On the Monday, it was doing it embedded. We improvised and then London caught up.

That ten-day period is a period I will never forget. It was a historic time to be there. I mean, you had the prime minister down there, you had the deputy prime minister. You had US two-stars coming down. It was an incredible kind of surge into Basra. I'll never forget it was the first morning Gen. Flynn was down, so I would guess that would be three days or four days in, but we had a big meeting with the Iraqi Security Forces guys Camp MAK at the time. . . . Then from that meeting we were waiting for the helicopter to come in and were waiting on the concrete and Gen. Flynn rolled out a map of Basra. You had his three US colonels with him and the British one-star with him and I was kind of standing over his shoulder. He rolled out of the map and was, I can't remember exactly which unit took what, but it was something like, "82d [Airborne] you take the eastern bank of the river. 101st [Airborne] you take the southwest. Marines you take the center and the Brits will catch up when they can. This is what we're going to do. Move your MiTT units to these areas. We're going to surround the Jaish al Mahdi and we're going to establish our lines of communication. We're going [to] get into a position of dominance. Once we [do] that we'll then see where the politicians want to take things. Once we've done that then we're on the up." I remember looking at the British brigade commander, he had sunglasses on and he was chewing gum, I remember looking at him and just shaking my head. It was an unspoken thing between us, he was nodding as if he was a part of this process. To be fair, I mean, he was, but he was only a part of the process because he made the effort to be there. They could have done that all entirely themselves . . .

I put up the J2 slide and it was a very, very red slide of Basra. It basically showed red surrounding the city, purple a little bit being fought over and then two very small patches where the Iraqi Security Forces bases were. There was a palpable intake of breath, because it kind of said, "Look, this is how bad things actually are." Then the operations officer (J3) guys who followed me might as well just have put up a question mark on a slide for where the Iraqi Security Forces were, because they're like, "Just don't know. Don't know where they are." The Corps headquarters put up with that nonsense for about 72-hours. Then they said, "Right, we don't know what's going on down there. This is not satisfactory. We're going to send down," they called it, "Corps tactical operations center (TOC)." They sent 100 staff officers with a two-star commander who was one of the deputy force commanders, [I] think it was Gen. [George] Flynn of the US Marines—absolutely great officer, great guy. Our division headquarters was only 100 strong anyway and it was under a two-star commander. So, kind of looked at them and thought, "You're replacing us aren't you? You are rightly replacing us, because we are not adequate to the task that faces us." We weren't. We were quite unequivocal about it at the time, that the military reputation of this headquarters is not high right now, because we are unable to produce satisfactory answers to any questions. The most basic one being, "What is going on?" . . .

All of the sudden you could have the Iraqi Security Forces actually fighting in the streets with Americans in close support where you could give them fire support, different platforms, and get situational awareness of what they were doing . . . We began to take the initiative back internally. We were like, "Right, let's organize these guys. The prime minister's come down. He's commanding operations from a mobile phone in Basra palace. Let's engage with him, let's add some value, let's try and get the military forces pulling all together in the same direction. Let's try and not get chucked into a meat grinder, but maybe take the lines of communication to the city, establish ourselves in a firm operational footing and then go in and take the tactical advantage. So, we began to sort ourselves and then just sent us an e-mail and told us how to support them. He was stepping up to engage and add value, which was good. The reason I looked at him, because I was looking at him and I thought, "You know the same thing I know that this is failure for us. For our campaign to have got to this stage, where the Iraqis are having to reinvade their own city, because it was in such a bad condition and the only people who can give them the support they need right now are the Americans. We have failed. How did this happen?" That was a real bitter moment. It was a bitter moment, because I was glad that they were there, because we'd done such a bad job. I was relieved to see someone who was going to come down and take it seriously. That was remarkable experience to be a part of that and it was then good to then see things turn around.

So, in the next set of 20 days we turned things around and things got an awful lot better. Then that tour was the only one that had any professional and personal satisfaction, because over the course of it we did all the things right that we'd been doing wrong in the previous six years.

Source: Stephen Campbell. Interview by Lisa Beckenbaugh, August 27, 2013. Interview Transcript. Courtesy of the Operational Leadership Experiences Digital Collection, Combat Studies Institute, Fort Leavenworth, KS. Available at: http://cgsc.contentdm.oclc.org/cdm/singleitem/collection/p4013coll13/id/3100/rec/1 (accessed July 23, 2015).

AFTERMATH

Basra combined with the fighting in Sadr City ended the Jaysh al-Mahdi as a major irritant for the coalition forces and the government of Iraq. This was a powerful display of Iraqi commitment to assert government control over militias—in this case, militias from a political block that had supported the prime minister. This was very serious and it worked.

The British handed over their responsibility for their sector in 2009 and British forces departed Iraq. Until the time of writing this book the war in Iraq is a highly sensitive issue in British politics. The level of sensitivity was demonstrated in late 2014 and early 2015 when the British minister of defense sent a few British soldiers to Iraq as part of the coalition to fight the Islamic State with a promise to send more. That promise was shortly rescinded by the British prime minister, who in the midst of a national election, could not be seen as supporting Iraq even though the plan was to send trainers to teach the Iraqis how to deal with IEDs. This wasn't because of the sensitivity of the mission or the opponent, but because of the place. Iraq was toxic in British politics.

ASK YOURSELF

1. Why did the British pull back so much? Was this all about casualty avoidance? The impact of domestic politics on the behavior of specific coalition participants was significant throughout the war.
2. Americans get a lot of criticism internationally for being brash, muscling in, and taking charge. Much of this may be rightly deserved. In this instance one can see the benefits of aggressive action and taking charge. What empowered the American leadership to act boldly?

TOPICS TO CONSIDER

1. The change in loyalty or perceived loyalty of parties and religious sects was powerful in Iraq. Moqtada al-Sadr supported Nuri al-Maliki for prime minister and the Sadrists were generally supporters early on in his administration. The prime minister's attack into Basra was an attack on Shia and risked alienating his base of support. He did it anyway. It is worth reflecting on the importance of political support and perceived government legitimacy and which trumps which.

Further Reading

Bolger, Daniel P. *Why We Lost: A General's Inside Account of the Iraq and Afghanistan Wars.* Boston: Houghton Mifflin Harcourt, 2014.

Broadwell, Paula. *All In: The Education of General David Petraeus.* New York: Penguin Press, 2012.

Mansoor, Peter. *Surge: My Journey with General David Petraeus and the Remaking of the Iraq War.* New Haven, CT: Yale University Press, 2013.

Robinson, Linda. *Tell Me How This Ends: General David Petraeus and the Search for a Way Out of Iraq.* New York: PublicAffairs, 2008.

Sky, Emma. *The Unraveling: High Hopes and Missed Opportunities in Iraq.* New York: PublicAffairs, 2015

Films and Television

American War Generals. Executive producers: Peter Bergen, Tresha Mabile, Jonathan Towers. National Geographic Channel, 2014.

Frontline: Bush's War. Director: Michael Kirk. PBS, 2008.

32. Brigade Commander in Sadr City: John Hort

INTRODUCTION

In 2015 senior U.S. military leaders suggested that the Battle of Sadr City in 2008 was the battle to study in preparation for fighting the Islamic State in the city of Mosul. This chapter addresses why what happened in Sadr City was different. Events in early 2008 in Iraq turned the Iraq War in several ways. As explained in the previous chapter there were two major areas of conflict—Basra and Sadr City. The fighting began in Basra between the Iraqi security forces and Shia militias. Nearly simultaneously the fighting spread to Sadr City. Some have suggested that the success of the surge and the implementation of the Baghdad Security Plan were critical to the actions in this battle in that there was little to no concurrent threat from Sunni tribes, cities, or villages allowing the U.S. and Iraqi forces to focus solely on the Shia issues raised with the uprising in Basra and the near simultaneous uprising in Sadr City.

The Battle of Sadr City began on March 23, 2008, though it was not immediately apparent for U.S. forces that this was a major battle as all of the behaviors demonstrated by Jaish al Mahdi (JAM) were behaviors seen in the previous weeks and months both individually and in aggregate. JAM launched rockets into the International Zone (IZ) and attacked to defeat or destroy Iraqi Army outposts in and around Sadr City as well as nearby neighborhoods. As a result it took 3rd Brigade Combat Team (BCT), 4th Infantry Division until March 25 to begin a response in detail.

Sadr City is a neighborhood of Baghdad with a population of approximately 2.5 million. As a result it is not possible to fully isolate the neighborhood. It sits north-east of the IZ and on the eastern side of the Tigris River. Prior to the battle, U.S. ground forces were not allowed to enter the city and during the battle Prime Minister Maliki maintained a restriction of U.S. ground movement northeast of Al Quds Road (Route Gold). The Iraqi Army units were initially run off from their outposts, but these units returned to the fight because they were experienced and they had a positive relationship with the BCT and its subordinate unit leaders.

JAYSH AL-MAHDI

Jaysh al-Mahdi literally translates as the army of the guided one. The Mahdi is believed in Shia Islam to be one who will come from hiding (occultation) at the end of days to rule the world in peace and justice. The name for the group was given to seminary students in 2003 by Moqtada al-Sadr. They initially provided security and social welfare for Shia living in Sadr City. Throughout their existence they have been heavily supported from Iran which is where al-Sadr has fled at various times for protection both under the regime of Saddam Hussein and during the coalition occupation. Over the course of the occupation they grew in strength and influence until they reached into nearly every major Shia community in Iraq. In 2004, there was a general uprising of Shia that somewhat coincided with fighting going on in Fallujah. By June 2004, Moqtada al-Sadr called for a truce and his forces withdrew from most of the areas where they were fighting. Jaysh al-Mahdi continued to be one of the largest and most influential groups in the insurgency though unlike al-Qaeda in Iraq al-Sadr used his forces to gain political influence. In 2008, Moqtada al-Sadr tested the strength of the coalition and the Iraqi government by initiating conflict in both Basra and Sadr City and downtown Baghdad by the use of rockets fired from Sadr City. The response from the government of Iraq and the coalition forces was such that by the end of the year the Jaysh al-Mahdi was disbanded. In 2010, al-Sadr's party won 40 of 325 seats in parliament and he called for a reinstatement of the organization. They were officially reformed in 2014, now called Peace Companies, to protect Shia shrines from the advance of the Islamic State.

Prime minister Maliki ordered U.S. and Iraqi forces into Sadr City (with U.S. forces limited to Route Gold) to stop the rockets being fired into the IZ. The battle took place in two phases: Operation Striker Denial (March 26–April 14) and Operation Gold Wall (April 15–May 15). Striker Denial was the isolation of Sadr City at Route Gold from other neighborhoods and Gold Wall was the construction of the 12-foot T-Wall Barrier.

KEEP IN MIND AS YOU READ

1. The Mahdi militia led by Moqtada al-Sadr was one of the most powerful and influential Shia militias in Iraq throughout the Iraq War or at least until 2008. The fighting discussed in this chapter effectively controlled them as many of their fighters were killed in the battle.
2. During the battle the U.S. forces combined surveillance and targeting at a level previously not seen. The brigade commander had the ability to control the cycle of targeting from decide to detect to deliver and assess which included the use of unmanned aerial vehicles as well as target acquisition radar to track the ballistic trajectories of rockets being fired into the Green Zone. This unprecedented linkage empowered the brigade to rapidly turn information into battlefield effects.

Document 32: Excerpt from Interview with John Hort, Commander, 3rd Brigade, 4th Infantry Division, 2008–2009

When we came in, the surge was on its way out the door. . . . [W]e decided to take risk in the central part of Baghdad and I was pushed over to the east side. . . .

I had the Adhamiyah District, which is predominately Sunni, and then the Shaab/Sadr City District was predominately Shia, if not all Shia, as you went farther east. Then, up to the north, I had a similar problem in the Isqital province with Sunni to the west and Shia to the east. . . . [T]he second concern I had was the population density in Sadr City, 2.5 million people estimate wise, and our inability to really operate in there based off of previous agreements, as well as the Iraqi Security Forces' inability to operate in there as well. This area was really a safe haven or sanctuary for some of the senior leaders of the Jaysh al-Mahdi militia special groups, splinter groups from JAM, and, obviously, there were some other groups in there, one of which was Hezbollah. . . . [T]he third would be the Iraqi Security Forces (ISF). The 11th Iraqi Army (IA) Division was a fairly new division and having kind of the Shia extremist militia still operating and influencing on this side of Baghdad there was a concern of how influenced 11th IA were in their ability to conduct objective operations against that particular element of the security problem. . . .

I was concerned about this threat. . . . I was concerned and did have a gut feeling we would see a significant uptick in violence from that particular group. Ironically from March through May of 2008, we fought JAM and the other Shia extremist in a very conventional type urban warfare in East Baghdad, with Sadr City as the epicenter of all that. The al-Qaeda threat was a weakened threat from my first deployment in 2005 and 2006 to my arrival in December 2007. Based off what we observed RIP'ing out with 2–82, al-Qaeda was a significantly weakened force. . . . I would even argue that by the time we left that we had, at least in the eastern part of Baghdad, defeated AQI (al-Qaeda in Iraq). . . .

Question: . . . Previous brigades in the Sadr City had certain restrictions on them, placed on them predominately, I guess, by the MOD (Ministry of Defense) or maybe even [Prime Minister] Maliki himself. Did you experience any of that when you took over?

Answer: I did. That was, like I said, my initial concern, kind of the safe haven concept that was going on inside Sadr City and there were definitely some rational reasons why that was done, based off some sensitivities from previous events that had occurred in Sadr City. So, that was in place when I arrived and that abruptly ended on 25 March [2008] when the Jaysh al-Mahdi militia lifted the cease fire and began to attack all Government of Iraq security locations and primarily, for us, in and around Sadr City.

Question: [T]hat new offensive, if you will, or that renewal of heavy fighting in Sadr City was a direct result of the Operation CHARGE OF THE KNIGHTS down in Basra?

Answer: . . . The Sadr City piece started on or about 25 March and was called Operation STRIKE RESOLVE for us at the brigade level. . . .

[T]hey started the kinetic activity, at least in terms of their attacks against the Iraqi Government, starting in the middle of March [2008]. That was when we began to see a steady increase in rocket attacks coming out of Sadr City. Then, on 24 or 25 March [2008], it escalated tenfold. Within about a four-day period of time, between 24–28 March [2008], they fired close to 90–100 rockets at the Green Zone and this was not just special groups. This was main stream Jaysh al-Mahdi militia. . . .

Question: Can you describe for me kind of the situation, mission, and execution of STRIKE RESOLVE?
Answer: . . . So, on 25 March [2008], not only were the rockets being shot against the Green Zone but Sadr launched an offensive operation against all the security checkpoints, particularly in and around Sadr City against the Iraqi Army and National Police and most of those checkpoints succumbed to the attacks by the militia. Either they were captured, killed, or run off, as kind of the three scenarios that happened. So, we were directed to conduct a counterattack to seize those checkpoints, those that had fallen, and reinforce those that had not. That was kind of the first phase of Operation STRIKE RESOLVE and that happened within about four or five hours or, actually, a half day and maybe a day, in one case, that it took us to get back in there and reestablish that and take that back from Jaysh al-Mahdi militia. The second phase of this was to defeat the rocket threat emanating from Sadr City and that took about 45 days to really accomplish, in terms of our ability to defeat the rocket teams, and it was a ground assault into South Sadr City with a Stryker battalion initially, followed by a reinforced armored battalion in order to seize the primary points of origin (sites that the rockets were originating from), and then UAV (unmanned aerial vehicle), Apache helicopter, and fixed wing assets on top to acquire, fix, and kill the rocket teams that were operating north of an area called Route Gold, which was kind of our limit of advance for the ground forces, not to say that those assets weren't used south of Route Gold. . . .

I mentioned to you earlier that the Iraqi Security Forces had been overrun and most of their checkpoint operations in and around Sadr City had been given an isolation mission prior to that to control the accelerants as well as enemy activity moving in and out of there. That was part of that restrictive box. We kind of had a box around Sadr City but not inside of it. But, once Moqtada al-Sadr lifted his cease fire, the Iraqi Security Forces situation deteriorated very rapidly in terms of the ability to conduct offensive operations. So, initially, everything I describe to you on the ground side, going into South Sadr City, was unilateral in nature. . . .

[O]nce we initiated contact and maintained contact and began to have effects on the enemy, the Iraqi Security Forces quickly, I would say, regenerated themselves, fired some battalion commanders, replaced other battalions, and we began to see much more competent and capable Iraqi military units arrive into the Sadr City fight for us. And I'm describing something to you that happened over about a two-week or maybe three-week period of time, starting, like I said, in late March [2008] until about the 10th or so of April [2008], that we went through kind of a unilateral phase, followed by a joint phase with us in the lead, and then, by the end, as we declared the cease fire again, or I should say MNF-I (Multi-National Force-Iraq) working with Maliki's government and Sadr's forces, the 11th IA became the lead and entered into the northern part of Sadr City for the first time, I think, since the start of the war. This was the GOIs first bona fide security element that was controlling the population, supporting the population, and bringing peace. I would say peace in terms of how the government saw it. So, that was all very good news at the end but, at the beginning, it was kind of a very difficult situation in terms of what was going on with the Iraqi military and then that changed based off of US forces setting the example and they followed and joined up with us within about three weeks into the process. . . .

We defeated, destroyed you might say, in terms of the rocket teams all but one, was kind of how we looked at it, and I think there were 700 plus enemy KIA (killed in action), Jaysh al-Mahdi militia along with special groups intermixed in that, and, like I said, we were in control of Sadr City for the first time by around 15 May [2008] and began also, in that process as we were fighting, to conduct a significant amount of infrastructure reconstruction support, working initially unilaterally based off of limited government dialogue going on between us and Sadr City but also the Government of Iraq and the local governance. But, that progressed extremely well as we went through it and reconstruction was a major part of this operation. Infrastructure damage in and around the neighborhoods, we would proceed with some significant amount of civil-military assistance to ensure that it wasn't a long term wait to get the war torn look that some of the Sadr City residents were seeing out of the picture and focused more on what Sadr City should have looked like all along, which is clean streets, electricity, water, and other things working. That became our major effort even as we were fighting and we pursued that line of operation throughout the entire post-May [2008] period to when we redeployed. . . .

We shot 800 tanks rounds. It was a very, very kinetic fight and we fought a conventional enemy too. It kind of shows you the evolution of JAM for us, at least in our 15 months, where they were kind of this hidden force attacking us on the roadways and then all of sudden coming out to fight us and for about two months very heavy contact and then dropping off almost down to zero largely because they had been attrited so much inside Sadr City. . . .

Source: John Hort. Interview by Steve Clay, December 10, 2009. Interview Transcript. Contemporary Operations Study Team. Courtesy of the Operational Leadership Experiences Digital Collection, Combat Studies Institute, Fort Leavenworth, KS.

AFTERMATH

The fighting in Sadr City ended the Jaysh al-Mahdi as a major irritant for the coalition forces and the government of Iraq. As Colonel Hort described the battle resulted in the deaths of hundreds of their fighters. The Battle of Sadr City brought together a powerful combination of precision fires, target acquisition, and surveillance and reconnaissance to result in significant U.S. technological advantage. The prime example is when JAM fired a rocket its position of origin was identified by counterfire radars and this information was passed rapidly to unmanned surveillance aircraft to visually identify the firing element. This information was again passed to precisions fires to engage and destroy the element. As the battle progressed those conducting this fight developed the patience to follow firing units back to storage or command and control facilities before launching precision strikes thus killing more than just the operators. Over the course of the battle this tactical patience paid off with the reduction of nearly the entirety of JAM leadership either through kinetic action or the flight of the enemy. This linkage of target acquisition to firing element was made possible by the subordination of all of these assets to the brigade commander.

The construction of the wall of T-walls along Route Gold created engagement opportunities for U.S. precision fires and Iraqi Army direct fires. The wall represented isolation for JAM. Both the United States and JAM perceived the wall in the same way; therefore, JAM felt it necessary to directly attack the construction of the wall. This brought JAM personnel out of buildings and into areas where they could be identified, followed, and targeted. This facilitated the rapid destruction of the remaining fighters and leadership. In many ways this was a battle of attrition as JAM lost nearly all of their fighters and all of their will to fight by the time Moqtada al-Sadr announced a ceasefire. JAM initially engaged the wall with effective sniper fire, to include caliber .50 systems, against personnel and construction equipment. US forces adapted to provide counter-sniper teams that were instrumental in regaining the initiative.

Iraqi Army units that fled at the beginning of the fighting reconstituted and became integral to the success in the middle and end of the battle as their engagements along Route Gold effectively reduced JAM's capability. This unit responded this way because they had previous battlefield experience and a positive relationship with their American partners. Once they knew they were not going to be left alone in the fight they rejoined with energy.

ASK YOURSELF

1. The transformation of this fighting was not isolated to Sadr City. As stated, this was linked to events happening in Basra as well. What led the leadership of the militias to believe that the Iraqi government was weakening? Was it the departure of *Surge* brigades or was it a general tone of violence?
2. Cooperation between the Iraqi security forces and the coalition was significant in this battle to the point that Iraqi forces were in the lead in clearing insurgents from parts of the city at the end. What empowered this transformation in the partnership?

TOPICS TO CONSIDER

1. JAM's weapon of significance was rockets—able to track to a point of origin—and they were easy to track and follow from firing position to storage and command and control locations. This brought JAM into the open to fire and they were susceptible to observation and engagement.
2. This battle features symmetry of understanding as JAM and the United States both saw al-Quds Road (Route Gold) as decisive terrain and they were both willing to exert resources toward controlling it. This brought JAM into the open where they were susceptible to observation and engagement.
3. Moqtada al-Sadr had a stake in Iraq and he ultimately sought political influence and power within the government. This always meant that there was leverage toward political accommodation, even if only to a small degree.

Further Reading

Bolger, Daniel P. *Why We Lost: A General's Inside Account of the Iraq and Afghanistan Wars.* Boston: Houghton Mifflin Harcourt, 2014.

Johnson, David E., M. Wade Markel, and Brian Shannon. *The 2008 Battle of Sadr City: Reimagining Urban Combat.* Santa Monica, CA: RAND Corporation, 2013.

Ludwig, Konrad R. K. *Stryker: The Siege of Sadr City.* La Cañada Flintridge, CA: Roland-Kjos Publishing, 2013.

Sky, Emma. *The Unraveling: High Hopes and Missed Opportunities in Iraq.* New York: PublicAffairs, 2015.

Films and Television

American War Generals. Executive producers: Peter Bergen, Tresha Mabile, Jonathan Towers. National Geographic Channel, 2014.

Frontline: Bush's War. Director: Michael Kirk. PBS, 2008.

Frontline: Losing Iraq. Director: Michael Kirk. PBS, 2014.

33. Status of Forces Agreement, November 17, 2008

INTRODUCTION

A Status of Forces Agreement (SOFA) is a common framework to discuss the rules associated with the stationing of foreign forces on sovereign soil. The U.S. government typically views a SOFA as necessary to protect the legal rights of its citizens serving in foreign countries. The agreement is designed to establish ground rules and jurisdiction for prosecution of crimes committed by U.S. forces. This can make a SOFA controversial if it is seen as placing U.S. law above that of local law; it also can be perceived as treating U.S. lives and interests as more important than those of the host nation.

This particular SOFA also placed time limitations on U.S. presence in Iraq and U.S. presence in specific places in Iraq, which makes the document more than a SOFA. In this last sense it also served as a roadmap for operational behavior. U.S. forces were directed to pull out of cities by June 2009 (only about seven months from the signing of the document) and depart the country by the end of 2011.

The document was signed by Iraqi foreign minister Hoshiyar Zebari and U.S. ambassador Ryan Crocker in an official ceremony on November 17, 2008. It was ratified by the Iraqi Parliament on November 27, 2008, and later signed by President Bush.

This is a heavily edited document because of the legal tone and technical language. Some articles are entirely omitted due to technical language and specific issues: definition of terms, tax exempt status, claims, etc.

KEEP IN MIND AS YOU READ

1. SOFAs exist because U.S. citizens want the protections afforded by U.S. law and want to avoid treatment in foreign justice systems that may be perceived as capricious or extrajudicial. This very reason for a SOFA tends to place U.S. law as superior to host nation law. Consider the implications of this when host nation law is based significantly on religious law. In such cases the local people see their laws as coming from God and therefore they are superior to any law created by man. Ideally the inherent conflict between a SOFA and what is sometimes called *sharia* law is then made clearer.

Document 33: Excerpt from Agreement between the United States of America and the Republic of Iraq on the Withdrawal of U.S. Forces from Iraq and the Organization of Their Activities during Their Temporary Presence in Iraq (Signed in Iraq on November 17, 2008)

Preamble

The United States of America and the Republic of Iraq, referred to hereafter as "the Parties":

> Recognizing the importance of: strengthening their joint security, contributing to world peace and stability, combating terrorism in Iraq, and cooperating in the security and defense spheres, thereby deterring aggression and threats against the sovereignty, security, and territorial integrity of Iraq and against its democratic, federal, and constitutional system;
>
> Affirming that such cooperation is based on full respect for the sovereignty of each of them in accordance with the purposes and principles of the United Nations Charter;
>
> Out of a desire to reach a common understanding that strengthens cooperation between them;
>
> Without prejudice to Iraqi sovereignty over its territory, waters, and airspace; and
>
> Pursuant to joint undertakings as two sovereign, independent, and coequal countries;
>
> Have agreed to the following:

Article 1: Scope and Purpose

This Agreement shall determine the principal provisions and requirements that regulate the temporary presence, activities, and withdrawal of the United States Forces from Iraq.

Article 3: Laws

1. While conducting military operations pursuant to this Agreement, it is the duty of members of the United States Forces and of the civilian component to respect Iraqi laws, customs, traditions, and conventions and to refrain from any activities that are inconsistent with the letter and spirit of this Agreement. It is the duty of the United States to take all necessary measures for this purpose. . . .

Article 4: Missions

1. The Government of Iraq requests the temporary assistance of the United States Forces for the purposes of supporting Iraq in its efforts to maintain security and stability in Iraq, including cooperation in the conduct of operations against

al-Qaeda and other terrorist groups, outlaw groups, and remnants of the former regime.

2. All such military operations that are carried out pursuant to this Agreement shall be conducted with the agreement of the Government of Iraq. Such operations shall be fully coordinated with Iraqi authorities. . . .

3. All such operations shall be conducted with full respect for the Iraqi Constitution and the laws of Iraq. Execution of such operations shall not infringe upon the sovereignty of Iraq and its national interests, as defined by the Government of Iraq. It is the duty of the United States Forces to respect the laws, customs, and traditions of Iraq and applicable international law.

4. The Parties shall continue their efforts to cooperate to strengthen Iraq's security capabilities including, as may be mutually agreed, on training, equipping, supporting, supplying, and establishing and upgrading logistical systems, including transportation, housing, and supplies for Iraqi Security Forces.

5. The Parties retain the right to legitimate self-defense within Iraq, as defined in applicable international law.

Article 5: Property Ownership

1. Iraq owns all buildings, non-relocatable structures, and assemblies connected to the soil that exist on agreed facilities and areas, including those that are used, constructed, altered, or improved by the United States Forces.

2. Upon their withdrawal, the United States Forces shall return to the Government of Iraq all the facilities and areas provided for the use of the combat forces of the United States, based on two lists. The first list of agreed facilities and areas shall take effect upon the entry into force of the Agreement. The second list shall take effect no later than June 30, 2009, the date for the withdrawal of combat forces from the cities, villages, and localities. The Government of Iraq may agree to allow the United States Forces the use of some necessary facilities for the purposes of this Agreement on withdrawal. . . .

Article 6: Use of Agreed Facilities and Areas

1. With full respect for the sovereignty of Iraq, and as part of exchanging views between the Parties pursuant to this Agreement, Iraq grants access and use of agreed facilities and areas to the United States Forces, United States contractors, United States contractor employees, and other individuals or entities as agreed upon by the Parties.

2. In accordance with this Agreement, Iraq authorizes the United States Forces to exercise within the agreed facilities and areas all rights and powers that may be necessary to establish, use, maintain, and secure such agreed facilities and areas. . . .

3. The United States Forces shall assume control of entry to agreed facilities and areas that have been provided for its exclusive use. . . .

Article 9: Movement of Vehicles, Vessels and Aircraft

1. With full respect for the relevant rules of land and maritime safety and movement, vessels and vehicles operated by or at the time exclusively for the United States Forces may enter, exit, and move within the territory of Iraq for the purposes of implementing this Agreement. . . .

2. With full respect for relevant rules of safety in aviation and air navigation, United States Government aircraft and civil aircraft that are at the time operating exclusively under a contract with the United States Department of Defense are authorized to over-fly, conduct airborne refueling exclusively for the purposes of implementing this Agreement over, and land and take off within, the territory of Iraq for the purposes of implementing this Agreement. The Iraqi authorities shall grant the aforementioned aircraft permission every year to land in and take off from Iraqi territory exclusively for the purposes of implementing this Agreement. United States Government aircraft and civil aircraft that are at the time operating exclusively under a contract with the United States Department of Defense, vessels, and vehicles shall not have any party boarding them without the consent of the authorities of the United States Forces. . . .

3. Surveillance and control over Iraqi airspace shall transfer to Iraqi authority immediately upon entry into force of this Agreement.

4. Iraq may request from the United States Forces temporary support for the Iraqi authorities in the mission of surveillance and control of Iraqi air space.

5. United States Government aircraft and civil aircraft . . . shall not be subject to payment of any taxes, duties, fees, or similar charges, including overflight or navigation fees, landing, and parking fees at government airfields. Vehicles and vessels owned or operated by or at the time exclusively for the United States Forces shall not be subject to payment of any taxes, duties, fees, or similar charges, including for vessels at government ports. Such vehicles, vessels, and aircraft shall be free from registration requirements within Iraq.

6. The United States Forces shall pay fees for services requested and received.

7. Each Party shall provide the other with maps and other available information on the location of mine fields and other obstacles that can hamper or jeopardize movement within the territory and waters of Iraq.

Article 12: Jurisdiction

Recognizing Iraq's sovereign right to determine and enforce the rules of criminal and civil law in its territory, in light of Iraq's request for temporary assistance from the United States Forces set forth in Article 4, and consistent with the duty of the members of the United States Forces and the civilian component to respect Iraqi laws, customs, traditions, and conventions, the Parties have agreed as follows:

1. Iraq shall have the primary right to exercise jurisdiction over members of the United States Forces and of the civilian component for the grave premeditated felonies enumerated pursuant to paragraph 8, when such crimes are committed outside agreed facilities and areas and outside duty status.

2. Iraq shall have the primary right to exercise jurisdiction over United States contractors and United States contractor employees.

3. The United States shall have the primary right to exercise jurisdiction over members of the United States Forces and of the civilian component for matters arising inside agreed facilities and areas; during duty status outside agreed facilities and areas; and in circumstances not covered by paragraph 1.

4. At the request of either Party, the Parties shall assist each other in the investigation of incidents and the collection and exchange of evidence to ensure the due course of justice.

5. Members of the United States Forces and of the civilian component arrested or detained by Iraqi authorities shall be notified immediately to United States Forces authorities and handed over to them within 24 hours from the time of detention or arrest. Where Iraq exercises jurisdiction pursuant to paragraph 1 of this Article, custody of an accused member of the United States Forces or of the civilian component shall reside with United States Forces authorities. United States Forces authorities shall make such accused persons available to the Iraqi authorities for purposes of investigation and trial.

6. The authorities of either Party may request the authorities of the other Party to waive its primary right to jurisdiction in a particular case. The Government of Iraq agrees to exercise jurisdiction under paragraph 1 above, only after it has determined and notifies the United States in writing within 21 days of the discovery of an alleged offense, that it is of particular importance that such jurisdiction be exercised.

7. Where the United States exercises jurisdiction pursuant to paragraph 3 of this Article, members of the United States Forces and of the civilian component shall be entitled to due process standards and protections pursuant to the Constitution and laws of the United States. Where the offense arising under paragraph 3 of this Article may involve a victim who is not a member of the United States Forces or of the civilian component, the Parties shall establish procedures through the Joint Committee to keep such persons informed as appropriate of: the status of the investigation of the crime; the bringing of charges against a suspected offender; the scheduling of court proceedings and the results of plea negotiations; opportunity to be heard at public sentencing proceedings, and to confer with the attorney for the prosecution in the case; and, assistance with filing a claim under Article 21 of this Agreement. As mutually agreed by the Parties, United States Forces authorities shall seek to hold the trials of such cases inside Iraq. If the trial of such cases is to be conducted in the United States, efforts will be undertaken to facilitate the personal attendance of the victim at the trial.

8. Where Iraq exercises jurisdiction pursuant to paragraph 1 of this Article, members of the United States Forces and of the civilian component shall be entitled to due process standards and protections consistent with those available under United States and Iraqi law. . . .

9. Pursuant to paragraphs 1 and 3 of this Article, United States Forces authorities shall certify whether an alleged offense arose during duty status. In those cases where Iraqi authorities believe the circumstances require a review of this determination, the Parties shall consult immediately through the Joint Committee, and United States Forces authorities shall take full account of the facts and circumstances and any information Iraqi authorities may present bearing on the determination by United States Forces authorities.

10. The Parties shall review the provisions of this Article every 6 months including by considering any proposed amendments to this Article taking into account the security situation in Iraq, the extent to which the United States Forces in Iraq are engaged in military operations, the growth and development of the Iraqi judicial system, and changes in United States and Iraqi law.

Article 13: Carrying Weapons and Apparel

Members of the United States Forces and of the civilian component may possess and carry weapons that are owned by the United States while in Iraq according to the authority granted to them under orders and according to their requirements and duties. Members of the United States Forces may also wear uniforms during duty in Iraq.

Article 24: Withdrawal of United States Forces from Iraq

Recognizing the performance and increasing capacity of the Iraqi Security Forces, the assumption of full security responsibility by those Forces, and based upon the strong relationship between the Parties, an agreement on the following has been reached:

1. All the United States Forces shall withdraw from all Iraqi territory no later than December 31, 2011.
2. All United States combat forces shall withdraw from Iraqi cities, villages, and localities no later than the time at which Iraqi Security Forces assume full responsibility for security in an Iraqi province, provided that such withdrawal is completed no later than June 30, 2009.
4. The United States recognizes the sovereign right of the Government of Iraq to request the departure of the United States Forces from Iraq at any time. The Government of Iraq recognizes the sovereign right of the United States to withdraw the United States Forces from Iraq at any time.
5. The Parties agree to establish mechanisms and arrangements to reduce the number of the United States Forces during the periods of time that have been determined, and they shall agree on the locations where the United States Forces will be present.

Article 25: Measures to Terminate the Application of Chapter VII to Iraq

Acknowledging the right of the Government of Iraq not to request renewal of the Chapter VII authorization for and mandate of the multinational forces contained in United Nations Security Council Resolution 1790 (2007) that ends on December 31, 2008;

Taking note of the letters to the UN Security Council from the Prime Minister of Iraq and the Secretary of State of the United States dated December 7 and December 10, 2007, respectively, which are annexed to Resolution 1790;

Taking note of section 3 of the Declaration of Principles for a Long-Term Relationship of Cooperation and Friendship, signed by the President of the United States and the Prime Minister of Iraq on November 26, 2007, which memorialized Iraq's call for extension of the above-mentioned mandate for a final period, to end not later than December 31, 2008:

Recognizing also the dramatic and positive developments in Iraq, and noting that the situation in Iraq is fundamentally different than that which existed when the UN Security Council adopted Resolution 661 in 1990, and in particular that the threat to international peace and security posed by the Government of Iraq no longer exists, the Parties affirm in this regard that with the termination on December 31, 2008 of the Chapter VII mandate and authorization for the multinational force contained in Resolution 1790, Iraq should return to the legal and international standing that it enjoyed prior to the adoption of UN Security Council Resolution 661 (1990), and that the United States shall use its best efforts to help Iraq take the steps necessary to achieve this by December 31, 2008.

Article 26: Iraqi Assets

1. To enable Iraq to continue to develop its national economy through the rehabilitation of its economic infrastructure, as well as providing necessary essential

services to the Iraqi people, and to continue to safeguard Iraq's revenues from oil and gas and other Iraqi resources and its financial and economic assets located abroad, including the Development Fund for Iraq, the United States shall ensure maximum efforts to:

    a. Support Iraq to obtain forgiveness of international debt resulting from the policies of the former regime.

    b. Support Iraq to achieve a comprehensive and final resolution of outstanding reparation claims inherited from the previous regime, including compensation requirements imposed by the UN Security Council on Iraq.

2. Recognizing and understanding Iraq's concern with claims based on actions perpetrated by the former regime, the President of the United States has exercised his authority to protect from United States judicial process the Development Fund for Iraq and certain other property in which Iraq has an interest. The United States shall remain fully and actively engaged with the Government of Iraq with respect to continuation of such protections and with respect to such claims.

3. Consistent with a letter from the President of the United States to be sent to the Prime Minister of Iraq, the United States remains committed to assist Iraq in connection with its request that the UN Security Council extend the protections and other arrangements established in Resolution 1483 (2003) and Resolution 1546 (2004) for petroleum, petroleum products, and natural gas originating in Iraq, proceeds and obligations from sale thereof, and the Development Fund for Iraq.

Article 27: Deterrence of Security Threats

In order to strengthen security and stability in Iraq and to contribute to the maintenance of international peace and stability, the Parties shall work actively to strengthen the political and military capabilities of the Republic of Iraq to deter threats against its sovereignty, political independence, territorial integrity, and its constitutional federal democratic system. To that end, the Parties agree as follows:

1. In the event of any external or internal threat or aggression against Iraq that would violate its sovereignty, political independence, or territorial integrity, waters, airspace, its democratic system or its elected institutions, and upon request by the Government of Iraq, the Parties shall immediately initiate strategic deliberations and, as may be mutually agreed, the United States shall take appropriate measures, including diplomatic, economic, or military measures, or any other measure, to deter such a threat.

2. The Parties agree to continue close cooperation in strengthening and maintaining military and security institutions and democratic political institutions in Iraq, including, as may be mutually agreed, cooperation in training, equipping, and arming the Iraqi Security Forces, in order to combat domestic and international terrorism and outlaw groups, upon request by the Government of Iraq.

3. Iraqi land, sea, and air shall not be used as a launching or transit point for attacks against other countries.

Article 28: The Green Zone

Upon entry into force of this Agreement the Government of Iraq shall have full responsibility for the Green Zone. The Government of Iraq may request from the United States

Forces limited and temporary support for the Iraqi authorities in the mission of security for the Green Zone. Upon such request, relevant Iraqi authorities shall work jointly with the United States Forces authorities on security for the Green Zone during the period determined by the Government of Iraq.

Article 30: The Period for Which the Agreement Is Effective

This Agreement shall be effective for a period of three years, unless terminated sooner by either Party pursuant to paragraph 3 of this Article.

Source: U.S. Department of State. Agreement Between the United States of America and the Republic of Iraq On the Withdrawal of United States Forces from Iraq and the Organization of Their Activities during Their Temporary Presence in Iraq. Available at: http://www.state.gov/documents/organization/122074.pdf (accessed July 17, 2015).

AFTERMATH

This document was seen as a threat to Iraqi sovereignty by many within Iraq. This was especially true for those who were supporters of Moqtada al-Sadr. The Shia senior religious leader in Iraq, Grand Ayatollah Ali al-Sistani voiced concern that this agreement violated Iraqi sovereignty. His opinion had significant influence and this empowered many in the Iraqi Parliament to oppose the agreement. As stated earlier, it was signed and approved, but this general sense of disapproval went a long way to discourage future efforts in 2010 and 2011 to amend the agreement or create a new agreement to extend U.S. forces beyond the dates given here.

Prime Minister Nuri al-Maliki and others suggested to U.S. officials in 2010 and 2011 that a less formal agreement would suffice to maintain a larger U.S. presence in Iraq, but the U.S. government insisted on the full SOFA. Therefore, no extension was agreed upon and no additional troops remained in Iraq.

In the United States the political criticism of the agreement was not as loud or widespread. During the withdrawal of forces in 2011 and more intensely during the success of the Islamic State and in the heat of the 2016 U.S. presidential elections the criticism of the agreement became more intense. The consistent comment was that if the United States kept more forces in Iraq then the Islamic State would not have been as successful. President Obama's response was consistently that this was not a unilateral U.S. decision, but that our departure was part of the agreed to framework between the United States and Iraq as stated in the above-mentioned document.

ASK YOURSELF

1. Are the protections afforded to U.S. citizens under the Constitution worth all of this legal hassle? What protections do you think the document is referring to? Consider the first ten amendments typically referred to as the Bill of Rights.
2. Why might the people and leaders of Iraq see this document as a threat to their sovereignty?
3. What are the stated purposes of the document?

TOPICS TO CONSIDER

1. In reading the agreement above there are comments about protecting Iraq's airspace and helping it if it is threatened by external attack. At the time of the document's signature Iraq did not have any radar coverage of its territory to even know if a friendly or enemy aircraft was flying over the country. All of this capability was provided by USF-I. The security of a state includes more than weapons. It also includes the information and observation of the territory of the state. What are the major issues associated with knowledge of borders and state sovereignty faced by the U.S. government today?

Further Reading

Al-Ali, Zaid. *The Struggle for Iraq's Future: How Corruption, Incompetence and Sectarianism Have Undermined Democracy*. New Haven, CT: Yale University Press, 2014.

Woodward, Bob. *The War Within: A Secret White House History*. New York: Simon & Schuster, 2008.

Woodward, Bob. *Obama's Wars*. New York: Simon & Schuster, 2010.

Films and Television

American War Generals. Executive producers: Peter Bergen, Tresha Mabile, Jonathan Towers. National Geographic Channel, 2014.

Frontline: Bush's War. Director: Michael Kirk. PBS, 2008.

Frontline: Losing Iraq. Director: Michael Kirk. PBS, 2014.

A NEW ADMINISTRATION AND WITHDRAWAL: OPERATION NEW DAWN (2009–2011)

34. A New Policy: Barack Obama

INTRODUCTION

President Back Obama won the election in 2008 running on a platform of ending the wars in Iraq and Afghanistan. He assumed office on January 20, 2009. On February 27, 2009, he traveled to Camp Lejeune, North Carolina, where he addressed members of the U.S. Marine Corps (USMC) and provided his vision for accomplishing his campaign promises with respect to the wars he inherited from his predecessor.

It is important to note what he does and does not promise in this endeavor. As with his predecessor he does not suggest rapid change. This speech serves as the point of transition from one administration to the next.

KEEP IN MIND AS YOU READ

1. Presidents often select military installations to deliver speeches on major national security policy issues. Camp Lejeune serves as one of the largest USMC bases in the United States. It was home to the 2nd Marine Division and a variety of other organizations. The president acknowledges that among the Marines in the audience are many who will shortly deploy to Iraq.
2. The change in presidential administration typically signals dramatic changes in U.S. military policy, especially in the case of ongoing combat operations.
3. President Barack Obama did not serve in the military and had not previously interacted with military personnel to any significant degree prior to his inauguration.

Document 34: Excerpt from Presidential Speech Given at Camp Lejeune, February 27, 2009

Next month will mark the sixth anniversary of the war in Iraq. . . .

Today, I have come to speak to you about how the war in Iraq will end.

To understand where we need to go in Iraq, it is important for the American people to understand where we now stand. Thanks in great measure to your service, the situation in Iraq has improved. Violence has been reduced substantially from the horrific sectarian killing of 2006 and 2007. Al Qaeda in Iraq has been dealt a serious blow by our troops and Iraq's Security Forces, and through our partnership with Sunni Arabs. The capacity of Iraq's Security Forces has improved, and Iraq's leaders have taken steps toward political accommodation. The relative peace and strong participation in January's provincial elections sent a powerful message to the world about how far Iraqis have come in pursuing their aspirations through a peaceful political process.

But let there be no doubt: Iraq is not yet secure, and there will be difficult days ahead. Violence will continue to be a part of life in Iraq. Too many fundamental political questions about Iraq's future remain unresolved. Too many Iraqis are still displaced or destitute. Declining oil revenues will put an added strain on a government that has had difficulty delivering basic services. Not all of Iraq's neighbors are contributing to its security. Some are working at times to undermine it. And even as Iraq's government is on a surer footing, it is not yet a full partner—politically and economically—in the region, or with the international community.

In short, today there is a renewed cause for hope in Iraq, but that hope rests upon an emerging foundation.

On my first full day in office, I directed my national security team to undertake a comprehensive review of our strategy in Iraq to determine the best way to strengthen that foundation, while strengthening American national security. I have listened to my Secretary of Defense, the Joint Chiefs of Staff, and commanders on the ground. We have acted with careful consideration of events on the ground; with respect for the security agreements between the United States and Iraq; and with a critical recognition that the long-term solution in Iraq must be political—not military. Because the most important decisions that have to be made about Iraq's future must now be made by Iraqis.

We have also taken into account the simple reality that America can no longer afford to see Iraq in isolation from other priorities: we face the challenge of refocusing on Afghanistan and Pakistan; of relieving the burden on our military; and of rebuilding our struggling economy—and these are challenges that we will meet.

Today, I can announce that our review is complete, and that the United States will pursue a new strategy to end the war in Iraq through a transition to full Iraqi responsibility.

This strategy is grounded in a clear and achievable goal shared by the Iraqi people and the American people: an Iraq that is sovereign, stable, and self-reliant. To achieve that goal, we will work to promote an Iraqi government that is just, representative, and accountable, and that provides neither support nor safe-haven to terrorists. We will help Iraq build new ties of trade and commerce with the world. And we will forge a partnership with the people and government of Iraq that contributes to the peace and security of the region.

What we will not do is let the pursuit of the perfect stand in the way of achievable goals. We cannot rid Iraq of all who oppose America or sympathize with our adversaries. We cannot police Iraq's streets until they are completely safe, nor stay until Iraq's union is perfected. We cannot sustain indefinitely a commitment that has put a strain on our military, and will cost the American people nearly a trillion dollars. America's men and women in uniform have fought block by block, province by province, year after year, to give the Iraqis this chance to choose a better future. Now, we must ask the Iraqi people to seize it.

The first part of this strategy is therefore the responsible removal of our combat brigades from Iraq.

As a candidate for President, I made clear my support for a timeline of 16 months to carry out this drawdown, while pledging to consult closely with our military commanders upon taking office to ensure that we preserve the gains we've made and protect our troops. Those consultations are now complete, and I have chosen a timeline that will remove our combat brigades over the next 18 months.

Let me say this as plainly as I can: by August 31, 2010, our combat mission in Iraq will end.

As we carry out this drawdown, my highest priority will be the safety and security of our troops and civilians in Iraq. We will proceed carefully, and I will consult closely with my military commanders on the ground and with the Iraqi government. There will surely be difficult periods and tactical adjustments. But our enemies should be left with no doubt: this plan gives our military the forces and the flexibility they need to support our Iraqi partners, and to succeed.

After we remove our combat brigades, our mission will change from combat to supporting the Iraqi government and its Security Forces as they take the absolute lead in securing their country. As I have long said, we will retain a transitional force to carry out three distinct functions: training, equipping, and advising Iraqi Security Forces as long as they remain non-sectarian; conducting targeted counter-terrorism missions; and protecting our ongoing civilian and military efforts within Iraq. Initially, this force will likely be made up of 35–50,000 U.S. troops.

Through this period of transition, we will carry out further redeployments. And under the Status of Forces Agreement with the Iraqi government, I intend to remove all U.S. troops from Iraq by the end of 2011. We will complete this transition to Iraqi responsibility, and we will bring our troops home with the honor that they have earned. . . .

Source: The White House. "Remarks of President Barack Obama; Responsibly Ending the War in Iraq." Available at: https://www.whitehouse.gov/the-press-office/remarks-president-barack-obama-ndash-responsibly-ending-war-iraq (accessed July 10, 2015).

AFTERMATH

This was a politically controversial announcement. Many criticized the president by saying that announcing an end date was effectively telling your opponent when you would cease contesting and leave the field. This argument further stated that such an announcement would then empower the opponents of the United States and Iraq to simply wait out the U.S. deployment schedule and then conduct more aggressive attacks once the United States departed.

On June 4, 2009, President Obama addressed the Muslim world from Cairo, Egypt. In that speech he extended a hand to Muslims and laid out his vision of positive relationships between the United States and Muslims across the globe. In that speech he criticized going into Iraq and referred to it as a "war of choice." His words were greeted with positive response. That response turned negative as few policies changed from administration to administration. It is also important to note the events referred to as the Arab Spring began during the time designated for the U.S. withdrawal from Iraq. The linkages are tenuous, but there are connections between U.S. policies that were initially laid out in this speech and these other events in the Middle East.

It is important to remember that the withdrawal of all U.S. forces by the end of 2011 was a date negotiated by the Bush administration with the government of Iraq.

Forces departed Iraq as stated by President Obama. Combat forces withdrew by 31 August and the operation changed names from Operation Iraqi Freedom to Operation New Dawn, effective September 1, 2010. All U.S. forces departed Iraq by December 2011.

During the successful rise of the Islamic State many criticized the decisions to unilaterally (so they argued) depart Iraq in 2011 and not to stay longer to offer a greater opportunity for the Iraqi government to become more stable and to empower a more inclusive and less sectarian government.

ASK YOURSELF

1. Politicians often get criticized for not living up to campaign promises. The election of 2008 offered a clear choice with respect to national security issues. In this speech President Obama lays out his promise and how he intended to fulfill it. As referenced several times in this book Carl von Clausewitz instructed that war is an extension of politics. Why should people be surprised that decisions about war have political motivations and expressions?

TOPICS TO CONSIDER

1. In this speech President Obama laid out three parts of his policy. Only one of the elements is contained in the text mentioned earlier. The second part was "sustained diplomacy on behalf of a more peaceful and prosperous Iraq." The third part was "comprehensive American engagement across the region." This third part included the nuclear weapons talks with Iran as well as a host of other initiatives. Looking over the entire Middle East, how effective was this policy?
2. The transition from one president to another during times of war was not that common before World War II. They have become more common since as nearly every major war has crossed administrations. Review the wars and their timelines and note the changes in policy when one president replaced another.

Further Reading

Al-Ali, Zaid. *The Struggle for Iraq's Future: How Corruption, Incompetence and Sectarianism Have Undermined Democracy*. New Haven, CT: Yale University Press, 2014.

Bolger, Daniel P. *Why We Lost: A General's Inside Account of the Iraq and Afghanistan Wars*. Boston: Houghton Mifflin Harcourt, 2014.

Woodward, Bob. *Obama's Wars*. New York: Simon & Schuster, 2010.

Films and Television

American War Generals. Executive producers: Peter Bergen, Tresha Mabile, Jonathan Towers. National Geographic Channel, 2014.

Frontline: Losing Iraq. Director: Michael Kirk. PBS, 2014.

35. CONFUSION IN LANGUAGE: MOHAMED AL-SHARA

INTRODUCTION

This chapter presents not simply the problems with translation, but also the difficulty in understanding simple mistakes when the expectations are so high. The expectation is that the American leaders know a lot and that they do not make simple mistakes. When mistakes are made this can sometimes create hours of problems trying to explain a simple mistake.

Mohamed al-Shara was a cultural advisor to a senior U.S. Army officer at the time of the story he is relating below.

KEEP IN MIND AS YOU READ

1. Watch American television or movies that portray technology with respect to surveillance, either through observation or listening, movies like *Enemy of the State* or the movies including the Jason Bourne character or James Bond (admittedly not American). In these movies western agencies are portrayed as having an ability to see and know everything.

Document 35: Excerpt from Interview with Mohamed al-Shara, Cultural Advisor

You know, you're not just here fighting ISIL [Islamic State in Iraq and the Levant] and then once you beat it, that's it, it's done. No you need to understand it's just so complicated. So complicated. You've gotta understand the politics, you've gotta understand the religion, you've gotta understand the history in order for you to work in this environment. So I think that's the biggest thing. I've seen a lot of officers come in where they really get it, and they can adapt to it. And I've seen a lot of officers, "Nah, I'm just here for my twelve months. Here's my job, here's my talking points, and that's it. I'm out." And that's, I think a very important thing.

There was a big meeting. Uh, senators came in to meet with Abd al-Qadir (the Iraqi Minister of Defense at the time of the meeting) and one of the senators looks at Abd al-Qadir and says, "Well, Minister, congratulations, because we heard the Taliban are not doing well here in Iraq." Abd al-Qadir leans over and asks, "Did he just say 'Taliban?' Did he just say 'Taliban?'" And, so, I'm-I'm confused. You know, Abd al-Qadir's confused. So Abd al-Qadir takes it, "okay."

This is a big deal. This is a U.S. Senator. You know, from the—from the U.S. So there's no way he's making a mistake where he's confused. So Abd al-Qadir looks at his intelligence guy and says, "Hey, there must be a Taliban in here. You better check on that." So then he's respectful because he has senators there, and you have a senator asking about Taliban, then . . . They keep talking and the minister just didn't know how to respond to it. So he finally responded with, "The Iraqi Security Forces with the support of the U.S. are doing well." So they move on to another talking point and after the meeting, Abd al-Qadir keeps talking about that Taliban comment. You know, every time. And then finally, we explain it to him that "these guys (the senate delegation) probably came from Afghanistan"—which they did not.

It just shows you how just one word, like Taliban, whether that senator wanted to say Al-Qaida or he wanted to say some other group. Just one word can get a guy like a minister or somebody—can get him spun up. And they were checking on it. They (the Iraqi Ministry of Defense) thought the Senator really knew what he was talking about. They were thinking "this guy must know something. There's Taliban in here (Iraq). You know, this guy must know something," because if it comes out of a U.S. guy's mouth then it must be 100% accurate and true. Because the U.S. knows what's going on. They don't—they don't make any mistakes. You try to explain it to the Iraqis, saying it was just a mistake, but Noooo, no. How can—how can they make a mistake?! I tell them that I promise you, this is just a mistake—I'm just telling you. Nope. The Iraqi believes there's gotta be something behind it. They believe that there is something that you are not telling them.

Part of the problem is that the minister spoke a little English and Taliban is also a word in Arabic so he heard it and he knew what he heard. If it was someone else it could have been a lot easier, because I could have said it was a mistranslation. Yeah, but I kid you not, man. That got—that got the Iraqis spinning, because they really thought the Taliban were here in Iraq. Which is funny.

Source: Mohamed al-Shara, interview by author, Baghdad, Iraq, February 23, 2015. Reprinted with permission.

AFTERMATH

Abd al-Qadir and others in the Iraqi government were caught up in the turbulent times following the end of the U.S. presence in Iraq. He was not the minister of defense in the second Maliki prime ministership as Nuri al-Maliki served as the prime minister, the minister of defense, and the minister of interior simultaneously. Essentially he held all of the security force decision-making positions at the same time. This story is indicative of the problems of perception and imprecision in combination.

In most Arab countries, and certainly in Iraq, political leaders did not share everything they knew. Therefore, when they shared a piece of intelligence information it was always only a small part of what they knew—the tip of the information iceberg. Thus, there was a lot more they were not saying. In this story the problem is that the Iraqi thinks the American is behaving like an Iraqi and revealing only a small part of what he knows. He has difficulty believing in the possibility that it was just a simple mistake.

ASK YOURSELF

1. What role do congressional elections play in international politics? Should they play a role? What was this senator doing in Iraq? What right has he to address high government officials if he doesn't even know the circumstances of the nation he's visiting?

TOPICS TO CONSIDER

1. One of the biggest challenges in cross-cultural communication is a behavior called mirror imaging. This is when participants see themselves or their culture in the behavior and words of the counterpart. They see what they would mean or intend if they were saying the words and doing the actions. This may be a useful communication technique when in a common cultural environment, but dangerous in a foreign culture.

Further Reading

Al-Ali, Zaid. *The Struggle for Iraq's Future: How Corruption, Incompetence and Sectarianism Have Undermined Democracy.* New Haven, CT: Yale University Press, 2014.

Bolger, Daniel P. *Why We Lost: A General's Inside Account of the Iraq and Afghanistan Wars.* Boston: Houghton Mifflin Harcourt, 2014.

Shadid, Anthony. *Night Draws Near: Iraq's People in the Shadow of America's War.* New York: Henry Holt and Company, 2005.

Steed, Brian L. *Bees and Spiders: Applied Cultural Awareness and the Art of Cross-Cultural Influence.* Houston: Strategic Book Publishing & Rights Agency, LLC, 2014.

Woodward, Bob. *State of Denial: Bush at War,* Part III. New York: Simon & Schuster, 2006.

Woodward, Bob. *Obama's Wars.* New York: Simon & Schuster, 2010.

Films and Television

Lawrence of Arabia. Director: David Lean. Columbia Pictures, 1962.
Zero Dark Thirty. Director: Kathryn Bigelow. Columbia Pictures, 2012.

36. Unmanned Aerial Vehicles (UAV)/Drones: Albert Scaperotto

INTRODUCTION

One of the most long-ranging tactics and technologies to come from the global war on terrorism is the use of drone aircraft. There are a lot of different words used for what are commonly called drones. The U.S. Air Force uses the term remotely piloted vehicles primarily because they want to emphasize the importance of pilots in the action. The U.S. Army referred to them as unmanned aerial vehicles (UAVs) throughout the fighting in Iraq. None of these terms communicate fully the nature of these systems. These are aircraft that do not have a pilot present onboard. The aircraft is flown or piloted remotely. The distance between pilot and aircraft depends on the size of the aircraft and the nature of the missions. Some of the aircraft only have short ranges so the pilots are close by. Some, as described in the excerpts below are piloted from a different continent.

Major Albert Scaperotto was commissioned in 2000 as an officer in the U.S. Air Force. He began his career as an F-16 pilot. In 2008 he was selected to fly the MQ-9 Reaper. This is a large aircraft with a long range and long loiter time. This means it can stay airborne for a long time. It carries numerous sensors and can carry weapons that can be used to engage targets identified by the cameras and other on-board sensors. As a reaper pilot Major Scaperotto worked to support U.S. overseas contingency operations in Iraq, Afghanistan, and other locations remotely.

KEEP IN MIND AS YOU READ

1. The global war on terrorism was not the first use of drones in combat. Drones began as reconnaissance platforms to provide targeting data for naval gunfire and for ground-based artillery. Interestingly enough this is the same way that airplanes were first utilized in military service. Drones followed a similar progression. The first armed strike by a drone came in Afghanistan relatively early in the fighting. By the time the U.S. military entered Iraq drones were common for reconnaissance and became more and more common as armed vehicles.

2. The primary advantage of drone aircraft is their ability to provide long-term surveillance without risk to a human pilot. This allows for better understanding of

the target which can limit the loss of civilian life. That said, there have been numerous incidents of drones targeting and killing civilians. Sometimes the victims were misidentified as combatants. Other times the civilians were unintended casualties.

3. Drone aircraft have reduced the number of casualties than were experienced by civilian populations in conflict in previous wars. They also add a psychological component which did not exist in previous conflicts. Because the aircraft can loiter for hours or days, the people in the villages being watched believe they are under constant threat.

Document 36: Excerpt from Interview with Albert Scaperotto, RPV Pilot

Question: Because I've heard so many different things about the future of unmanned flight, what do you see as the future? Is this going to only expand? Is this going to make all fighters obsolete? You hear so much, but what are your thoughts on that?

Answer: Yeah. I've heard everything, because we get pitched ideas from contractors looking to make money for the next 50 years. There is going to be—you like wear a helmet and gloves and it's all virtual and you're like in the cockpit and you're controlling like multiple airplanes and you're giving orders to multiple different unmanned platforms and they are all stealth and they all carry precision weapons and that's that future of warfare. I mean, when I hear stuff like that I just kind of nod and smile, because maybe, I don't know, sure I guess that could happen like in 50 years. When you do look at the history and the technological leap of air power, which is relatively new, a lot has happened in say 100 years or so. So, it's not outside the realm of possibility, but the one thing I've learned and I'm glad I had the experience I did flying a manned fighter, being over a—not a combat battlespace—but when we're training, to be over the battlespace. The most important thing I think that people need to acknowledge and recognize is it's not the technology, it's not the platform, it's the individuals. It's the man, it's the woman that's not just in the loop, but making the decisions. So, I don't even like calling it in the loop, because that kind of give the connotation that the machine is making the decision and you just say, "Yes or no," to that and let things happened. That's, again, a misnomer of when the news says that drones are attacking things in foreign countries and it's drone, drone, drone. Well, what they don't understand, the current state of technology is that it's all about a human being making a decision. Yes, they are disconnected from the technology, but nothing happens without a human being, a man or a woman, making a tactical decision in a very dynamic environment. It's the same thing as flying a manned fighter, you just happened to be separated. So, if, again, we come up with these cosmic ideas of how to use the technology and we do goofy stuff like that where you're controlling eight different planes at a time, you will lose the human being as the primary decision maker or at least it will be lessened in terms of the human being making it work, making the decisions. So, whatever happens with this community,

I think that needs to be the baseline understanding of what's most important then everything else can kind of build around that.

Question: I know the term drone almost means mindless, like the person is not making the decision. It's the technology doing it and I think that's a misnomer.

Answer: Yeah. Absolutely. I mean, you think about just the average American that doesn't know anything about this kind of stuff. If I was that guy, I would lead to believe that the machine is droning around and when it sees something on the ground that meets an algorithm or something, then the missile comes off. Obviously, that couldn't be further from the truth. Not that that won't happen in 50 years or something. Again, if it does then I think we've—I mean, all war and combat is a human endeavor and if we take the human out, then we're going to suffer the consequences, I guarantee it. Right now, the state of technology allows that the human being has to make all the decisions and treats it—at least I do—treat it just like I was flying a fighter. I try to make the same type of decisions. I try to think the same. I try to build the same mental picture, so that it helps get over the fact that I'm 6,000 miles away, because I am still in control of what happens with the platform and the decisions that or the requested effect comes from the decisions that I make. I think if we start to stray away from that then we're probably going to be—I don't know what the right word is, but I don't think that's the right course of action. I don't think you can ever take the human being out of the execution of combat, of war, it's just not going to work. So, that's my personal view on it.

Source: Albert Scaperotto. Interview by Lisa Beckenbaugh, January 31, 2014. Interview Transcript. Courtesy of the Operational Leadership Experiences Digital Collection, Combat Studies Institute, Fort Leavenworth, KS. Available at: http://cgsc.contentdm.oclc.org/cdm/singleitem/collection/p4013coll13/id/3162/rec/1 (accessed July 13, 2015).

AFTERMATH

Drone use grew significantly during the Obama administration. It has continued to increase throughout the prosecution of the Global War on Terrorism. As a result it has become more and more controversial. It has been used regularly in Yemen, Afghanistan, and Pakistan. In all three of these cases drones operate outside of direct support of U.S. ground forces. The use of drones in Iraq was typically linked to specific missions in support of U.S. and coalition forces on the ground or in the pursuit of designated terrorists like Abu Musab al-Zarqawi. This is arguably one of the most long-term influential aspects of technology development in the Global War on Terrorism, and industry is developing greater and greater drone capability.

ASK YOURSELF

1. Is it good to kill a human being with a drone? Numerous popular science fiction books and movies depict the rise of machines and artificial intelligence to fight humanity. Does the use of drones support this darker future?

2. What are the benefits of drones? Human pilots are placed in less danger, of course, but are there other benefits to the belligerents in the conflict?

TOPICS TO CONSIDER

1. How do people perceive the use of drones? There are numerous surveys of the U.S. perspective that typically shows a great deal of support for drones. What about how they are perceived around the world?
2. A review of casualty figures for military and civilians will show that fewer people are being killed per number of military personnel involved and for the tonnage of explosives used. This communicates something in favor of those who say drones make war less horrific.

Further Reading

Bolger, Daniel P. *Why We Lost: A General's Inside Account of the Iraq and Afghanistan Wars.* Boston: Houghton Mifflin Harcourt, 2014.

Singer, P.W. *Wired for War: The Robotics Revolution and Conflict in the 21st Century.* New York: The Penguin Press, 2009.

Woodward, Bob. *Obama's Wars.* New York: Simon & Schuster, 2010.

Websites

The Bureau of Investigative Journalism: Covert Drone War. https://www.thebureau investigates.com/category/projects/drones/ (accessed July 13, 2015).

Currier, Cora. "Everything We Know So Far About Drone Strikes." ProPublica: Journalism in the Public Interest. http://www.propublica.org/article/everything-we-know-so-far-about-drone-strikes (accessed July 13, 2015).

Drone Wars UK: Information and Comment on the Use of Drones. http://dronewars.net/drone-wars-library/ (accessed July 13, 2015).

Films and Television

American War Generals. Executive producers: Peter Bergen, Tresha Mabile, Jonathan Towers. National Geographic Channel, 2014.

Frontline: Losing Iraq. Director: Michael Kirk. PBS, 2014.

37. End of Combat Operations: Barack Obama

INTRODUCTION

The Iraq War did not end on August 31, 2010. The United States transitioned from Operation Iraqi Freedom to Operation New Dawn. In this new operation the intent was to train and advise the Iraqi security forces and to move the remainder of U.S. forces out of Iraq. This was a herculean task as it meant closing more than a hundred bases, transferring equipment to the Iraqis or removing it from the country, and moving all personnel out of the country. With the change in the operation one of the primary tasks for the U.S. Forces-Iraq was to get out of Iraq.

KEEP IN MIND AS YOU READ

1. President Obama was elected to end the war in Iraq. This was a campaign pledge and a recurring comment from the president.
2. Moving forces and equipment is a difficult task. The logistics associated with getting out of Iraq was as demanding, or more so, as any combat operation. To accomplish this feat the U.S. military closed down and transferred to Iraq hundreds of bases, moved tens of thousands of vehicles from the country, transferred millions of items of property from United States to Iraqi control and responsibility. This involved millions upon millions of tons of material. All of this was done while maintaining function for the U.S. Forces-Iraq headquarters and continuing to advise and assist Iraqi forces in contact with insurgents.

Document 37: Excerpt from Presidential Address on the End of Combat Operations in Iraq

Good evening. Tonight, I'd like to talk to you about the end of our combat mission in Iraq, the ongoing security challenges we face, and the need to rebuild our nation here at home.

I know this historic moment comes at a time of great uncertainty for many Americans. We've now been through nearly a decade of war. We've endured a long and painful recession. And sometimes in the midst of these storms, the future that we're trying to build for our nation—a future of lasting peace and long-term prosperity—may seem beyond our reach.

But this milestone should serve as a reminder to all Americans that the future is ours to shape if we move forward with confidence and commitment. It should also serve as a message to the world that the United States of America intends to sustain and strengthen our leadership in this young century.

From this desk, seven and a half years ago, President Bush announced the beginning of military operations in Iraq. Much has changed since that night. A war to disarm a state became a fight against an insurgency. Terrorism and sectarian warfare threatened to tear Iraq apart. Thousands of Americans gave their lives; tens of thousands have been wounded. Our relations abroad were strained. Our unity at home was tested.

These are the rough waters encountered during the course of one of America's longest wars. Yet there has been one constant amidst these shifting tides. At every turn, America's men and women in uniform have served with courage and resolve. As Commander-in-Chief, I am incredibly proud of their service. And like all Americans, I'm awed by their sacrifice, and by the sacrifices of their families.

The Americans who have served in Iraq completed every mission they were given. They defeated a regime that had terrorized its people. Together with Iraqis and coalition partners who made huge sacrifices of their own, our troops fought block by block to help Iraq seize the chance for a better future. They shifted tactics to protect the Iraqi people, trained Iraqi Security Forces, and took out terrorist leaders. Because of our troops and civilians—and because of the resilience of the Iraqi people—Iraq has the opportunity to embrace a new destiny, even though many challenges remain.

So tonight, I am announcing that the American combat mission in Iraq has ended. Operation Iraqi Freedom is over, and the Iraqi people now have lead responsibility for the security of their country.

This was my pledge to the American people as a candidate for this office. Last February, I announced a plan that would bring our combat brigades out of Iraq, while redoubling our efforts to strengthen Iraq's Security Forces and support its government and people.

That's what we've done. We've removed nearly 100,000 U.S. troops from Iraq. We've closed or transferred to the Iraqis hundreds of bases. And we have moved millions of pieces of equipment out of Iraq.

This completes a transition to Iraqi responsibility for their own security. U.S. troops pulled out of Iraq's cities last summer, and Iraqi forces have moved into the lead with considerable skill and commitment to their fellow citizens. Even as Iraq continues to suffer terrorist attacks, security incidents have been near the lowest on record since the war began. And Iraqi forces have taken the fight to al Qaeda, removing much of its leadership in Iraqi-led operations.

This year also saw Iraq hold credible elections that drew a strong turnout. A caretaker administration is in place as Iraqis form a government based on the results of that election. Tonight, I encourage Iraq's leaders to move forward with a sense of urgency to form an inclusive government that is just, representative, and accountable to the Iraqi people. And when that government is in place, there should be no doubt: The Iraqi people will have a strong partner in the United States. Our combat mission is ending, but our commitment to Iraq's future is not. . . .

Ending this war is not only in Iraq's interest—it's in our own. The United States has paid a huge price to put the future of Iraq in the hands of its people. We have sent our young men and women to make enormous sacrifices in Iraq, and spent vast resources abroad at a time of tight budgets at home. We've persevered because of a belief we share with the Iraqi people—a belief that out of the ashes of war, a new beginning could be born in this cradle of civilization. Through this remarkable chapter in the history of the United States and Iraq, we have met our responsibility. Now, it's time to turn the page.

As we do, I'm mindful that the Iraq war has been a contentious issue at home. Here, too, it's time to turn the page. This afternoon, I spoke to former President George W. Bush. It's well known that he and I disagreed about the war from its outset. Yet no one can doubt President Bush's support for our troops, or his love of country and commitment to our security. As I've said, there were patriots who supported this war, and patriots who opposed it. And all of us are united in appreciation for our servicemen and women, and our hopes for Iraqis' future. . . .

Indeed, one of the lessons of our effort in Iraq is that American influence around the world is not a function of military force alone. We must use all elements of our power—including our diplomacy, our economic strength, and the power of America's example—to secure our interests and stand by our allies. And we must project a vision of the future that's based not just on our fears, but also on our hopes—a vision that recognizes the real dangers that exist around the world, but also the limitless possibilities of our time. . . .

Part of that responsibility is making sure that we honor our commitments to those who have served our country with such valor. As long as I am President, we will maintain the finest fighting force that the world has ever known, and we will do whatever it takes to serve our veterans as well as they have served us. This is a sacred trust. That's why we've already made one of the largest increases in funding for veterans in decades. We're treating the signature wounds of today's wars—post-traumatic stress disorder and traumatic brain injury—while providing the health care and benefits that all of our veterans have earned. And we're funding a Post-9/11 GI Bill that helps our veterans and their families pursue the dream of a college education. Just as the GI Bill helped those who fought World War II—including my grandfather—become the backbone of our middle class, so today's servicemen and women must have the chance to apply their gifts to expand the American economy. Because part of ending a war responsibly is standing by those who have fought it.

Two weeks ago, America's final combat brigade in Iraq—the Army's Fourth Stryker Brigade—journeyed home in the pre-dawn darkness. Thousands of soldiers and hundreds of vehicles made the trip from Baghdad, the last of them passing into Kuwait in the early morning hours. Over seven years before, American troops and coalition partners had fought their way across similar highways, but this time no shots were fired. It was just a convoy of brave Americans, making their way home.

Of course, the soldiers left much behind. Some were teenagers when the war began. Many have served multiple tours of duty, far from families who bore a heroic burden of their own, enduring the absence of a husband's embrace or a mother's kiss. Most painfully, since the war began, 55 members of the Fourth Stryker Brigade made the ultimate sacrifice—part of over 4,400 Americans who have given their lives in Iraq. As one staff sergeant said, "I know that to my brothers in arms who fought and died, this day would probably mean a lot."

Those Americans gave their lives for the values that have lived in the hearts of our people for over two centuries. Along with nearly 1.5 million Americans who have served in Iraq, they fought in a faraway place for people they never knew. They stared into the darkest of human creations—war—and helped the Iraqi people seek the light of peace.

In an age without surrender ceremonies, we must earn victory through the success of our partners and the strength of our own nation. Every American who serves joins an unbroken line of heroes that stretches from Lexington to Gettysburg; from Iwo Jima to Inchon; from Khe Sanh to Kandahar—Americans who have fought to see that the lives of our children are better than our own. Our troops are the steel in our ship of state. And though our nation may be travelling through rough waters, they give us confidence that our course is true, and that beyond the pre-dawn darkness, better days lie ahead.

Thank you. May God bless you. And may God bless the United States of America, and all who serve her.

Source: The White House. "Remarks by the President in Address to the Nation on the End of Combat Operations in Iraq." Available at: http://www.whitehouse.gov/the-press-office/2010/08/31/remarks-president-address-nation-end-combat-operations-iraq (accessed July 16, 2015).

AFTERMATH

Despite the assurance of no combat forces, 66 more coalition soldiers died before the complete force was withdrawn. The war was not over just because the president said it was. More than 40,000 soldiers remained in Iraq up until the last two months of 2011.

ASK YOURSELF

1. When do wars end? This has been a recurring question in this book for good reason. Both presidents told the American people that the war wouldn't end like other wars. This begs the question asked at the beginning of this paragraph. If wars end because we withdraw and say they are over then the follow-up question should be: why wait?
2. What takes precedence, the sovereignty of a foreign nation or the interests of your own nation? In a more "enlightened" environment the answer seems obvious, but why fight wars at all? Clearly there are interests that supersede the sovereignty of another state. In what circumstances does one take precedence over the other?

TOPICS TO CONSIDER

1. How is conflict resolved? Actually resolved. Research various conflicts that have come to an end to see how they were resolved. The fighting in Sri Lanka or Malaya are a couple of examples where the fighting ended. Were the conflicts resolved?

Further Reading

Al-Ali, Zaid. *The Struggle for Iraq's Future: How Corruption, Incompetence and Sectarianism Have Undermined Democracy*. New Haven, CT: Yale University Press, 2014.

Bolger, Daniel P. *Why We Lost: A General's Inside Account of the Iraq and Afghanistan Wars.* Boston: Houghton Mifflin Harcourt, 2014.

Woodward, Bob. *Obama's Wars.* New York: Simon & Schuster, 2010.

Films and Television

American War Generals. Executive producers: Peter Bergen, Tresha Mabile, Jonathan Towers. National Geographic Channel, 2014.

Frontline: Losing Iraq. Director: Michael Kirk. PBS, 2014.

38. Defense Secretary at the End: Leon Panetta

INTRODUCTION

The Iraq War consisted of several significant phases as identified in this book. The last phase began on September 1, 2010, when the operation changed names from Operation Iraqi Freedom to Operation New Dawn. Technically, August 31, 2010, was the end of combat operations and all remaining forces had the mission of advising and assisting the Iraqi Security Forces. This interview points out some of the challenges associated with that idea of change.

Leon Panetta was the third U.S. secretary of defense to guide the war effort and the second in the Obama administration. He took over as secretary of defense on July 1, 2010, only ten days before this interview. He came into the defense department from a position as the director of Central Intelligence in the Central Intelligence Agency.

This interview occurred while Secretary Panetta was traveling in Iraq.

KEEP IN MIND AS YOU READ

1. President Obama promised the American voters that he would get the United States out of Iraq and Afghanistan in 2007. Much of his efforts with respect to Iraq in his first administration were focused on fulfilling this campaign promise.
2. The Iraqi people wanted the United States to leave Iraq because they generally believed the U.S.-led coalition was responsible for the chaotic and violent environment in Iraq.

Document 38: Excerpt from NBC Interview with Defense Secretary Leon Panetta, July 11, 2011

MR. MIKLASZEWSKI: Thanks for joining us, Mr. Secretary. Just today, three or four rockets landed in the Green Zone. Fifteen American soldiers were killed last month. I mean, it sounds like the war is back on. What's going on?

SEC. PANETTA: Well, there's some concerns, obviously. We did lose an awful lot of troops last month, and we're continuing to see attacks. And a lot of this that we think can be tracked to Iran and their supplying of weapons to insurgents here who are conducting these kinds of attacks. That raises a lot of concerns.

So my view is that, bottom line, it's they have the responsibility and the authority to ensure they do everything necessary to protect the troops—and that leaves us, if I ask the Iraqis, as a partner in this, to go after those who are attacking troops, that we want to be partners with them in that effort and conduct those kinds of operations. But we have a responsibility to defend our soldiers, and that's exactly what I'm going to do.

MR. MIKLASZEWSKI: Mr. Secretary, I talked to soldiers this morning who told me, they're coming after us again. But yet, they feel like their hands are somewhat tied because they don't feel the Iraqis have actually done enough, and in fact, are not willing to do enough, according to some soldiers. So what can the U.S. do if that's going to be the case? How are you going to protect those soldiers?

SEC. PANETTA: Well, you know, the point I have to make to the leadership here is that this is not just about protecting our soldiers; it's about protecting your country. And when these kinds of attacks are happening, it weakens Iraq.

And if you allow this kind of violence to go on, then it sends a signal to the world that you haven't developed the kind of security that needs to be done. So they have a responsibility. They have to respond to these attacks, as well. And that's the message that we're sending them. And it's also the responsibility that they're going to have to take on if they're going to be able to have a country that they can secure and defend.

MR. MIKLASZEWSKI: Now, the U.S. troops have the authority to defend themselves, but does that include unilateral action, if necessary? That is, can the U.S. respond unilaterally against that threat?

SEC. PANETTA: Well, you know, I don't want to go into the particulars of what steps we would take in order to do that, but what I'll tell you is I do have the authority and the responsibility to defend U.S. soldiers. And if necessary, we will take what actions are necessary to do that.

MR. MIKLASZEWSKI: Iran has been thumbing its nose at the U.S. for years on any number of fronts. You know that very well. So what possibly could the U.S. to do to prevent Iran from shipping those highly lethal weapons to [Iraq]?

SEC. PANETTA: You know, I think—I think it's very important to let them know that, you know, we do not appreciate their support for terrorism, here or anyplace else in the world. And they've been in engaging in basically not only equipping terrorists but supporting them.

And you know, that's not just a responsibility that we have; I think it's a responsibility that the world has to send the signal to Iran that we're not going to tolerate that—they can't just go around supporting terrorism in the world. The world is going to respond to that kind of behavior. If they want to be a member of the family of nations, they've got to act like it.

MR. MIKLASZEWSKI: The Iraqis have to make a decision sometime soon on whether they want additional U.S. troops to stay here in the country after the deadline for withdrawal at the end of this year. You said this morning, "Damn it, make a decision." I mean, that's pretty tough talk, no?

SEC. PANETTA: Well, I think the time has come to make a decision. You know, obviously, there's been a lot of sacrifices made by U.S. men and women here and there have been a lot of casualties, but I think we've also put this country on the right path towards the future.

They are, in fact, able to secure and defend themselves and they are governed, at this time. But if this is going to continue—continue on the right path—then I think that partnership has to continue. And one of the keys to that is making the tough decisions that you have to make when you govern a country. If they want our support in the future, then they've got to ask for it.

MR. MIKLASZEWSKI: And one of those tough decisions for President Obama was, do we keep additional forces here? Is the U.S. leaning to doing that to help the Iraqis in terms of security and training?

SEC. PANETTA: Well, right now, we are on track to withdraw our forces—pursuant to the agreement—to withdraw our forces by the end of this year. That's the track we're on, and we're going to begin that process in August. And we will follow that. If they do make a request, then obviously, the president—has indicated we will consider it. But the longer this goes on, the more difficult it is to consider it because, frankly we'd be on the way out.

Source: Department of Defense. NBC News Broadcast Presenters: Secretary of Defense Leon Panetta and Jim Miklaszewski, NBC News, July 11, 2011. Available at: http://archive .defense.gov/transcripts/transcript.aspx?transcriptid=4851 (accessed December 26, 2015).

AFTERMATH

U.S. forces withdrew from Iraq as prescribed by the agreement signed under the Bush administration. No additional forces remained. The United States kept only 157 personnel in the U.S. Embassy and elsewhere in Iraq to conduct the existing foreign military sales cases and provide purchased training and support. The 157 were uniformed personnel with hundreds more contractors providing the actual training and support. Unlike during the war the U.S. forces who remained following the withdrawal were constrained to only a handful of locations and needed to coordinate all movements under strict security procedures. No longer did they move about the country as they wished.

Should the United States have left more forces in Iraq? Why didn't the Government of Iraq request more forces to stay behind? These things have continued to serve as political discussion points since the withdrawal of forces. For 2012 and 2013 as the issue of Iraq took a backseat to election politics and other foreign policy concerns. The rise and success of the Islamic State in 2014 and 2015 brought the issue back into the spotlight with many questioning whether or not having greater U.S. involvement and presence in Iraq would have made a difference. There continues to be a debate in both political and military circles about who lost the Iraq War.

ASK YOURSELF

1. Why not have additional U.S. forces in Iraq? What drove the decisions to depart? President Obama challenged the notion that it was a U.S. decision to leave more forces by stating that the U.S. withdrawal was in accordance with agreements between the United States and Iraq signed during the Bush administration. Former Vice President Cheney challenged that notion by pointing out that it was within President Obama's ability to renegotiate the agreement if he felt so inclined.
2. What are the U.S. interests in Mesopotamia? What lengths should the United States pursue to maintain those interests?

TOPICS TO CONSIDER

1. Mesopotamia has served as a zone of collisions and conflict for centuries of human history. In the latest period it served as a bulwark against perceived Iranian/Persian cultural and religious imperialism. In this sense it is useful to understand the historical link between geography and conflict and understand why conflicts happen in a given space and time.
2. The government of Prime Minister Nuri al-Maliki became more sectarian after the departure of U.S. forces. This move toward greater persecution of Sunnis in Iraq and exclusion of Sunnis from power and dignity was credited as one of the primary reasons for the rise of the Islamic State and their success in making inroads in Iraq. What causes societies to fragment or atomize? Can foreign forces prevent those situations from occurring?

Further Reading

Al-Ali, Zaid. *The Struggle for Iraq's Future: How Corruption, Incompetence and Sectarianism Have Undermined Democracy*. New Haven, CT: Yale University Press, 2014.
Bolger, Daniel P. *Why We Lost: A General's Inside Account of the Iraq and Afghanistan Wars*. Boston: Houghton Mifflin Harcourt, 2014.
Panetta, Leon. *Worthy Fights: A Memoir of Leadership in War and Peace*. New York: Penguin Group, 2014.
Woodward, Bob. *Obama's Wars*. New York: Simon & Schuster, 2010.

Films and Television

American War Generals. Executive producers: Peter Bergen, Tresha Mabile, Jonathan Towers. National Geographic Channel, 2014.
Frontline: Losing Iraq. Director: Michael Kirk. PBS, 2014.

IMPACT

39. Posttraumatic Stress Disorder: Ashley Pullen

INTRODUCTION

The conduct of day-to-day operations as violence progressed throughout Iraq was dominated by the function of transportation. Simply moving from place to place became a significant operation with planning and preparation. Units coordinated their movement with higher headquarters to ensure that they could call for assistance if contacts were made. Contact became expected. As will be discussed in later chapters, this near-constant stress when outside of the forward-operating bases played some role in the high incidences of posttraumatic stress disorder suffered by so many who deployed to Iraq and Afghanistan.

Ashley Pullen was a specialist in the National Guard when her unit deployed to Iraq in November 2004. On March 20, 2005, while serving as the driver for Charlie Team, 2nd Squad, 4th Platoon, 617th Military Police Company, her squad encountered an enemy ambush south of Bagdad, Iraq, along Main Supply Route Detroit where they were acting as route patrol for a convoy. Ashley's squad placed their armored Humvees between the insurgents and the convoy, dismounted and launched a counterattack that resulted in the death of 27 insurgents and capture of seven more. Ashley, who received the Bronze Star for her actions that day, shares her experience protecting and assisting a wounded comrade during the ambush.

KEEP IN MIND AS YOU READ

1. This interview offers the unique perspective of a female junior enlisted soldier in direct combat where she and another woman were later recognized for the quality of their soldierly conduct. For that reason it is worth thinking over the role of women in combat and the preconceived notions regarding such things.

Document 39: Excerpt from Interview with Ashley Pullen, Military Police, March 20, 2005

Over all the gunfire and racket, I heard yelling on the radio. I looked at Sergeant Hester and told her I was going to get the radio because I didn't know what it was; and as soon as I went to get that, I stood up and was just standing there at the passenger's side door—the side of main contact—just listening to the radio. Just standing there! It's a miracle I didn't get shot that day. I was standing there and Staff Sergeant Nein had just said we needed aerial support at a specific grid location . . . I picked up the handheld and Specialist Mike was yelling on it that he needed help and that everybody was down. I looked down and saw Sergeant Rivera rolling around on the ground and I didn't see Specialist Haynes—the gunner at the time—or Specialist Mack, or Mike for that matter. All I saw was Sergeant Rivera on the ground and I said, "Oh shit!". . . I told him I was on my way and that was when Sergeant Hester was running back down to the berm. I shut my door—as I was standing facing oncoming fire—and ran around the front of the vehicle. I went to tell Staff Sergeant Nein as he was climbing up this 10-foot tall berm, wondering what he was doing and thinking he can't go alone; and right about the time he had thrown a grenade and was coming down, I said, "Sergeant Rivera is down, everybody's down and Mike needs help. I'm going." He said, "Okay, you do what you got to do," and went running off towards the berm and Sergeant Hester.

[Sergeant Rivera] was up by the driver's side tire [of his truck]. He was rolling around in a puddle of mud. I got back into my vehicle and I told Ordunez to hold on, that we were going to help Rivera, but I don't even know if he heard me because he was in the process of turning and firing on that two-story house. I threw the vehicle into reverse, did a 180 and went to where I originally should have been between the two vehicles. I went midway down between our two vehicles.

. . . I know I put my vehicle right in between the other two and that was the best spot because it would help cover both Specialist Haynes and Cooper. I got out of the vehicle on the contact side and ran with my rifle to where Sergeant Rivera was on the ground. I had my back towards the fire and wasn't even thinking about where the fire was coming from. I knelt down beside him and said, "Mike, what do you need me to do?" and he said, "Tend to Rivera. I've got everything else covered." I looked down at Sergeant Rivera and asked him where it hurt. He didn't have his rifle because Specialist Mike had picked it up and put it inside the truck, or Specialist Mike was using it. I'm not sure. The first thing that went through my head was that I needed bandages. Because Sergeant Rivera didn't have a weapon, I left my weapon in his hands in case he needed it because I had my nine millimeter and the rifle would slow me down when I was running. I didn't think about the fact that there was a combat life saver (CLS) bag in the truck that was right beside me. Instead, I ran all the way back to the truck that I came from. I got the CLS bag out of that truck and then ran back to Sergeant Rivera under heavy fire, because it hadn't calmed down at all. I remember Sergeant Rivera screaming that he couldn't feel his legs and I told him to calm down, that he needed to help me. He helped me take off his vest and I pushed up his battle dress uniform (BDU) top and shirt and he was bleeding from this hole in his stomach. I told him there was an entry wound and I had to see if there was an exit wound in the back, because there was a lot of blood everywhere. I told him I needed him to turn over so I could look at his back, he did, and I saw that there was indeed an exit wound. Right about that time, I heard Specialist Mike yell on the radio, "AT4! Backblast area! Clear!" I jumped on Sergeant Rivera to cover him, because I could reach out and grab Mike's leg. He was that close to us. The repercussion of the AT4—because he was standing right beside the closed door of the vehicle—knocked me off of Sergeant Rivera.

. . . At this time, the only thing I was focused on was Sergeant Rivera because Mike had told me that everybody else was taken care of. My main objective was Sergeant Rivera and helping him. For some reason, I remember hearing some firing was going on and Sergeant Hester just popped up out of nowhere asking what I needed, and I told her I needed a bandage. I was holding a bandage on his stomach and I needed another one. I didn't think to take the one off of his vest or anything, because we all carried at least two bandages on us . . . I had already dumped out the CLS bag to get to the bandages because I didn't know where they were. I'm not CLS qualified at all. I have the basic first aid training . . .

. . . Rivera was screaming at me to get off him because I was hurting him and here I was trying not to cry—and I'm not a big crier, but I didn't know what to do to calm him down. I told him to think about his little boy, think about home and his mom and Kentucky, think about the beautiful trees and the green grass, just anything but here. When I was doing this, I believe this was when the 623rd showed up. I remember looking at them and they all just sat there.

I remember looking back and Mike was there doing something, I'm still hearing all this firing going on, and then I'm looking at the guy sitting in the driver's seat of the vehicle that pulled up next to Sergeant Rivera's vehicle. I looked at Mike and said, "Get him out of there and make him do something!" He was just sitting there looking at me in total and utter shock. So Mike physically hauled him out of the vehicle, and Mike's a big boy. I remember sitting there with Sergeant Rivera screaming at me to get off him and seeing two or three guys pop up beside me—and they're just watching me! Here we are being fired upon and I said, "If you're not going to help me, go shoot somebody or something; but just don't stand there and stare at me!" We were being fired upon—or at least there was still fire going on somewhere—and they were all just standing there looking at me and it pissed me off, which is very difficult to do. At that time, somebody else came up to me. He was a black guy with a green vest, whereas everybody else had brown vests, so I assume he was in the 1075th Transportation Company . . . I think he was a sergeant.

He's not much taller than me and he had a mustache. If I saw him today, I would walk up to him and give him a big fat kiss. I remember exactly what he looks like but I never knew his name. If I could tell him thank you for what he helped me do that day, I would, but I haven't seen him or talked to him since. He said to me, "What can I do to help you?" and I said, "We need to move him, get him out of the mud and get him to a truck." And he said, "Okay." I asked Mike to help us move him. He grabbed Sergeant Rivera's feet, this Sergeant Brown grabbed Sergeant Rivera's arms, I was holding the bandages on and we moved him out of the mud and closer to one of the trucks. I don't know which truck it was. I just know it was one of the ones close by. I believe it was the one right behind Sergeant Rivera's truck, which I believe was a 623rd truck.

. . . Ordunez took his guardian angel that his fiancé had sent him, gave it to Sergeant Rivera and looked at me and asked if he was going to be okay. Ordunez was upset and crying and I said, "I'm not going to let them do anything to him. He's going to be okay. Trust me. I'm going to go with him." He said, "Okay," and he went back to doing whatever he was doing . . . I felt like Sergeant Rivera was bleeding to death in my hands . . . I remember looking out the window and seeing two or three of the armored sport utility vehicles

(SUVs) that our guys drive blown up, and trucks blown up . . . I remember seeing all this and just the total destruction.

. . . I remember getting there [to the landing zone] and just as we did the helicopter was landing . . . I remember telling Sergeant Rivera that I wasn't going to leave him alone—and he had this death grip on my hand. I hadn't been in the squad long enough to form a really good bond with anybody because I was new to the unit; and then after being in the unit for a month and a half, I was new to the squad so I hadn't been with them long at all. I had just really gotten a good bond with Sergeant Rivera. We took him up to the helicopter and they asked me what was wrong. I told them he had an entry and an exit wound in his stomach and I was going to crawl up into the helicopter with him, but they wouldn't let me go. At that time I was irritated because I had told Sergeant Rivera that I wasn't going to leave him and I wasn't going to let anything happen to him—and I understand now why they wouldn't let me go. They took off and, before they got off the ground, I remember looking at the guys who were in that truck—the gunner and that one mystery sergeant—and I said, "If you're coming with me, I'm going because my guys are still under fire so you better get your asses in," and they got in. I looked at Mike and gave him a hand signal telling him I was going back. He looked at me and waved and nodded and we took off back down to where the ambush was.

. . . It was definitely an adventure that I'm not sure I'd want to repeat. I don't talk to anybody I was deployed with anymore. Considering the fact that I've been diagnosed with severe post-traumatic stress disorder (PTSD), I actually don't talk to people about it at all. My parents actually talk to people about it more than I do because of what it does to me. It really affected me and that's because they pulled me from a completely different company and threw me in with people I didn't know. It was just like I was fresh out of Basic Training going into this company. That's what it felt like. I was in one company one day and then five minutes later I was in a completely different company. They say that's the reason I got PTSD. I had a hard time bonding with people over there. I got close to a couple people, but other than that I don't talk to or interact with anyone I was there with.

Source: Ashley Pullen. Interview by Tom Bruscino, August 16, 2006. Interview Transcript. Courtesy of the Operational Leadership Experiences Digital Collection, Combat Studies Institute, Fort Leavenworth, KS. Available at: http://cgsc.contentdm.oclc.org/cdm/singleitem/collection/p4013coll13/id/256/rec/1 (accessed July 20, 2015).

AFTERMATH

The incident described by Specialist Pullen is what the military often calls a complex ambush. As a result of the actions, as stated above 27 Iraqis were killed and seven more were captured. No U.S. soldiers were lost during the encounter, although two were wounded. Three U.S. or coalition civilians were killed.

Ashley received the Bronze Star for valor. This is an unusually high award for a junior ranking soldier. Ashley's squad leader, Staff Sergeant Timothy F. Nein, received the Distinguished Service Cross (upgraded from a Silver Star), an award for valor surpassed only by the Medal of Honor, for his actions during the ambush. Sergeant Leigh Ann Hester, also mentioned in Ashley's account, has the distinction of being the first woman to receive the Silver Star for direct combat action against the enemy. Another member of the Squad, Specialist Jason Mike (medic) also received the Silver Star for his role in the 20 March encounter.

For Specialist Pullen and many of her fellow Iraq War veterans, both male and female, the battle did not end upon her return home. Her experiences in Iraq left her with post-traumatic stress disorder. At the tender age of 22 she faced a daily battle for normalcy which may affect her for the rest of her life.

ASK YOURSELF

1. What should be the role of women in combat? Are they physically capable of doing all of the same things men can do? If not, does that matter?
2. What are the attributes that have value in combat situations? Which is more important: physical strength and capability or emotional leadership and the ability to function and make key decisions in tremendously stressful circumstances?

TOPICS TO CONSIDER

1. What causes posttraumatic stress? This is a challenging dilemma that most people, including experts, do not fully understand. Is it caused by a single traumatic event or is it the day in and day out stress and fear of imminent danger?
2. While women have been associated with the American military since 1775, it is only recently that they have begun to take on many of the duties that were exclusively reserved for men. It wasn't until 2013 that women were allowed to serve directly in combat units. (Keep in mind that Specialist Pullen and Sergeant Hester, both mentioned in this chapter, were members of the military police that is not considered a combat unit. Look into the history of women in the U.S. military. At what point were women allowed to attend the different military academies? When were women first trained as pilots? Some jobs within the military are still not open to women. What are those jobs? Why might women be restricted from pursuing them?

Further Reading

Holmstedt, Kirsten. *Band of Sisters: American Women at War in Iraq.* Mechanicsburg, PA: Stackpole Books, 2008.
Holmstedt, Kirsten. *The Girls Come Marching Home: Stories of Women Warriors Returning from the War in Iraq.* Mechanicsburg, PA: Stackpole Books, 2011.

Websites

Cohen, Sharon. "Heroic in war, she's tormented at home." *Los Angeles Times*, December 24, 2006. http://articles.latimes.com/2006/dec/24/news/adna-hero24 (accessed July 20, 2015).
Freedberg, Sydney J. "Timothy Nein, Leigh Ann Hester, and Jason Mike." *National Journal*, January 13, 2007. http://www.nationaljournal.com/magazine/timothy-nein-leigh-ann-hester-and-jason-mike-20070113 (accessed July 20, 2015).
Morris, Dustin. Interview by Tom Bruscino, July 19, 2006. Interview Transcript. Combat Studies Institute Operational Leadership Experience Collection, Fort Leavenworth, KS. http://cgsc.contentdm.oclc.org/cdm/singleitem/collection/p4013coll13/id/237/rec/4 (accessed July 20, 2015).

Nein, Timothy F. Interview by Tom Bruscino, July 18, 2006. Interview Transcript. Combat Studies Institute Operational Leadership Experience Collection, Fort Leavenworth, KS. http://cgsc.contentdm.oclc.org/cdm/singleitem/collection/p4013coll13/id/256/rec/1 (accessed July 20, 2015).

Ordunez, Jesse. Interview by Tom Bruscino, June 28, 2006. Interview Transcript. Combat Studies Institute Operational Leadership Experience Collection, Fort Leavenworth, KS. http://cgsc.contentdm.oclc.org/cdm/singleitem/collection/p4013coll13/id/235/rec/3 (accessed July 20, 2015).

Films and Television

Frontline: Bush's War. Director: Michael Kirk. PBS, 2008.

40. Sexual Assaults: Kirsten Gillibrand

INTRODUCTION

Sexual assault is an underreported crime because of the shame and humiliation faced by the victim associated with the crime. For the military this was not treated with great seriousness until pressure came down from Congressional hearings. The military was a predominantly male enterprise for many decades and even at the time of writing the percentage of women in the military was about 14 percent for enlisted ranks and 16 percent for officer ranks. It is important to note that military leaders never encouraged and only in the rarest of incidences condoned sexual harassment or sexual assault. What did happen was a lack of systemic support for the victims. It is possible that a lot of the problems associated with sexual assault and sexual harassment stem from ignorance on the part of leaders and commanders than on malicious intent.

The Iraq War did not create the problem of sexual assault in the military nor did it put men and women together for the first time. What it did provide was longevity of proximity under stressful conditions. U.S. military personnel tended to deploy to Iraq for months at a time depending on the branch of service. The U.S. Air Force and U.S. Navy typically deployed personnel for about six months with some spending as long as a year in theater. The U.S. Army sent people into theater for anywhere from 12 to 15 months.

Senator Kirsten Gillibrand was a freshman senator who had success in moving legislation to rescind the "don't ask don't tell" policy for the U.S. military which was widely seen as discriminatory toward homosexuals. This legislation was passed in 2011. In 2013 the senator went after the military on sexual assault issues with her objective being to remove prosecutorial authority for sexual assault cases from the military chain of command. This challenged the standing Uniform Code of Military Justice and the existing culture of commanders and service members in terms of enforcement of good order and discipline. It is in this context that the below excerpt was given.

KEEP IN MIND AS YOU READ

1. The close contact associate with military life combined with the nature of military deployments and a culture of power, control, and violence contributes to the potential for sexual harassment and sexual assault.

2. There is a difference between perception and statistics. The majority of press coverage of these issues tends to revolve around the cases that featured an abuse of position and authority—drill instructors assaulting recruits, commanders assaulting subordinates, etc. The statistics show that half of the cases involve perpetrators who are junior enlisted soldiers and who have no authority.

3. The military chain of command exists to facilitate core missions that include combat duties. The commander has been given authority to administer justice within his or her sphere of authority to facilitate the good order and discipline of her or his unit. This system facilitates a rapid and personal style of justice with the intent of having a combat-effective unit that can successfully execute wartime missions.

Document 40: Excerpts from Senate Subcommittee Hearing Opening Comments of Senator Kirsten E. Gillibrand, March 13, 2013

. . . The issue of sexual violence in the military is not new. It has been allowed to go in the shadows for far too long. The scourge of sexual violence in the military should be intolerable and infuriating to all of us. Our best, brightest, and bravest join our Armed Forces for all the right reasons: to serve our country, to protect our freedom, and to keep America safe.

The U.S. military is the best in the world and the overwhelmingly, vast majority of our brave men and women serving in uniform do so honorably and bravely, but there is also no doubt that we have men and women in uniform who are committing acts of sexual violence and should no longer be allowed to serve.

Too often, women and men have found themselves in the fight of their lives not in the theater of war but in their own ranks, among their own brothers and sisters and ranking officers in an environment that enables sexual assault.

After an assault occurs—an estimated 19,000 sexual assaults happened in 2011 alone according to DOD's own estimates—some of these victims have to fight all over again with every ounce of their being just to have their voice heard, their assailant brought to any measure of justice, and then to fight for the disability claims they deserve to be fulfilled.

Congress would be derelict in its duty of oversight if we just shrugged our shoulders at these 19,000 sons and daughters, husbands and wives, mothers and fathers and did nothing. We simply must do better by them.

When brave men and women volunteer to serve in our military, they know the risks involved, but sexual assault at the hands of a fellow servicemember should never be one of them because not only does sexual assault cause unconscionable harm to the victim, but sexual assault is also reported to be the leading cause of posttraumatic stress disorder (PTSD) among women veterans. Sexual assault in the military also destabilizes our military, threatens our unit cohesion and national security. Beyond the enormous human costs, both psychologically and physically, this crisis is costing us significant assets, making us weaker both morally and militarily. . . .

I am hopeful that we can build on some of these initial changes which include: one, ensuring that all convicted sex offenders in the military are processed for discharge or dismissal from the Armed Forces regardless of which branch they serve in.

Second, we removed case-disposition authority from the immediate commanding officer in sexual assault cases, which is one of the issues we will look into today as to whether we need to remove such disposition authority entirely from the chain of command and place it with a trained prosecutor instead.

We pushed the Pentagon to lift the combat ban that prevents women from officially serving in many of the combat positions that can lead to significant promotion opportunities. By opening the door for more qualified women to excel in our military, we have increased diversity in top leadership positions, improving response from leadership when it comes to preventing and responding to sexual assault. . . .

We passed an amendment . . . which means that troops who do become pregnant as a result of a rape no longer have to pay out of pocket for those pregnancies to be terminated. . . .

Despite some very dedicated Judge Advocate General (JAG) officers, I do not believe that the current system adequately meets our standard. The statistics on prosecution rates for sexual assault in the military are devastating. Of 2,439 unrestricted reports filed in 2011 for sexual violence cases, only 240 proceeded to trial. Nearly 70 percent of these reports were for rape, aggravated sexual assault, or nonconsensual sodomy.

A system where less than 1 out of 10 reported perpetrators are taken to trial for their alleged crimes is not a system that is working. That is just the reported crimes. DOD itself puts the real number closer to 19,000. A system where in reality closer to 1 out of 100 alleged perpetrators are faced with any accountability at all is entirely inadequate and unacceptable.

My view is that emphasizing institutional accountability and the prosecution of cases is needed to create a real deterrent to criminal behavior. The system needs to encourage victims that coming forward and participating in their perpetrator's prosecution is not detrimental to their safety or their future and that it will result in justice being done because currently, according to DOD, 47 percent of servicemembers are too afraid to report their assaults because of fear, retaliation, harm, or unjust punishment. Too many victims do not feel that justice is likely or even possible.

We need to take a close look at the military justice system and we need to be asking the hard questions with all options on the table, including moving this issue outside of the chain of command so that we can get closer to a zero tolerance reality in the armed services. . . .

Source: Kirsten E. Gillibrand. Opening Comments for Testimony on Sexual Assaults in the Military. Given before U.S. Senate Subcommittee on Personnel, Committee on Armed Services, March 13, 2013. Washington, D.C. Available at: www.gpo.gov/fdsys/pkg/CHRG-113shrg88340/pdf/CHRG-113shrg88340.pdf (accessed July 25, 2015).

AFTERMATH

The bill proposed by Senator Gillibrand was defeated by a filibuster. Prosecutorial and judicial authorities remain within the control of the uniform chain of command. As a result of the attention brought to this issue by Senator Gillibrand, Department of Defense personnel currently undergo significantly increased training on sexual assault prevention and response. In addition, more trained personnel are in place to receive reports and to counsel with victims. The emphasis on this problem has made a distinct impact on the culture of the military. Despite this statement there are still thousands of cases of sexual harassment and assault reported every year.

ASK YOURSELF

1. When the statistics get reviewed the numbers continue to increase even after the attention on the issue is increased. Is this because the number of real incidents increased or because the reporting of incidents increased? In other words, do people in the new more open and supportive environment now feel more comfortable coming forward to report what had been a silent shame?

TOPICS TO CONSIDER

1. Military personnel commit violent crimes at a rate much reduced from that of the general populace. There are many reasons for this reduction—a selection process that removes criminals, an emphasis on discipline and training, steady employment and earning potential, etc. The reduction in the general violent crime is much greater than it is for rape. Why might this be the case? What leads to sexual assault and other sexually violent crimes? Explore the root factors associated with sexual crimes versus other types of violent crime in order to explain this discrepancy within the military.

Further Reading

Benedict, Helen. *The Lonely Soldier: The Private War of Women Serving in Iraq*. Boston: Beacon Press, 2009.

Holmstedt, Kirsten. *Band of Sisters: American Women at War in Iraq*. Mechanicsburg, PA: Stackpole Books, 2008.

Hunter, Mic. *Honor Betrayed: Sexual Abuse in America's Military*. Fort Lee, NJ: Barricade Books, 2007.

Websites

Cooper, Helen. "Pentagon Study Finds 50% Increase in Reports of Military Sexual Assaults." *New York Times*, May 1, 2014. http://www.nytimes.com/2014/05/02/us/military-sex-assault-report.html?_r=1 (accessed July 29, 2015).

Protect our Defenders. "Facts on United States Military Sexual Violence." www.protectour defenders.com, Washington, DC. http://protectourdefenders.com/downloads/Military_Sexual_Violence_Fact_Sheet_Final_150710.pdf (accessed July 29, 2015).

Sexual Assault Prevention and Response Office. *Department of Defense Annual Report on Sexual Assault in the Military, 2014*. U.S. Department of Defense: Washington DC. http://sapr.mil/public/docs/reports/FY14_Annual/FY14_DoD_SAPRO_Annual_Report_on_Sexual_Assault.pdf (accessed July 29, 2015).

U.S. Commission on Civil Rights. *Sexual Assault in the Military*. U.S. Commission on Civil Rights: Washington, DC, September 2013. http://www.usccr.gov/pubs/09242013_Statutory_Enforcement_Report_Sexual_Assault_in_the_Military.pdf (accessed July 29, 2015).

Williams, Kayla. "Seven Misconceptions about Military Sexual Assault." *The Daily Beast*, 6 April 2013. http://www.thedailybeast.com/articles/2013/06/04/seven-misconceptions-about-military-sexual-assault.html (accessed July 29, 2015).

Films and Television

The Invisible War. Director: Kirby Dick. Chain Camera Pictures, 2012.

41. WikiLeaks: John Conyers Jr., and Louie Gohmert

INTRODUCTION

In 2006, Australian born activist Julian Assange started a project called WikiLeaks through an organization called Sunshine Press in Iceland. The intent of the project was to provide information and allow people to understand information based on the source documents. This entire project was controversial from beginning to its current manifestation. The first document was published by the website in December 2006. As with all wiki sites, WikiLeaks functions through the collaborative editing of its users who provide documents to the site by uploading the material through a dropbox. This process protects the site from the legal ramifications associated with actually acquiring the documents. It does not, however, protect the individuals who do provide them and by so doing violate the laws of their home nations.

The website has produced numerous documents that have made front page or headline news. The single biggest trove of information on the site was provided by a U.S. Army soldier then named Bradley Manning who was serving in Iraq. Manning provided hundreds of thousands of documents that included gun-camera footage and diplomatic cables. This created a firestorm of diplomatic issues as U.S. State Department assessments of world leaders became public.

Some of the gun-camera footage was edited by WikiLeaks to produce a video in 2010 called "Collateral Murder" that showed the killing of two journalists who the attack helicopter pilots believed to be armed Iraqi insurgents. The full video showed three attacks all of which resulted in the killing of civilians. In several incidents the people targeted were clearly identified as wounded. The dialogue on the video demonstrated the challenges of the rules of engagement as pilots encouraged the wounded man to pick up a weapon thus making him a legitimate target.

The WikiLeaks release created a discussion at every level of the nature of government secrecy and the purpose of classified information in a free society.

John Conyers has served in the U.S. House of Representatives since 1965 and Louie Gohmert has served since 2005. Both men have prior military service. Representative Gohmert was a lawyer and judge before entering national politics.

KEEP IN MIND AS YOU READ

1. War is horrible. Videos of war visually communicate the horror of war in a way that words alone do not.

2. What is the purpose of classified communication? The idea is that keeping assessments outside of public access frees the people writing the assessments to be candid and provide honest and open opinions that are assumed to be beneficial to national leaders in understanding the people with whom they meet and the context of the meetings themselves.

3. There are varying levels of classification in nearly every nation. In the United States the classifications range from "for official use only" to "sensitive, but unclassified" to "confidential" all the way to "Top Secret" and code word classifications. Each level has rules and purposes. Some of the lower levels are technically not even classifications, but they exist to protect sensitive information. One example of classified information is travel details of senior military and government leaders. This is intended to protect the important people from potential attack by restricting those who have access to the details of the travel. Some government workers do most of their email traffic on classified systems. The sender of the email is expected to classify each message sent on a classified system. In some cases the default is to indicate the message as classified even though scrutiny would indicate it should be unclassified. In such cases it is common for messages that contain no classified information to gain a classification just by simple omissions. This leads to the "over classification" problems often discussed.

Document 41: Excerpts from Committee on the Judiciary House of Representatives by John Conyers Jr., and Louie Gohmert, December 16, 2010

John Conyers Jr.: . . . Today the Committee will consider the WikiLeaks matter. The case is complicated, obviously. It involves possible questions of national security, and no doubt important subjects of international relations, and war and peace. . . .

. . . [T]here is no doubt that WikiLeaks is in an unpopular position right now. Many feel their publication was offensive. But unpopularity is not a crime, and publishing offensive information isn't either. And the repeated calls from Members of Congress, the government, journalists, and other experts crying out for criminal prosecutions or other extreme measures cause me some consternation.

Indeed, when everyone in this town is joined together calling for someone's head, it is a pretty sure sign that we might want to slow down and take a closer look. And that is why it was so encouraging to hear the former Office of Legal Counsel, Jack Goldsmith, who served under George W. Bush caution us only last week. And he said, I find myself agreeing with those who think Assange is being unduly vilified. I certainly do not support or like his disclosure of secrets that harm U.S. national security or foreign policy interests. But as all the handwringing over the 1917 Espionage Act shows, it is not obvious what law he has violated.

Our country was founded on the belief that speech is sacrosanct, and that the answer to bad speech is not censorship or prosecution, but more speech. And so whatever one thinks about this controversy, it is clear that prosecuting WikiLeaks would raise the most fundamental questions about freedom of speech about who is a journalist and about what the public can know about the actions of their own government.

Indeed, while there's agreement that sometimes secrecy is necessary, the real problem today is not too little secrecy, but too much secrecy. . . .

. . . As to the harm caused by these releases most will agree with the Defense Secretary, Bob Gates, his assessment. Now, I have heard the impact of these releases on our foreign policy described as a meltdown, as a game changer, and so on. I think those descriptions are fairly significantly overwrought. And Mr. Gates continues, is this embarrassing? Yes. Is it awkward? Yes. Consequences for U.S. policy? I think fairly modest.

So the harm here, according to our Republican Defense Secretary, is fairly modest. . . .

Louie Gohmert: . . . [T]he release last month by WikiLeaks of over 250,000 classified and diplomatic U.S. documents threatens our national security, our relations with foreign governments, and continued candor from embassy officials and foreign sources. Many have applauded the Web site and its founder, Julian Assange, as a hero advocating the continued release of classified and sensitive government documents. But to do so is both naive and dangerous. Web sites such as WikiLeaks and the news publications that reprint these materials claim to promote increased government transparency.

But the real motivation is self-promotion and increased circulation to a large extent. They claim to be in pursuit of uncovering government wrongdoing but dismiss any criticism that their actions may be wrong or damaging to the country. As long as there have been governments, there have been information protected by those governments. There have clearly been documents classified that should not have been classified. While there is legitimate dispute over the extent to which information is protected and classified, it is simply unrealistic to think that the protection of information serves no legitimate purpose.

Much attention has been given to this most recent WikiLeaks release. Many dismiss that any negative repercussions resulted from the leak arguing that the documents, while embarrassing to the U.S., did no real harm to the country. But what about previous leaks by this Web site? On July 25, 2010, WikiLeaks released confidential military field reports on the war in Afghanistan. This site released Iraq war-related documents on October 23, 2010. Both of these leaks reveal sensitive military information that endanger military troops and may have bolstered our enemy's campaigns against us. . . .

. . . [T]oday we are confronted with a new kind of media, the Internet blog. What are the boundaries of free speech, how do we balance this freedom with the Government's need to protect some information. The drafters of the 1917 Act could not have foreseen that nearly 100 years later, sensitive information could have been transmitted to a global audience instantaneously . . . This time the leak involved primarily diplomatic cables, but previous leaks disclosed even more sensitive information.

And the next leak could be even more damaging. It could disclose [coordinates] of where military personnel are located overseas or even reveal the next unannounced visit to Iraq or Afghanistan by President Obama. This isn't simply about keeping government secrets secret, it is about the safety of American personnel overseas at all levels from the foot soldier to the commander-in-chief. . . .

Source: John Conyers Jr., and Louie Gohmert. Opening Statements for Espionage Act and the Legal and Constitutional Issues Raised by Wikileaks. Given before Committee on the Judiciary House of Representatives, One Hundred Eleventh Congress, Second Session, Serial No. 111–160, December 16, 2010. Washington, DC. Available at: http://www.gpo .gov/fdsys/pkg/CHRG-111hhrg63081/pdf/CHRG-111hhrg63081.pdf (accessed July 28, 2015).

AFTERMATH

Julian Assange has been accused of various crimes including violations of the U.S. Espionage Act of 1917. He has yet to be convicted of a crime. WikiLeaks is still an active site as of this writing and it continues to release documents from Manning and numerous others about a wide range of topics, many of which disclose secrets from numerous countries.

Bradley Manning was sentenced in August 2013 to 35 years in prison for violations of the espionage act and other violations of the Uniformed Code of Military Justice. He has since changed his name to Chelsea Manning and is seeking hormone replacement therapy to change gender. Chelsea currently is incarcerated at the U.S. Disciplinary Barrack at Fort Leavenworth, Kansas.

In the spring and summer of 2013 another major release of classified documents occurred. This time it was not through WikiLeaks, but through major newspapers. This information was released by Edward Snowden. Snowden's release of material revealed a widespread monitoring and collection of phone and data records by the U.S. National Security Administration (NSA). It is uncertain how much the Manning connection with WikiLeaks influenced Snowden, but these two releases of documents had a dramatic impact on the discussion of U.S. behaviors.

It is probable that what Manning released to WikiLeaks enhanced the emphasis on departing Iraq in the political discourse.

ASK YOURSELF

1. Should governments keep secrets? From whom should they keep these secrets?
2. What is the value, if any, of government secrets?

TOPICS TO CONSIDER

1. Throughout World War II very few people knew of the Manhattan project and the development of the nuclear weapons. Many of the people who worked on the project were not aware of the intent of their work as so much of the project was compartmentalized. If one accepts that the use of the nuclear devices against Japan facilitated the end of the war in August 1945 (a debatable proposition) then isn't this an argument for the importance of secrets?

Further Reading

Greenwald, Glenn. *No Place to Hide: Edward Snowden, the NSA, and the U.S. Surveillance State*. New York: Metropolitan Books, 2014.

Nicks, Denver. *Private: Bradley Manning, WikiLeaks, and the Biggest Exposure of Official Secrets in American History.* Chicago: Chicago Review Press, Incorporated, 2012.
WikiLeaks. *The WikiLeaks Files: The World According to US Empire.* New York: Verso, 2015.

Website

WikiLeaks. https://wikileaks.org/index.en.html (accessed July 29, 2015).

Films and Television

Frontline: Wikisecrets. Director: Marcela Gaviria. PBS, 2011.
The Fifth Estate. Director: Bill Condon. DreamWorks Pictures, 2013.
We Steal Secrets: The Story of WikiLeaks. Director: Alex Gibney. Universal Pictures, 2013.

APPENDIX 1: BIOGRAPHICAL SKETCHES OF IMPORTANT INDIVIDUALS MENTIONED IN THE TEXT

Abadi, Nasier: Iraqi army lieutenant general recalled from military retirement to serve as deputy chief of staff for the Iraqi Joint Forces following the U.S. invasion of Iraq in 2003. In this position, he served as the senior Iraqi advisor to the Coalition Military Assistance Training Team (CMATT) during the formation and development of the new Iraqi Joint Forces. He is a decorated Iraqi Air Force veteran with over 4,200 flying hours operating more than fifty different types of aircraft.

Abizaid, John: He served as commander of U.S. Central Command (CENTCOM) during Operation Iraqi Freedom from July 2003 to March 2007. In this position General Abizaid oversaw the wars in both Iraq and Afghanistan simultaneously.

Alawi, Ayad: Shia Muslim political leader in Iraq who spent thirty years in exile prior to the U.S. overthrow of Saddam Hussein. From 2004 to 2005 he served as interim prime minister of Iraq. In 2014, he became vice president of Iraq. Considered a moderate centrist.

Al-Majid, Ali Hassan: A member of the Ba'athist Party in Iraq. Under Saddam Hussein he held positions as a military commander, defense minister, interior minister, and chief of the Iraqi Intelligence Service. He became known as "Chemical Ali" for his role in carrying out mass killings through the use of chemical weapons in order to quell rebellions among the Kurds in the north of Iraq.

Al-Maliki, Nouri: As a member of the Islamic Dawa Party in Iraq he opposed the Saddam Hussein regime and was forced to go into exile in 1979. In exile he coordinated anti-Saddam activities. He returned to Iraq following the overthrow of Hussein and was elected prime minister of Iraq in 2006 where he served two terms until September 8, 2014.

Al-Sadr, Mohammed Mohammed (Grand Ayatollah): Twelver Shia cleric who sought government reform under Saddam Hussein. He was shot while traveling in a car on February 19, 1999. He is considered to be a martyr of the Saddam regime amongst the Shia community in Iraq.

Al-Sadr, Moqtada: Iraqi Shiite Islamic leader who promoted retribution against Sunni Muslims in Iraq following the U.S. invasion. Al-Sadr led an Islamic militant group known as the Jaysh al-Mahdi (Mahdi Army) which opposed U.S. presence in Iraq and demanded the establishment of an Iraqi government which was in no way connected to the Ba'ath Party. He was instrumental in inciting insurgency in places like Sadr City and Basra.

Al-Sahhaf, Mohammed Saeed: He served as Iraqi information minister under Saddam Hussein during the 2003 U.S. invasion of Iraq. U.S. troops nicknamed him "Baghdad Bob" in mockery of the outrageously exaggerated propaganda broadcasts he gave both before and during the war in an attempt to convince the Iraqi people of the fortitude of the Iraqi Army and the invincibility of the regime.

Al-Sistani, Ali (Grand Ayatollah): The senior and most respected Twelver Shia cleric in Iraq. He has promoted the democratic process in Iraq following the overthrow of Saddam Hussein and encouraged his followers to be active participants in it.

Al-Zarqawi, Abu Musab: Born Ahmad Fadeel al-Nazal al-Khalayleh, Abu Musab al-Zarqawi (father of Musab from Zarqa) was a militant Islamist from Jordan. In the 1990s he formed a jihadist group known as al-Tawhid wal-Jihad. He ran a paramilitary camp in Afghanistan. Following the U.S. invasion in 2003 he began working in Iraq to undermine and protest U.S./coalition efforts there. He claimed responsibility for numerous acts of violence including bombings, beheadings, and the taking of hostages. He swore allegiance to Osama bin Laden in late 2004 and his organization became known as Tanzim Qaidat al-Jihad fi Bilad al-Rafidayn or al-Qaeda in Iraq (AQI). He was killed in a targeted bombing conducted by joint U.S. forces in 2005.

Austin, Lloyd III: The last commanding general of U.S. Forces Iraq serving until September 1, 2010, to December 15, 2011, and then as the commander, U.S. Central Command from March 22, 2013, to the present.

Bremer, L. Paul: U.S. diplomat who served as U.S. ambassador to Iraq from 2003 to 2004. In this capacity he served as head of the Coalition Provisional Authority, designed to function as an interim government following the U.S. invasion of Iraq.

Bush, George H.W.: He served as the 41st president of the United States from 1989 to 1993. Before becoming president, he served as the nation's 43rd vice president for eight years (1981–1989) under Ronald Reagan. Bush also served as a Congressman, ambassador to the United Nations, and director of the Central Intelligence Agency. In his early years, he served as a naval aviator in World War II.

Bush, George W.: Son of U.S. president George H.W. Bush and 43rd president of the United States (2001–2009). Bush also served as governor of Texas for five years (1995–2000). A graduate of Harvard Business School, Bush was also a prominent businessman. Included among his business ventures was co-ownership of the Texas Rangers baseball team prior to his election as governor. Bush also served as a pilot in the Texas Air National Guard.

Casey, George: Served as commanding general, Multi-National Forces-Iraq from June 2004 to February 2007 and then as chief of staff of the United States Army from April 2007 to April 2011.

Chalabi, Ahmed: Controversial Iraqi politician. While in exile from the Saddam Hussein regime, he served as head of the Iraqi National Congress (INC), a Washington, D.C., based group that lobbied for the U.S. overthrow of Saddam Hussein. Much of the information sited prior to the invasion relating to weapons of mass destruction and supposed ties between the regime and Al-Qaeda was provided by the INC. Following the invasion Chalabi served as Iraqi oil minister for the interim government. He also held the position of deputy prime minister for a time, but in the December 2005 elections he failed to win a seat in the Iraqi parliament and was not chosen for a cabinet-level position.

Crocker, Ryan: Served as a career ambassador for the U.S. Foreign Service, a rank which must be nominated by the president and approved by the U.S. Senate. He has served as U.S. ambassador to Lebanon, Kuwait, Syria, Pakistan, Iraq (2007–2009), and Afghanistan (2011–2012).

Garner, Jay: Retired U.S. Army Lieutenant General who was appointed to lead the Office for Reconstruction and Humanitarian Assistance (ORHA) in Iraq following the U.S. invasion in 2003. Within a month of its inception the organization and its leader were replaced by the Coalition Provisional Authority headed by newly appointed Ambassador Paul Bremer.

Hussein, Saddam: Leader in the Arab Socialist Ba'ath Party and participated in the coup that brought the party to power in Iraq in 1968. He served as vice president (and de facto ruler of the country) under the ailing General Ahmed Hassan al-Bakr for several years before ascending to the presidency. Saddam Hussein was the president of Iraq from 1979 to 2003 when he was deposed by the United States. Under Saddam's rule his supporters enjoyed lavish lifestyles while those who opposed him suffered torture and execution. He used extreme methods, including chemical weapons, to control certain segments of the population.

Kay, David: Served as chief weapons inspector for the United Nations following the first Gulf War. Later he was appointed to lead the search for weapons of mass destruction in Iraq following the 2003 invasion.

Negroponte, John: U.S. diplomat. He enjoyed a lengthy career in the U.S. foreign service that included serving as ambassador to Honduras, Mexico, the United Nations and the Philippines. In 2004, he replaced Paul Bremer as ambassador to Iraq, and in 2005 Negroponte was sworn in as the first ever U.S. Director of National Intelligence. Prior to his retirement from government Negroponte served as the U.S. deputy secretary of state from 2007 to 2009.

Odierno, Raymond: Served as commanding general of U.S. Forces Iraq from September 2008 to September 2010 and then as the U.S. Army chief of staff from May 30, 2011 to August 31, 2015.

Petraeus, David: Appointed by President George W. Bush to lead the U.S. surge in Iraq in 2007 in an attempt to quell the insurgency. In this capacity he was known as the commanding general for Multi-National Forces-Iraq. He served in this position until the fall of 2008 when he assumed command of U.S. Central Command (CENTCOM). In June 2010 President Barak Obama appointed Petraeus commander of U.S. Forces in Afghanistan and then in 2011 the president nominated him as director of the Central Intelligence Agency where he served for fourteen months.

Rumsfeld, Donald: An American politician and businessman who holds the dual distinction of being both the youngest and the oldest person to serve as secretary of defense for the United States. Rumsfeld served in the position under President Gerald Ford (1975–1977) and again under President George W. Bush (2001–2006) during which time he oversaw Operation IRAQI FREEDOM.

Von Clausewitz, Carl (1780–1831): A Prussian General and military theorist whose theories regarding conflict are still studied to this day. He was a rationalist who studied the European Enlightenment. His theories emphasize the moral and political aspects of war.

Appendix 2: Glossary of Terms Mentioned in the Text

al-Qaeda: a global militant Islamic organization founded by Osama bin Laden which opposes Western culture and influence.

AQI: al-Qaeda in Iraq.

Asymmetric Warfare Group: a U.S. Army unit created during the Global War on Terrorism with the purpose of mitigating threats from terrorism.

Ba'ath Party: a political party founded in Syria and expanded into Iraq which favors the unification of the Arab world into one state and opposes non-Arab control and influence. Saddam Hussein, ruler of Iraq prior to the U.S. invasion, was a Ba'athist.

Balkanization: used to describe the fragmentation or division of a region or state into smaller groups which are often opposed to one another.

Bradley Fighting Vehicle: American armored vehicle designed to transport infantry or scouts, which is armed with a 25-mm cannon, twin missile launchers for TOW antitank missiles, and a coaxial 7.62-mm medium machine gun.

Bureaucratic: relating to the business of running an organization or government.

Capos: short for caporegime or capodecina and is a term used to refer to senior-ranking mafia members.

Charge of the Knights: the name of the Iraqi Army operation designed to drive the Jaysh al-Madi out of Basra in southern Iraq in 2008.

CJTF: Combined Joint Task Force.

CMATT: Coalition Military Assistance Training Team—responsible for organizing, equipping, and training the Iraqi Army.

CPA: Coalition Provisional Authority.

CPATT: Civilian Police Assistance Training Team.

Deep Attack: this is a helicopter operation that has an objective beyond the forward line of troops or "deep in the enemy rear."

Doctrine: a set of standards and procedures designed to create a common frame of reference for military actions.

EFP: explosively formed penetrator—a shaped charge designed to penetrate armor from a distance.

EOD: Explosive Ordinance Disposal.

Fedayeen: term used to refer to an Arab commando group. In English the word means "those who sacrifice themselves."

Fiefdom: an organization in which a dominant person or group assumes control.

Green Zone: a heavily fortified "safe" zone, 10 kilometers square, in central Baghdad which served as the area of operations for the Coalition Provisional Authority and remains the center of international operations within Iraq.

HMMWV: high-mobility multi-wheeled vehicle.

IAEA: International Atomic Energy Agency.

ICDC: Iraqi Civil Defense Corps.

IED: improvised explosive devise—bombs that are constructed and detonated in nonconventional ways, often used as roadside bombs.

Imam: an Islamic leader commonly responsible for leading the worship at a mosque.

Insurgent: someone who rises in active revolt as in the case of those opposed to the U.S. invasion/occupation of Iraq in 2003.

IO: information operations—actions taken to affect adversary information and information systems while defending one's own information and information systems.

ISF: Iraqi Security Forces.

Islamic State: generally speaking, the term refers to a type of government based on Sharia law. Specifically, it is one of several terms used to refer to the militant group that invaded Iraq in 2014. It adopted this name in June 2014 when it declared itself to be the new successor state or Caliphate for Islam. The previous name by which the organization was known was the Islamic State of Iraq and al-Sham (ISIS).

JAM: Jaysh al-Mahdi.

JIEDDO: Joint Improvised Explosive Device Defeat Organization.

Jihadist: generally speaking, the term refers to anyone engaged in jihad (holy war) which can include the quest for self-perfection. Often used to refer to a person who participates in opposition against Western influence and authority.

Kurds: an ethnic group that numbers more than 30 million worldwide but is concentrated in the Middle East particularly in parts of Turkey, Iraq, and Syria. Kurds make up the majority of the population in Iraqi Kurdistan, a semiautonomous region of northern Iraq.

M113: American armored personnel carrier that can be fitted with a variety of weapons systems, the most common being a single .50 caliber M2 machine gun.

Madean Sabeans: a gnostic religious group living in southern Iraq.

Mausoleum: an elaborate building designed to house a tomb or tombs.

Mesopotamia: an area of the eastern Mediterranean considered to be the cradle of civilization. The name comes from Ancient Greek and means "between two rivers," in this case the Tigris and Euphrates Rivers. This ancient region included modern day Iraq as well as parts of Kuwait, Iran, Syria, and Turkey and was home to the Sumerian, Akkadian, Babylonian, and Assyrian empires.

MiTTs: Military Transition Teams—10–15 man teams designed to train Iraqi military units.

MLRS: Multiple Launch Rocket Systems.

MND-S: Multi-National Division South.

MNF-I: Multi-National Forces-Iraq. The name of the military command during the 2003 invasion of Iraq.

MNSTC-I: Multi-National Security Transition Command-Iraq.

MTOE: Modified Table of Organization and Equipment.

Mujahedeen: the plural form of mujahid, one who participates in jihad. In English the term is also used to refer to Muslim guerilla fighters who opposed the Soviets in Afghanistan.

National Guard of the United States: part of the U.S. reserve military force with units in each state as well as the territories of Guam, the Virgin Islands, Puerto Rico, and the District of Columbia. National Guard units are under the dual control of both the state and the federal government. National Guard soldiers typically serve one weekend a month in addition to one two-week period during the year. Units can be activated in order to assist with national security as well as domestic issues such as natural disasters or riots.

Northern Alliance: The Afghan Northern Alliance or United Islamic Front for the Salvation of Afghanistan came into existence in 1996 and fought a defensive war against the Taliban.

Operation Anaconda: the first large-scale battle in the U.S. war in Afghanistan. It was fought by U.S. military, CIA paramilitary officers, and Afghan military forces in an attempt to destroy al-Qaeda and the Taliban.

Operation Desert Fox (December 16–19, 1998): U.S. military-named operation conducted by the United States and the United Kingdom against Iraq as a consequence of Iraq's refusal to comply with UN Security Council Resolutions and its lack of cooperation with UN Inspectors sent to document the production of weapons of mass destruction.

Operation Desert Storm (January 17, 1991–February 28, 1991): U.S. military-named operation for the expulsion of Iraqi forces from Kuwait. This operation is often paired with its immediate predecessor, Operation Desert Shield (August 2, 1990–January 17, 1991) which was designed to secure the Arabian Peninsula from attack by the Iraqi military in 1990–1991.

Operation Enduring Freedom (January 17, 1991–February 28, 1991): U.S. military-named operation given to the U.S. military action in Afghanistan which began on October 7, 2001.

Operation Inherent Resolve (June 15, 2014–Current): U.S. military-named operation to coordinate coalition military actions against the Islamic State.

Operation Iraqi Freedom (March 20, 2003–August 31, 2010): U.S. military-named operation for the invasion of Iraq in order to overthrow the regime of long-time dictator Saddam Hussein and seize purported stockpiles of weapons of mass destruction.

Operation New Dawn (September 1, 2010–December 31, 2011): U.S. military-named operation for the advice and assist effort of the Iraqi security forces and U.S. withdrawal from Iraq.

PRT: Provincial Reconstruction Teams.

Republican Guard: an elite branch of the Iraqi military under Saddam Hussein which was mostly composed of Sunni Arabs and was better trained, disciplined, equipped, and paid than ordinary Iraqi soldiers.

Revolution in Military Affairs: A major change in the nature of warfare brought about by the innovative application of technologies which, combined with dramatic changes in military doctrine, and operational concepts, fundamentally alters the character and conduct of operations.

Sadrist Movement: a Shia Iraqi Islamic political movement led by Muqtada al-Sadr which favors a society governed by religious laws and tribal customs.

Salafist: refers to Muslim groups who adhere to an interpretation of Islam that hearkens back to the original generations of the faith and the period in which Islam advanced across the Middle East and North Africa in a seemingly miraculous fashion.

Seabee: Naval engineering construction units.

Sectarianism: a form of discrimination based on perceived differences between subdivisions within a group, such as between different denominations of a religion or political movement.

Sharia Law: Islamic law—refers to the compilation of laws governing public and some aspects of private law in a legal system based on the tenants of Islam. Sharia law is derived from a combination of the Koran, the statements of the Prophet Mohamed (*hadith*), the patterns of behavior of the Prophet Mohamed (*sunna*), and Islamic jurisprudence (*fiqh*).

SIGIR: Special Inspector General for Iraq Reconstruction—an inspector general is an investigative officer in a civil or military organization whose job is to provide quality control.

Sons of Iraq: coalitions of Iraqi citizens, particularly former Iraqi Army officers, who aligned themselves in order to maintain order in their communities and drive out insurgents.

Sovereignty: authority of a state to govern itself.

Sunni Awakening: a movement in which Sunni tribesmen formerly opposed to the U.S. occupation of Iraq realigned themselves to work with coalition forces to fight other insurgent elements, particularly al-Qaeda in Iraq.

Taliban: Islamic fundamentalist political movement in Afghanistan.

Theater: militarily speaking it is an area in which military operations take place.

Theocratic: rule of religion—a form of government in which God or a deity is recognized as the supreme civil ruler and God's laws are interpreted by religious authorities.

UN: United Nations—an international governmental organization composed mainly of sovereign states designed to promote international cooperation.

United States Reserve Components: part of the U.S. reserve military force designed to augment and support active duty units as needed. Reserve components exist for all four branches of military service as well as the U.S. Coast Guard. Reserve soldiers typically serve one weekend a month in addition to one two-week period during the year. Units can be activated in order to assist with national security as well as domestic issues such as natural disasters or riots.

UNMOVIC: United Nations Monitoring, Verification, and Inspection Commission. Created through UNSCR 1284 on December 17, 1999, to verify Iraq's compliance to rid itself of weapons of mass destruction.

UNSC: United Nations Security Council—an organization within the United Nations which is responsible for maintaining international peace and security. In addition, the security council is responsible for accepting new members to the United Nations, approving changes to the UN charter, establishing peacekeeping operations, instituting sanctions, and authorizing military action through Security Council Resolutions. The security council has five permanent members who hold veto power: the United States, the United Kingdom, Russia, China, and France. In addition, ten nonmember nations are elected on a regional basis to serve two-year terms.

UNSCR: United Nations Security Council Resolution—in order for a resolution to be adopted by the security council, the branch of the United Nations responsible for peacekeeping and security, at least nine of the 15 council member states must vote in favor of the resolution and it must not be vetoed by any of the five permanent member states (United States, United Kingdom, Russia, China, and France).

WIAS: worldwide individual augmentation system—designed to fill temporary duty assignments or assignments that require individuals who possess a specific skill set.

Yazidis: an ethnic group living primarily in northern Iraq (primarily in the Nineveh Province) and northeastern Syria. They are oftentimes linked ethnically to the Kurdish community with a distinct culture and religion which has its roots in ancient Zoroastrianism.

BIBLIOGRAPHY

BOOKS

Abrams, David. *Fobbit*. New York: Grove Press, Black Cat, 2012.

Al-Ali, Zaid. *The Struggle for Iraq's Future: How Corruption, Incompetence and Sectarianism Have Undermined Democracy*. New Haven, CT: Yale University Press, 2014.

Atkinson, Rick. *Crusade: The Untold Story of the Persian Gulf War*. New York: Houghton Mifflin Company, 1993.

Atkinson, Rick. *In the Company of Soldiers: A Chronicle of Combat*. New York: Henry Holt and Company, 2004.

Bellavia, David. *House to House: An Epic Memoir of War*. New York: Pocket Star, 2008.

Bolger, Daniel P. *Why We Lost: A General's Inside Account of the Iraq and Afghanistan Wars*. Boston: Houghton Mifflin Harcourt, 2014.

Bremer, L. Paul. *My Year in Iraq: The Struggle to Build a Future of Hope*. New York: Threshold Editions, 2006.

Broadwell, Paula. *All In: The Education of General David Petraeus*. New York: Penguin Press, 2012.

Bush, George W. *Decision Points*. New York: Random House, Inc., 2010.

Buzzell, Colby. *My War: Killing Time in Iraq*. New York: Berkley, 2006.

Chandrasekaran, Rajiv. *Imperial Life in the Emerald City: Inside Iraq's Green Zone*. New York: Vintage Books, 2007.

Clay, Fil. *Redeployment*. New York: Penguin Books, 2015.

Clinton, Hillary. *Hard Choices*. New York: Simon & Schuster Inc, 2014.

Danner, Mark. *Torture and Truth: America, Abu Ghraib, and the War on Terror*. New York: New York Review of Books, 2004.

Drogin, Bob. *Curveball: Spies, Lies, and the Con Man Who Caused a War*. New York: Random House, 2007.

Ervin, David. *Leaving the Wire: An Infantryman's Iraq*. New York: BookBaby, 2013.

Fick, Nathan. *One Bullet Away: The Making of a Marine Officer*. New York: Mariner Books, 2006.

Filkins, Dexter. *The Forever War*. New York: Vintage, 2009.

Finkel, David. *The Good Soldiers*. New York: Picador, 2010.

Fontenot, Gregory, E.J. Degen, and David Tohn. *On Point: The United States Army in Operation Iraqi Freedom*. Fort Leavenworth, KS: US Army Command and General Staff College Press, 2004.

Frederick, Jim. *Black Hearts: One Platoon's Descent into Madness in Iraq's Triangle of Death*. New York: Broadway Paperbacks, 2010.

Friedman, Brandon. *The War I Always Wanted: The Illusion of Glory and the Reality of War: A Screaming Eagle in Afghanistan and Iraq*. New York: Zenith Press, 2007.

Gallagher, Matt. *Kaboom: Embracing the Suck in a Savage Little War*. Boston: Da Capo Press, 2011.

Gates, Robert M. *Duty: Memoirs of a Secretary at War*. New York: Alfred A. Knopf, Inc., 2014.

Gedes, John. *Highway to Hell: Dispatches from a Mercenary in Iraq*. New York: Broadway, 2008.

Gentile, Gian. *Wrong Turn: America's Deadly Embrace of Counterinsurgency*. New York: The New Press, 2013.

Gomez-Granger, Julissa, ed. *CRS Report for Congress: Medal of Honor Recipients: 1979–2008* (updated June 4, 2008). Congressional Research Service: Washington, DC, 2008.

Gordon, Michael R. and Bernard Trainor. *Cobra II: The Inside Story of the Invasion and Occupation of Iraq*. New York: Pantheon Books, 2006.

Gordon, Michael R. and Bernard Trainor. *The Endgame: The Inside Story of the Struggle for Iraq from George W. Bush to Barack Obama*. New York: Vintage, 2013.

Hersh, Seymour. *Chain of Command: The Road from 9/11 to Abu Ghraib*. New York: HarperCollins Publishers Inc., 2004.

Holmstedt, Kirsten. *Band of Sisters: American Women at War in Iraq*. Mechanicsburg, PA: Stackpole Books, 2008.

Holmstedt, Kirsten. *The Girls Come Marching Home: Stories of Women Warriors Returning from the War in Iraq*. Mechanicsburg, PA: Stackpole Books, 2011.

Hughes, Christopher P. *War on Two Fronts: An Infantry Commander's War in Iraq and the Pentagon*. Philadelphia: Casemate, 2007.

Isikoff, Michael. *Hubris: The Inside Story of Spin, Scandal, and the Selling of the Iraq War*. New York: Broadway, 2007.

Johnson, David E., M. Wade Markel, and Brian Shannon. *The 2008 Battle of Sadr City: Reimagining Urban Combat*. Santa Monica, CA: RAND Corporation, 2013.

Kagan, Kimberly. *The Surge: A Military History*. New York: Encounter Books, 2008.

Kaplan, Fred. *The Insurgents: David Petraeus and the Plot to Change the American Way of War*. New York: Simon & Schuster, 2014.

Keegan, John. *The Iraq War*. New York: Vintage, 2005.

Kilcullen, David. *Counterinsurgency*. Oxford: Oxford University Press, 2010.

Kilcullen, David. *The Accidental Guerilla: Fighting Small Wars in the Midst of a Big One*. Oxford: Oxford University Press, 2011.

Kukis, Mark. *Voices from Iraq: A People's History, 2003–2009*. New York: Columbia University Press, 2011.

Kyle, Chris and Scott McEwen. *American Sniper: The Autobiography of the Most Lethal Sniper in U.S. Military History*. New York: HarperCollins, 2013.

Lacey, James G. *Takedown: The 3rd Infantry Division's Twenty-One Day Assault on Baghdad*. Annapolis, MD: Naval Institute Press, 2007.

Ludwig, Konrad R. K. *Stryker: The Siege of Sadr City*. La Canada, Flintridge, CA: Roland-Kjos Publishing, 2013.

Mansoor, Peter. *Surge: My Journey with General David Petraeus and the Remaking of the Iraq War*. New Haven, CT: Yale University Press, 2013.

McCann, Colum. *Fire and Forget: Short Stories from the Long War*. Boston: Da Capo Press, 2013.

McChrystal, Stanley. *My Share of the Task: A Memoir*. New York: Penguin Group, 2013.

McCool, John, and Kendall D. Gott. *Eyewitness to War, V. 1: US Army in Operation AL FAJR: An Oral History*. Government Printing Office, 2006. http://1.usa.gov/19vFnjH (accessed June 15, 2015).

McCool, John, and Kendall D. Gott. *Eyewitness to War, V. 2: US Army in Operation AL FAJR: An Oral History*. Government Printing Office, 2006. http://1.usa.gov/1h8UDHi (accessed June 15, 2015).

Montalvan, Luis Carlos. *Until Tuesday: A Wounded Warrior and the Golden Retriever Who Saved Him*. New York: Hachette Books, 2011.

Morrell, Michael. *The Great War of Our Time: The CIA's Fight against Terrorism—From al Qa'ida to ISIS*. New York: Hatchet Book Group, 2015.

Nagl, John A. *Learning to Eat Soup with a Knife: Counterinsurgency Lessons from Malaya and Vietnam*. Westport, CT: Praeger Publishers, 2002.

Nagl, John A. *Knife Fights: A Memoir of Modern War in Theory and Practice*. New York: Penguin Press, 2014.

O'Donnell, Patrick. *We Were One: Shoulder to Shoulder with the Marines Who Took Fallujah*. Boston: Da Capo Press, 2007.

Packer, George. *The Assassins' Gate: America in Iraq*. New York: Farrar, Straus and Giroux, 2005.

Panetta, Leon. *Worthy Fights: A Memoir of Leadership in War and Peace*. New York: Penguin Group, 2014.

Power, Kevin. *The Yellow Birds*. New York: Back Bay Books, 2013.

Prince, Erik. *Civilian Warriors: The Inside Story of Blackwater and the Unsung Heroes of the War on Terror*. New York: Penguin Group LLC, 2013.

Raddatz, Martha. *The Long Road Home: A Story of War and Family*. New York: The Penguin Group, 2008.

Ricks, Thomas. *Fiasco: The American Military Adventure in Iraq*. New York: Penguin Books, 2007.

Ricks, Thomas. *The Gamble: General David Petraeus and the American Military Adventure in Iraq, 2006–2008*. New York: Penguin Press, 2009.

Robinson, Linda. *Tell Me How This Ends: General David Petraeus and the Search for a Way Out of Iraq*. New York: PublicAffairs, 2008.

Rumsfeld, Donald. *Known and Unknown: A Memoir*. New York: Penguin Group, 2011.

Sanchez, Ricardo S. and Donald T. Phillips. *Wiser in Battle*. New York: HarperCollins, 2008.

Scahill, Jeremy. *Blackwater: The Rise of the World's Most Powerful Mercenary Army*. New York: Nation Books, 2007.

Scales, Robert H. *Certain Victory: The US Army in the Gulf War*. Fort Leavenworth: US Army Command and General Staff College Press, 1993.

Shadid, Anthony. *Night Draws Near: Iraq's People in the Shadow of America's War*. New York: Henry Holt and Company, 2005.

Singer, P. W. *Wired for War: The Robotics Revolution and Conflict in the 21st Century*. New York: The Penguin Press, 2009.

Sky, Emma. *The Unraveling: High Hopes and Missed Opportunities in Iraq*. New York: PublicAffairs, 2015.

Smith, Ray, and West, Bing. *The March Up: Taking Baghdad with the 1st Marine Division*. New York: Bantam, 2003.

Steed, Brian L. *Armed Conflict: Lessons of Modern Warfare*. New York: Ballantine Books, 2003.

Steed, Brian L. *Piercing the Fog of War: Recognizing Change on the Battlefield: Lessons from Military History, 216 BC through Today*. Minneapolis: Zenith Press, 2009.

Steed, Brian L. *Bees and Spiders: Applied Cultural Awareness and the Art of Cross-Cultural Influence*. Houston: Strategic Book Publishing & Rights Agency, LLC, 2014.

Swain, Richard M. *"Lucky War": Third Army in Desert Storm*. Fort Leavenworth: US Army Command and General Staff College Press, 1994.

United Nations Security Council. "Resolution 1441 (2002)." United Nations, November 8, 2002.

Weinberger, Caspar W., Wynton C. Hall (May 29, 2007). *Home of the Brave*. New York: Macmillan. pp. 201–217.

West, Bing. *No True Glory: A Frontline Account of the Battle for Fallujah*. New York: Bantam Books, 2005.

West, Bing. *The Strongest Tribe: War, Politics, and the Endgame in Iraq*. New York: Random House, 2009.

Williams, Kayla. *Love My Rifle More than You: Young and Female in the U.S. Army*. New York: W. W. Norton & Company, 2006.

Woodward, Bob. *The Commanders*. New York: Simon & Schuster, 1991.

Woodward, Bob. *Bush at War*. New York: Simon & Schuster, 2002.

Woodward, Bob. *Plan of Attack*. New York: Simon & Schuster, 2004.

Woodward, Bob. *State of Denial: Bush at War, Part III*. New York: Simon & Schuster, 2006.

Woodward, Bob. *The War Within: A Secret White House History*. New York: Simon & Schuster, 2008.

Woodward, Bob. *Obama's Wars*. New York: Simon & Schuster, 2010.

Wright, Donald P. and Timothy R. Reese. *On Point II: Transition to the New Campaign: The United States Army in Operation Iraqi Freedom May 2003–January 2005*. Fort Leavenworth: US Army Command and General Staff College Press, 2008.

Wright, Evan. *Generation Kill*. New York: Berkley, 2008.

Zogby, James. *Arab Voices: What They Are Saying to Us, and Why It Matters*. New York: Palgrave Macmillan, 2012.

Zucchino, David. *Thunder Run: The Armored Strike to Capture Baghdad*. New York: Atlantic Monthly Press, 2004.

ARTICLES

Ackerman, Spencer. "Over $8B of the Money You Spent Rebuilding Iraq was Wasted Outright." Wired. http://www.wired.com/2013/03/iraq-waste/ (accessed July 9, 2015).

Aesho, Caroline. "Iraq in Process of Signing Joint Partnership, Cooperation Agreement with EU". Al-Forat TV. June 15, 2011.

Amos, Deborah. "Turkey Flexes Economic, Political Muscle in Iraq". *NPR*. December 31, 2010. http://www.npr.org/2010/12/31/132475910/turkey-flexes-economic-political-muscle-in-iraq (accessed August 13, 2015).

Arango, Tim. "Through Political Prism, Iraqis Grieve." *The New York Times*. April 5, 2011. http://www.nytimes.com/2011/04/06/world/middleeast/06tikrit.html?_r=0 (accessed August 13, 2015).

Arango, Tim, and Michael S. Schmidt. "Should U.S. Stay or Go? Views Define Iraqi Factions." *The New York Times*. May 10, 2011. http://www.nytimes.com/2011/05/11/world/middleeast/11iraq.html (accessed August 13, 2015).

Arango, Tim, and Michael S. Schmidt. "Anger Lingers in Iraqi Kurdistan After a Crack-down." *The New York Times.* May 19, 2011. http://www.nytimes.com/2011/05/19/world/middleeast/19iraq.html?_r=1&pagewanted=2 (accessed August 6, 2015).

Axe, David. "Axe to Navistar: I Hate Your Blast Resistant Vehicle." WarIsBoring.com. June 10, 2011.

Barnard, Anne. "Inside Fallujah's War: Empathy, Destruction Mark a Week with US Troops." *The Boston Globe*, November 28, 2004. http://www.boston.com/news/world/articles/2004/11/28/inside_fallujahs_war/?page=full (accessed August 12, 2015).

Barnard, Anne. "Returning Fallujans Will Face Clampdown." *The Boston Globe*, December 5, 2004. http://www.boston.com/news/world/articles/2004/12/05/returning_fallujans_will_face_clampdown?pg=full (accessed August 12, 2015).

BBC News. "US Surge has Failed—Iraqi Poll." http://news.bbc.co.uk/2/hi/middle_east/6983841.stm (accessed July 7, 2015). Specific poll data at http://news.bbc.co.uk/1/shared/bsp/hi/pdfs/10_09_07_iraqpollaug2007_full.pdf (accessed July 7, 2015).

Benn, Tony. "Full Text of Benn Interview with Saddam." BBC News. February 4, 2003, http://news.bbc.co.uk/2/hi/uk_politics/2726831.stm (accessed June 10, 2015).

Bennett, John T. "Iraq Not Ready to Stand on Own, Lawmakers Say." The Hill. June 2, 2011. http://thehill.com/homenews/house/164367-iraq-not-ready-to-stand-on-own-lawmakers-say. (accessed August 13, 2015).

Biden, Jr., Joseph R. "What We Must Do For Iraq Now." *The New York Times.* November 20, 2010. http://www.nytimes.com/2010/11/21/opinion/21biden.html (accessed August 13, 2015).

Burns, Robert. "Gate Blasts NATO, Questions Future of Alliance." *The Washington Times.* http://www.washingtontimes.com/news/2011/jun/10/gates-blasts-nato-questions-future-alliance/?page=all (accessed August 13, 2015).

Capaccio, Tony. "U.S. Lagging on 'Key Milestones' in Iraq Transition Plan." Bloomberg. June 2, 2011. http://www.bloomberg.com/news/articles/2011–06–01/u-s-lagging-on-key-milestones-in-iraq-transition-plan-1- (accessed August 13, 2015).

Chivers, C. J. "The Secret Casualties of Iraq's Abandoned Chemical Weapons." *The New York Times.* October 14, 2014. http://www.nytimes.com/interactive/2014/10/14/world/middleeast/us-casualties-of-iraq-chemical-weapons.html (accessed May 14, 2015).

Chivers, C. J. "12 Years Later, a Mystery of Chemical Exposure in Iraq Clears." *The New York Times.* May 14, 2015, http://www.nytimes.com/2015/05/15/world/middleeast/12-years-later-a-mystery-of-chemical-exposure-in-iraq-clears-slightly.html?_r=1 (accessed May 14, 2015).

Cohen, Sharon. "Heroic in War, She's Tormented at Home." *Los Angeles Times*, December 24, 2006. http://articles.latimes.com/2006/dec/24/news/adna-hero24 (accessed July 20, 2015).

Cooper, Helen. "Pentagon Study Finds 50% Increase in Reports of Military Sexual Assaults." *The New York Times*, May 1, 2014. http://www.nytimes.com/2014/05/02/us/military-sex-assault-report.html?_r=1 (accessed July 29, 2015).

Cordesman, Anthony H., Marissa Allison, Vivek Kocharlakota, Jason Lemieux, and Charles Loi. "Afghan and Iraqi Metrics and the IED Threat." Center for Strategic and International Studies, November 10, 2010. http://csis.org/files/publication/101110_ied_metrics_combined.pdf (accessed July 14, 2015). Supporting website is http://csis.org/publication/afghan-and-iraqi-metrics-and-ied-threat-afghanistan (accessed July 14, 2015).

Currier, Cora. "Everything We Know So Far About Drone Strikes." ProPublica: Journalism in the Public Interest. http://www.propublica.org/article/everything-we-know-so-far-about-drone-strikes (accessed July 13, 2015).

Dagher, Sam. "Iraq Wants the U.S. Out." *The Wall Street Journal.* December 28, 2010. http://www.wsj.com/articles/SB10001424052970204685004576045700275218580 (accessed August 13, 2015).

Davis, Aaron C. "Iraq's Maliki Inches toward U.S. Troop Decision." *The Washington Post.* May 11, 2011. https://www.washingtonpost.com/world/war-zones/iraqs_maliki_inches_toward_us_troop_decision/2011/05/11/AFDpiAsG_story.html (accessed August 13, 2015).

Davis, Aaron C. "In Iraq, an Internal Shiite Battle May be Key to U.S. Troop Extension." *The Washington Post.* May 13, 2011. https://www.washingtonpost.com/world/war-zones/in-iraq-an-internal-shiite-battle-may-be-key-to-us-troop-extension/2011/05/13/AFQ4wm2G_story.html (accessed August 13, 2015).

Davis, Aaron C. "In Iraq, Military Still Seen as Dysfunctional." *The Washington Post.* June 10, 2011. https://www.washingtonpost.com/world/middle-east/in-iraq-military-still-seen-as-dysfunctional/2011/06/07/AGaBk7MH_story.html (accessed August 13, 2015).

El Gamal, Rania, and Suadad al-Salhy. "Scenarios: What's Next for Iraq After Sadr's Comeback?" *Reuters.* January 5, 2011. http://www.reuters.com/article/2011/01/06/us-iraq-politics-sadr-scenarios-idUSTRE7053CW20110106 (accessed August 13, 2015).

Freedberg, Sydney J. "Timothy Nein, Leigh Ann Hester, and Jason Mike." *National Journal,* January 13, 2007. http://www.nationaljournal.com/magazine/timothy-nein-leigh-ann-hester-and-jason-mike-20070113 (accessed July 20, 2015).

Goodwin, Liz. "More Than $6 Billion in Iraq Reconstruction Funds Lost." *Yahoo news.* June 13, 2011. http://news.yahoo.com/blogs/lookout/more-6-billion-iraq-reconstruction-funds-lost-174047033.html (accessed August 13, 2015).

Gutman, Roy. "U.S. Lawmakers, Iraq's Maliki Clash over Killing of Iranians." *McClatchy Newspapers.* June 10, 2011.

Healy, Jack. "As U.S. Leaves, Iraqis Suffer Economic Toll." *The New York Times.* December 6, 2010. http://www.nytimes.com/2010/12/06/world/middleeast/06withdraw.html?pagewanted=all (accessed August 13, 2015).

Healy, Jack, and Omar Al-Jawoshy. "As Iraqi Militants Flee, Families are Targets of Blood Reckoning." *The New York Times.* June 4, 2011. http://www.nytimes.com/2011/06/05/world/middleeast/05iraq.html?_r=0 (accessed August 6, 2015).

Healy, Jack, and Michael S. Schmidt. "Iraqi Delay Hinders U.S. Planning." *The New York Times.* March 15, 2011. http://www.nytimes.com/2011/03/16/world/middleeast/16iraq.html (accessed August 13, 2015).

"Iraq, Bahrain and the Region: Sectarian Bad Blood." *The Economist.* March 31, 2011. Print edition. http://www.economist.com/node/18491700 (accessed August 13, 2015).

"Iraq Conducts Major Artillery Exercise with U.S." *World Tribune.* June 7, 2011. http://www.worldtribune.com/worldtribune/WTARC/2011/me_iraq0687_06_06.asp (accessed August 6, 2015).

Jakes, Lara. "US Troops Face Increasing Dangers from Shiite Militias in Southern Iraq." *Associated Press.* May 17, 2011. http://www.aina.org/news/20110517135440.pdf. (accessed August 13, 2015).

Kelland, Kate. "Civilian Death Study Rates 'Dirty War' in Iraq." *Reuters.* February 16, 2011. http://www.reuters.com/article/2011/02/16/us-civilian-death-idUSTRE71F3KL20110216 (accessed August 13, 2015).

Kennedy, Kelly. "Could the Dust Be the Cause of War Vets' Ailments?" *USA Today.* May 12, 2011.

Lando, Ben. "Iraqi Forces End a Deadly Siege." *The Wall Street Journal.* June 15, 2011. http://www.wsj.com/articles/SB10001424052702303714704576385024210944518 (accessed August 13, 2015).

Leland, John, and Duraid Adnan. "Last Christmas Ponder Leaving a Hometown in Iraq." *The New York Times.* January 20, 2011. http://www.nytimes.com/2011/01/20/world/middleeast/20christian.html (accessed August 13, 2015).

Lessig, Hugh. "Honoring the Fallen: 'We Will Get Them Home.'" *Newport News Daily Press.* May 28, 2011. http://articles.dailypress.com/2011–05–27/news/dp-nws-cp-dover-honoring-fallen-main-20110527_1_military-families-sign-husband (accessed August 13, 2015).

Londono, Ernesto. "Iraq's Sunnis View Justice System as Cudgel." *The Washington Post.* November 23, 2010. http://www.washingtonpost.com/wp-dyn/content/article/2010/11/22/AR2010112206379.html (accessed August 13, 2015).

Londono, Ernesto. "Barren Iraqi Park Attests to U.S. Program's Flaws." *The Washington Post.* January 3, 2011. http://www.washingtonpost.com/wp-dyn/content/article/2011/01/02/AR2011010203520.html (accessed August 13, 2015).

MacQuarrie, Brian. "Mission: Seemingly Impossible." *The Boston Globe.* May 30, 2011. http://www.boston.com/news/nation/washington/articles/2011/05/30/dismantling_war_machine_is_final_us_campaign_in_iraq/ (accessed August 13, 2015).

McEvers, Kelly. "In Surprise, Iraq May Enforce Withdrawal Deadline." *NPR.* January 4, 2011. http://www.npr.org/2011/01/04/132632709/in-surprise-iraq-may-enforce-withdrawal-deadline (accessed August 13, 2015).

McQuarrie, Brian. "Winding Down an Almost Forgotten War." *The Boston Globe.* May 29, 2011. http://www.boston.com/news/world/middleeast/articles/2011/05/29/winding_down_an_almost_forgotten_war_in_iraq/ (accessed August 6, 2015).

"Mr. Maliki's Power Grab." *The New York Times.* March 13, 2011. http://www.nytimes.com/2011/03/14/opinion/14mon1.html (accessed August 13, 2015).

"Navy Christens Newest Arleigh Burke-Class Ship Jason Dunham," http://www.Navy.mil/submit/display.asp?story_id=47354 (accessed April 1, 2015).

Palast, Greg. "Jay Garner." *BBC Newsnight.* http://news.bbc.co.uk/2/hi/programmes/newsnight/3552737.stm (accessed June 12, 2015).

Pincus, Walter. "Iraqi Defense Ministry Woefully Unprepared." *The Washington Post.* November 23, 2010. http://www.washingtonpost.com/wp-dyn/content/article/2010/11/22/AR2010112207023.html (accessed August 13, 2015).

Pincus, Walter. "U.S. Inspector General Calls for Halt in Funding $26 Million Iraqi Academy." *The Washington Post.* January 25, 2011. http://www.washingtonpost.com/wp-dyn/content/article/2011/01/25/AR2011012506690.html (accessed August 13, 2015).

Pincus, Walter. "State Department Report on U.S. Withdrawal From Iraq Cites Lack of Money, Other Problems." *The Washington Post.* June 4, 2011. http://www.washingtonpost.com/national/national-security/state-department-report-on-us-withdrawal-from-iraq-cites-lack-of-money-other-problems/2011/06/01/AGwdsQIH_story.html (accessed August 13, 2015).

Ramsey, Robert D. III. *Advice for Advisors: Suggestions and Observations from Lawrence to the Present. Global War on Terrorism Occasional Paper 19.* Fort Leavenworth, KS: Combat Studies Institute Press, 2006. http://1.usa.gov/16fYgn9 (accessed June 16, 2015).

"Sadrist Movement: We Have Armed Resistance Against American, AAH Works for Free." *Al-Sumaria News.* June 7, 2011.

Schmidt, Michael S. "For Iraqis and U.S. Troops, a Question Is Still Unanswered." *The New York Times*. May 18, 2011. http://atwar.blogs.nytimes.com/2011/05/18/for-iraqis-and-u-s-troops-a-question-is-still-unanswered/ (accessed August 13, 2015).

Schmidt, Michael S. "U.S. Braces for Withdrawal along Iraqi Road." *The New York Times*. June 7, 2011. http://www.nytimes.com/2011/06/07/world/middleeast/07iraq.html?_r=2 (accessed August 6, 2015).

Schmidt, Michael S. and Jack Healy. "Iraq Shuts Office of Protest Organizers." *The New York Times*. March 7, 2011. http://www.nytimes.com/2011/03/08/world/middleeast/08iraq.html (accessed August 13, 2015).

Schmidt, Michael S. and Jack Healy. "Shiite Militia Claims Responsibility for Attack in Baghdad." *The New York Times*. June 10, 2011. http://www.nytimes.com/2011/06/11/world/middleeast/11iraq.html (accessed August 13, 2015).

"SECNAV Names New Zumwalt-Class Destroyer USS Michael Monsoor," http://www.defense.gov/releases/release.aspx?releaseid=12320 (accessed April 1, 2015).

Seib, Gerald F. "Biden Grows Optimistic About Iraq." *The Wall Street Journal*. December 28, 2010. http://www.wsj.com/articles/SB10001424052970203568004576044632913086772 (accessed August 13, 2015).

Shuster, Mike. "Special Series: the Partisans of Ali." National Public Radio. http://www.npr.org/series/7346199/the-partisans-of-ali (accessed December 22, 2015).

Shuster, Mike. "U.S. Works to Help Iraq's Air Force Take Off." *NPR*. April 2, 2011. Weekend edition. http://www.npr.org/2011/04/03/135043139/u-s-works-to-help-iraqs-air-force-take-off (accessed August 13, 2015).

Sly, Liz. "Maliki's Governing Style Raises Questions about Future of Iraq's Fragile Democracy." *The Washington Post*. December 21, 2010. http://www.washingtonpost.com/wp-dyn/content/article/2010/12/21/AR2010122106870.html (accessed August 13, 2015).

"Statement on Libya." Press Release. June 8, 2011. http://www.nato.int/cps/en/natohq/news_75177.htm (accessed August 13, 2015).

Stewart, Rory. *The Prince of the Marshes*. New York: Recorded Books, LLC, 2007.

Synnott, Hilary. *Bad Days in Basra: My Turbulent Time as Britain's Man in Southern Iraq*. New York: Palmgrave Macmillan, 2008.

Tilghman, Andrew. "I Came over Here Because I Wanted to Kill People." *Washington Post*, 30 June 2006. http://i.cdn.turner.com/cnn/2009/images/05/28/statement.pdf (accessed June 16, 2006).

"US Congressman Says Iraq Should Repay War Costs." *Yahoo News*. June 10, 2011. http://news.yahoo.com/s/afp/20110610/pl_afp/iraquspoliticsdiplomacyfinance (accessed August 6, 2015).

Williams, Kayla. "Seven Misconceptions about Military Sexual Assault." *The Daily Beast*, April 6, 2013. http://www.thedailybeast.com/articles/2013/06/04/seven-misconceptions-about-military-sexual-assault.html (accessed July 29, 2015).

WEBSITES

Blackwater USA Hearing. Given before U.S. House of Representatives Committee on Government Reform, October 2, 2007. Washington, DC. https://house.resource.org/110/org.c-span.201290-1.1.pdf (accessed June 17, 2015).

The Bureau of Investigative Journalism: Covert Drone War. https://www.thebureauinvestigates.com/category/projects/drones/ (accessed July 13, 2015).

Charter of the United Nations. "Preamble." United Nations. http://www.un.org/en/documents/charter/preamble.shtml

Coalition Provisional Authority. "Coalition Provisional Authority Order Number 1: De-Ba'athification of Iraqi Society." May 16, 2003. http://nsarchive.gwu.edu/NSAEBB/NSAEBB418/docs/9a%20-%20Coalition%20Provisional%20Authority%20Order%20No%201%20-%205–16–03.pdf (accessed June 12, 2015).

Coalition Provisional Authority. "Order Number 2: Dissolution of Entities." May 23, 2003. http://www.iraqcoalition.org/regulations/20030823_CPAORD_2_Dissolution_of_Entities_with_Annex_A.pdf (accessed June 12, 2015).

Cordesman, Anthony H., Sam Khazai, and Daniel Dewit. *Shaping Iraq's Security Forces: US-Iranian Competition Series*. Center for Strategic & International Studies. December 16, 2013. csis.org/files/publication/131213_Iraq_Security_Forces.pdf

Council on Foreign Relations. "The Sunni-Shia Divide." Council on Foreign Relations. http://www.cfr.org/peace-conflict-and-human-rights/sunni-shia-divide/p33176#!/

Democratic Policy and Communications Center. "Iraq by the Numbers." December 19, 2011. www.dpc.senate.gov/docs/fs-112–1–36.pdf (accessed June 12, 2015).

Drone Wars UK: Information and Comment on the Use of Drones. http://dronewars.net/drone-wars-library/ (accessed July 13, 2015).

Gallup. "Presidential Approval Ratings—Gallup Historical Statistics and Trends." Gallup. http://www.gallup.com/poll/116677/presidential-approval-ratings-gallup-historical-statistics-trends.aspx

Green, Steven D. Court Statement of Steven D. Green as part of the court martial for the rape and murder of Abeer Qasem Hamza. http://i.cdn.turner.com/cnn/2009/images/05/28/statement.pdf (accessed June 16, 2015).

Home of Heroes. "U.S. Army Awards of the Silver Star." http://www.homeofheroes.com/valor/08_WOT/ss_GWOT/citations_USA-M.html (accessed June 12, 2015).

Iraq Coalition Casualty Count, icasualties.org. "Operation Iraqi Freedom." http://icasualties.org/Iraq/index.aspx (accessed June 12, 2015).

Morris, Dustin. Interview by Tom Bruscino, July 19, 2006. Interview Transcript. Combat Studies Institute Operational Leadership Experience Collection, Fort Leavenworth, KS. http://cgsc.contentdm.oclc.org/cdm/singleitem/collection/p4013coll13/id/237/rec/4 (accessed July 20, 2015).

Nein, Timothy F. Interview by Tom Bruscino, July 18, 2006. Interview Transcript. Combat Studies Institute Operational Leadership Experience Collection, Fort Leavenworth, KS. http://cgsc.contentdm.oclc.org/cdm/singleitem/collection/p4013coll13/id/256/rec/1 (accessed July 20, 2015).

Ordunez, Jesse. Interview by Tom Bruscino, June 28, 2006. Interview Transcript. Combat Studies Institute Operational Leadership Experience Collection, Fort Leavenworth, KS. http://cgsc.contentdm.oclc.org/cdm/singleitem/collection/p4013coll13/id/235/rec/3 (accessed July 20, 2015).

Protect our Defenders. "Facts on United States Military Sexual Violence." www.protectourdefenders.com, Washington, DC. http://protectourdefenders.com/downloads/Military_Sexual_Violence_Fact_Sheet_Final_150710.pdf (accessed July 29, 2015).

Sexual Assault Prevention and Response Office. *Department of Defense Annual Report on Sexual Assault in the Military, 2014*. U.S. Department of Defense: Washington, DC. http://sapr.mil/public/docs/reports/FY14_Annual/FY14_DoD_SAPRO_Annual_Report_on_Sexual_Assault.pdf (accessed July 29, 2015).

Special Inspector General for Iraq Reconstruction. Archived Site. http://cybercemetery.unt. edu/archive/sigir/20130930184730/http://www.sigir.mil/ (accessed July 9, 2015).

The War Profiteers—War Crimes, Kidnappings & Torture. "The Massacre of Haditha—The Revenge Killing of 24 Iraqi Civilians." The War Profiteers—War Crimes, Kidnappings & Torture, Killing of Iraqi Civilians Index. http://www.expose-the-war-profiteers. org/DOD/iraq_II/haditha.htm (accessed June 16, 2015).

The White House. "Saddam Hussein's Defiance of United Nations Resolutions." The White House of President George W. Bush official site. http://georgewbush-whitehouse. archives.gov/infocus/iraq/decade/sect2.html

United Nations. "Convention against Torture and Other Cruel, Inhuman or Degrading Treatment or Punishment." United Nations Human Rights, Office of the High Commissioner for Human Rights. Adopted by General Assembly resolution 39/46 of 10 December 1984. http://www.ohchr.org/EN/ProfessionalInterest/Pages/CAT.aspx (accessed June 13, 2015).

United Nations Security Council Resolution 1441. "U.S. Explanation of Vote." United Nations. http://www.un.org/webcast/usa110802.htm

United States Congress Joint Resolution. "Public Law 107–40, 107th Congress." Government Printing Office. http://www.gpo.gov/fdsys/pkg/PLAW-107publ40/pdf/PLAW-107publ40.pdf

U.S. Commission on Civil Rights. *Sexual Assault in the Military.* U.S. Commission on Civil Rights: Washington, DC, September 2013. http://www.usccr.gov/pubs/09242013_Statutory_Enforcement_Report_Sexual_Assault_in_the_Military.pdf (accessed July 29, 2015).

U.S. Department of Defense. Measuring Stability and Security in Iraq, Quarterly Reports. http://www.defense.gov/home/features/Iraq_Reports/Index.html (accessed June 18, 2015).

U.S. Army Human Resources Command. "Awards and Decorations by Conflict." https://www.hrc.army.mil/TAGD/Awards%20and%20Decorations%20Statistics%20by%20Conflict (accessed June 12, 2015).

FILMS AND TELEVISION

Movies

The A Team. Director: Josh Carnahan. 20th Century Fox, 2010.
Allegiance. Director: Michael Connors. Five by Eight Productions, 2012.
American Sniper. Director: Clint Eastwood. Warner Bros, 2014.
American Son. Director: Neil Abramson. Map Point Pictures, 2008.
Battle for Haditha. Director: Nick Broomfield. Channel Four Films, 2007.
Body of Lies. Director: Ridley Scott. Warner Bros, 2008.
Buried. Director: Rodrigo Cortez. Versus Entertainment, 2010.
Conspiracy. Director: Adam Marcus. Stage 6 Films, 2008.
Djihad. Director: Felix Olivier. Noe Productions, 2006.
Fair Game. Director: Doug Liman. River Road Entertainment, 2010.
GI Jesús. Director: Carl Colpaert. Cinefrontera, 2006.
Grace Is Gone. Director: James C. Strouse. Plum Pictures, 2007.
Green Zone. Director: Paul Greengrass. Universal Pictures, 2010.

Harsh Times. Director: David Ayer. Andrea Sperling Productions, 2005.

Home of the Brave. Director Irwin Winkler. Metro-Goldwyn-Mayer, 2006.

The Hurt Locker. Director: Kathryn Bigelow. Voltage Pictures, 2009.

In the Valley of Elah. Director: Paul Haggis. Warner Independent Pictures, 2007.

Jarhead. Director: Sam Mendes. Universal Pictures, 2005.

Lawrence of Arabia. Director: David Lean. Columbia Pictures, 1962.

The Lucky One. Director: Scott Hicks. Warner Bros, 2012.

The Lucky Ones. Director: Neil Burger. Lionsgate, 2008.

Manticore. Director: Tripp Reed. United Film Organization, 2005.

The Marine. Director: John Bonito. 20th Century Fox, 2006.

The Mark of Cain. Director: Marc Munden. Red Production Company, 2007.

The Men Who Stare at Goats. Director: Grant Heslov. BBC Films, 2009.

The Messenger. Director: Oren Moverman. Oscilloscope Laboratories, 2009.

Nothing Like the Holidays. Director: Alfredo Rodriguez de Villa. 2DS Productions, 2008.

Redacted. Director: Brian De Palma. Film Farm, 2007.

Return. Director: Liza Johnson. 2.1 Films, 2011.

Saving Jessica Lynch. Director: Peter Markle. Daniel L. Paulson Productions, 2003.

Sella Turcica. Director: Fred Vogel. TOETAG, 2010.

Shadows in Paradise. Director: J. Stephen Maunder. Aberto Entertainment, 2010.

The Situation. Director: Philip Haas. Shadow Distribution, 2006.

Stir of Echoes: The Homecoming. Director: Ernie Barbarash. Lionsgate Entertainment, 2007.

Stop-Loss. Director: Kimberly Peirce. Paramount Pictures, 2008.

Taking Chance. Director: Ross Katz. HBO Films, 2009.

The Tiger and the Snow. Director: Roberto Benigni. Melampo Cinematografica, 2005.

The Trial of Tony Blair. Director: Simon Cellan Jones. Daybreak Pictures, 2007.

Turtles Can Fly. Director: Bahman Ghodabi. Mij Film Co., 2004.

Valley of the Wolves: Iraq. Director: Serdar Akar, Sadullah Senturk. Pana Films, 2006.

Zero Dark Thirty. Director: Kathryn Bigelow. Columbia Pictures, 2012.

Documentaries

About Baghdad. Director: Sinan Antoon. InCounter Productions (2004).

American War Generals. Executive producers: Peter Bergen, Tresha Mabile, Jonathan Towers. National Geographic Channel (2014).

Arlington West. Director: Peter Dudar, Sally Marr. Laughing Tears Productions (2005).

Baghdad ER. Director: Jon Alpert. HBO Documentary Films (2006).

Baghdad or Bust. Director: Matt Frame. NA (2004).

Baker Boys: Inside the Surge. Director: Kern Konwiser. GigaPix Studios (2010).

BattleGround: 21 Days on the Empire's Edge. Director: Stephen Marshall. Artists/Media Cooperation (2004).

Bearing Witness. Director: Bob Eisenhardt. Cabin Creek Films (2005).

Body of War. Director: Phil Donahue. Mobilus Media (2007).

The Boys from Baghdad High. Director: Ivan O'Mahoney, Laura Winter. Arte, BBC (2007).

Breaking the Silence: Truth and Lies in the War on Terror. Director: Steve Connell, John Pilger. Carlton Television (2003).

Brothers at War. Director: Jake Rademacher. NA (2009).

Bush Family Fortunes: The Best Democracy Money Can Buy. Director: Steven Grandison. Disinformation Company (2004).

Control Room. Director: Jehane Noujaim. Noujaim Films (2004).

Cysgod Rhyfel. Director: John Evans. Cwmni Da (2014).

The Dreams of Sparrows. Director: Haydar Daffar, Haydar Mousa Daffar. Harbinger Productions (2005).

Fahrenheit 9/11. Director: Michael Moore. Fellowship Adventure Group (2004).

Ghosts of Abu Ghraib. Director: Rory Kennedy. HBO Documentary Film (2007).

The Ground Truth. Director: Patricia Foulkrod. Plum Pictures, Radioaktive Film (2006).

Gunner Palace. Director: Petra Epperlein, Michael Tucker. Nomados (2004).

Heavy Metal in Baghdad. Director: Surosh Alvi, Eddy Moretti. VBS.TV, Vice Films (2007).

In the Shadow of the Palms. Director: Wayne Coles-Janess. Ipso Facto Productions Pty. Ltd. (2005).

Inside Iraq: The Untold Stories: N/A, Mike Shiley (2004).

The Invisible War. Director: Kirby Dick. Chain Camera Pictures (2012).

Iraq for Sale: The War Profiteers. Director: Robert Greenwald. Brave New Films (2006).

Iraq in Fragments. Director: James Longley. Daylight Factory (2006).

Leading to War. Director: Barry J. Hershey. Walden Woods Film Company (2008).

The Liberace of Baghdad. Director: Sean McAllister. British Broadcasting Corporation (2005).

Lioness. Director: Meg McLagan, Daria Sommers. Room 11 Productions (2008).

The List. Director: Beth Murphy. Principle Pictures (2012).

Meeting Resistance. Director: Molly Bingham, Steve Connors. Nine Lives Documentary Productions (2007).

My Country, My Country. Director: Laura Poitras. N/A (2006).

Nice Bombs. Director: Usama Alshaibi. Artvamp (2006).

No End in Sight. Director: Charles Ferguson. Red Envelope Entertainment (2007).

Occupation: Dreamland. Director: Ian Olds, Garrett Scott. GreenHouse Pictures (2005).

Of Men and War. Director: Laurent Becue-Renard. Alice Films (2014).

Operation Homecoming: Writing the Wartime Experience. Director: Richard Robbins. Documentary Group (2007).

Poison Dust. Director: Sue Harris. N/A (2005).

The Prisoner or: How I Planned to Kill Tony Blair. Director: Petra Epperlein, Michael Tucker. Pepper and Bones (2006).

The Prosecution of an American President. Director: David J. Burke, Dave Hagen. Lost Soldier Films (2012).

Reserved to Fight. Director: Chantelle Squires. Reserved To Fight (2008).

Return to the Land of Wonders. Director: Maysoon Pachachi. Falafel Daddy Productions (2004).

The Road to Fallujah. Director: Mark Manning, NA (2009).

Severe Clear. Director: Kristian Fraga. Sirk Productions (2009).

Shadow Company. Director: Nick Bicanic, Jason Bourque. Purpose Films (2006).

The Short Life of José Antonio Gutierrez. Director: Heidi Specogna. Ps Film Zurich (2006).

Soldiers Pay. Director: Tricia Regan, David O. Russell. Warner Bros (2004).

Soundtrack to War. Director: George Gittoes. Gittoes & Dalton Productions Pty Ltd (2005).

Standard Operating Procedure. Director: Errol Morris. Participant Media (2008).

Taking Liberties. Director: Chris Atkins. S2S Productions (2007).

The Triangle of Death. Director: Folleh Shar Tamba. Wolf Dog Films (2009).

Uncovered: The War on Iraq. Director: Robert Greenwald. Cinema Libre Studio (2004).

The Unreturned. Director: Nathan Fisher. N/A (2010).

Voices of Iraq. Director: Martin Kunert. Booya Studios (2004).
War Feels like War. Director: Esteban Uyarra. In Focus Productions (2004).
The War Tapes. Director: Deborah Scranton. SenArt Films (2006).
The War You Don't See. Director: Alan Lowery. Dartmouth Films (2010).
We Are Many. Director: Amir Amirani. Amirani Media (2014).
We Iraqis. Director: Abbas Fahdel. Agat Films & Cie (2004).
When I Came Home. Director: Don Lohaus. Lohaus Films (2006).
Why We Fight. Director: Eugene Jarecki. BBC Storyville (2005).
Year at Danger. Director: Steve Metze, Don Swaynos. Scum Crew Pictures (2007).

Television

Frontline: Blair's War. Director: Eamonn Matthews. PBS, 2003
Frontline: Beyond Baghdad. Exec Producer: David Fanning. PBS, 2004.
Frontline: Chasing Saddam's Weapons. Exec Producer: David Fanning. PBS, 2004.
Frontline: The Invasion of Iraq. Director: Richard Sanders. PBS, 2004.
Frontline: Son of Al Qaeda. Director: Don Knox. PBS, 2004.
Frontline: Al Qaeda's New Front. Director: Ruthie Calarco, Neil Docherty. PBS, 2005.
Frontline: Private Warriors. Producer: Martin Smith. PBS, 2005.
Frontline: The Soldier's Heart. Director: Raney Aronson, Miri Navasky. PBS, 2005.
Frontline: The Torture Question. Director: Michael Kirk, 2005.
Frontline: The Lost Year in Iraq. Director: Michael Kirk. PBS, 2006.
Frontline: Gangs of Iraq. Exec Producer: David Fanning. PBS, 2007.
Frontline: Bad Voodoo's War. Director: Deborah Scranton. PBS, 2008.
Frontline: Bush's War. Director: Michael Kirk. PBS, 2008.
Frontline: Rules of Engagement. Exec Producer: David Fanning. PBS, 2008.
Frontline: The Wounded Platoon. Director: Daniel Edge. PBS, 2010.
Frontline: Fighting for Bin Laden. Director: Daniel Edge. PBS, 2011.
Frontline: Al Qaeda in Yemen. Director: Safa Al Ahmad. PBS, 2012.
Frontline: Losing Iraq. Director: Michael Kirk. PBS, 2014.
Frontline: The rise of ISIS. Director: Martin Smith. PBS, 2014.
10 Days to War. Exec Producer: Colin Barr. BBC, 2008.
Gary: Tank Commander. Exec Producer: Colin Gilbert. Comedy Unit, 2009.
Generation Kill. Director: Susanna White, Simon Cellan Jones. Blown Deadline Productions, 2008.
House of Saddam. Director: Alex Holmes, Jim O'Hanlon. BBC, 2008.
The Kill Point. Director: Steve Shill, Josh Trank. Lionsgate Television, 2007.
Occupation. Director: Nick Murphy. BBC America, 2009.
Over There. Exec Producer: Steven Bochco. 20th Century Fox Television, 2005.

Index

About the Author

Brian L. Steed is currently a U.S. Army lieutenant colonel and a military history instructor at the U.S. Army Command and General Staff College and a Middle East foreign area officer. Steed has written numerous books on military theory and military history and cultural awareness. His most recent book is *Bees and Spiders: Applied Cultural Awareness and the Art of Cross-Cultural Influence* (Strategic Book Publishing & Rights Agency, 2014), about using cultural awareness to develop empathy and ultimately influence.